... the winner of ...
... d, *Tars*, and the critically acclaimed ...
Waterloo. Tim is also an Associate Fellow of the University of Warwick and a Fellow of the Society of Antiquaries. He worked at the British Museum as co-curator of the exhibition *Bonaparte and the British*, which marked the 200th anniversary of the Battle of Waterloo.

'What an astonishing story it all is, alternately inspiring and disturbing, a challenging addition to the Napoleonic canon ... Clayton writes with a fine eye for detail. You smell the sewers in which these men (and some women) hid or escaped, the cells in which they were confined and sometimes died – and the fear' *Spectator*

'In the era of fake news, this fascinating tale has obvious contemporary resonances' *Times Literary Supplement*

'Well-researched and well-written ... breaks new ground, going much deeper into the subject than any previous account' Andrew Roberts, *Sunday Times*

This Dark Business

The Secret War
Against Napoleon

TIM CLAYTON

ABACUS

First published in Great Britain in 2018 by Little, Brown
This paperback edition published in 2020 by Abacus

1 3 5 7 9 10 8 6 4 2

Maps drawn by John Gilkes

A CIP catalogue record for this book
is available from the British Library.

ISBN 978-0-349-14238-8

Typeset in Caslon by M Rules
Printed and bound in Great Britain by
Clays Ltd, Elcograf S.p.A.

Papers used by Abacus are from well-managed forests
and other responsible sources.

In memory of my close friend
David Bradshaw and of my mother
Avice Clayton; and for her close
friend Anny Cousin and her family.

Contents

List of Maps — ix

Cast of Characters — xiii

3 *nivôse*, year IX — I

1 Fair is Foul, and Foul is Fair — 9

2 Responding to Cataclysm — 24

3 *Bellum Internecinum* — 42

4 The Modern Alexander — 58

5 The English Conspiracy — 79

6 The Infernal Machine — 95

7 The Character of Bonaparte — 109

8 The Peace and the Press — 125

9 Rousing the Nation — 146

10 Grand Conspiracy — 170

11 Reactivating the Spies — 185

12 Atrocities of the Corsican Demon — 201

13 Landing the Assassins — 222

14 Méhée de la Touche — 236

15 Paris in Panic   255

16 Worse than a Crime   277

17 The Eagle Does Not Catch Flies   292

18 Trials and Executions   312

19 The Emperor Napoleon   326

20 Epilogue   343

    Acknowledgements   357

    Notes   359

    Select Bibliography   385

    Index   405

Maps

Northern Europe   x–xi

Northern France   184

Strasbourg   276

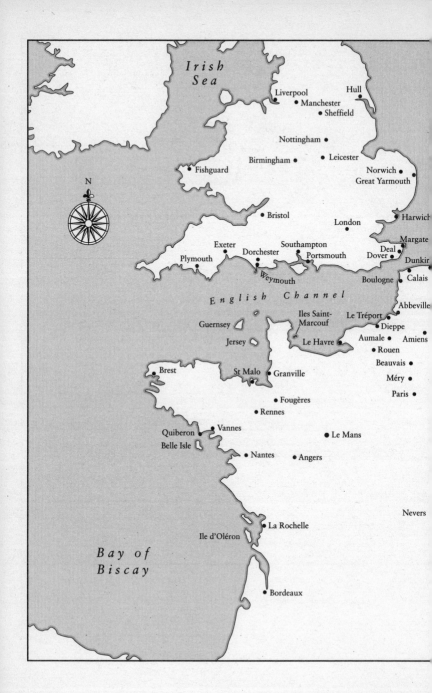

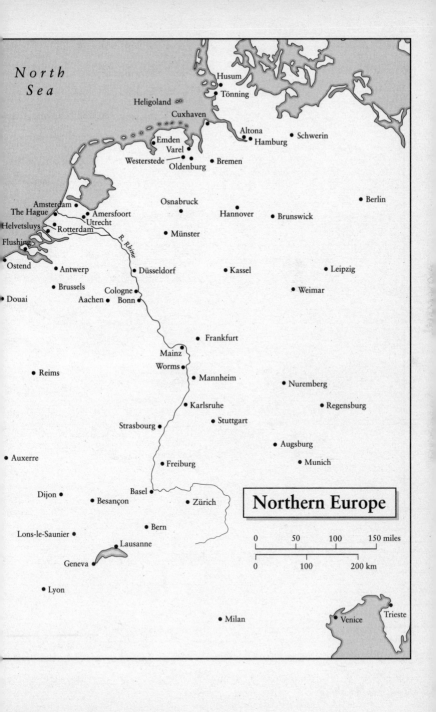

North Sea

Husum
Tönning
Heligoland
Cuxhaven
Altona
Emden   Schwerin
Varel   Hamburg
Westerstede   Bremen
Oldenburg

Amsterdam   Osnabruck   Berlin
The Hague   Hannover   Brunswick
Amersfoort
Helvetsluys   Utrecht
Rotterdam   Münster
Flushing
R. Rhine
Ostend   Düsseldorf   Kassel   Leipzig
Antwerp
Brussels   Cologne   Weimar
Douai   Aachen   Bonn

Reims   Frankfurt
Mainz
Worms
Mannheim   Nuremberg
Karlsruhe   Regensburg
Strasbourg   Stuttgart
Auxerre   Augsburg
Freiburg   Munich
Basel
Dijon   Besançon   Zürich

Northern Europe

Bern
Lons-le-Saunier   Lausanne
Geneva

0	50	100	150 miles
0	100		200 km

Lyon

Milan   Venice   Trieste

Cast of Characters

The Bonaparte Family

Napoleon Bonaparte, born 1769, general of the Army of Italy
    1796, First Consul 1799

His brothers Joseph (born 1768), Lucien (born 1775), Louis (born
    1778), Jérôme (born 1784)

His sisters Elisa (born 1777), Pauline (born 1780), Caroline
    (born 1782)

His mother Letizia, born 1750

His wife, previously Rose de Beauharnais, known as
    Josephine, born 1763

Her son Eugène (born 1781) and daughter Hortense (born 1783)

Bourbons

Louis Stanislas Xavier de Bourbon, comte de Provence, born
    1755, lived in Warsaw as 'comte de Lille' 1801–4; self-styled
    Louis XVIII

Charles, comte d'Artois, born 1757; after 1789 lived in Turin, then
    Edinburgh, then London

Louis Joseph de Bourbon, prince de Condé, born 1736; emigrated to Coblenz 1791 and raised a royalist army; to London 1800

Louis-Antoine-Henri de Bourbon, duc d'Enghien, Condé's grandson, born 1772

French politicians

Maximilien Robespierre, born 1758, 'the Incorruptible', a leader of the Jacobins and mastermind of the Terror until his execution in 1794

Paul, vicomte de Barras, born 1755, Provençal nobleman, the most important of the five Directors who ruled France from 1795 until Bonaparte's coup in 1799

Joseph Fouché, born 1759, son of a Nantes slaver; teacher at the Oratory school then Jacobin politician; minister of police in summer 1799–1802 and 1804–

Charles Maurice de Talleyrand-Périgord, born 1754; bishop of Autun 1789, excommunicated 1791; to Britain 1792 but expelled; America 1793–6; minister for foreign affairs 1797–

Alexandre-Maurice Blanc d'Hauterive, born 1754, professor before the revolution; consul at New York 1790-98; foreign ministry 1798–

François-Marie (marquis de) Barthélemy, born 1747, French minister in Switzerland; Director 1797; exiled 1797, rescued and came to England; returned after *Brumaire*; senator

Louis-Guillaume Otto, born 1754, French representative in London 1800–2; minister to the Palatinate 1803–4

Michel Regnaud de Saint-Jean-d'Angély, born 1761, lawyer and state counsellor

Pierre-François Réal, born 1757, lawyer, state counsellor and special investigator

Claude Ambroise Régnier, born 1736, Grand Judge and minister of justice 1802–

Louis Antoine Fauvelet de Bourrienne, born 1769, school friend and private secretary to Bonaparte

Henri Shée, born 1739, prefect of the Bas-Rhin 1802–

Amé Masclet, born 1760, sub-prefect of Boulogne 1800–

André Dumont, born 1764, sub-prefect of Abbeville 1799–

Antoine-François Bertrand de Moleville, born 1744, minister of marine to Louis XVI; exiled to London

Emmanuel-Henri-Louis de Launay, comte d'Antraigues, born 1759, agent of Louis XVIII

Louis-Antoine-Marc-Hilaire de Conzié, born 1732, bishop of Arras, head of Artois's council

Armand de Polignac, born 1771, raised at Versailles, went to London in 1800, courtier to Artois

Jules de Polignac, born 1780, his brother, courtier to Artois

Jean-François Dutheil, financial agent for Artois, manager of secret service and link with British government

Charles-François de Riffardeau, marquis de Rivière, born 1765, first aide to Artois

French armed forces

Jean-Charles Pichegru, born 1761, sergeant-major of artillery before revolution; general in 1793 and commanded the army of the Rhine; army of the North 1794; changed sides and exiled 1797; escaped to Britain

Auguste Thévenet dit Danican, born 1764, as lieutenant colonel in Parisian national guard fought royalists in the Vendée 1793; suspected of treachery after defeats; denounced colleagues; led revolt in Paris in 1795; fled to London and became royalist publicist

Amédée Willot, born 1755, private 1771; republican general 1793 in Pyrenees and in Vendée 1795; exiled 1797 and escaped with Pichegru to Britain

Jean Victor Marie Moreau, born 1763, lieutenant colonel of Breton volunteers 1791; served as general under Pichegru in Flanders 1794; commander of the army of the Rhine 1795-7; dismissed with Pichegru 1797; commanded in Italy 1799, then army of the Rhine and victor of Hohenlinden 1800

Frédéric Lajolais, born 1765, volunteer 1778; general 1793 under Pichegru; arrested 1794 over Pichegru's supposed treachery; acquitted but not re-employed

Henri Rolland, born c.1758, old acquaintance of Pichegru and of Moreau

Charles-Léon Tinseau d'Amondans, born 1748, aide to Artois, military engineer and royalist publicist

Athanase-Hyacinthe Bouvet de Lozier, born 1770, adjutant-general of royal army

Etienne-François Rochelle, born c.1768, royalist officer

Jacques Jean-Marie François Boudin de Tromelin, born 1771, fought at Quiberon, then assisted Sidney Smith before returning to France in 1802

Bon-Adrien Jeannot de Moncey, born 1754, commissioned 1778; general of the Army of the Western Pyrenees 1794; suspected royalist; led a corps under Bonaparte 1800; inspector-general of the gendarmerie 1802–

Anne Jean Marie René Savary, born 1774, staff messenger to Pichegru, then to Moreau; aide to Desaix, then to Bonaparte; commander of the Gendarmes d'Élite of the Consular Guard 1801

French police

Louis Nicolas Dubois, born 1758, prefect of police for Paris 1800–

Pierre Marie Desmarest, born 1764, Fouché's assistant from 1799, chief of the secret police; astronomer, botanist, novelist

Pierre Fardel, investigated Hyde's network in 1800 and the Boulogne network in 1803

Charles Pasques, said to be a sadistic colossus

Pierre Hugues Veyrat, an enthusiastic police chief inspector

Joseph Mengaud, born c.1750, envoy to Switzerland 1797–8; police commissioner for Manche and Pas-de-Calais 1801–4

Hanoverians

George III, born 1738, King of Great Britain (after 1801 the United Kingdom of Great Britain and Ireland) and Elector of Hanover

Queen Charlotte, born 1744

George, Prince of Wales, born 1762

Frederick, Duke of York and Prince-Bishop of Osnabrück, born 1763

British politicians

Henry Addington, born 1757, Viscount Sidmouth 1805; Speaker of the House of Commons 1789–1801; First Lord of the Treasury and Chancellor of the Exchequer 1801–4

John Hiley Addington, born 1759, Lord or Secretary of the Treasury 1800–3; paymaster-general 1803–4

George Canning, born 1770, Foreign Office undersecretary 1796–9; commissioner of the Board of Control 1799–1801; joint paymaster-general 1800–1; treasurer of the navy 1804–6

William Cavendish-Bentinck, Duke of Portland, born 1738, Home Secretary 1794–1801

Francis Drake, born 1764, envoy to Genoa 1793–7; envoy to the Elector Palatine 1799–1804

Henry Dundas, born 1742, Home Secretary 1791–4; Secretary for War and the Colonies 1794–1801; Viscount Melville 1802

Charles William Flint, born 1777, acting superintendent of aliens 1797, joint superintendant 1798; joint undersecretary for Ireland 1802

Charles James Fox, born 1749, leader of the Whig opposition

Francis Freeling, born 1764, Secretary of the Post Office 1797– and part-owner of the *Sun*

John Hookham Frere, born 1769, undersecretary for Foreign Affairs 1799–1800; minister to Portugal 1800–2, to Spain 1802–4

William Wyndham Grenville, 1st Baron Grenville, born 1759, Home Secretary 1789–91; Foreign Secretary 1791–1801

George Hammond, born 1763, minister plenipotentiary to USA 1791–5; undersecretary for Foreign Affairs 1795–1806

James Harris, born 1746, Earl of Malmesbury 1800; led peace negotiations with France 1796–7 then retired owing to deafness but was widely consulted

Robert, Lord Hobart, born 1760, Secretary for War and the Colonies 1801–4

William Huskisson, born 1770, superintendent of aliens 1793; undersecretary for War 1795–1801

Robert Jenkinson, born 1770, Lord Hawkesbury 1796–1808, Earl of Liverpool 1808; Foreign Secretary 1801–4; Home Secretary 1804–

John King, born 1759, undersecretary Home Office 1791–1806

John Maddison, head of the Secret Office of the Post Office

Evan Nepean, born 1752, Home Office undersecretary 1782–94; undersecretary for War and the Colonies 1794; Secretary of the Admiralty 1794–1804

Thomas Pelham, born 1756, Lord Pelham 1801; Home Secretary July 1801–August 1803

William Pitt, born 1759, First Lord of the Treasury and
    Chancellor of the Exchequer 1783–1801 and 1804–6
John Reeves, born 1752, treasurer of the Westminster magistrates
    and founder of the Association for Preserving Liberty and
    Property against Republicans and Levellers; superintendent
    of aliens 1802
Sir George Rumbold, born 1764, minister in Hamburg to the
    Hanse towns
Richard Brinsley Sheridan, born 1751, Whig MP close to Prince
    of Wales, dramatist and theatre impresario
George, 2nd Earl Spencer, born 1758, First Lord of the
    Admiralty 1794–1801
Robert Stewart, Viscount Castlereagh, born 1769, acting chief
    secretary for Ireland 1798–1801; president of Board of Control
    1801–4; Secretary for War 1804
Charles Whitworth, born 1752, ambassador St Petersburg 1788–
    1800; mission to Copenhagen 1800; ambassador Paris 1802–3
William Wickham, born 1761, superintendent of aliens 1794;
    minister to Switzerland 1794–8; undersecretary Home
    Office 1798–1801; chief secretary to Lord Lieutenant of
    Ireland 1802–4
William Windham, born 1750, Secretary at War 1794–1801
Charles Philip Yorke, born 1764, Secretary at War 1801–3; Home
    Secretary 1803–4

Royal Navy

John Jervis, born 1735, Earl St Vincent 1797; commander
    Mediterranean 1795–9; Channel fleet 1800–01; First Lord of
    the Admiralty 1801–4
Horatio Nelson, born 1758, rear-admiral Mediterranean
    1797-1800; vice-admiral Baltic and anti-invasion 1801;
    commander-in-chief Mediterranean 1803–

George Elphinstone, 1st Viscount Keith, born 1746, commander in Mediterranean 1800–2; commander of North Sea fleet 1803–6

John Markham, born 1761, captain, on Board of Admiralty

Robert Montagu, born 1763, rear-admiral Downs station 1803

Philippe d'Auvergne 'prince de Bouillon', born 1754, commodore Channel Islands

The Smiths

John Smith, Sidney's father, captain in the Guards and gentleman-usher to Queen Charlotte

General Edward Smith, Sidney's uncle

Colonel Charles Douglas Smith, born 1761, Sidney's brother, governor of Dover Castle

Captain Sir Sidney Smith, born 1764

John Spencer Smith, born 1769, Sidney's brother, secretary at Constantinople 1795–8; plenipotentiary 1798–1801; envoy extraordinary to Württemberg 1802–4

John Wesley Wright, born 1769, naval officer and spy, Sidney's principal assistant

Spies

John Alexander Keith, nephew of the banker William Herries and cashier of Herries & Co. of Paris

Antoine Marstin Viscovitch, a mysterious spy probably of Dalmatian origin

Richard Cadman Etches, born c.1765, wine merchant and ship owner; made a Danish citizen in 1789, working for Nepean

Louis Bayard (aka Duval), born 1769, agent of Wickham who became a British spy in Paris

François-Louis Rusillon, born 1751, Swiss soldier and agent
of Wickham
Louis Fauche (aka Fauche-Borel), born 1762, a bookseller
from Neuchâtel
Guillaume Hyde de Neuville, born 1776, royalist agent in
Paris 1799–1800
Louis-Charles-Joseph Dupérou, born 1770, British paid plant in
the French police
Antoine Omer Talon, born 1760, British paid plant in the
French police
Arabella Williams, born 1745, British courier
Justin Ratel, born 1758, codenamed 'The Monk',
Anglo-royalist agent
Julienne Spère (aka Derlan), his mistress
Lelièvre de Saint-Rémy (aka Pruneau), assistant to Ratel
Julien Leclerc, born 1762, professor turned lawyer turned
Anglo-royalist agent
Pierre-Marie Poix, born c.1765 (aka La Rose, Durieux) of
l'Ecuelle-Trouée, wholesale pedlar and estate manager, and
his brothers Claudin, Joachim, Antoine and sister Celestine
Jean-Claude Méhée de la Touche, born 1762, republican
journalist
Martin Laubéypie of the Bank of France
Michelle de Bonneuil, born 1748, a beautiful and
charming woman
François-Xavier-Désiré Joliclerc, born 1770

Chouans

Georges Cadoudal, born 1771, commander Morbihan
Pierre Guillemot, born 1759, adjutant-general to Cadoudal
Joseph Picot de Limoëlan, born 1768, major-general to Cadoudal

Charles d'Hozier, born 1775, son of the royal genealogist, served
 under Limoëlan

François-Jean Carbon, born 1755, servant to Limoëlan

Aimé-Augustin-Alexis Joyaux aka Villeneuve, born c. 1777, from
 Morbihan, aide to Cadoudal

Michel Roger, born c.1769, commander of Cadoudal's cavalry

Pierre Robinault de Saint-Régent, born 1768, commander of
 Cadoudal's legion of la Trinité-Porhoët

Jean-Marie Hermilly, born c.1770, aide to Cadoudal,
 from Morbihan

Jean-Baptiste Coster de Saint-Victor, born c.1771, from Epinal,
 commanded in pays de Vitré

Edouard de la Haye Saint-Hilaire, born c.1777, Breton from the
 border with Normandy who fought under Cadoudal

Louis Picot, born c.1774, servant to Cadoudal

Louis de Sol de Grisolles, born 1761, commanded Cadoudal's
 4th legion

François-Noel de Prigent, born c.1760, courier between
 Cadoudal and the British

Pierre Querelle, a former naval surgeon

Louis de Ghaisne de Bourmont, born 1773, commander of Maine

Louis de Frotté, born 1766, commander of lower Normandy

Charles-Nicolas de Margadel, born 1765, aide and
 major-general to Frotté

Louis Guérin de Bruslart, born 1752, adjutant to Frotté,
 commander after his death

Jean Picot, 'the butcher of the Blues', senior officer under Frotté

Fortuné Guyon, comte de Rochecotte, born 1765, commander of
 upper Normandy

François Mallet, born 1765, agent of Wickham from Geneva,
 commander of upper Normandy

Raoul Gaillard, born c.1770, from Rouen, senior officer in
 upper Normandy

Armand Gaillard, born c.1773, his brother

Charles Lebourgeois, keeper of coffee-house at Rouen, officer under Maillet

Antoine de Phélippeaux, born 1767, officer in Condé army, then agent of Wickham in Vendée and aide to Sidney Smith

Antoine Caron, born c.1744, a perfumer

Pierre-Antoine Spin, born c.1755, a builder

Victor Couchery, born 1772, worked in the office of General Moncey

The Boulogne network

Claude-Guillaume-Victor du Wicquet, baron d'Ordre, born 1752, of the château of Macquinghen

Rosalie le Camus of Saint-Martin-Boulogne

Mme Combremont, concierge of Godincthun

Mlle Duchâtelet of the manoir d'Escault at Offrethun

Louis Delaporte, born c.1766, a priest

Godefroy, chevalier de Roussel de Préville, born 1776, of the château of Mont-Lambert

Nymphe de Préville, born 1785, 'la Belle', his sister

Louis Lefevre, wine merchant on the main street in Boulogne

Fishermen: Captain Verlingues, Louis Delpierre, Robert Lefort, Sauvage and Pierre Tuttelet

The Trocherie

Michel Troche, born c.1745, clockmaker of Eu

Gaston Troche, born c.1780, his son

Jacques-Joseph Duponchel, born 1770, schoolmaster and municipal secretary of Le Tréport

Jean-Louis Philippe, born 1771, grocer, commander of the shore battery at Le Tréport

Marie-Françoise Bachelier, born 1767, his wife

Jean Antoine Gallien, born 1760, oyster park manager at
    Le Tréport

Jean Dieppois, born 1761, fisherman

Prosper Quennehen, born 1750, curate at Bellancourt

Publicists

John Aikin, born 1747, editor of the *Monthly Magazine* 1796–1807

James Aitken, born ?c.1770, caricature printseller

James Asperne, born 1757, bookseller and proprietor of the
    European Magazine

William Vincent Barré, born c.1760, translator for the French
    government, then anti-Bonaparte publicist in London

John Bowles, born 1751, high Tory anti-Jacobin publicist

William Cobbett, born 1763, loyalist political journalist; editor
    the *Porcupine* (1800–1), *Political Register* (1802–)

Samuel Taylor Coleridge, born 1772, liberal journalist for the
    Morning Post and poet

Jean-Baptiste Couchery, born 1768, politician and journalist

Samuel William Fores, born 1761, Tory printseller in Piccadilly

Friedrich Gentz, born 1764, anglophile German publicist
    and diplomat

John Gifford, born 1758 'John Richards Green', editor of the
    Anti-Jacobin Review

William Gifford, born 1756, satirical poet and editor of the
    Anti-Jacobin

James Gillray, born 1756, caricaturist

John Ginger, bookseller favoured by the Prince of Wales

Lewis Goldsmith, born c.1763/4, radical author, editor of the
    Paris *Argus*, then spy for France

John Hatchard, born 1769, Piccadilly bookseller favoured by
    government

John Heriot, born 1760, editor of the *Sun* and the *True Briton*

William Holland, born 1757, Whig caricature printseller

Jacques Mallet du Pan, born 1749, Genevan exile; editor of
    Mercure britannique 1798-1800

François-Dominique-Reynaud de Montlosier, born 1755, editor
    of *Courier de Londres* 1797–1802, then *Bulletin de Paris* 1802–

John Parry, proprietor of the *Courier* until 1799

Jean-Gabriel Peltier, born 1760, editor of *Les Actes des Apôtres*;
    fled to London after fall of monarchy; editor *Paris pendant
    l'année* (1795–1802); *l'Ambigu* (1802–)

James Perry, born 1756 'Pirie', editor and proprietor of the
    Morning Chronicle

Sampson Perry, born 1747, proprietor of the *Argus*

Richard Phillips, born 1767, Whig bookseller in Leicester then
    London, proprietor of the *Monthly Magazine*

Jacques Regnier, born c.1760, editor of the *Courier de Londres*

James Ridgway, born c.1755, Whig bookseller

Ludwig, Count von Starhemberg, born 1762, Austrian
    ambassador to Britain 1793–1807 and publicist

Daniel Stuart, born 1766, proprietor and editor of the *Morning
    Post* 1795–1803 and joint editor and proprietor with Peter
    Street of the *Courier* 1799–

Henry Delahay Symonds, born 1741, Whig bookseller

Robert Wilson, born 1777, maverick soldier and publicist

John Wright, born c.1770, ministerial bookseller in Piccadilly,
    publisher of the *Anti-Jacobin* and first publisher of the
    Anti-Jacobin Review; after a bankruptcy in 1802 he worked
    for Cobbett

Henry Redhead Yorke, born 1772 'Redhead', radical then
    ministerial publicist

3 *nivôse*, year IX

Paris in the year IX of the new era – 1800; the third day of the month of snow. In England it was Christmas Eve, but Christmas had been abolished in revolutionary France. Wednesday, a dark night of light rain.

The *beau monde* of Paris was making its way to the Théâtre de la République et des Arts in the rue de la Loi for the first Paris performance of Josef Haydn's *Creation*. The famous singer Pierre Garat was making a one-night return from retirement to sing the part of the Angel Gabriel; the performance had sold out and the theatre filled early. It was the custom of young people with boxes in the theatre to meet up beforehand and dine in a group at a *cabaret* so as to arrive at the theatre when the doors opened. Everybody who was anybody was heading to the theatre on this special night to see and to be seen, for the room was brightly lit during the performance.

Haydn's music was already more than a year old, but tonight's performance was to unveil a new French libretto written by the talented intellectual soldier Louis-Philippe, comte de Ségur, one of the influential noblemen that Bonaparte had charmed into his camp, his future master of ceremonies. The *Creation* had first been performed at the Burgtheater in Vienna on 19 March 1799, and earlier in 1800 it had been published in German and in English-language versions, but this French version would be bigger and better. The huge chorus of 250 singers, the Opéra chorus having been reinforced by singers from the Théâtre Feydeau, was directed by the veteran Jean-Baptiste Rey, who had first taken his post as master of music to Louis XVI.

It was time for the performance to begin, and the First Consul was late. The curtain rose without him to reveal Garat dressed in his signature style, flamboyant beyond caricature – 'his collar rose above his head, and his face, not unlike a monkey's, was barely visible amid a forest of curls'. Beside him Lavinie Barbier-Walbonne was dressed with contrasting simplicity.[1] 'In the beginning God created the heaven and the earth. And the Earth was without form and void and darkness was upon the face of the deep . . . ' The orchestra played twenty bars of the opening description of 'Chaos' before being interrupted by the noise of a huge, rumbling boom from somewhere outside.

At eight o'clock César had Bonaparte's carriage ready outside the Tuileries Palace, half a mile from the theatre; as usual, the coachman had dined well. Bonaparte had been working all day and was not keen on going out, but the women were all dressed up and determined to go, and so he joined the party. At quarter past eight the First Consul and generals Lannes, Bessières and Berthier drove away towards the theatre about half a mile away in the rue de la Loi (it was in what is now the Square Louvois in the rue de Richelieu). Napoleon's wife Josephine, her daughter Hortense and Napoleon's sister Caroline were to follow in a second carriage, escorted by his handsome aide Jean Rapp, but they left a little later. Josephine had just been given a magnificent Ottoman shawl from Constantinople which she was wearing for the first time, and either Bonaparte or Rapp told her that she had not folded it as gracefully as she usually did. It was probably Rapp and

Josephine flirting; she asked him to arrange it in the way that an Egyptian lady would wear it, which took some time. Napoleon's carriage drove off and Caroline, anxious that they would miss the beginning of the performance, told them that they were being left behind; by the time they had settled in their carriage, Napoleon was already crossing the place du Carrousel.

The *chouans* had arrived early. The name had been adopted by the royalist insurgents of western France – bandits or heroes depending on your point of view. It means silent one or owl, but the application is obscure – possibly in their own region they used owl calls as signals. There had been *chouan* armies in most regions of western France until Bonaparte had forced their surrender earlier in the year. Most of the leaders had made their peace with the First Consul, but the most determined *chouan* general, Georges Cadoudal, had fled to London, and two of these men were officers of his, who had ventured away from their native Brittany to hide out in Paris. They were waiting, with a soldier servant, in the rue Saint-Nicaise at the end of the place du Carrousel in front of the Tuileries Palace.

Wearing blue workmen's smocks over dirty jackets, they had driven their cart with the empty barrel they had had made a few days earlier, from its shed in the *faubourg* – the suburb – southward to the northern gate to Paris proper, the Porte Saint-Denis. Near Louis XIV's monumental gate two more *chouans* had taken away the barrel and brought it back half an hour later transformed into a bomb, filled with two hundred pounds of gunpowder mixed with sharp stones. The journey south-west along the rues Neuve-Égalité, Croix des Petits-Champs and Saint-Honoré to the rue Saint-Nicaise had gone without a hitch, and now, with time to kill, the Bretons were attempting to look inconspicuous. First they took off the rainproof tarpaulin, as if to check the load: in reality they were putting in place a fuse impregnated with saltpetre. The barrel was concealed by a load of dung, hay, straw and a sack of oats. At the front was a pile of rubble and paving slabs.

Joseph Picot de Limoëlan, who drove the cart, was a former army officer whose father had been guillotined and his brother killed fighting for the *chouans*, after which he had joined them himself, leading a band in northern Brittany. Thirty-two years old, blue-eyed, with a long, thin nose, his blond hair was cut in the short-cropped ancient Roman style *à la Titus* and he normally wore a blue coat and trousers, boots and a hat with a mother-of-pearl buckle; he was the tallest of the three, being the same height as Napoleon Bonaparte, the First Consul. His servant was a Parisian who knew his way around, forty-five-year-old François-Jean Carbon, known as Little Francis, a former seaman, not much over five foot tall, blond, bearded, blue-eyed, with a scar over his left eye. He had been confidential servant to the *chouan* commander of lower Maine, but for the last two months he had been employed by Limoëlan; a week before he had bought the horse and cart from a grain merchant. Their leader was the diminutive Pierre Robinault de Saint-Régent, aged thirty-two, commander of Cadoudal's legion of la Trinité-Porhoët, normally a dapper dresser in blue coat, black velvet waistcoat with textured stripes and grey trousers, with chestnut hair and big blue eyes. He was a former naval artillery officer, expert in explosives, who fled to England in 1794, fought at Quiberon in 1795, was wounded at Locminé in 1796 and accompanied Cadoudal to England in 1798. Only five foot tall, he had once been captured dressed as a woman, but had broken out through the roof of his prison. He was adept at disguising himself as a peasant and living wild in the woods and had a reputation for being daring, violent and merciless. His name appears in 'A list of Persons who receive an Allowance from the British government for their Services on the coast of France', in the papers of the Secretary at War, William Windham, paid at the senior officer rate of 3 shillings a day.[2]

They looked at a lemonade shop, then had a drink in the crowded café d'Apollon on the corner of the rue Marceau. A wine merchant and a grill also had many customers, for the rue Saint-Nicaise was a lively street and many of the rooms on the side facing the Carrousel were rented out to prostitutes.[3] The church clock rang eight. They made as if to repair the road near the corner of the rue Saint-Nicaise, piling up some stones and rubble there as an obstacle, and Limoëlan walked off across the square towards the Tuileries Palace so that he could signal to Saint-Régent when the Consul's coach was leaving, to give him time to light the fuse, which would take several seconds to burn. Saint-Régent, who had positioned the cart so that it partly blocked the road, reckoned he just had time to get round the corner of the street before the bomb went off; he offered a young girl 12 sous to hold the docile old mare for a few minutes while he stood by the barrel.

Leaving the Tuileries gate, César began to cross the place du Carrousel, but he could see that the entrance into Saint-Nicaise and the rue Marceau was blocked. Inside the coach, Bonaparte was dozing, but General Lannes pulled the cord to instruct César to slow down, and he did so: a cart drawn by a black horse, facing the Tuileries, was obstructing a cab that was coming out of the rue Marceau and trying to turn right towards the rue Saint-Honoré. Twenty yards ahead of the coach, the leading outrider, a horse grenadier of the Consular Guard, pushed his big, powerful horse between the two vehicles to create a gap, forcing the little black mare towards the wall, and, threatening the driver of the cab with his drawn sabre, urged him to move on fast; in the commotion his horse hurt its leg. César, who was slightly drunk, saw the gap open just wide enough, and without waiting for instruction, knowing they were late for the performance, whipped his splendidly trained horses on through the traffic at top speed, into the rue Marceau and then sharp left, northwards, towards the opera.[4]

All this happened in seconds. In the confusion Saint-Régent lost sight of Limoëlan and failed to light the fuse before the grenadier was on top of him. Afterwards he claimed to have been knocked over by the grenadier's horse, but, if so, the grenadier didn't notice; possibly the cab was part of the plan and he had been intended to escape in it; at any rate, there was a slight delay before Saint-Régent lit the fuse and fled down the rue Marceau.

Just after César turned right into the rue de la Loi the bomb exploded. Saint-Régent, running for his life, was thrown into the air and landed against the wicket-gate to the Louvre. The horse and the girl holding it were blown to pieces by the explosion; only the legs of the girl and the front half of the horse were found intact. The landlady of the café d'Apollon, who had rushed to her door to see the First Consul pass, had both her breasts ripped off by a piece of flying debris; she died three days later. One of her waiters was killed, the other wounded. Pieces of cart and stone and horse shot into the air and fell on the rooftops, bringing down a shower of tiles. The buildings in nearby streets shook as if in an earthquake – those closest to the explosion were gutted and windows smashed as far away as the Tuileries. Forty-five houses were so badly damaged that they were no longer inhabitable. Almost nobody who was in the rue Saint-Nicaise escaped uninjured: seven people were killed and twenty seriously injured. Several were blinded; those who could still walk tried to get away from the shrieks and wailing and the smoke and dust.

Bonaparte's carriage was thrown onto one wheel and the windows smashed. César's horses bolted momentarily, but he regained control and reined them in at the Théâtre de la République on the corner of the rue Saint-Honoré. The Consul called over the commander of his escort to ask if there had been casualties, but only one horseman had been hurt by a falling tile. He sent someone back to find out what had happened to Josephine and, if she was still alive, to reassure her that he too had survived, and they drove on to the performance.

Josephine's coach had only just reached the palace gate when the bomb went off: flirtation had saved her life. Its windows also broke as the ground shook, the women screamed and a shard of glass cut Hortense's hand. Rapp jumped from the coach to find the street ahead a chaos of smoke, dust, corpses and debris from ruined walls and houses. Bonaparte's coach was nowhere to be seen. Uncertain what to do, he ran back to Josephine's coach, but one of the outriders cantered up to summon them on to the opera, saying that the Consul was unhurt. They drove on, anxious, wondering what had really happened and what would happen next.

When Rapp reached the royal box above the left of the stage, Bonaparte, impassive, was calmly surveying the audience through his lorgnette. The audience was applauding wildly. Seeing Rapp, he asked: 'Josephine?' She appeared at that moment and his question tailed off. 'Those bastards tried to blow me up,' he remarked calmly. 'Have someone bring me the libretto of Haydn's oratorio.'

1

Fair is Foul, and Foul is Fair

The *machine infernale* detonated in the rue Saint-Nicaise on 24 December 1800 in an attempt to kill Napoleon Bonaparte was the first of its kind – the first terrorist act of mass killing, targeted at an individual but indiscriminate in its effect, the first 'IED' (improvised explosive device), the first time a bomb had been used for assassination.[1] It was called a terrorist bomb at the time, but that was because at first everybody thought it had been planted by Jacobins responsible for the Terror; in fact, it had been detonated by royalists secretly sponsored by the British government. This had been a French bomb, placed by French royalists, to blow up the man who was head of state in France, but William Pitt's British government paid for the operation and naval vessels transported most of the conspirators from Britain to France. Three years later there was a second and far larger-scale plot to assassinate Bonaparte and overturn his government. The unscrupulous people who directed these operations believed that this was a new kind of war, that French innovation must be met with an unprecedented ruthlessness whose full extent remains relatively unexplored and remarkably little known.

During the same period, and partly in order to justify their unscrupulous schemes, figures in or allied to the British government developed sophisticated propaganda directed against Napoleon Bonaparte personally, using techniques that survive and flourish today.[2] It is to these efforts that we owe our enduring perception of Napoleon as a dwarfish megalomaniac who could not rest content unless he was fighting a war.

This is a book about propaganda, spying and covert operations. In *This Dark Business* I shall tell the story of the British leadership's determination to destroy Napoleon Bonaparte by any means possible. We have been taught to think of Napoleon as the aggressor – a man with an unquenchable thirst for war, conquest and glory. This may have been so, but the perception is the product of propaganda fabricated at this time. What if the reverse were true: what if the British refusal to make peace either with revolutionary France, or with this man who claimed to personify the revolution, was the real reason this great war continued for more than twenty years? During this pivotal period, when Britain consolidated its place as number one world power, its king and ruling aristocracy were ruthless. To secure the continuation of Britain's hierarchic but relatively liberal social structure, the British (with the help of French royalists) invented an evil enemy, the perpetrator of countless dark deeds. They blackened Napoleon's name, destroyed his reputation and turned him into a Satanic demon against whom disparate nations might unite. They also tried to assassinate him.

Their campaign determined how a war came to be fought not against a nation or a system but against an individual: the Napoleonic War, as the British called it, was the first war against one man. At the time people found this unusual. An eminently sensible soldier and military historian commented:

But the most remarkable feature of the time was the flame which burst forth and spread its light over the whole of Britain. It was not merely the flame of patriotism, or of indignation at the bare idea that England should lie at the proud feet of a conqueror; it appeared to be fed and rendered intense by a passionate hatred of Napoleon personally. There had suddenly blazed up in the breasts of millions a fierce, uninquiring, unappeasable detestation of the individual.[3]

My argument is that this flame did not burst forth spontaneously, but rather was deliberately ignited, and then fuelled by a concerted and sometimes conspicuously crude propaganda campaign whose origins can be traced to people in or around the ministries of William Pitt and Henry Addington.

We are dealing here with the beginnings of propaganda in the modern sense, aimed at the widest possible public. The word 'propaganda' derives from the counter-reformation *congregatio de propaganda fide* – the congregation for propagating the faith – founded in 1622. This was sometimes known as 'the propaganda', and the word 'propaganda' came into wider use in the 1790s as a noun designating similar institutions. So one anti-Jacobin writer referred to a speech by Bonaparte being 'perfectly conformable to the doctrine of the famous propaganda of the revolutionary leaders, Marat, Robespierre, &c.' This 'revolutionary propaganda at Paris' was originally 'the Jacobin Committee of Correspondence and of Propaganda' (where the word is used in the modern way for the product that was propagated by the committee). The French grand judge's announcement of Bonaparte's wish to secure established governments against '*toute espèce de propagandes et de complots*' was translated for Cobbett as 'every kind of propagandas and plots', although it is susceptible to translation as 'all sorts of propaganda and plots'.[4] The word 'propagating', as in 'propagating the infernal principles of Jacobinism', or 'propagating the most offensive and unfounded calumnies against his Majesty and his government', was very much a favourite word during this period, and the word 'propaganda' was gradually shifting in application from the committee that did the propagating, to its product.

In the 1790s the importance of public opinion was a new concern for politicians and the idea of manipulating it on such a huge scale was a novelty. British anti-Bonaparte propagandists used techniques that have now been defined and named, such as 'Big Lie', 'ad nauseam', 'flag waving', 'bandwagon' and 'appeal to fear' as well as 'demonizing the enemy'.

Through their propaganda strategy the British made the central issue the question of whether or not Napoleon was really a villain – ground over which biographers are still arguing. By doing so they succeeded in deflecting attention away from the question of what the British themselves were up to (one that Napoleon attempted to pose unavailingly in his own propaganda), and whether it was a good thing that Europe should continue to be ruled by kings, princes, clerics and – as grew more and more evident under Pitt and subsequent British ministries – bankers. *This Dark Business* is not a defence of Napoleon but an explanation of how and why the British government turned him into a monster – and of how astonishingly successful in the long term that gambit proved to be. Although it is utterly obvious that such a thing happened, the story has never been told. There is still a gap in Napoleonic literature at precisely this point: how Napoleon was painted black.[5]

Ultimately, this policy was highly successful. At times it was also executed with considerable skill, and much of the nation's literary and artistic talent rallied to its narrative and was reinforced by talent from other nations. This book emphasises the role of the British government in forcing Bonaparte into courses of action that it could then portray in a bad light as evidence of insatiable ambition and warmongering. Its constant plotting, spying and shrill, mendacious propaganda persuaded him to call Fouché back into action after he had attempted to relax police supervision during and after the Peace of Amiens and, in accordance with traditional continental practice, to suppress hostile journals (which were all subsidised by the British government). The British dubbed this tyranny in action and the suppression of free speech – a view that survives to this day. Yet Pitt's government had systematically suppressed and intimidated opposition voices in Britain. Propaganda is always more effective if it is not seen to be propaganda, and the government took great pains to proclaim the independence of the British press and to disguise their involvement in and influence over the production of newspapers, periodicals, pamphlets and caricatures. The illusion of spontaneous expression was massively effective and it was also partly true – there was no formal system of censorship, and very few organs of communication were fully in a ministry's control.

In laying stress on this pattern I am conscious that I shall oversimplify a complex story and single out one thread of a complex pattern in a polemical manner, but that is inevitable. I should emphasise that I am not trying to paint Napoleon Bonaparte white – satire and propaganda are most effective when exaggerating a grain of truth, and if there is nothing there to start with, no feature to be caricatured, the design will not work. Like caricature, propaganda is about degrees of exaggeration, fomenting a climate in which anything is credible, so that something much worse than the truth is taken for the truth.

The British people seem still to love exaggeration and caricature. The appetite that took such works as *The Revolutionary Plutarch* into multiple editions lives on – uninquiring and unquenchable – in the lively but censorious journalism of the *Daily Mail*, as the simpler, more salacious and sensational writing of the *Atrocious Life* is still lapped up in the *Sun* and, until recently, the *News of the World*. The evil machinations and corruption of Europeans, and especially the French, continue to appeal to a British public that is ever ready to rally to fend off the wickedness beyond its shores.

In Britain propaganda had been deployed successfully

before – notably, for instance, in Britain's own revolutionary wars of the previous century and against Louis XIV. The demonising of an individual was unprecedented in its extent, but not novel in itself. However, during the long and intense wars against revolutionary France and against Napoleon, patterns formed, departments were created, techniques crystallised: the war behind the Napoleonic battlefields saw the development of political propaganda into the powerful instrument that generates 'fake news' and 'alternative truth', and the growth in Britain of systems of espionage and agencies for destabilisation and regime change that are now equally familiar. In particular, that student of history Winston Churchill investigated the methods used by Pitt and his people against Napoleon and revived them for use against the continental power of Hitler's Germany: he nurtured resistance movements and instructed his SOE to do to Nazi-occupied Europe what Pitt had done to Napoleon's Empire. Winston Churchill's methods have been copied in their turn, and similar techniques have been used more recently against the Ayatollah and Gaddafi, and most notably against Saddam Hussein, who had to be transformed from American-armed hero of the Western stand against Iran to ruthless thug armed with weapons of mass destruction. This is a very modern story of secret committees, slush funds, assassination and black propaganda. The compilation of evidence to justify a predetermined course of action rings loud bells in the wake of the war against Iraq.

The issues of free speech and seditious libel are equally alive today – if not more so. In Britain during these wars a tradition of robust rudeness came up against challenges not only from polite-ness but also from the sometimes paranoid fears of a broad-based ruling class that was determined to stamp out sedition. 'Political correctness' and 'hate speech' are anachronistic terms for the period under discussion, but the issues to which they respond were as urgent then as now.

The fight to the death against Napoleon was the culminating episode in a hundred-year struggle for global primacy between France and Britain, and we need to appraise both the long- and the short-term background to the problem of Napoleon in order to grasp why the British government responded to him in the way that it did. In terms of policy, when Napoleon appeared Pitt's government was already travelling down a certain road. How did it come to make that choice? Reactions to him were also influenced by obvious, long-term instincts: the gut reflex to 'French' was 'enemy'; 'brilliant French general' spelled 'fear'. Britain's most able and influential diplomat James Harris, Earl of Malmesbury, remarked that it was 'a truth inculcated into John Bull with his mother's milk, viz. that France is our natural enemy'.[6]

In 1815 Britain emerged triumphant as the leading economic power on the globe, with a huge empire; before long English was to replace French as the international language, and that status persists to this day, even though that language is now more truly American. But at the end of the seventeenth century, when one might argue that the struggle began, Britain was very much the underdog and France seemed far more powerful. Armed conflict blew up in the wars of Spanish and Austrian succession; from the Seven Years War (1756–63) Britain emerged triumphant as the dominant naval and commercial power; in the War of Independence France got a measure of revenge as a divided Britain lost her American colonies.

The King, George III, was widely blamed for this debacle. Unlike his grandfather and great-grandfather, George III spoke English and made it a point of pride to prioritise Britain over his ancestral lands in Hanover, where he was Elector. However, as his wife Charlotte's English was less accomplished, the court still often spoke French. George III was well-meaning but not terribly bright, and he lacked judgement in choosing advisers. He was guided by his concept of rectitude of conduct, unswayed by popular or parliamentary opinion, and deeply obstinate. He was aware that Britain was different from Germany, but remained glued to Germanic notions of aristocratic precedence and protocol – here his wife was even less flexible. Compromise with American rebels was never easy for him, and he was at his most English in his attitude to the French. He was also manipulative, and quite capable of using royal influence and patronage ruthlessly, either to support or to undermine a minister. He loathed and hated the most gifted and charismatic Whig politician, the reformer Charles James Fox, for his opposition and mockery during the American War when Fox had dressed habitually in the blue and buff uniform of George Washington's army.

His eldest son George, Prince of Wales, followed the tradition of Hanoverian heirs in setting up in opposition to his father. He drank, wenched, gambled and spent remarkably freely in the company of leading opposition politicians, notably Richard Brinsley Sheridan and Charles James Fox (who were universally admitted to be good company). In 1787 the House of Commons voted £161,000 in a futile attempt to clear his debts, together with £60,000 to pay for his London residence, Carlton House.

Despite the setback in America, the years between 1763 and 1789 were economically and culturally rich for Britain, and many Europeans had come to admire the institutions and achievements of the liberal rising power where press freedom and free speech were considered touchstones of liberty. 'Anglomania' was widespread in continental Europe and even Marie-Antoinette decorated her private rooms with English prints that took their subjects from English history, literature and the classical world.[7] Novelists like Laurence Sterne and Oliver Goldsmith were familiar across the Continent, and Shakespeare was universally admired, becoming a model for German dramatists. There was a craze for the supposed ancient Celtic poet 'Ossian', for whose work Napoleon and Josephine shared a passion. When the French staged a revolution in 1789 it was greeted with enthusiasm in Britain, where most assumed that the French would take Britain as their model.

Charles James Fox, progressive leader of the Whigs in Parliament, welcomed the French Revolution as 'one of the most glorious events in the history of mankind' and many Englishmen agreed with him, thinking, as at first it seemed, that France was following the English example and bringing in a limited monarchy. The future Pittite politician George Canning, then at Christ Church, Oxford, was an enthusiast. James Gillray the caricaturist, who will later feature in this book as one of the leading patriotic publicists, designed, engraved and in 1790 co-published a large and pretentious engraving, *Le Triomphe de la Liberté en l'élargissement de la Bastille*, which he dedicated, as an admirer, to '*la Nation Françoise*' (*The Triumph of Liberty in the freeing of the Bastille*, dedicated to the French Nation by their respectful admirers James Gillray and Robert Wilkinson).[8] The young poets Samuel Taylor Coleridge, Robert Southey and William Wordsworth were even more determined in their enthusiasm.

But as it grew clear that the revolution would not follow a moderate, circumscribed course towards a British model, alarm bells began to sound. The shrillest came from the Whig reformer Edmund Burke, who, remarkably early on, in 1790, prophesied the imminent destruction of European civilisation and demanded a crusade to root out the revolution and restore the Bourbon monarchy and the *ancien régime*. In a phrase that was widely remembered, he predicted that learning would be trodden down 'under the hoofs of the swinish multitude'.

The leading British politician William Pitt the younger was just thirty when the French Revolution broke out. He had come to power in 1783 as a reforming twenty-four-year-old with a famous father and allies in the financial world. He was highly intelligent, clear-thinking and a brilliant speaker. Pitt was very slim, with a long, pointed nose that soon became distinctly red, for he drank a great deal of wine and port, especially with his chum, the hearty Scot Henry Dundas, who was his treasurer of the navy and then his Home Secretary from 1791 until 1794. Dundas was a pragmatic strategist who generally wished to pursue sensible policies, especially imperial, trade-driven policies, but he was also a gifted political fixer and helped his Scottish clients ruthlessly, which made him unpopular with those who resented his domination of government patronage, especially in the navy.

The third member of the triumvirate at the core of Pitt's ministry after the revolution was his domineering cousin William, Lord Grenville, who was his foreign secretary. Grenville was also able, but austere, arrogant, dogmatic and obstinate. Blind to the other person's point of view or the other side of an argument, he acted on what he conceived to be correct principles. Grenville was a few months younger than his cousin, but large, overbearing, and growing increasingly fat. Widely known as 'Boguey', he was not much liked. He bullied Pitt, who was remarkably pliable, and Dundas (who was often in opposition to Grenville on policy) complained that this had 'often, too often, led him to give up his better judgement to the persevering importunity of Lord Grenville'.[9] Others also complained of Grenville's influence over Pitt.

The British government was broadly supportive of the revolution in its earliest stages, and Pitt was determined to preserve peace. However, the British were outmanoeuvred, and as the revolution became more extreme so the government became more hostile – the King especially so. It was the pious hope of most British politicians that the revolution would weaken France, but the government was reluctant to join European absolutist princes in a war to restore an absolutist monarch in France. It is notorious that even as late as February 1792 Pitt told the House of Commons that 'unquestionably, there never was a time in the history of this country, when, from the situation of Europe, we might more reasonably expect fifteen years of peace, than we may at the present moment'.[10] Along with Grenville, he believed that the French Revolution had weakened France to the point where it could not pose a threat for the foreseeable future. Neither of them saw the revolution itself as a reason to go to war, and they did not join Prussia and Austria in their attack on France in July. These powers' general, the Duke of Brunswick, threatened to execute civilians who fired on his troops and to destroy Paris if any harm came to the royal family in an unprecedented violation of the rules of war that first introduced the idea that France's enemies saw this as a war of principle in which normal conventions did not apply.

Ostensibly, it was the French republic's invasion of the Low Countries – a threat to vital British economic and strategic interests – that changed Pitt's attitude to a war that he had sought to avoid. To a considerable extent he agreed with his friend Henry Dundas, then Home Secretary, that the war was about the security and improvement of Britain's economic interests. But, from the beginning, some of Pitt's allies and future allies saw the war in a quite different light. The King shared the views of unsophisticated Francophobes and denounced the French as 'that dangerous and faithless nation' and 'the enemies of mankind'.[11] He harboured a grudge against them for treacherously supporting the American rebels, but at the same time he was concerned for his Bourbon 'cousins' and determined to preserve monarchy and aristocracy. So, along with many British aristocrats and Anglican Churchmen, he shared the view expressed by the great orator Edmund Burke in Parliament that the aim of the war was 'the entire destruction of the desperate horde which gave it birth'.[12] Burke, previously allied to Fox, crossed the floor of the house, and in 1793 was given two pensions each worth £1200 a year, followed by more money in 1795, but died in 1797.

It should be remembered that the ministry in office were the King's servants: he chose his ministers and his views were not to be taken lightly by them. He was a driving force and a source of funds for covert operations: it may indeed not merely have been convenient financial subterfuge that led to much secret activity being paid for from the privy purse. He saw himself as a patriotic Briton and was sympathetic to the value that the British placed on their constitution, with its limited monarchy, and to their abhorrence of absolutism, although as Elector of Hanover he was also responsible for a large part of northern Germany where attitudes to bloodlines and protocol were more respectful. Above all George III was deeply religious and conservative and took his responsibilities very seriously.

Public expression by the British of a wish to restore monarchy in France was likely to be unpopular in France – at least in Paris; indeed, it was liable to damage the Bourbon cause in French eyes, for the revolution was essentially nationalist, and if the Bourbons were seen to be in league with the enemies of France they would never be accepted.[13] Public expression of a desire to restore the Bourbon monarchy with all the trappings of absolutist tyranny was liable also to be unpopular in Britain, since the vast bulk of British opinion favoured a limited monarchy and loathed from long tradition Bourbon absolutism. Pitt had to be circumspect about how he defined Britain's war aims, was generally reluctant to do so at all, and was especially unwilling to state publicly that he was committed to regime change in France. At one point he was goaded by the opposition into an unusually frank admission that 'the idea of interference with the government of France had been implicit since the beginning of the war'.[14]

When he first came to power in 1783 Pitt had weak support in the Commons and had used government patronage and royal patronage and bullying in order to buy votes. Over the years the continuation of this policy had introduced many 'placemen' into the Commons and the Lords. Once the Portland Whigs came over to his side, Pitt's majority in the Commons became unassailably huge, with the result that opponents saw Commons debate as essentially futile – at best a way of making a noise that could achieve no concrete result. Pitt's efforts in 1795 to crush extra-parliamentary debate in the name of the constitution were thus seen by opponents as a way of removing all means to effect change.

In the later 1790s conventional opposition was to a large degree cowed and silenced, and as France grew stronger and more dangerous, so it was liable to look ever more unpatriotic to voice opposition. With each refusal to make peace the chasm widened.

The writing and the pictures of the time often relied on historical analogies that were familiar to contemporary audiences but are far less well known today. For this reason I offer some explanations here.

The French Revolution was very frequently compared with the seventeenth-century English Revolution. After a civil war (1642–6) between forces loyal to King Charles I and forces loyal to Parliament, and a second in which the Scots supported the King (1648–9), Charles I was tried for treason and in 1649 executed. His death was followed by a period of republican government – the Commonwealth – which was ended when Oliver Cromwell dispersed Parliament and took power, effectively as a military dictator, until his death in 1658. In 1660, after infighting between rival generals, General George Monck orchestrated the Restoration of King Charles II. Parallels were drawn between the fates of Louis XVI and Charles I and between Bonaparte and either Cromwell or Monck.

This period of English history was very familiar to educated Frenchmen. Rapin de Thoyras's *History of England* (1724–7) was a major bestseller in both English and French, and the French translation of Hume's Tory *History of England* in 1788 enjoyed spectacular success with conservatives in France on account of its argument for the retention of a monarchy in preference to a republic. The key episodes of the period were also very well known from prints which had a large international sale. The leading French constitutionalist the comte de Mirabeau's *Sur la liberté de la presse* (1788) was a rough translation of Milton's *Areopagitica*. Mirabeau helped to translate Catharine Macaulay's republican *History of England* (1791–2) and wrote a *Théorie de la Royauté, d'après la doctrine de Milton* (1789). The works of Milton, Nedham (*The Excellency of a Free State*, 1756), Harrington and Algernon Sidney were translated and discussed. 'Levelling' in the sense of '*niveler tous les rangs*' was a term borrowed from the English Revolution. On the royalist side the *Relation véritable de la mort cruelle et barbare de Charles Ier* was republished in 1792, while on that of the republicans the pamphlet *Killing No Murder* (1657), which justified the killing of a tyrant – originally Oliver Cromwell – was republished in 1792 in London and in Paris in 1793, in order to justify the execution of Louis XVI.[15]

Another analogy that is liable to be even less familiar is that which likened France to republican Rome and Britain to Carthage. Three long wars between Rome and Carthage over a period of about two hundred years ended in the total eradication of the North African city state. Carthage in Latin literature was a naval power that founded colonies and built an enormous mercantile imperial network founded on maritime trade. Its enormously wealthy, tasteless, luxury-loving people were interested only in money, made and sold cheap, shoddy goods, appreciated other people's art but made nothing worth mentioning of their own, were utterly untrustworthy and employed mercenaries to fight their wars.[16] 'Punic faith' (Punic is the adjective for Carthaginian) was also what you got from 'perfidious Albion'. The parallels with Britain were irresistible, even down to the concept that the Carthaginians had a mixed constitution that was reckoned the best in the antique world and was likened most closely to Britain's. So as early as August 1793 the Committee of Public Safety was being assured that 'The modern Carthage will be destroyed'. The French meanwhile saw themselves as possessing the austere virtue of republican Rome, with citizen soldiers drawn from an independent peasantry. The pursuit of luxury and the equation of prosperity with affluence was to be rejected with revulsion as commercial, Carthaginian, English.[17]

Napoleon signed himself Buonaparte until he invaded Egypt, when he Frenchified his name to Bonaparte. Once crowned Emperor he became Napoleon. One can gauge the degree of a British writer's hostility to him by what he is called: 'the Corsican Usurper', Buonaparté, Buonaparte, Bonaparte ... So, from 1800 the *Monthly Magazine* used the form Bonaparte, the anti-Jacobin papers Buonaparté.

Bonaparte claimed to embody the revolution; the crusaders claimed that he still represented the revolution and Jacobin principles. To understand we must start with the revolution and the ideas that so frightened the British establishment, and to which they responded with repression, propaganda and covert operations aimed at regime change.

2

Responding to Cataclysm

B ritain was not ready for the sort of unprecedented total war that the French seemed to be calling for when their revolution was threatened.

Until the winter of 1792 responsibility for British espionage and counter-espionage had rested in the hands of the overworked Home Office undersecretary, Evan Nepean, whose appointment to that newly invented department dated from the closing months of the American War of Independence in 1782. Born in the Green Dragon, St Stephens by Saltash, Cornwall, the son of an affluent innkeeper, Nepean became a purser in the navy, and during his twelve years running the police department of the Home Office he developed a small network of agents and domestic spies. He was a keen botanist – an interest that played a part in his organisation of voyages by Bligh, Vancouver and Phillip to various unfamiliar parts of the globe. He was very much trusted by both Pitt and the King, and George III liked him so much that he dealt with him direct despite his lack of noble blood. Nepean's experience in office also gave him considerable influence over William Grenville, Home Secretary 1789–91, and Henry Dundas (1791–94), who was said, behind his back, to be 'the mere funnel of Nepean'. Very hard-working, respected and prized by his superiors, primarily loyal to Pitt, Nepean was the key figure in home and foreign secret service and masterminded most covert operations.[1]

As a result of the French Revolution Nepean's workload exploded in volume and urgency. The government soon became worried that large numbers of people in Britain might be prepared to follow the French example and overturn the established structure of society. When Edmund Burke's *Reflections on the Revolution in France* attempted to justify the *ancien régime* in 1790 it provoked an avalanche of answering pamphlets and caricatures, for few Englishmen shared Burke's apparent adulation for the Bourbons. One caricaturist famously ridiculed Burke as 'Don Dismallo, the Knight of the Woeful Countenance', a crypto-Catholic, Don Quixote figure of the age of chivalry. Another produced *The Aristocratic Crusade*, unambiguously anti-Burke and pro-French Revolution in its hatred of aristocratic privilege.[2] These were minor sallies, however: the most famous and influential reply to Burke's pamphlet was Thomas Paine's *The Rights of Man*, of which the first part appeared in 1791 and the second, more incendiary, part in 1792. It sold very rapidly and widely and was markedly republican in tendency. Part one had asked: 'What is monarchy? Is it a thing, or is it a name, or is it a fraud? Is it "a contrivance of human wisdom", or of human craft to obtain money from a nation? . . . It appears to be a something going much out of fashion.'

In July 1791 a thirty-four-year-old artist called James Gillray etched a daring caricature called *The Hopes of the Party* showing Charles James Fox about to execute the King. Published eighteen months before the French executed their king, it was ostensibly hostile to the Whigs, but it was subversive: George III was shown saying stupidly: 'What! What! What! – what's the matter now?'[3] Part two of Paine's *Rights of Man*, published in 1792, cast further scorn on the nature of monarchy, with clear reference to George III: 'Whether the person be wise or foolish, sane or insane, a native, or a foreigner, matters not. ... The people must be hood-winked and held in superstitious ignorance by some bugbear or other; and what is called the crown answers this purpose.'

With an obstinate, eccentric and occasionally mad king, who had made himself very unpopular during the American Revolution, and an heir and siblings who indulged themselves regardless of cost or consequence, Britain might have seemed ripe for revolution. This was the message of another bestseller of 1792, Charles Pigott's *The Jockey Club*, which was a series of salacious biographical sketches of prominent aristocrats led by the Prince of Wales, who had cost the nation £220,000 in 1787 and was now once more in debt to the tune of £400,000. Pigott's preface explained that: 'our purpose will be in a great degree accomplished, if we can succeed, by taking dust out of the eyes of the multitude, in lessening that aristocratic influence which so much pains are now taking to perpetuate', although he 'feared that a revolution in government can alone bring about a revolution in morals; while it continues the custom to annex such servile awe and prostituted reverence to those who are virtually the most undeserving of it, and whose sole merit consists in their birth or titles ... what happy result can be expected?'[4] *The Jockey Club* was published by Henry Delahay Symonds in late February 1792 and went into a fifth edition in early May. A second part in which George III was the lead biography was published in April, and then a third. When eventually the prince himself read *The Jockey Club* he wrote to his parents demanding a prosecution, which followed swiftly.

It was not just the bloated Prince of Wales who found such bold attacks on royalty and aristocracy alarming. Prime Minister William Pitt, though sympathetic in principle to parliamentary reform, was utterly opposed to such attacks on the established structure of society in Britain, derived, as he saw it, from French Jacobins. Literally speaking, Jacobins were members of a left-wing club that met in a former monastery in the rue Saint-Jacques in

Paris and became notorious for its extreme republican views. The term soon came to embrace in current usage all those who might support extreme republican measures, especially among artisans and common people; and so, for Pitt, Jacobinism was 'that monstrous doctrine under which the weak and the ignorant, who are most susceptible of impression by such barren abstract propositions, were attempted to be seduced to overturn government, law, property, religion, order and everything valuable in this country'. There was much that was valuable in the way that eighteenth-century Britain was run, and it was run far better than eighteenth-century France, but the terms under which the prime minister proposed to defend its merits pitted the ruling class against the ignorant and impressionable masses – Burke's 'swinish multitude' – terms in which the struggle was envisaged by certain aristocrats, including George III.

The spread of French levelling to Britain had to be opposed at all costs, and on 21 May the King issued a proclamation against 'wicked and seditious Writings', directed chiefly at Thomas Paine. To enforce the royal threat the policing of the capital was much expanded. The Westminster Police Bill, which passed the Lords in June, provided for seven new police offices in addition to the existing Bow Street office, each assigned three stipendiary magistrates appointed and dismissed by the King. This expanded police force was the brainchild of John Reeves, a lawyer educated at Eton and Christ Church, Oxford, who had studied the police in Paris in 1783. He was appointed a magistrate and given control of the funding.

The twin goals of the Westminster police organisation were to keep an eye on the vast numbers of immigrants flooding into the country and to prevent revolution. In response to an escalation in violence against aristocrats and priests, the incarceration of the royal family, and the declaration that France was now a republic, four thousand French refugees fled to Britain between

August and October 1792 alone, and they represented a source of great anxiety because the government had precious little idea of who these people were – any number of them might be spies or revolutionary agitators. Britons had always associated the continental system of police, as it existed in pre-revolutionary France, with absolutism, popery and wooden shoes. State surveillance had been regarded as un-English, incompatible with civil liberty, and possibly unconstitutional, but the public mood was changing, and the more conservative of those with something to lose backed wholeheartedly a clampdown on free expression as a means to suppress radical agitation.

By the autumn of 1792 relations between the British government and the French Convention were deteriorating and Pitt had already begun the process of naval rearmament. The Convention's declaration of fraternal help to those struggling for liberty in other countries helped to stimulate an atmosphere of paranoia and panic and a short-lived but apparently genuine fear in December of an imminent revolution in Britain.

In this atmosphere Reeves, paymaster of the Westminster magistrates, also founded the Association for Preserving Liberty and Property against Republicans and Levellers. Reeves claimed that his society was independent of government and founded without government knowledge, but this was at best only partly true, since he had used police funds to pay for its handbills.[5] The first advertisements were placed by Evan Nepean with John Heriot, editor of the *Sun*, a newspaper founded privately in 1792 by George Rose of the Treasury and Francis Freeling of the Post Office, both government officials party to secret information. It was subsequently proved that the secretary, 'John Moore', was not a real person and that the resolutions of the foundation 'meeting' of 20 November were drafted by Reeves.[6]

The *raison d'être* of the Association was 'discouraging and suppressing Seditious Publications' – a sort of informal censorship through denunciation. Reeves welcomed communications relating to these goals and hoped that similar societies would be set up all over the provinces to pursue the same aims. His hopes were realised: the Association rapidly won massive support from a whole range of people who believed in the benefits of the existing system of permeable hierarchy in prosperous Britain (albeit many supporters, especially Churchmen, had much to lose from a revolution), and he received numerous denunciations of persons said to be promoting seditious publications. During December and January loyal declarations came in from most parts of the country, promising, in the words of Oxford loyalists printed in the local newspaper, to help to suppress locally 'all seditious, treasonable, inflammatory Publications, whether in News-papers, printed Hand-Bills, ludicrous or caricature prints or in any other Mode'.[7] Reeves soon found himself at the head of a nationwide army of ready vigilantes, so that the radical poet and journalist Samuel Taylor Coleridge dubbed him 'captain of the spy-gang'.

Much of the information that his correspondents sent in related to those who published or promoted the works of Thomas Paine, but informants spread their net much wider. Beyond the newspapers, handbills and caricatures mentioned by the worthies of Oxford, they must also look out for books, pamphlets, medals and tokens, songs, broadsheets, printed fans, printed pottery and any other ingeniously imagined vehicle for seditious messages.[8] On 4 December the Association recommended householders and the keepers of inns, taverns and coffee-houses to discontinue and discourage the circulation of disloyal and seditious newspapers. On 6 December it cautioned 'all sellers of Newspapers, Newscarriers, persons delivering hand-bills for club-meetings, and the like, that if such papers are seditious or treasonable, *they* are also guilty'; it also published laws relating to treason, reminding people, for instance, that it was treasonable to drink to the pious memory of a traitor or to curse the King. The *Evening Mail* for 7–10

December pointed out 'certain print-shops which abound with the most scandalous and libellous caricatures', especially one kept by 'a great Jacobin in Oxford Road, who has lately imported some prints from Paris, strongly bordering on Treason. They are labelled with decrees of the National Convention, and quotations from *Paine's Rights of Man*.' On 11 December, having received several other complaints about the 'licentiousness of certain Print-shops, wherein libellous pictures and engravings are daily exhibited', the Association printed the libel laws relating to pictures 'by way of caution to the proprietors of these shops'.[9]

On 17 December the 'great Jacobin', a printseller called William Holland, was arrested with the reformist bookseller James Ridgway, and on 23 February 1793 Holland was sentenced to a year in prison, fined £100, and ordered to find £200 surety for good behaviour for selling Paine's *Letter Addressed to the Addressers*. Ridgway, who had earlier in 1792 published a highly provocative edition of *Killing No Murder*, the pamphlet traditionally republished to accompany an invitation to overthrow a tyrant, was fined £200 and sentenced to four years in prison for publishing *The Jockey Club*, Paine's *Letter* and *The Rights of Man*. Another bookseller, Henry Delahay Symonds, was fined a total of £200 and imprisoned for four years for publishing the same seditious works.[10] Other booksellers had already been imprisoned, and prominent targets, such as Paine himself, had fled to France.

To prevent Evan Nepean from 'killing himself by his labours' in dealing with this increased workload, an apprentice had been found by Lord Grenville, then Home Secretary, in the shape of John King, just turned thirty, a contemporary and friend of Grenville's from Christ Church, Oxford, and protégé of the dean, Cyril Jackson, who played a central role in recruiting operatives for Pitt's secret service.[11] King, a Yorkshireman, was the son of a curate whose family had close connections with Edmund Burke. He was an amiable, hard-working factotum – when George Canning first

dined with him in December 1793 he found him 'one of the worthi-
est and friendliest and best sort of men in the world'.[12] Appointed
clerk in 1791 and then co-undersecretary in 1792, King took on
much of the work produced by the new Westminster Police, but
they alone were not enough to deal with the ever-increasing influx
of Frenchmen, who had become an acute problem as war with
France became merely a matter of who declared it first.

In a further bid to gain some control over the spate of potentially
subversive immigrants, the Aliens Act was passed in January 1793,
requiring foreigners to register and suspending Habeas Corpus
for them, and the twenty-two-year-old William Huskisson joined
the team as the first superintendent of aliens. Highly intelligent,
Huskisson had just returned from Paris, where he had spent his
teenage years, before working as an assistant to the ambassador. As
superintendent he initially shared the rooms of the Secret Office of
the Post Office, working with one clerk under him 'in the smallest
Garret in the Home Office' in Whitehall.[13] Residential accommodation for agents as well as prisoners was added in 1794; from there
state prisoners were usually transferred to Cold Bath Fields prison,
which became known as 'the English Bastille'. The Alien Office,
created in 1793, instructed the Post Office to open mail from France
as a matter of course and worked closely with the Post Office head,
instructing him which mail that had been opened was to be forwarded to its intended recipient and which mail was to be detained.

The Secret Office of the Post Office had long been responsible
for monitoring foreign correspondence, employing decipherers and
translators under the 'foreign secretary'. Ironically, in the course
of reforms in 1793 the necessity for a 'foreign secretary' was questioned and, since the true occupation of the incumbent could not
be revealed, the post was abolished as a sinecure; but despite his
official abolition, John Maddison continued as head of the Secret
Office, doing the job he had done since 1787 when he took over
from his uncle.

His main work was to supervise the opening and transcribing of foreign correspondence, sending intercepted letters to the confidential undersecretaries in packets marked 'Private and Most Secret'. As Maddison's uncle had explained in 1753 when appealing for assistance, the opening and resealing of the letters so that the recipients remained unaware that they had been opened was easily the most difficult part of the business.[14] Those in plain language went straight to the King and those in cipher were taken by hand or special messenger to a small Deciphering Branch, which passed them to the King once decoded. Letters sometimes reached the King within twenty-four hours of being sent; after that they were passed to the secretaries of state for circulation to selected ministers. The Secret Office also prepared 'plant' letters for foreign courts or agents, searched correspondence with special 'liquors' for invisible ink, and kept an eye out for cipher cribs, which they passed to the deciphering branch. In 1801 Maddison controlled a staff of ten. The Hanoverian government also maintained a 'secret bureau' of openers and decipherers at Nienburg, working in close contact with London, exchanging information and visits.[15]

From 1793, Maddison's office also opened suspicious inland correspondence as potential troublemakers were identified either by information coming to the Alien Office, or to Reeves's 'Association for Preserving Liberty', or through confidential local information drawn by Francis Freeling from trusted provincial postmasters.[16] Freeling was a Bristolian, born in 1764, who shared with Maddison a passion for collecting books. Originally employed in Bristol, he came to London in 1785 and supervised the implementation of the new mail coach service as 'resident surveyor', but from 1792 he was the dominant figure in the Post Office, 'advising' the aristocrats who were nominally in charge. He was appointed joint secretary of the Post Office in 1797, and sole secretary the following year, and he ran the organisation until his death in 1836.

While the government and its auxiliaries were concerned to

suppress all hints at sedition, they were also keen to nourish support for their own views. Reeves's Association took on a prop-aganda role, aiming 'to explain those topicks of public discussion which have been so perverted by evil-designing men' and recom-mending to its branches that the Association 'should by reasoning, and by circulating cheap books and papers, endeavour to undeceive those poor people who have been misled by the infusion of opin-ions dangerous to their own welfare and that of the State'.

It issued numerous handbills, pamphlets and prints, the best-known print being Thomas Rowlandson's *The Contrast*, a loyalist caricature showing on one side 'British Liberty' personified by Britannia holding Magna Carta and the scales of justice and guarded by a sleeping lion, and on the other 'French Liberty', a rampaging, snake-haired fury wielding a dagger and a trident on which a head and hearts were impaled. Several plates were made in order to print huge numbers of this print, which the Association sold at a quarter of the normal price in an attempt to extend its circulation; they offered a hundred prints for a guinea to wealthy men who might give them away. *The Contrast* was reproduced on printed pottery and as a woodcut on the cover of the *Antigallican Songster*, a collection of loyal songs.[17]

Secret service payments were used as an incentive or reward to those who contributed to the cause. Secret service payments from the Civil List had become controversial during the war of American Independence, and were reformed by a bill brought in by Edmund Burke in 1782 by which Parliament agreed to pay for foreign secret service to a maximum of £100,000 a year, while home secret service continued to be paid from the Civil List but was limited to £10,000 a year.[18] Burke himself continued to be an important crusading pamphleteer against the revolution until shortly before his death in 1797, but the most prolific of the pamphleteers in government pay was John Bowles, author of one of the earliest pamphlets paid for and circulated by Reeves, his

Protest against Paine's 'Rights of Man' (1792). Bowles was by nature far more reactionary than Burke: after secret service payments of £115 in 1792 and 1793 he received a pension of £100 a year for his journalism, then a post as commissioner of bankrupts worth £3–400 per annum, and finally in 1795, a colossal reward as one of five commissioners for the sale of Dutch prizes.[19] Bowles believed wholeheartedly in the cause he wrote for, but he made a fortune from his work as a government publicist.

Blaming foreigners, in a time-honoured English manner, Bowles described 'a deep and vast conspiracy against all the ancient institutions of Europe, civil, political, and religious' stemming from Voltaire's infidel philosophy and from 'licentious' German writing. He feared 'Treachery, Conspiracy, Revolt and Insurrection' and regarded all opposition politicians as Jacobins. He approved of repressive legislation and promoted 'dictatorial powers'. His goal was the complete destruction of the revolutionary machine and the restoration of lawful authority. To Bowles, interference in France was almost a matter of duty; he was totally committed to the restoration of the Bourbons, wanted the government to recognise Louis XVII, then XVIII, and to give all possible support to royalist rebels in France, for the enemy was not the French nation but French revolutionary principles. This was a new kind of war – for which traditional means were inadequate and 'new evils must be encountered by new remedies'. He regarded all peace-mongering as seditious, since its proponents 'look forward to a Republican Peace as to a Republican Triumph'.[20]

A periodical and two government newspapers gave dependable support to Pitt's views. Tory Churchmen Robert Nares (paid £50 from the secret service fund in 1792 and 1793) and William Beloe established the *British Critic* as an anti-Jacobin, anti-dissent opponent of the Whiggish *Monthly*, *Critical* and *Analytical* reviews.[21] The founding of the *Sun* and the *True Briton* is shrouded in mystery, but it is generally acknowledged that the Treasury played some part and those newspapers remained under the influence of Treasury undersecretaries George Rose and Charles Long, both close friends of Pitt. John Heriot, who had been recruited as a government pamphleteer when the King went mad in 1788, was installed as first editor of the *Sun* and was rewarded with a double commissionership of the lottery worth £5–600 a year. The *True Briton* took over the Catherine Street office and presses of Sampson Perry's radical *Argus* (1789–92) after Perry had fled to France to avoid trial for seditious libel and the government had declared him an outlaw and seized his property.[22] The *True Briton*'s first editor may also have been Heriot, but he was eventually replaced by John Gifford, whose anti-Jacobin *History of France* (1791–3) had caught Pitt's eye along with his pamphlet *A Plain Address to the Common Sense of the People of England* (1792).

Gifford, born John Richards Green, had squandered a fortune as a young man, fled to France to escape his creditors, and changed his name.[23] He returned just before or during the revolution and, somewhat bizarrely, aged thirty-four, was appointed one of the new Westminster magistrates, with a stipend of £400. As well as writing ministerial anti-Jacobin history and pamphlets, Gifford translated pamphlets by *émigrés*. He received £170 2s. 6d. from the secret service account in 1794, £210 in 1795 and £240 in 1796, after which he was in regular government employment as editor first of the *True Briton* and then of the *Anti-Jacobin Review*.

In France, meanwhile, the months between September 1793 and July 1794 were those of the Terror and of dechristianisation, a concept appallingly shocking to Protestant Britons, however much they might despise the French Catholic Church. In France this was year zero: in October 1793 the Christian calendar was replaced by one that reckoned time from the revolution. Clerical property was seized, worship was closed down, Christmas was abolished. Notre Dame in Paris became the Temple of Reason. There were savage reprisals against Lyon, which had revolted against rule from Paris, and thousands more executions under the Reign of Terror which came to a close with the execution in June 1794 of Maximilien Robespierre himself.

This godless chaos was too much for most Britons, and in July 1794 the bulk of the Whig party, led by Lord Portland, joined the government in order to support the war against the French Revolution. The Whig aristocrats who joined the ministry with Lord Portland all took Edmund Burke's crusading view: their object was the overthrow of the French republic. 'They see that their titles & possessions are in danger, & they think that their best chance for preserving them is by supporting Government & joining me,' Pitt wrote, somewhat cynically, in 1793.[24] Portland received assurances that the administration sought the restoration of the Bourbon monarchy, and the Whigs tried to cooperate with the royalist *émigrés*. Grenville had always favoured this approach, in contrast to Dundas, who preferred to keep out of France but seize French colonies, and his hand was strengthened by the reinforcement of Portland's like-minded friends.

At the Home Office, the ministry Portland took over, John King became undersecretary in chief when Nepean and Huskisson left with Dundas for a newly created Ministry for War and the Colonies. An important new face was William Wickham, a Westminster stipendiary magistrate, then aged thirty-three, who took over as superintendent of aliens. His father was a lieutenant colonel in the Foot Guards, which endeared him to the King, and through Christ Church, Oxford he had become another protégé of Dean Cyril Jackson. He studied law in Switzerland and married a woman from a Genevan banking family. It was John King, a Yorkshire neighbour, who introduced Wickham to Grenville, who had been a distant acquaintance of Wickham at Oxford, and at Grenville's request Wickham had spent the previous year investigating the London Corresponding Society. Nepean received Wickham's (rather overexcited) report on 8 May 1794, and four days later the

Society's leaders were arrested, with Habeas Corpus suspended the following week: Pitt explained that the corresponding societies aimed at the 'total subversion of the Constitution, the annihilation of Parliament and the destruction of the King himself'.[25]

Wickham quite quickly became the most notorious British spymaster and recruited people who played important roles in the secret war. His familiarity with Switzerland recommended him to Grenville when a confidential emissary had to be sent there in October 1794 in response to an approach from the former president of the Constituent Assembly and the former editor of the *Mercure de France*, who claimed to be in contact with the president of the National Convention, who was willing to facilitate the restoration of the Bourbon monarchy, a goal to which Grenville was now firmly committed. Wickham arrived in Bern on 1 November 1794, but a few questions revealed that the project was less than substantial and he judged it imprudent to invest funds. Grenville approved of Wickham's handling of the negotiations and, as he was anxious to open any channel that might bring him reliable information on affairs within France, he required Wickham to remain in Switzerland as minister plenipotentiary and explore potential links with Paris.[26] Grenville already received royalist intelligence reports from Paris through Francis Drake, the consul at Genoa, and his contact the comte d'Antraigues, who acted for the comte de Provence (uncle of Louis XVII), but as d'Antraigues acted principally for the Spanish, his was not a network that Grenville trusted entirely.[27]

One of Wickham's contacts recommended an engineer from the Jura called Louis Bayard as an agent, and during the following year Bayard established lines of communication to Paris, and from there to the Vendée. Wickham eventually established and funded a 'Paris Committee' of royalist agents who supplied him with information through Bayard, who became Wickham's most reliable assistant and ultimately Britain's leading spy in Paris.[28]

Grenville sent Wickham an assistant, the eighteen-year-old

Charles William Flint, the son of a King's Messenger who had died in 1793 while on official duty. Grenville made himself responsible for the orphan and had given him a clerk's job at the Foreign Office before sending him to Wickham as someone 'who bore the character of much diligence and intelligence'.[29] Flint was a pretty, straw-blond boy who looked even younger than his age, but was hard-working, invariably good-humoured, charming, resourceful and cool under pressure. He became the most dependable British spymaster, and a crucial figure in winning the long war.

Support for French dissidents in the western provinces of France was directed by William Windham, who, after joining the ministry with Lord Portland, became secretary at war in 1794, and was made responsible for liaison with the *émigrés*, specifically planning help for the royalists in western France. Windham was a highly educated and civilised scholar who possessed one of the best collections of Hogarth's satires in the country. He had been a great enthusiast for the revolution in its early stages of constitutional monarchy, but, influenced by Burke, he turned violently against it in its apparent descent to chaos, terror, atheism and levelling. The diplomat Lord Malmesbury, who was a shrewd judge of character, admired Windham but distrusted his judgement:

> Windham is uncommonly and classically clever, but has the very fault he attributes to Pitt – no real knowledge of mankind; not from not living in the world, but from not being endowed with those qualities (inferior in themselves) which would enable him to judge of their real designs and character. From this reason he was the dupe of every emigrant who called on him; and he still persists in the idea of the *bellum internecinum*, and the invading of France. Burke spoilt him, and his genius still rules him. He is withal the most honourable and most sensible of the cabinet, and with many very great and amiable private virtues – a first-rate scholar, and quite of the right school.[30]

Windham's principal front-line operative was the naval officer Philippe d'Auvergne, who in June 1794 had been put in charge of the sea defence of Jersey with a fleet of gunboats. He was Evan Nepean's choice and was also instructed to provide material aid to the *chouan* rebels in Brittany and Normandy and 'to open communications with the enemy so as to obtain early information of hostile movements of the enemy', to which end he established an elaborate spy network known as 'the Channel Islands correspondence'.

D'Auvergne had been a midshipman in the same arctic expedition in which the young Horatio Nelson had taken part, and from which illness had forced Windham to withdraw early. During the American War of Independence he was promoted three times, making post captain in 1783. He was captured by the French in 1779 and during a period on parole in France so impressed and charmed the French prince Godefroy Charles Henri de la Tour d'Auvergne, duc de Bouillon, that Bouillon adopted him as his heir in 1787, having persuaded himself and the French official genealogist that Philippe was a distant cousin. By 1794 the British naval officer Philippe d'Auvergne was officially prince de Bouillon in France, and acknowledged as such by George III. A distinguished mathematician and scientist and a Fellow of the Royal Society, in Jersey the prince lived partly on his flagship, partly in two rooms in Mont Orgueil castle, and partly in a Gothic tower that he built on Hogue Bie, given to him by his uncle, and he began to build up extravagant debts based on his enormous expectations.

Bouillon established resident correspondents in strategic locations, whose reports were picked up by his boats from prearranged hiding places in the rocks. For instance, packets were buried twice a week on the islets of Chausey off the Normandy port of Granville fifty miles from Mont Orgueil, picked up by a Granville fisherman and given to a girl called Pipette. There was another postbox on the Roches du Sac de Pirou on the French coast opposite Mont Orgueil – a boy would swim to find any packet and give it to Madame de Bougainville, wife of the circumnavigator. Bouillon was constantly required to land spies and royalist agents and established landing places with routes from safe house to safe house to *chouan* centres. One landing place was nine miles east of Saint-Brieuc at the foot of a rock into which steps had been cut; guides led parties to a lonely farm, then eight miles inland to a friendly village; then past Moncontour and through the forest of Loudéac to Pontivy.[31]

Bouillon's responsibilities did not stop at landing arms and money to support insurgency. In summer 1793 the British government decided to wage economic war on France by forging its paper currency – a further indication that this total war was to be waged in unconventional as well as conventional ways. Three paper mills were devoted to making paper with forged French watermarks, and although someone tried to raise the matter in Parliament and Thomas Bewick the wood engraver 'very honourably declared he would have no hand in such business' the project went ahead. 'The war of assignats', wrote a royalist general, 'is capable of destroying the Republic.' One of Bouillon's lieutenants was Armand de Chateaubriand, cousin of the writer, and his first job for Bouillon in December 1794 was to land false *assignats* in Normandy. The practice was exposed in a case in King's Bench on 18 November 1795 where an engraver admitted forging French *assignats* after being assured by Colonel Smith, agent to the Duke of York's army, that the secretaries of state had approved the commission.[32] As one historian wryly observed, it meant that the government 'could pay their agents in France very handsomely with currency that cost little more than the paper on which it was printed'.[33]

The great British military effort of 1794 in Europe, however, had gone into a campaign to defend the Austrian Netherlands, but in the end the Duke of York's British army had not fared well and during the winter of 1794–5 the allies were defeated. The duke retreated to Bremen while, riding over the ice, General

Jean-Charles Pichegru's republican French hussars captured the Dutch fleet, as well as Amsterdam, and the Prince of Orange fled to London. Republicans triumphed in Holland, which joined France; Prussia and Spain made peace with France, and Spain soon after changed sides. Conventional approaches had failed against the remarkable brilliance of the republican armies and their general, Pichegru, but the Bourbon princes could point to clear signs of support for their cause in parts of France and they were keen to put another strategy in place.

3

Bellum Internecinum

The next year, 1795, those who wanted to support insurrection in France got their way, and on both the western and eastern borders preparations were made to support uprisings within France and invasions by Frenchmen to bring about counter-revolution. They produced the first of several highly complicated and over-ambitious plans for synchronised attacks from several different directions. In the west a force of *émigrés* equipped in Britain and supported by British soldiers and ships was to land at Quiberon in Brittany and link up with *chouan* insurgents, drawing republican troops away from the eastern frontier. In the east Foreign Secretary Lord Grenville ordered his agent William Wickham to negotiate to subsidise the army of French *émigrés* led by the prince de Condé, an experienced soldier of the blood royal, and Condé and Wickham opened negotiations with the opposing republican general, none other than the brilliant Jean Charles Pichegru, victor of the campaign in the Netherlands, now commander of the French army of the Rhine, who was dissatisfied with the current republican government. The plan for the east was for the Austrians to break through with the prince de Condé's British-paid army as spearhead, General Pichegru having agreed to allow Condé through; this invasion would coincide with an attack in the south-east from Piedmont, a rising in Lyon and a coup in Paris.

The timing went wrong from the start. The Austrians made no move until long after the Anglo-royalist Quiberon expedition, landed in June, had been crushed in July by the republican army. However, despite the catastrophe at Quiberon, some royalists were still active in the west. In particular, Louis de Frotté made his way to his native Normandy to organise resistance in the bocages.

In order to cooperate with Frotté, to blockade the river Seine leading to Paris, and to harry the French in that quarter, in March 1795 Captain Sir Sidney Smith was given a naval command to the eastward of the prince de Bouillon's. Smith was a cousin of both Grenville and Pitt and, with his brothers, he had been brought up at court, where their father was gentleman usher to Queen Charlotte.[1] This meant that the Smiths were personally acquainted with George III and blood relations of Pitt and Grenville, and as they were also poor and ambitious they were ideal material for operations involving daring and gallantry. Sidney Smith had been allocated a career in the navy, where his excellent royal patronage and other connections won him posts on flagships, rapid promotion and a Swedish knighthood.

In spring 1793 Smith had been at Smyrna, researching Russian and Turkish naval capabilities for Lord Grenville, while ostensibly serving as a volunteer in the Turkish navy, when he heard of the outbreak of war with France.[2] Instantly (and leaving his young brother Spencer behind to take up a post as secretary of legation at Constantinople) he bought a coaster, hired forty British seamen and set sail westward. Learning that Admiral Hood's Anglo-Spanish fleet was at Toulon, he steered for that port. By the time he arrived he found that Toulon was about to be evacuated; Smith volunteered for the task of burning the magazine and naval equipment in the dockyard together with those French ships that could not be sailed away. He accomplished this arson tolerably well, according to his own account, despite obstruction from Spanish colleagues who didn't approve, the danger from explosions, enemy artillery, and finally musketry from republican soldiers as they broke in to the dockyard.

On return to London he was eventually given the frigate *Diamond* and the job of taking Earl Spencer to Flushing (Vlissingen) in the Netherlands. During the voyage he treated the First Lord of the Admiralty to some of his ideas on how to win the war. Spencer wrote to Windham:

> He is certainly an odd, eccentric man, but he is very clever and has a great deal of contrivance about him and if he could somehow be put into activity without giving offence to the more regular and orderly sort of Geniuses, who I believe all look upon him as a fellow of the College of Physicians does upon a Quack doctor, he might be of great service.[3]

Smith commanded an inshore squadron consisting of *Diamond*, two smaller frigates, some gunboats, fireships, a floating battery and two cutters. In July, as a base for his operations, he occupied the uninhabited Iles Saint-Marcouf, off the eastern side of the Cotentin peninsula in Normandy, leaving some of his gunboats and his floating battery to guard them. Gradually, he fortified the islands, building redoubts, and established a naval garrison five hundred strong under Lieutenant Charles Price, who lived on the islands with a prostitute he had brought from Portsmouth. The islands provided Smith with a firm base for his harrying and his more secret duties landing agents and supplies for Norman royalists.[4] He made contact with Frotté, they set up a correspondence with London via the Marcouf islands, and Smith landed money, muskets and officers for Frotté's small force.

Smith's team included several resourceful assistants. John Wesley Wright was brought up in Minorca, where his father was paymaster. He served at the great siege of Gibraltar, but in peacetime left the navy to be a clerk in the City and then spent five years in Russia, before returning to the navy as secretary to Smith in 1794. Wright had probably always been a spy, but certainly served Smith in this capacity, linking up with Frotté and fighting with him on land. Jacques Boudin de Tromelin, a twenty-four-year-old Breton royalist officer, took charge of correspondence from the Marcouf islands where he was normally based, but he also ran missions to Frotté, and Smith also had another Breton and an emigrant from Toulon to act as emissaries and couriers on shore.

On the eastern border negotiations with Pichegru had gone well, and he played his part in allied plans, losing deliberately and retreating with minimum resistance, without being suspected by the French government. However, the planned coup in Paris of 5 October 1795 (13 *vendémiaire*), which was probably less royalist in nature than the British had been led to believe by their royalist correspondents, failed thanks to the betrayal of the plans and the decisive intervention of General Bonaparte, who deployed artillery against the royalist force that was advancing on the Tuileries, and the other initiatives also collapsed. The Austrians cancelled the attack from Piedmont and the Lyon rising was compromised by the capture of incriminating papers.

These failures only increased the unpopularity of the ministry and its war at home, where a poor harvest, a harsh winter and disruption to trade with Holland and Germany had produced poverty and hardship. Membership of the radical London Corresponding Society grew; petitioners and rioters campaigned against the war. Parliament's grant of £125,000 annual income to the newly married Prince of Wales provided he allocated some of it to paying off a debt that had now reached £630,000 added insult to injury. In July a mob broke the windows of 10 Downing Street while Pitt was hosting a dinner party; when he went to open Parliament

George III was abused by a mob said to be 200,000 strong and something broke the window of his coach.

Despite the opposition of the 'crusaders', and the reluctance of the King, Pitt opened negotiations with the Directory, the five-man executive now governing France; overtures passed between Wickham and the French minister in Switzerland François Barthélemy, but the British approach was couched in insulting terms and the Directory's 'haughty and inadmissible demands' only confirmed George III's disdain for the 'perfidious nation'. George III deplored any talk of making peace, and although he did not try to veto peace negotiations, he made it clear to all concerned that he was relying on their failure.[5]

Riots and unrest inspired Pitt's ministry to introduce even more repressive measures to restrict criticism in print. In autumn 1795 the Treasonable and Seditious Practices Act extended the definition of treason to include speaking and writing, even if no subsequent actions followed, and made treasonable bringing the King or his government into contempt: hostile portrayals of the King were effectively outlawed from this time. Another act banned 'seditious meetings'. The bestselling Whig satirist John Wolcot published the wonderfully titled *Liberty's Last Squeak*, a collection of poems including 'Ode to an Informer', and 'Crumbs of Comfort for the Grand Informer', which registered delight when Fox and others persuaded the attorney general to prosecute John Reeves for a 'libel on the British Constitution' contained in his *Thoughts on the English Government* (it had likened the British constitution to a tree, monarchy, from which the branches legislature, Lords and Commons could be lopped off without harm). Wolcot's *Convention Bill: an Ode* carried the epigraph, supposedly Pitt's translation of Horace, 'Be padlocks plac'd on ev'ry Briton's tongue!'[6]

The 'Gagging Acts' provoked hostile caricatures showing a ragged *Freeborn Englishman* bound and gagged or with his mouth padlocked shut in *A Lock'd Jaw for John Bull* and *A Sociable Meeting*, or with the Convention Bill stuffed down his throat with the butt of a musket in *Talk of an Ostrich!* [7] However, they were effective in silencing critics; as Sampson Perry pointed out in the preface to another *Argus*, written in Newgate prison and bravely published in 1796 by H. D. Symonds, 'the latitude which an Attorney General may give to an act of Parliament, so worded, has occasioned a number of booksellers to decline disposing of any work which animadverts upon government, however pertinently or warily.' [8]

Moreover, those who had irritated loyalists with their political publications could often be prosecuted for other offences. The printseller James Aitken, whose shop had displayed many prints attacking Pitt and ridiculing the royal family, was convicted in November 1795 of publishing a directory of prostitutes that had come out annually for forty years. [9] Soon afterwards in January 1796 Aitken's shopman was arrested, along with the publisher Samuel William Fores and the engraver James Gillray, for selling *The Presentation – or – The Wise Mens Offering* on a charge of blasphemy. [10] Later, while Aitken was incarcerated in Newgate, his wife Ann was convicted through evidence provided by a member of the Society for the Suppression of Vice 'of carrying on the same nefarious trade that constituted his offence'. He proved that 'she kept, for sale, a large collection of the most indecent prints and drawings, out of above *two hundred* of which another witness proved the purchase of one at the price of *one guinea*.' She was sentenced to a year's hard labour, and by 1803, after a further conviction, Aitken had been driven out of business. [11]

The risk involved in publishing prints that crusading magistrates might deem either seditious or indecent was brought sharply home by Aitken's case, and the commercially vulnerable caricature printsellers, a mere handful of people, were bullied into line. It might look as if people whose main offence was political were being arrested for unrelated moral crimes, but this is to miss the point. Loyalists believed that enlightenment free-thinking encouraged loose morals in the same way that it encouraged loose politics, that the trends were directly linked, and that they aimed towards destroying the moral and structural bonds of traditional society. The association of Jacobin principles with vice was one that the anti-Jacobins were determined to make stick in the public mind. The prime mover in this crusade was John Bowles, an energetic committee member both of the Proclamation Society (which became the Society for the Suppression of Vice in 1802) and of Reeves's Association. Post Office Secretary Francis Freeling was also on the Vice Society committee.

Once Church and state and especially Church had closed ranks against the revolution, and once the revolution had gone through its phase of dechristianisation and terror, it became difficult to depict it sympathetically or to promote the cause of moderate reform. Once Fox was pictured in the public mind as a pro-French, Jacobin traitor, it was difficult to show him as a forward-thinking cosmopolitan, and with the country at war, opponents of 'loyalism' were liable to appear unpatriotic into the bargain. As the reformist London tailor Francis Place recalled:

Infamous as these laws were, they were popular measures. The people, ay, the mass of shopkeepers and working people may be said to have approved them without understanding them. Such was their terror of the French regicides and democrats, such was the fear that 'the throne and the altar' would be destroyed.[12]

The willingness of juries to convict made sure that these laws ended the robust tradition of free expression that writers and political artists had often been able to get away with until 1795. From then on people began to get used to much more restrictive libel laws and varieties of 'political correctness'.

Meanwhile, off the west coast of France the efforts of d'Auvergne and Smith to preserve 'the throne and the altar' continued.

Rapaciously hungry for both glory and prize money, Smith pulled off some daring enterprises, but his luck ran out in April 1796 while conducting a secret mission in Le Havre. During the night he went out in the frigate's boats with a large number of his men, and with characteristic audacity bordering on foolhardiness they attempted to cut out a notorious French privateer, *Le Vengeur*. Smith's men succeeded in overpowering the French crew, but as they attempted to sail their prize out to sea the wind dropped away unexpectedly and despite all their efforts the changing tide swept the captured *Vengeur* several miles up the estuary of the Seine. Dawn revealed them to the French and, facing overwhelming force, Smith eventually surrendered and was taken to the Abbaye prison in Paris. There was probably more to the incident than met the eye: perhaps this unfortunate piece of military bravado that went so disastrously wrong had been intended to distract the attention of the French authorities from Smith's main mission that night. When he was captured he had both Wright and Tromelin with him. They had no business in a boat attack and it is likely that his main purpose had been to pick up Wright and drop off Tromelin, or to communicate with somebody on shore.[13] The British hoped that Frotté might rescue Sir Sidney without delay, but his band was scattered and he was forced to flee to London in June. Smith and his fellow prisoners were transferred from the Abbaye to the Temple prison in July, and Wickham allocated £1000 to royalist agents in Paris to secure his release.[14]

The year went badly for the allies: the royalist risings in the west were stamped out, and although the Austrians drove back a French offensive in Germany, General Bonaparte inflicted a series of defeats on them in Italy. In December 1796 General Hoche even managed to launch an invasion of Ireland: a fleet carrying fourteen thousand men escaped the blockade of Brest and evaded the British fleet, but winter storms scattered Hoche's ships. Most of them reached Bantry Bay, but his own ship did not; the weather was so bad that the French couldn't land, and with their leaders driven miles off course they were uncertain what to do and eventually returned to France. The invasion was a flop, but it had come close enough to convince people in Britain that another attempt might succeed. One of the diversionary forces, 1400 strong, intended to march on Bristol, actually landed at Fishguard in February 1797, and caused a run on the Bank of England before they were rounded up. In these circumstances, the mutinies in the Channel fleet at Spithead in April and May and at the Nore in May and June 1797 caused great alarm. Such were the fears of the French plan to seize Bristol that the Home Office sent its best spy, James Walsh, to investigate the suspicious coastal walks of the 'Jacobin' poets Samuel Coleridge and William Wordsworth, who had been joined in Somerset by John Thelwall, a leading London radical.

The failures of 1795 and 1796 highlighted intrinsic difficulties in working with French royalists. One was that their different factions would not cooperate with each other, even within the deposed royal family itself, for Monsieur, the comte de Provence, who declared himself regent after the execution of Louis XVI, was not on good terms with his younger brother the comte d'Artois. Artois, based at first in Edinburgh and after 1800 in London, was the more significant figure to ministers, as it was his council that directed royalists operating from Britain. 'Once the most gay, gaudy, fluttering, accomplished, luxurious, and expensive, Prince in Europe', he was 'beloved by the courtiers, but execrated by the people', much more so than his obese but scholarly elder brother, who led a wandering life on the Continent.[15] At first their supporters sought to undermine each other, but eventually Artois was appointed to be Louis's military commander. One of the few things the brothers and their bickering courtiers agreed on was that the old monarchy should be restored in undiluted absolutist form. This was fundamentally unacceptable to constitutional monarchists who wanted a limited monarchy and a balanced constitution, following the British model. Having been outmanoeuvred by the Jacobins in the early phases of the revolution, the constitutional-ists now hoped for British support for a moderate revolution. The 'ultras' or *'purs'* (as the absolutists were called) hated them, but the constitutionalists commanded broader sympathy in Britain.

A Bourbon restoration was still not official British policy, and after the death in June 1795 of the young prince, known to royalists as Louis XVII, Britain chose not to recognise his uncle the comte de Provence, then in Verona, as Louis XVIII. But the British minis-try was split in its views, with some, such as Windham and George III, deeply committed to the *purs*, while Wickham, for instance, was known personally to favour constitutionalist views. He, at least, soon realised that royalists usually vastly overestimated the extent of support for their cause in France, and he grew quickly disenchanted with the intransigence of those surrounding the self-styled Louis XVIII.

Patriotism also played a major part in complicating negotiations with Frenchmen, and in this respect it was the constitutionalists whose anglophobia most frustrated Wickham. Desperate as they were for British financial support, all French factions distrusted British motives, and especially any British plan that encouraged civil war in France, suspecting that the unspoken aim of Pitt was to weaken France as much as possible. As a British diplomat remarked to Grenville of the royalist factions, 'however they hate one another, they *all* in the bottom detest *us*'.[16]

Thrown onto the defensive militarily, the British turned away from violence towards a 'war of opinion' as the best hope for a royalist settlement within France, and Wickham and his agents formed a plan to manipulate the elections of 1797 through bribery in order to get royalists elected to key positions, creating 'philan-thropic institutes' throughout France to organise locally.[17] It was hoped that General Pichegru would play a key role in this plan and might engineer a peaceful takeover. After his inglorious campaign

in 1795 Pichegru had been deprived of his command and had
retired to his estates, where he was visited by one of Wickham's
most trusty agents, a Swiss royalist officer called François-Louis
Rusillon. After smoking a pipe or two with him, Rusillon reported
Pichegru trustworthy and still well disposed. Pichegru stood for
election as president of the Council of Five Hundred, the lower
house of the legislature of France under the Constitution of
the Year III. François Barthélemy, formerly French minister in
Switzerland, but a secret constitutional monarchist, had also joined
the conspiracy, standing for election as a Director, a member of the
ruling five-man executive.

But the conspiracy faced problems from the start. In February
1797 three members of the royalist Paris Committee were betrayed
and arrested, although, crucially, their papers were saved by the
swift action of a junior associate called Julien Leclerc, who was
soon to become a key British agent.[18] In a similarly mysterious episode in Italy, where royalist agents had been sounding out General
Bonaparte, the papers of the comte d'Antraigues, which betrayed
Pichegru's past treacherous defection to the Anglo-royalist cause,
fell into Bonaparte's hands, and after some editing he passed them
to the Director Paul Barras, his political patron and the leader of
the government.[19] It turned out later that, among other difficulties,
rogue 'ultra' royalists from Louis XVIII's court were sabotaging the
prospects of the constitutionalists linked to London.

The three members of the Paris Committee joined Smith in the
Temple prison, and the recovery of this large group of agents became
a priority. The comte de Rochecotte, senior royalist general in western France, assembled a team to rescue them, involving Antoine
de Phélippeaux, a royalist officer that Wickham had selected to
fight in the Vendée, and the twenty-one-year-old royalist agent
Guillaume Hyde de Neuville, but a first plan involving a tunnel
failed. Despite the disruption of the organising Paris Committee,
the elections went well, with Pichegru elected president of the Five

Hundred and another royalist elected president of the upper house, the Council of Ancients. Although the extent of royalist support was nothing like as great as pure royalists hoped and pretended, there was a majority that opposed the Directory, favoured peace and looked to create a moderate government.[20]

At Lille, meanwhile, a British team, led by James Harris, Earl of Malmesbury and his secretary George Ellis, was again attempting to negotiate a peace, this time with much greater sincerity, albeit against the better judgement of the King and Lord Grenville, and against the background of a plot to produce a royalist coup. But Pitt wanted peace and Malmesbury and Canning supported him, so that relations between them and their haughty boss Lord Grenville became strained. In the end the outcome of the power struggle in Paris dictated the result of the peace negotiations.

By late August 1797 Paris was very tense; *chouan* generals and Anglo-royalist agents were gathered there ready for a coup, but a pure royalist coup was not what most deputies wanted. The Directors acted more decisively, and on 18 *fructidor* (4 September 1797) troops led by General Pierre Augereau, Bonaparte's envoy, arrested Pichegru.[21] The royalist leaders Pichegru, François Barthélemy, General Amédée Willot and others were deported to Sinnamary in French Guiana along with two members of the royalist Paris Committee from the Temple prison (the third had cracked under interrogation and convicted his colleagues).

At Lille new French plenipotentiaries took a much harder line after the 4 September crisis, and faced with intransigent hostility the British peace negotiator Malmesbury left France. The new French envoy to Switzerland, Joseph Mengaud, delivered a note to the Swiss government demanding the ejection of William Wickham, whose part in various plots that had nothing to do with diplomatic duties in Switzerland had been revealed by captured correspondence, and he left the country before the Swiss authorities told him to.

Remarkably, Pichegru, together with a group of exiles who had been most closely associated with the British, soon escaped from Sinnamary, on their own initiative according to the published story, and arrived in Sheerness in a British frigate in October 1798.[22] It was then that the young George Canning first met Pichegru and was very impressed, finding him 'simple, modest, wholly unlike a Frenchman, talking in a quiet narrative style ... chattering his teeth with a shivering ague-fit by Wickham's fire in Duke Street ... He is so much the greatest man that the Revolution has produced!'[23]

Rescuing Pichegru proved easier than rescuing Sir Sidney Smith. After the failure of the September coup, Nepean threw in the principal agent run by the Admiralty, Richard Cadman Etches. The details of the plan masterminded by Etches remain mysterious, but it certainly involved bribery: it would seem that the government paid at least £10,000 to secure the escape of Smith and Wright. Two more spies, Antoine Viscovitch (who had experience in extracting and laundering bribes for figures in the French government) and John Keith (Etches' operative, related to the Herries banking family to whom Etches gave 95,000 livres to bribe somebody), dealt with the financial side of things, and the plot turned on a blank sheet of official paper signed by the minister of marine which one of them obtained.[24]

The escape itself was undertaken by Tromelin, Phélippeaux and two royalist assistants. When Smith was captured, Tromelin had successfully eluded execution as a traitor by pretending to be Smith's Canadian servant 'John Bromley'; he was freed in July 1797 and he and his wife then joined forces with the other royalists. On 23 April 1798 one of them presented the gaoler of the Temple with an order, signed by the minister of marine, for the transfer of the prisoners Smith and Wright to a different prison. They were released to a fiacre waiting outside the gate. Tromelin was on the box beside the driver and Phélippeaux was inside. They drove to a safe house in Paris and then to the house at Rouen of the abbé Justin Ratel, a leading royalist agent, crossed via Le Havre, and reached London on 8 May 1798.[25]

The day before Smith reached London the French launched an amphibious assault on the base he had established at Saint-Marcouf. Fifty-two gun brigs and landing craft and some 5–6000 troops attacked at a time when wind and tide prevented British naval forces interfering, but even so, the attack was a disaster. Despite casualties, the boats got to within fifty yards of the shore, but then the British artillery switched to canister (a tin can packed with musket balls, from which they sprayed like shotgun pellets); six or seven boats were sunk with all hands and nearly 1000 French troops were killed. The result reassured those who feared a French invasion, as the title of a short pamphlet on the two coincidental triumphs made plain: *Glorious defeat of the French gun-boats! . . . To which is added, a true and circumstantial account of the escape of that gallant hero Sir Sidney Smith, from a French prison; . . . By a perusal of this book it may be seen how little old England has to fear from the boasted French invasion.* The pamphlet's account of Smith's escape was a fictional cover story for the real events.

Smith returned to his previous station off the French coast, from where he tried to re-establish an intelligence network in Paris – the previous one had been severely disrupted in September 1797 – and a line of communication to London via the Normandy coast. His first attempt, using the route to the Saint-Marcouf islands, had been compromised by the arrest of the comte de Rochecotte, his first choice as master agent, who had been denounced by a subordinate who had not been paid on time. François Mallet, based at Rouen, was replacing Rochecotte. Mallet, 'a tall well looking young man' aged thirty-two, was a Genevan cousin of William Wickham's wife, originally sent by Wickham to be his agent in the Vendée, whence he had travelled with Louis Bayard. Smith, who was about to leave the station to undertake a new mission, had introduced Mallet to his successor and his secretary so that they were familiar with his true appearance and signature, and had sent John Wesley Wright to coordinate arrangements for delivery of packages between Mallet's boatmen and the naval squadron.[26]

Having appointed Mallet to look after the Rouen end of the correspondence operation, the man who had previously been in charge there, the abbé Ratel, was free to set off to Paris to arrange matters at that end with Wickham's agent Bayard (who had returned to the French capital in June), and to recover and use the £500 that Smith had sent to Rochecotte. Smith told Canning that he had promised Ratel and Bayard £2–3000 to pay for a clerk in each of the principal French government offices.[27]

Justin Ratel, then aged thirty-six, was of medium height and very good-looking, with blond hair and blue eyes and a slightly reddish tinge to a short beard. He was the son of a hatter from Saint-Omer with an uncle in the Church. Academically brilliant, he studied theology in Paris, was ordained a priest, and had a promising Church career ahead of him when the revolution broke out. After avoiding the Terror with his family in La Roche-Guyon he was recruited into the Anglo-royalist network at Paris, was an early correspondent of d'Antraigues and the author of a number of pamphlets. In 1795 he helped Frotté establish the Normandy network linked to Sir Sidney Smith's naval squadron in the islands of Saint-Marcouf and he had first attracted the attention of the French police in connection with the rising in Paris later that year. He had been Smith's host at Rouen during his recent escape from the Temple. In Paris he and Bayard began to assemble a team. This new spy network, recruited and paid by Englishmen, proved more reliable than any previous one, and reports were soon flowing in from 'Julie Caron', the codename adopted by Ratel.[28]

Sidney Smith was leaving the station because he and his brother Spencer had been appointed joint plenipotentiaries to the Turkish government, known as the Ottoman Porte. They were there to deal with the threat to Turkey, to Russian interests and to the British Empire in India posed by the presence in Egypt of the most dangerous and enterprising of French generals, Bonaparte.

The failure of the project for a peaceful accommodation with moderate revolutionaries in 1797 was a significant blow, perhaps the last hope for a republican France not ruled by a dictatorship.[29] It was brought down as much by interference from the far right – the pure royalists and such British aristocrats as Grenville, who did not trust any form of republicanism in France – as it was by force from the left, because French moderates did not want an outright Bourbon victory, and did not trust a Britain where the harsh voice of a Grenville sought to undermine the friendly overtures of a Malmesbury, a half-in, half-out attitude to European innovation that has also paralysed Anglo-European relations more recently. The failure weakened the moderate voices in Pitt's ear and strengthened Grenville's conviction that 'it would be ten thousand times safer . . . to face the storm than to shrink from it' – safer for aristocrats, of course.[30]

4

The Modern Alexander

After a series of victories in Italy and the imposition of a humiliating peace on the Pope in February 1797, General Buonaparte's name really registered with the British people for the first time. At this time he still spelled his name in the Italian manner, which went down well in Italy, and he was generally known as 'Buonaparte'. Those who were following the war had viewed his bewildering success in the previous year's campaigning with a degree of awe and admiration: in late May 1796 the British minister at Turin remarked of the young general to Commodore Horatio Nelson that 'if he was not a Jacobin I should call him a fine fellow for his Enterprise and Abilities'.[1] Even London-based French *émigré* writers took patriotic pride in his victories although they were opposed to his politics. The best-known of them, Jean-Gabriel Peltier, writing in his journal *Paris pendant l'année*, voiced admiration for 'this extraordinary man whose talents and activity place [him] amongst the greatest generals of the century' after the 'veritable miracles achieved by him in Italy'.[2] The short 'anecdotes on Bonaparte' that Peltier published in March 1797 were complimentary: he had now through glorious negotiation set the seal on his military success, in a manner reminiscent of the Roman generals of antiquity. He wrote of how, when he was still a general of artillery, Bonaparte used to frequent a tower near Monaco where Julius Caesar was said to have pondered whether or not to cross the Rubicon. Bonaparte was sombre and taciturn; his favourite book, which he always carried, was Ossian; he was extremely sober and once rejected a woman he loved solely because she tried to get him drunk. When he left for Italy a friend pointed out that he was very young to take on the experienced generals of Austria, who were old in war. His response was: 'In a year I shall be either dead or old.'[3]

The French-language newspapers and periodicals published in London by exiled Frenchmen were important because French was the international language. For this reason they might be read not only by French exiles and those people in France who could get hold of them, but by educated people all over Europe, whereas English-language publications were understood by relatively few outside Britain and America. Knowledge of the English language was increasing fast on the Continent, especially in Germany, but it remained relatively rare, whereas knowledge of French was almost universal amongst businessmen and educated people of the governing classes. Where it mattered for an English publication to reach a European audience it was translated into French, and the presence of *émigré* writers in London was particularly useful for this purpose. Only works that local publishers expected to sell beyond the French-speaking classes were translated into other languages.

In May Peltier printed a more substantial account of Buonaparte's background. Although it contained a number of mistakes – notably placing his birth in 1767 – it was quite well informed about his Corsican origins, and claimed that the nationalist hero Pasquale Paoli was Napoleon's godfather.[4] John Aikin, editor of the liberal *Monthly Magazine*, the highest-selling British periodical, with a circulation of 4500, used Peltier's piece as the core of a fuller life, which was probably the most widely read early biography of the French hero. After first appearing in the magazine it was republished in *Biographical Anecdotes of the Founders of the French Republic* (1797), in the liberal periodicals the *Edinburgh Review* and the *New Annual Register*, and even in the *New Jamaica Magazine*. Aikin (or perhaps the publisher Richard Phillips, who in 1792 had been incarcerated in Leicester gaol as a Jacobin) had checked Peltier's story with Paoli himself, as he was living in London, and Paoli confirmed that he was godfather to one of Charles Buonaparte's children, but could not remember which one.[5]

These liberals still had cautious hopes for the outcome of the French Revolution, and the preface to *Biographical Anecdotes* concluded:

> The dreadful waste of human talents and virtues, and even of human existence, which has accompanied this grand effort for the recovery of political freedom, must fill every benevolent mind with infinite regret. Nor can anything relieve the painful feelings excited by the first part of this distressing drama, but the 'trembling hope' of a happy termination, in which the VAST PRICE which has been paid for the purchase of liberty, will be abundantly recompensed in the happiness of COUNTLESS MILLIONS yet unborn.

Bonaparte was very much a part of that hope. Aikin told how Buonaparte's father Charles, a lawyer, had fought with Paoli for Corsican independence, but after the French invasion the governor, Charles Louis de Marboeuf, became a patron of the family. Nevertheless, Charles Buonaparte remained fiercely loyal to Paoli and had once travelled to Livorno to get the English consul to warn the Corsican of a French plot to assassinate him. Bonaparte was sent to study with distinction at the military academy and met Paoli again in Paris after his graduation. After returning to Corsica Napoleon found his loyalties split when Paoli opposed the execution of Louis XVI; he defended Paoli against the Jacobins, but left Corsica with his family when Paoli invited the British to capture the island, settling near Toulon. He directed the artillery in the reduction of Toulon and, having gained the confidence of Barras, he again won the day in the insurrection of *vendémiaire*, after which 'the moderation displayed ... is perhaps unequalled in the history of the civil wars of modern times!'

Appointed to command the French army of Italy, Buonaparte's five victories forced Sardinia to capitulate; his bravery in imitating Caesar by seizing a standard and standing in front led to the capture of the bridge of Lodi, after which he seized Verona, and then at Pavia defeated superstition 'clothed in cowls and surplices, brandishing a poniard in one hand, and a crucifix in the other'. A final victory at Arcola led to the capture of Mantua and completed the humiliation of Austria. Not even the Archduke Charles could match 'a hardy Corsican, brought up amidst perils, and breathing the spirit of the ancient republics'. He married 'Madame Beauharnois, a beautiful Frenchwoman, who had suffered a variety of persecutions, during the time of Robespierre'. He aspired to be a legislator as well as a general and had established a buffer zone of free republics between himself and the Austrians. Physically Buonaparte was small but well proportioned and robust (though a description by the orientalist Volney was also quoted to the effect that he was 'a man of middle stature').[6]

The hatred for the Papacy and Catholic 'superstition' evident in British nonconformist writing is a startling reminder of the enduring strength of British Protestant belief. Another pamphlet of this date also found that 'one great and important benefit has resulted to mankind from these victories of Buonaparte, in the destruction of the Papal Dominion', its author noting also that 'the great consideration with which he has uniformly treated all professors of the arts and sciences is universally known'.[7] Even Edmund Burke, at least in jest, valued 'the Protestant hero Bonaparte'.[8]

A first group of printed portraits of Napoleon reached London in spring and summer 1797, none of them very true to life. Although he had never seen Buonaparte, the *Monthly Magazine*'s editor recommended an Italian portrait sold in London by Gaetano Testolini, and the one painted in Verona for the Anglo-Italian artist Maria Cosway, which came out in July.[9] With portraits came caricatures, but these didn't even pretend to offer a likeness. Isaac Cruikshank's Bonaparte was a ragged, fierce, sans-culotte bandit humiliating the Pope and terrifying pampered Austrians. A similar fierce sans-culotte represented Napoleon in Richard Newton's *Buonaparte the Modern Alexander on his Journey round the World* and *Buonaparte the Ambassador of Peace*, both published in April 1797. Although all the images stressed Bonaparte's Jacobinism, he was still an unknown face in a France personified as Equality or the Great Nation.[10]

The publicity surrounding the brave young hero of Italy had breathed new life into the liberal cause in Britain, and the influence of Bonaparte's propaganda machine, as he turned his attention to England, was probably a factor in Pitt's decision to pay more attention to the subject.[11] He was persuaded to do so by George Canning, a very gifted twenty-six-year-old with a flair for satirical writing, who had in January 1796 taken a post as undersecretary at the Foreign Office, which put him at the heart of the intelligence machine. One of Canning's targets for recruitment was the outstanding caricaturist James Gillray, an internationally famous artist, who was first introduced to the politician within a month of his taking office. During that year Gillray engraved twenty plates for *Hollandia Regenerata*, a work designed to expose and invite international criticism of French activities in Holland, published in December 1796, probably at government expense, and quickly copied for distribution in Italy.[12]

After a discussion with Pitt at Walmer Castle in October 1797 Canning created the *Anti-Jacobin, or Weekly Examiner*, a new newspaper designed to counter the influence of the liberal press. He reported to his friend the diplomat George Ellis, their

> plan for a Secret Committee, of which you and Friou [John Hookham Frere] must be distinguished & active members – to superintend a new Paper which is to be full of sound reasoning, good principles, & good jokes, & to set the minds of the People right upon every subject. The Committee is to meet every Sunday during the session at dinner at Pitt's. We went over nine or ten names of persons who, I think, are very likely to do well.

The highly rated satirical poet William Gifford was appointed editor, and as well as Canning, Frere and Ellis, contributors included George Hammond and even Pitt himself.[13]

Gifford, being a professional literary person, was the public face of the enterprise, for the others were all politicians. George Ellis was a forty-three-year-old diplomat, a close friend and protégé of Lord Malmesbury, and had been his assistant in the negotiations with France that year. Frere was twenty-seven, like his friend Canning, and had just entered Parliament as a supporter of Pitt. He took over Canning's post at the Foreign Office in March 1799. George Hammond was another young diplomat, aged thirty-three, who had returned in 1795 from a post as minister to the United States, where he had married an American, to become a Foreign Office undersecretary. The ever-curious art-gossip Joseph Farington noted further details: 'Hoppner told me the Anti-Jacobin Newspaper is looked over at Cannings before publication, where Frere & Hamond reside. It is printed on Sundays at the Press of the *Sun* paper. Wright has a guinea a week for publishing.'[14]

Correspondence between Ellis and Canning reveals much about their modus operandi: whatever was rated not good enough or too extreme for the *Anti-Jacobin* was sent to the *Sun* or the *True Briton*, but they could not be sure when or whether Heriot, their editor, would choose to publish these offerings, as, although these papers were expected to speak for the ministry, they were not (unlike the *Anti-Jacobin*) under its immediate control. This sheds interesting light on politicians' view of what constituted a free press: although the ministry owned, or part-owned, newspapers, influenced the selection of editors, and supplied 'paragraphs', it did not completely dictate what was selected for publication, or when; and the advantage of this arrangement was that it provided a degree of deniability. For instance, when Ellis wrote to Canning, disappointed that his 'Ode to Lord Moira' had not appeared in the *Anti-Jacobin*, Canning explained that concerns had been voiced that Moira might write to Pitt demanding to know if he had countenanced its publication, as Moira had behaved like this before. So the poem had been sent to the friendly newspapers: 'In the Sun & T. B. there is no responsibility. It is therefore gone back to Heriot again, and I have been surprised and disappointed at its not coming out today.' Ellis agreed with their reasoning, replying that: 'If it can find its way into the T.B. it will do much more good there & in the Sun than it could do in a paper which is considered as to a great degree official.'[15]

In November 1797 Canning finally persuaded the caricaturist James Gillray to work directly for him. *The Friend of Humanity and the Knife-Grinder*, published on 4 December 1797, drew attention to a parody of a 'Jacobin' poem by Robert Southey that Canning and John Hookham Frere had written for the second issue of the *Anti-Jacobin* a week earlier, while Gillray's elaborate and brilliant *Apotheosis of Hoche*, a celebration of the French general's death in September, derived from Frere. On 7 December Canning's friend and Gillray's patron John Sneyd wrote to congratulate the caricaturist 'that what I had so long wished, has taken place': Gillray had been offered a pension of £200 a year to serve the ministry. Canning probably flattered Gillray into agreeing by arguing that his prints could make a significant and valuable contribution to the war effort, for Gillray seems to have relished his auxiliary role in 'skirmishing against the common enemy'.[16] £200 a year was reckoned to be enough to live comfortably in London with a servant, and so the pension ruled out financial worry and encouraged Gillray to devote time to more ambitious prints, such as *The Apotheosis of Hoche*.

The *Anti-Jacobin* ran only from 20 November 1797 to 9 July 1798. It was deft in its treatment of the opposition, and in its year of existence it said nothing impolite about Bonaparte personally. One of its favourite targets was English 'Jacobin' poetry, for criticism of the administration and its war took all kinds of oblique forms that included prints for display on the wall that sympathised with the plight of the rural poor, as well as more blatant anti-war poetry like Robert Southey's famous 'Battle of Blenheim' (1798) or Coleridge's 'Fire, Famine and Slaughter', published in the *Morning Post* on 8 January 1798 and a direct and savage indictment of Pitt's policy in France and Ireland. The *Anti-Jacobin* sought to challenge liberal possession of this cultural high ground, and its poems were successfully extracted and anthologised for loyalists. In the introduction to *Poetry of the Anti-Jacobin* Canning complained that whereas the Jacobin poet was happy to sing of Bonaparte's victories, finding 'nothing but trophies and triumphs, and branches of laurel and olive, phalanxes of Republicans shouting victory, satellites of despotism biting the ground', a British victory inspired from him 'nothing but contusions and amputations, plundered peasants and deserted looms'.[17] During the year of the *Anti-Jacobin*'s existence Gillray produced a series of caricatures that certainly originated with Canning, including projects such as *French Habits*, ridiculing Jacques Louis David's designs for official uniforms.

In October 1797 the Directory had appointed Bonaparte to command the Army of England, destined to invade and conquer the arch-enemy, but an inspection of the French naval forces left him with the feeling that an indirect attack on Britain might prove more fruitful. Instead of invading England or Ireland, where rebels had hoped for his help, he had led an expedition to Egypt, threatening Britain's ever-growing empire in India. He captured Malta, landed successfully at Alexandria, defeated the Mameluke rulers and captured Cairo, but was then marooned in Egypt by Admiral Nelson's victory at the battle of the Nile on 1–2 August 1798.

Canning's hand can be traced in the introduction to the first volume of *Copies of Original Letters from the Army of General Bonaparte* (1798), in which the government published correspondence that they claimed British or Turkish cruisers had captured on ships bound from Egypt to France. The introduction claimed that the expedition had been designed by the Directory to reward the Army of Italy with the fabled riches and plunder of Egypt, and the soldiers' bitter disappointment offered a precious opportunity to mock the 'stupid admirers' of Bonaparte. The government showed the collection to opposition journalists in order to convince them (with only partial success) that the letters were not fakes, and by giving them the impression that they intended to publish the entire correspondence, drew the *Morning Chronicle* into complaints that hinted at the content of private letters that the government ultimately withheld (possibly because they really were fakes). 'One of these letters', the *Chronicle* revealed, 'is from Bonaparte to his brother, complaining of the profligacy of his wife; another from young Beauharnois expressing his hopes that his dear Mamma is not so wicked as she is represented!' The *Chronicle*'s comments were published in footnotes to the introduction, another of which wondered what 'Madame Bonaparte's chastity has to do with her husband's Expedition through Egypt'.[18]

Some of James Gillray's Egyptian work was certainly made with guidance from Canning's circle. *Buonaparte hearing of Nelson's Victory swears by his Sword to extirpate the English from the Earth* of 8 December 1798 attributed to Bonaparte a speech published by one of his '*savants*', 'that atheistical driveller Volney', in the *Moniteur*, with Bonaparte's pacific intentions altered to a drive for universal conquest (followed by a peace imposed on European slaves minus the extirpated English). For *Siege de la Colonne de Pompée*, published on 6 March 1799, there exists a set of instructions written anonymously in a copperplate hand but undoubtedly issued by somebody closely familiar with Bonaparte's expedition. From these detailed instructions Gillray produced an extraordinarily brilliant print, and if his instructor was Canning, as is probable, then Canning knew what Gillray could do, and provided material that was exactly what Gillray would have chosen for himself.[19] Gillray was now neatly integrated into the administration's propaganda effort, for this was one of a series of Gillrays 'based on the original intercepted drawing', supposing that the designs had been drawn by a French artist in Egypt, as counterparts to the letters. A second volume of intercepted letters appeared in 1799, necessitated by 'the perverse obstinacy of Jacobinism', which insisted on treating the expedition as a triumph; in this, Bonaparte's attempt to curry favour with the locals by showing sympathy to Islam provided further scope to attack his hypocrisy.

Perversely obstinate liberals continued to venerate Buonaparte as a hero. The poet Helen Maria Williams, who had settled in Paris but fled to Switzerland for her own safety when her Girondin friends were defeated by Robespierre, before returning after his execution, took advantage of her exile to publish *A Tour in Switzerland*, part travel narrative, part political meditation. In it she waxed lyrical over Buonaparte, not just for his military achievements in 'scaling the Alps, and chasing the imperial eagle back to its haunts, after tearing from its beak its choicest prey', or for his devotion to arts and science, but as 'the benefactor of his race converting the destructive lightning of the conqueror's sword into the benignant rays of freedom, and presenting to vanquished nations the emblems of liberty and independence entwined with the olive of peace.' She reached a rousing conclusion:

'The glory of Buonaparte,' says the eloquent minister, 'belongs to the revolution, to his valorous soldiers, to France.' The glory of Buonaparte soars beyond these limits, however enlarged, or extended; he belongs not exclusively to France, or her revolution; like Homer, or Newton, Buonaparte belongs to the world.[20]

In the later eighteenth century Swiss society was regarded as a model of human liberty. But close scrutiny revealed darker aspects of Swiss life to Williams, who described a bitter divide between French-leaning liberals and what she saw as repressive aristocratic regimes, most notably in Bern (where the British spymaster Wickham was based). She sympathised with the efforts of the French-speaking Pays de Vaud to win independence from German-speaking Bern.

By the time her book was published in March 1798 French armies had intervened in support of revolts in Basel and Vaud, the old confederacy was dissolved and a Helvetic Republic established. In April Canning's *Anti-Jacobin* took exception to a sentence in the *Courier*, delighted that 'in *vain* have the little Despots of Berne urged the brave people of Switzerland to support their *tyrannic* claims.' In its weekly column of 'Misrepresentations', the *Anti-Jacobin* insisted that the people had supported the Council of Bern, but had been crushed by the French, and asked rhetorically on whose authority the *Courier* printed these falsehoods:

On Mrs Stone's!* On a Poissarde more bloody, on a st-mp-t more shameless than any which the *Halles* of Paris ever vomited forth ... who danced with all the fury of a drunken Bacchante round the mangled bodies of the faithful Swiss.[21]

In this war of public opinion it was vital to discredit the opposition, for their views still struck a chord with a large number of people who remained unconvinced by government arguments.

Whatever people's thoughts on Bonaparte personally, there was widespread scepticism about the necessity for war and complaint about the hardship it entailed. Repressive silencing continued. Between 1792 and 1794 the government had driven the editors of the *Argus*, the *Sheffield Register* and the *Manchester Herald* abroad. The editors of the *Leicester Herald* (Richard Phillips) and *Sheffield Iris* had been imprisoned, as well as two political printsellers and several booksellers. In 1798 two prominent Whig booksellers, Joseph Johnson and Jeremiah Jordan, were convicted of seditious libel for selling the Unitarian minister Gilbert Wakefield's *Reply to Some Parts of the Bishop of Llandaff's Address to the People of Great Britain*, which had attacked the bishop's defence of the war as 'just and necessary', as well as lambasting Pitt's system of packing Parliament with 'a prostitute majority of borough-mongers, loan jobbers, military officers, pensioners and official sycophants'.[22] Wakefield himself was given two years in Dorchester gaol, and Fox wrote to him, commiserating: 'The liberty of the press I consider as virtually destroyed by the proceedings against Johnson and Jordan, and what has happened to you I cannot but lament therefore the more, as the sufferings of a man whom I esteem in a cause that is no more.' £5000 was raised to support Wakefield's family, but two months after his release he died of typhus contracted in gaol.

In March 1799 Lord Grenville prosecuted the publisher, printer and John Parry, the proprietor of the *Courier*, for a paragraph stating 'the emperor of Russia to be a tyrant among his own subjects and ridiculous to the rest of Europe'.[23] Presumably his crime was to have insulted the head of a friendly state at a moment when his loyalty to the coalition against Bonaparte was wavering. Grenville followed this in May by arresting the editor of the *Cambridge Intelligencer*, Benjamin Flower, to answer a case of breach of privilege of the House of Lords for his 'libel on the Bishop of Llandaff'. This was an extraordinary move of dubious legality presumably intended to circumvent the necessity for a trial.

Flower, who continued to edit his paper from prison, reported that he thought that what had really offended ministers was a different paragraph from the one that had supported Wakefield's attack on the sycophantic bishop, for which he was punished. He thought it was this one:

> While our ministers have, for years past, been exerting them-selves, and squandering the blood and treasure of the British Empire, in supporting the old despotic governments of Europe, their endeavours have not been wanting at home, to render our constitution, (distinguished by the freedom of its genuine principles) more similar to those governments. After all the numerous abridgements of our liberties – After all the extraor-dinary powers committed to ministers – After the many severe prosecutions, and the verdicts of complaisant juries – After the repeated, the boasted acknowledgements of our national loyalty – After the annihilation, almost, of opposition in both houses of parliament, ministers it appears are not yet satis-fied. . . . From Mr. Pitt's speech, on the report of the committee of secrecy, our readers may form some idea of the ferocity, the implacability, the enmity to the principles of freedom, which reign in the heart of that apostate.[24]

In this offensive passage Flower went on to get personal about the hypocrisy of Pitt, this 'Sabbath Breaking duellist – (to say nothing of his Sunday drinking parties)', in prating about virtue. The poet Robert Southey, writing to his wife, echoed Fox's phrase about the extinction of English Liberty as he set off to visit Wakefield and Flower in prison, but reassured her light-heartedly that 'Buonaparte is making a home for us in Syria, and we may per-haps enjoy freedom under the suns of the east, in a land flowing with milk and honey'. At this time, for Southey and other liberals, Bonaparte still represented liberty in contrast to Pitt's tyranny.[25]

Bonaparte, however, was trapped in Egypt, and there Earl St Vincent, Admiral Nelson and even Earl Spencer were determined to keep him. His escape from this trap has always been a puzzling episode, usually blamed on a Nelson supposedly so dazzled and distracted by Emma Hamilton and by his intimacy with Neapolitan royalty that he was not concentrating on his job. At the time, perhaps, Bonaparte might not have been deemed so important a detainee as subsequent events make us think. However, it was not Nelson but Sir Sidney Smith who was in charge at Alexandria, and Sir Sidney had his own ideas about policy. Lord Grenville had sent him to join his brother Spencer at Constantinople, where they were appointed joint plenipotentiaries to treat with the Ottoman Porte. Smith had orders, but I wonder whether, once again, Grenville had appointed 'a reckless adventurer who nevertheless believed he was acting with implicit government sanction'.

In 1810 Lewis Goldsmith, then a government publicist, formerly a French spy, and before that a radical journalist, expressed a common suspicion when he wrote: 'I have heard it stated by different parties, that Bonaparte left Egypt with the permission of our Government, and that he had promised to restore the Bourbon family'; it is an interpretation that cannot be ruled out.[26] Accompanied by a whole team of spies, John Wesley Wright, Antoine de Phélippeaux, John Keith and Antoine Viscovitch, Smith sailed in his ship *Tigre* to Constantinople, stopping at Cadiz to report to St Vincent but missing Nelson. His naval orders, which are well known, made him subordinate to both of them, but his naval orders came close to conflicting with his political orders, which are less easy to come by now and puzzled everybody at the time.

Taking local naval command, and with authority from the Sultan to command Turkish forces, he successfully defended Acre against Bonaparte's army and thwarted whatever plans the French general might have had for further conquest. This was Smith's

moment of greatest triumph, and Acre transformed him into a
British hero with a status approaching Nelson's. But triumph was
rapidly followed by disaster when the Turkish army that Smith
then escorted from Rhodes to Aboukir to liberate Egypt was
heavily defeated by Bonaparte, who had returned in haste by land.
Smith then fell back on the plan that he had originally concerted
with the Turks in Constantinople.

When he had first arrived in Egypt in March 1799, he had
explained in letters to Nelson and Earl Spencer that he had decided
to offer Bonaparte 'a golden bridge' back to France, and also to
allow the French army to return home as British prisoners of war
on parole, and he had already printed proclamations to this effect
in Constantinople.[27] When this letter reached Nelson in Sicily the
admiral replied bluntly: 'this is in direct opposition to my opinion
which is never to suffer any one individual Frenchman to leave
Egypt – I must therefore strictly charge and command you never
to give any French ship or man leave to quit Egypt.' Earl Spencer
did not approve either, and said so to Lord Grenville. Grenville's
opinion was not revealed, but Smith's confident manner might
suggest that he had counted on his sympathy.[28] Although he had
distributed his proclamations before he learned that everybody else
disapproved of them, none of it mattered while he was winning.
After the Turkish defeat at Aboukir on 25 July 1799, however, he
was forced to fall back on guile, a quality in which he believed
himself to excel.

Smith sent his secretary John Keith to negotiate an exchange
of prisoners, and to give the French the newspapers that reported
the reverses their armies had suffered against Austria and Russia.
Keith also dropped the information that the blockading ships were
short of water and would shortly be leaving their station in order
to get new supplies.[29] It is more than possible, though it is speculation, that as some came to believe, Bonaparte had indicated to
Smith a willingness to restore monarchy in France and that he left

Egypt expecting his army to be allowed to follow him. Whatever agreement he thought he had reached, Smith sailed with his squadron for Cyprus on 9 August, deliberately allowing Bonaparte a clear run, as he later informed the French general's successor as commander in Egypt, General Kléber.[30] Failing to obtain supplies in Cyprus, he sent *Theseus* on westward and returned to Alexandria long after Bonaparte had embarked on the night of 22/23 August.

On 20 October Smith wrote to his brother Spencer:

> His intention to desert his army I had no doubt of – I gave an opening for his embarkation in order to catch him at sea and apprized Lord Nelson of that intention as soon as I could speak with certainty and if I had not considered the accomplishment of the objects of the campaign in concert with the Grand Vizier, by the emancipation of Egypt, of more consequence than the capture of his person and treasure I should have gone to the Westward with the Tigre rather than send the Theseus.[31]

His letters to Lords Spencer and Grenville had made no mention of any plan to capture Bonaparte at sea, and this letter to his brother is so full of bluster that it suggests that Smith may by October have realised that he might have blundered. He made a series of excuses about the unreliability of the Turks and the treachery of one of their officials, before claiming that he had prioritised Turkish success in Egypt over the capture of the French general, which was true. To allow Bonaparte to escape in order to catch him at sea was an alluring plan, no doubt, but one fraught with very high risk, even if Turkish 'treachery' had not ruined its timing. It would be rash to dismiss the possibility that Smith was foolhardy enough to have persuaded Bonaparte to go to sea in order to give himself a chance of capturing him, but it is not what he told Lord Spencer. It is more than possible that Smith believed that he had reached a private agreement with

Bonaparte that the general would return to France and pave the way for a Bourbon restoration.[32] I think this is quite likely; there was certainly wide expectation among royalists that Bonaparte would act in this way.

In any case, Bonaparte returned to France, served as figurehead in the coup known by its date as *Brumaire* (9 November), and quickly took the helm in the new government. He was thirty. The two most powerful and talented personalities in the group that brought him in, Joseph Fouché and Charles Maurice Talleyrand, became his chief instruments in government, hating each other in deadly rivalry and representing the two sides of France that Bonaparte sought to reconcile in order to produce stable government. Both inspired fear: you could hear Talleyrand coming because his congenitally deformed foot gave him a noisy limp; you could hear Fouché because his pulmonary condition made him cough and wheeze. But Fouché was the more obviously sinister: 'Ah Fouché,' Napoleon teased him, 'if you limped like Talleyrand, I would say that you were the devil.'[33]

At the time of *Brumaire* Fouché was forty, the highly intelligent son of a slave-trader from Nantes, with interests in money and cutting-edge science.

> Everybody knows this personage; his medium stature, his tow-coloured hair, lank and scanty, his active leanness, his long, mobile, pale face with the physiognomy of an excited ferret; one remembers his piercing keen glance, shifty nevertheless, his little, blood-shot eyes, his brief and jerky manner of speech which was in harmony with his restless, uneasy attitude.[34]

Ferret-like is the abiding impression, but with charm and great intelligence. Fouché was educated at the Oratory school in Nantes and became a teacher with the Oratorians (though, contrary to black propaganda, he never took orders as a priest). He taught science and determined to modernise the curriculum; he was fascinated with physics, with experiments with electricity and gas, was devoted to his pupils, and bought the best and latest instruments and equipment for the laboratory over which he presided. He was a Freemason, a partisan for the new, and threw himself into the revolution with enthusiasm.

He soon reached its forefront. While working at the Oratory college at Arras from 1788 to 1790 he got to know Robespierre and came close to marrying his sister.[35] Moving back to the college at Nantes, he became leader of the local Jacobin club, was elected to the Convention, and in 1793 was sent out as a representative *en mission*. He suppressed a royalist revolt around Nantes, returned to Paris as a prominent member of the Mountain (the extremist Jacobin group in the Assembly), spearheaded dechristianisation and social revolution in the Nièvre, and carried out violent reprisals after the suppression of the revolt in Lyon. At this date he was a populist ideologue, a passionate champion of the revolution. He was instrumental in the fall of Robespierre, who had become a deadly enemy, but was taken by surprise by the anti-terrorist reaction and went into hiding. After an amnesty, he attached himself to Barras and became his secretary. He also developed links with the financial world, especially with Guillaume Herries, a Scottish banker whose family resided chiefly in London.

In 1798 Fouché was sent as French representative to Milan but was recalled as too Jacobin. He was appointed head of the police in July 1799 and began at once to build a department with tentacles that stretched everywhere, including London.

Despite Fouché's demonic qualities, it was Charles Maurice de Talleyrand-Périgord who became known as '*le diable boiteux*', the limping devil, a name awarded not just for his limp but because Le Sage's character of that name was a civilised, witty and sophisticated devil with the gift of being able to look through the walls of any house to discern what was going on inside. Talleyrand liked to know what was happening everywhere: his informal spy network rivalled Fouché's.

Talleyrand's congenitally deformed foot ruled out the pursuit of his father's military career, and so instead he followed his powerful uncle, the archbishop of Reims, into the Church. Charles Maurice was a precociously intelligent financial whizz-kid, appointed in 1780 agent-general of the clergy, representing the Church to the Crown. On the Church's behalf, he drew up an inventory of Church property and presented a defence of their 'inalienable rights' to the King. He was made bishop of Autun in 1789 and represented the clergy in the Estates General. However, he embraced the revolution: he advised on the seizure of Church properties for the nation, drew up the Civil Constitution of the Clergy which subordinated them to the state rather than the Pope, and showed off his French state allegiance by celebrating mass during the Fête de la Fédération on 14 July 1790, which led to his excommunication in 1791. He was sent as part of a delegation to Britain in 1792 but was expelled and spent three years in America, returning to a safer France in September 1796. Having been appointed minister for foreign affairs in June 1797, he backed and befriended the rising star of Napoleon.

Writing later, of a man he had first admired in 1802 when in love with French politics, the mercenary turncoat Lewis Goldsmith drew a caustic portrait for Talleyrand's enemies:

From his appearance it could not be supposed that there is much energy of mind left; it is impossible to see a more lifeless, ill-shaped being. His debilitated frame is moved on by a club-foot, and all that is left are the remains of fire, which flash from a very fine blue eye.

I am persuaded that Talleyrand has more moral depravity than any Frenchman ever possessed, not even excepting Richelieu or Mirabeau, though he has less talent than either of these two. Such a mass of corruption and turpitude was never before collected in the person of one man. Yet there is a certain *je ne sçais quoi* about him which makes his company agreeable. He possesses the *suaviter in modo* to an extraordinary degree ... Carnot, speaking to me of Talleyrand, said, 'C'est de la M[er]de en bas de Soie!!' (T[ur]d in silk stockings.)[36]

Where Fouché stood for the old Jacobins and for revolutionary social change, Talleyrand was allied to the old nobility, and these deadly rivals detested each other. One of the few things they had in common, however, was a genuine desire for peace with Britain.

Talleyrand invited Guillaume Hyde (now the principal organiser of the comte d'Artois's network in Paris) and another senior royalist officer to a meeting with Bonaparte on 27 December 1799, and the royalists were hopeful at first. A number of people, including the writer Louis de Fontanes, had led London-based royalists to believe that Bonaparte might bring back the Bourbons.[37] 'Nobody feared more than a Cromwell and many, me included, hoped for a Monck,' recalled Hyde later, using the familiar analogy with the English Revolution which had ended in military dictatorship under Cromwell, after which General Monck had engineered the Restoration of Charles ii.[38] Bonaparte's government seemed extremely insecure, and the burning question was how long he would last. 'If he lasts a year he will go far!' Talleyrand remarked to Hyde in his coach on the way to a first meeting with the Consul. 'He is a man who believes that fortune is on his side and his astonishing confidence in his guiding star inspires his partisans with an equally astonishing sense of security.'[39] In the event, Bonaparte and the royalist envoys found common ground on the restoration of Catholic religion and of unsold aristocratic property, but agreed to differ on loyalty to the Bourbon monarchy. Bonaparte told Hyde that he had considered backing their restoration while the corrupt Directory was in power, but now found that neither France nor Europe wanted them.[40]

Having offered peace to the royalist leaders, Bonaparte made the same offer to the Austrians and to the British, writing to George III at Christmas: 'The war which for eight years has ravaged the four quarters of the world, must it be eternal? Are there no means of coming to an understanding?' His offer of peace was probably sincere, but he didn't expect a positive response, and this was a good way of laying the blame on the British. It is likely that he knew that writing direct to the King was not how things were done in England, and that he did it in order to emphasise that he was in control, and a leader of equal rank to King George.[41]

5

The English Conspiracy

At the time that Bonaparte seized power in Paris and at once began to talk about peace, Foreign Secretary Grenville was concerting plans with the Austrians and French royalists to 'make an immense effort against France', as he put it on 30 November 1799, in the next campaigning season.[1]

The sudden appearance of Bonaparte as head of state was a game changer, but nobody yet knew what to make of the change, or of him. There was genuine, widespread, anxiety that his regime was insecure, and that when he proposed peace he did it merely in order to play for time and sow distrust amongst the allies. The opposition leader Charles James Fox, on the other hand, thought Bonaparte sincere and that, whatever the government thought, the country agreed with him that 'Peace & Peace upon good terms might be had'. The evidence indicates that Bonaparte was, indeed, sincere in his wish to make peace.[2]

Within Pitt's ministry there was significant private debate about what attitude to take to him and whether to continue fighting, and it reveals much about the thinking of British politicians. Pitt was prepared to fall in with Grenville, Windham and Canning's demand to fight the next campaign, to which they were already heavily committed, whatever Bonaparte might do; but, he told Canning, 'I am not sanguine in the hope of giving by any Effort such a Tone to our Friends in the Country, as will make them long endure a separate War, if moderate terms should be offered, and Bonaparte's Power should appear to establish itself firmly and on Principles that can be distinguished from Jacobin.'[3] Pitt effectively allowed the proponents of the Bourbon cause one more year.

George Ellis went further and questioned whether his friend Canning's determination to continue fighting was still justifiable after Bonaparte's accession:

> [France] has found in Buonaparte a man patriotic enough, or if you please vain enough, to seek to conciliate the affections of the people and for that purpose desirous of concluding peace. He has effected an Anti-Jacobin Revolution (observe that the *Sun* inculcates this opinion every day), he has disclaimed all revolutionary measures, all pretensions of interfering with the government of other countries ... If such a government shall propose to Europe fair and honourable terms of peace, shall we, who have professed only an enmity to Jacobins, continue at war with a government, the enemy of those very Jacobins? And for what purpose?[4]

Ellis drew attention to the *Sun*'s promotion of the view that Bonaparte's was an anti-Jacobin revolution because the *Sun* normally said what Pitt wanted it to say, and so this indicated that Pitt really believed that the reason for fighting had gone and that there was a genuine opportunity to make peace. Pitt's chum Henry Dundas certainly opposed the views of Grenville and Canning on the grounds that continental victory was unattainable and that France no longer posed an ideological threat.

Pitt conceded to Canning his points that a premature peace might delay the restoration of monarchy, that another coup to

overturn Bonaparte would cause civil war and make every moderate a royalist, and that perhaps the best chance was that before
long Bonaparte would be willing through self-interest to negotiate
for the return of monarchy. Pitt told Canning that he thought 'all
this likely and desirable' but (and there was always going to be a
but) he could not rule out the opposite possibility that Bonaparte
would establish himself, subdue the Jacobins and extinguish the
hope of the royalists.

> If this were to happen; and it were to appear (as I think in such
> a Case it might) to be really his Interest both to make Peace and
> to maintain it when made, and if under such circumstances he
> were to offer honourable and advantageous Terms – I cannot
> see how on such a Supposition (no Matter for this Part of the
> Argument how improbable,) on what Grounds we could justify
> to ourselves a refusal to Treat, and much less how We could
> expect it to be supported by Public Opinion.

It is interesting to read this clear-sighted analysis from Pitt,
which reveals his ability as a political animal for whom strategic
advantage was at least as important as principle. How far he was
personally wedded to the Bourbon cause, or might have viewed
Bonaparte as somebody with whom he could do business, is
never revealed. However, he insisted to Canning that 'we ought
on no account to commit ourselves by any declaration that the
Restoration of Royalty is the sine quâ non Condition of Peace'.[5]
But his overbearing cousin Grenville was determined that
there could be no peace without a Bourbon restoration, and that
Bonaparte had always been, and still was, a Jacobin. Given that the
King was on Grenville's side as usual, Pitt bowed to the majority
view, and, with a foolish emphasis on protocol that was characteristic of him, Grenville issued an imperious and haughty reply
to Bonaparte's letter to the King, rejecting his proposal. He also

rejected bluntly a second polite offer sent on 14 January 1800, which was shortly followed by a peace envoy, Louis-Guillaume Otto, who arrived in London on 22 January. Bonaparte had hoped to dent British confidence and influence them towards peace by crushing Cadoudal's *chouans* while this offer was still under consideration, but it was rejected too fast, and right after this final snub he ordered the preparation of the army destined to invade Italy.[6]

The British government pursued its plans for war, feeling that victory was at last within its grasp. Once again, there was to be a three-pronged attack on France. The Royal Navy was to land General Willot with the Condé army in southern France while an Austrian army invaded from the east to support a planned royalist rising in the Midi. General Pichegru with another Austrian army was poised on the eastern border to exploit a royalist rising in Lyon.[7] The navy had been landing huge quantities of arms in Brittany and Normandy along with large sums of money, and 13,000 Russian troops were wintering in Jersey and Guernsey. In the west Grenville, Windham and the royalists planned the seizure of Brest and an invasion by an army accompanied by the comte d'Artois, as a focus for the rising of Normandy, Brittany and the Vendée. Meanwhile, in Paris, the chevalier de Margadel would deliver the *coup essentiel* – the assassination of Bonaparte by means of the armed band already put together by Guillaume Hyde.

It is no wonder that those who had planned this vast operation wanted to put it into practice. William Wickham's secret service expenditure for the first six months of 1800 for paying agencies, agents and the armies of Pichegru and Willot amounted to £3,682,520, more than the total sum promised by Britain to help pay Austrian and other foreign troops. Wickham's, though easily the largest, was only one of several concurrent secret service accounts at a time when, we may recall, the legal limit for foreign secret service expenditure was £100,000.[8] Wickham wrote to Grenville in the spring of his 'firm belief that we have force enough to beat all that Buonaparte can bring against us' and of 'a re-union of talents at the Austrian head-quarters such as has never been assembled before. If all this is destined to be beaten, I can only say God's will be done, ... and that He has some great object in view, beyond the reach of our faculties, of which the Consul is to be a leading Instrument.'[9]

The Austrian subsidy of £2,500,000 required parliamentary approval, and the debate in February reopened the question of why the British were fighting the war. Opposition MP George Tierney tried to trap Pitt into admitting that the aim was to restore the Bourbon monarchy, but Pitt insisted that the aim was 'security', as it always had been, since Jacobinism lived on, 'centred and condensed into one man who was reared and nursed in its bosom, whose celebrity was gained under its auspices, who was at once the child and champion of all its atrocities and horrors. Our security in negotiation is to be this Buonaparte, who is now the sole organ of all that was formerly dangerous and pestiferous in the Revolution.' Pitt's phrase went into legend as 'the child and champion of Jacobinism' and came back to haunt him later.[10]

Despite all opposition, the latest attempt to obtain security by crushing Jacobinism in France went ahead. Young Guillaume Hyde was secretary and front man of a royalist network in Paris, taking orders from the comte d'Artois via his go-between with the British, Jean-François Dutheil, and paid by the British government, that was relaunched on 11 December 1799 with a promise of 1000 *louis d'or* to be delivered by Ratel. He had charge of a small group of hit men under the leadership of Margadel, and a correspondence network linking Paris to London via François Mallet in Rouen and the Marcouf islands or the prince de Bouillon in Jersey. Hyde came from the Nièvre, where his father had a factory, from a family of English Catholic exiles, and first came to notice defending a royalist who had been denounced by Fouché when he had been sent *en mission* to the upper Loire. He had a strong interest in propaganda and was working with a number of writers and journalists who controlled several of the sixty political journals that Bonaparte suppressed on 17 January 1800 in order to control debate about his government that was spinning out of control.

Most of this writing (republican as well as royalist) sought to prepare the francophone public for the overthrow of the new tyrant. The second part of the *Code des Tyrannicides* (imprint Lyon, year VIII) was a translation (which had 'fallen into the hands of the printer by chance') of *Killing No Murder*, the pamphlet that had first been published to justify the assassination of Oliver Cromwell and then subsequently reissued whenever it seemed necessary to remove a ruler deemed by some party to be a tyrant.[11] The royalist author Jean François Michaud wrote two pamphlets, *Les Adieux à Bonaparte*, issued in Paris and London at the end of 1799, and *Les Derniers Adieux à Bonaparte Victorieux* of April or May 1800. The first was designed to persuade Bonaparte to 'descend from the throne which he has usurped, and to recall the lawful monarch' (as John Gifford put it in the *Anti-Jacobin Review*), and the second told the story of Cromwell and then compared Bonaparte first with Cromwell, and then with George Monck. Michaud explained the application of *Killing No Murder*: Cromwell 'knew the spirit of the people he had enchained; he was continually prey to the fear of assassination, and to cap his anxieties a book came out called *Killing No Murder* in which the author sought to prove that it was just to destroy him, whatever the means.'[12] In February 1800 Hyde launched the *Avant-Coureur*, a weekly, of which the first number also appeared in London in Jean-Gabriel Peltier's *Paris pendant l'année*, and a paper called *l'Invisible* to compensate for newspapers that Bonaparte had closed down.

Royalists were protected by a 'counter-police' supervised by Louis Dupérou, the son of a court official at Baden and destined for a career in diplomacy, fluent in five living languages, educated at Heidelberg and highly intelligent. Dupérou had worked in the

French intelligence services and foreign office, and was currently employed by Talleyrand. He was also working for Pitt by 1797 and was now reporting to Charles William Flint at the Alien Office, who was in charge of continental espionage.[13] He had bought the services of two badly paid police officials and provided a description of the organisation of the police within Paris and a list of some 251 policemen and their paid '*mouchards*' or spies.[14] With the help of his informers he was able to warn 230 people of police moves against them between 2 January and 9 March 1800.

Also working with Hyde was the abbé Justin Ratel, who had been Sir Sidney Smith's principal contact in Normandy. At the end of 1799 Ratel established a new route for correspondence via Amiens and Boulogne. The route controlled by Mallet was proving unreliable because Mallet, with his *chouan* band under attack, was often unavailable and his people refused to do anything without a direct order from him, which caused awkward delays. In principle, from about 5 January 1800 fishermen crossed the Channel from Boulogne to Dover twice a week on Monday and Thursday with identification that could only be provided by senior figures. They tried to arrange things so that Mallet's people made their journeys on different days.[15] In April, after some valuable correspondence had been thrown overboard by fishermen who feared that they were about to be arrested as spies by a British cutter, Dutheil instituted a system of numbered passports that was controlled at Dover by the chief customs officer.[16] Ratel had also rented a house in Paris for the use of visiting *chouan* officers.[17]

From 1798 developments in Paris and Brest were matched in importance to Britain by developments around Boulogne, which had become a potential base for an invasion of England, and Ratel established a spy network there, using people who were known to be loyal to the highly intelligent and popular *ci-devant* bishop of Boulogne, Jean-René Asseline. Ratel bought a town house in Boulogne, as well as an isolated country house, the manor of

Godincthun, four miles east and slightly north of Boulogne, a kilometre from Pittefaux, where he lived with his mistress Julienne Spère (if that was her real name), a woman who was witty, intelligent, brave, devoted to the royalist cause and very beautiful, hence her nickname 'Belle-peau'.[18] Godincthun was built on a hill but concealed by a screen of trees, commanding a wide view over fields and woodland. The house was equipped with secret underground rooms and passages that could be accessed from concealed entrances, one of which was hidden under the parquet flooring of the salon, so that in an emergency the occupant could disappear.

Ratel benefited from the local influence of Claude-Guillaume-Victor du Wicquet, baron d'Ordre, one of the most important men in the area. In 1799 Artois (who himself had been appointed lieutenant general of the royal army by his brother) appointed the baron royalist commander of the Boulonnais and, after a voyage to England in a fishing boat, Artois also appointed him commander of the secret organisation of royalists in the Boulonnais. It was probably also Ratel who established the route through Le Tréport, which was in use by 1799 when Hyde had landed at the nearby hamlet of Biville.

Their principal courier, for money and other matters too valuable to be trusted to fishermen, was Arabella Williams, the daughter of the poet David Mallet, and apparently the lover of another minor royalist agent. Mrs Williams was in her early fifties, but to judge from descriptions she must have looked younger. She was both attractive and resourceful, a wealthy woman who had spent much of her life in Paris, and when she pretended that the money she brought from England was income from her property there, she did have sufficient rental income for the lie to be plausible.[19]

Bonaparte just about lived up to Pitt's most pessimistic predictions. The *chouans* had risen prematurely in late autumn 1799, and as soon as he came to power Bonaparte took a series of measures to conciliate royalists. The anniversary of the King's execution was no longer to be celebrated. People were free to worship, the churches were opened with mass on Sundays, and priests no longer had to swear hatred to royalty, merely to be faithful to the constitution. Despite British supplies of arms and money, a fierce campaign against them, followed by an offer of generous terms for a pacification, persuaded *chouan* leaders to accept an amnesty in November or December 1799 and further defeats in January 1800 forced them to sign peace deals by the end of February. Louis, comte de Bourmont, the royalist commander in Maine, Frotté and Georges Cadoudal, known in London as 'General Georges', held out most obstinately, but Bourmont made peace after being wounded, Frotté was shot after Bonaparte sent explicit orders to have him taken dead or alive and to hunt down his deputies, and although Bonaparte sent similar orders regarding Cadoudal, he was forced to accept his negotiated surrender as a *fait accompli*.[20]

Bonaparte invited most of the *chouan* leaders to meet him, giving the more reputable ones dinner. Neither Bourmont nor Cadoudal was invited to dinner, but Bonaparte did offer them and their men roles in his army, which Bourmont turned down, while Cadoudal equivocated. Fouché was even cosier with Bourmont and did him a number of favours. The comte de Bourmont was as smooth as Fouché, and thought himself equally cunning, and the two played a devious game, their mutual loathing veiled by exchanges of compliments. Fouché hoped to infiltrate the *chouans* while Bourmont hoped to get warning of Fouché's plans and save his skin.[21]

Georges Cadoudal, a miller's son from Brittany, built like a bull, with a romantic streak despite his brutal violence (one thinks IRA perhaps), was not one to change sides. He didn't trust Bourmont, whom he regarded as a traitor, and certainly didn't trust Bonaparte. A short time later he and Hyde judged it expedient to make a dash for London, retreating to the baron d'Ordre's château at Macquinghen near Boulogne. Having told the authorities that he was going to Brittany, he sailed for England on 13 April and Windham told Pitt of Georges's arrival six days later. Bonaparte had thought that Cadoudal might be brought round, despite having told him that he would never acquiesce in the return of the Bourbons, but gave orders to arrest him once he had left Paris.[22]

From that moment the plans for 1800 began to unravel. The Russians dropped out of the alliance and removed their troops from the Channel Isles, so there was no force to invade Brittany. On 2 May an aged abbot was spotted by a police informant distributing one of Michaud's threatening pamphlets and followed to his lodging with a widow to whom Hyde had temporarily entrusted a large part of his correspondence (up to 4 February). The capture of the correspondence together with pamphlets, passports and documents from Dupérou led to the unravelling of almost the entire network of Anglo-royalists working in France. Fouché tried to arrest Justin Ratel that very day, but Ratel eluded him despite a huge police search.[23]

However, Louis Dupérou had gone to London in order to consult Flint and the Foreign Office about an offer that had been made from somebody at a high level, to betray French secrets for sums of money large enough for the whole matter to need special clearance. He landed at Dover on the fatal 2 May under the name of Pierre Geoffre, and when in London he assumed the name of Martin. Having seen Flint and John Hookham Frere, who had succeeded Canning as Foreign Office undersecretary, Dupérou sailed for France, disguised with spectacles and under a false passport in the name of Frédéric Dierhof, but Police Commissioner Mengaud arrested him on arrival in Calais on 24 May.[24]

Joseph Mengaud was a brute; 'of all the mastiffs that I have placed to guard the borders, Mengaud is my biggest; he is vicious, the dear man', wrote Fouché. His job in the Pas-de-Calais was to keep watch on all boats and cargoes and on all who came and went. He also handled the transfer of newspapers between the two countries and (for Fouché) supervised French propaganda in London. His weakness was that he was thoroughly corrupt, had an interest in smuggling and was willing to sell passports. He supplied Fouché with smuggled English goods as presents for Josephine.[25] Nor was he overzealous: Dupérou escaped from him, but was recaptured on 12 June and escorted into solitary confinement in the Temple.

In the Temple he wrote a memorandum about high-level treachery in Talleyrand's foreign office where documents were being offered to the English. Fouché complained to Bonaparte, who wrote from Italy to Talleyrand, who replied icily that by locking his best double agent in the Temple Fouché had ruined an elaborately laid plan to tempt the British into a potentially brilliant trap.[26] Dupérou was eventually released in 1802 into rustic exile, and it is difficult to tell just what had been going on. The use of double agents and the feline rivalry between Talleyrand and Fouché were both characteristic, making it very difficult to tell if anybody was telling the truth. It may be relevant that in February 1801 one of Talleyrand's principal employees was imprisoned and another fled via Hamburg to London.[27]

It is difficult to know whether it was through cracking Hyde's correspondence or by sheer chance that on the night of 8–9 May 1800 customs officers ambushed a landing just to the east of Le Tréport in which the authorities failed to recognise the significance of their coup. While they tackled decoy runners from what they thought was a band of smugglers, others made sure that six chests containing 1,500,000 francs in gold (about £75,000) that they were in the act of landing from a British boat were safely hidden at the base of the cliff. An English boat recovered the chests six days later and redelivered them safely to Mallet. The customs officers captured a number of wooden stakes, a twenty-metre rope ladder, and a portable crane with a rope and stretcher, but they missed the money. Nor, until two years later, did they capture the royalist agent who came in that night from an English cutter. Suspicion rightly fell on an affluent clockmaker, Michel Troche, because he left his hat behind and a cartridge that they found was wrapped in a letter addressed to him. It was he who had organised the landing, but he fled before he could be arrested. Troche came from Eu, a town two or three miles inland of Le Tréport and twice the size, which had owed its prosperity to an abbey and a major château, and he was indeed the principal local royalist organiser. His name was on a passport in Hyde's papers.[28]

Fouché put one of his top investigators, Pierre Fardel, in charge of the Hyde case. It was not easy to break the royalist codes and make sense of their letters, even when they had captured some of the ciphers and codenames. The police eventually learned what the royalists thought about their negotiation with Bonaparte and Talleyrand, and most of the details of the plans for the seizure of Brest and the landing in France. They learned a bit about plans for negotiations with Pichegru and his friend and Hyde's brother-in-law Isaac-Étienne de Larue, who had escaped with him from Sinnamary. From the code list they knew that Julie Caron was Ratel and that the courier code-named *le petit matelot* was a Mrs Williams, but wondered whether Mrs Williams might be the authoress Helen Maria Williams.

Reading the documents now, as decoded and interpreted by the French police, it is very difficult to be sure who is who unless you are familiar with the precise and immediate circumstances. Codenames and real names are mixed. One person had several codenames, one codename might represent more than one person, and the codename was often also the name of a real person who might or might not be completely irrelevant. People changed sexes too, so that Justin Ratel became Julie Caron or sometimes Godefroy Caron. As Julie, he might be 'la belle Julienne', but that might also be his mistress, Julienne, who is sometimes 'Mme Justine'. In this way it was quite easy for one person to become two or two to become one. Fouché's police, whatever all-seeing myths he might like to promulgate, were far from infallible, and they were very often to be found barking up the wrong tree.

However, Dupérou's capture and interrogation were a source of great anxiety in London. The French, in triumph, published the captured correspondence under the title *Conspiration anglaise* later in the year, and Joseph Mengaud claimed to have embedded four copies within *pâtés de canard* that Pitt had ordered for his private table.[29] Given the tidiness of most politicians in removing remotely incriminating evidence, it is slightly surprising that Charles William Flint's copy of the *Conspiration anglaise* survives in the British Library, the part relating to Dupérou annotated in pencil in his minute, meticulous, academic hand. For the benefit of somebody else who was familiar with the general pattern but not with the precise circumstances surrounding this episode – perhaps the Foreign or Home Secretary, or conceivably William Pitt – he decoded the codenames and explained the implications of the content. He confirmed that what was printed was essentially true and accurate, confirmed that Dupérou had indeed 'received £500 which Frere delivered to me by Lord Grenville's desire for his use', and that he himself had been Dupérou's English correspondent. A letter beginning '*Mon cher monsieur*', where the French could not identify the correspondent, was glossed: 'This letter was to me I presume – as all Duperou's communications were to pass through my hands.' In this letter Dupérou told Flint about his capture; he expected either to be executed or deported to Cayenne and asked Flint to look after his family if he was killed and to arrange for him to be sprung from his place of exile if deported. It is interesting that Dupérou expected this to be possible – an indication perhaps that Flint had been behind the simultaneous escape of the British agents Pichegru, Dossonville, Larue, Willot and Barthélemy from Sinnamary in Guiana.[30]

The final letter, thought by the French investigators to have been written to another Englishman with the codename Snem, was glossed by Flint: 'Snem – one of Dutheil's names. This shews I think that Dupérou did not make a full confession to the French Government.' From his analysis Flint concluded that Dupérou had not revealed his (Flint's) identity to Fouché or told the whole truth about his relations with the royalists, which came as some relief. Ratel's friend Julien Leclerc, who had escaped the general catastrophe in Paris, came to London for instructions and was put in charge of rebuilding the Paris network.

Despite the *chouan* surrenders and Russian desertion, the government decided to send a small British force to seize Belleisle as an offshore stronghold in Cadoudal's part of Brittany. One thousand men took the little island of Houat at the beginning of May and 3000 more followed a fortnight later. Cadoudal left Jersey in mid-May with £20,000 of British money and with his heart set on bigger things than the seizure of an island. His plan now was for an attack on Nantes led by Artois, followed by a march on Paris, where the *coup essentiel* would have prepared the way for a royalist rising. On 19 May he wrote to Frere to remind him that it was essential to make sure that Artois sent his aide Charles-François de Rivière along with Hyde to set in motion the *coup essentiel* in Paris, and on 6 June he repeated that they must not neglect the *coup essentiel* in the capital. Just what this essential blow was to be was not committed to paper, and royalists have taken it to mean a *coup d'état* or kidnapping or some sort of elaborately contrived hand-to-hand combat rather than an assassination.[31] In February Hyde wrote once of the 'removal of the Corsican' and once, in a hot-headed moment after hearing of the execution of a friend, that he would be proud to stab Bonaparte to death, but on paper people rarely committed themselves to more than a vague 'blow'.[32]

Cadoudal raised only a few recruits to help the British expeditionary force and then insisted that Belleisle was too strong to attack. He wanted a bolder policy, but after much vacillation the government decided on 16 June to send the expeditionary force to the Mediterranean. Unaware of this decision, Cadoudal wrote on 19 June that everything was ready; that he could raise the whole of the west with promise of great success so long as the *coup essentiel* at Paris did not fail; that the First Consul would go to Paris at the first sign of trouble, and that it was crucial to deal with him immediately he did so; that he was sending to Paris to find out the state of preparation for the coup and that he had sixty or so hitmen who could do the job.[33]

Then came the catastrophic news of Bonaparte's close-run but decisive victory at Marengo in northern Italy on 14 June 1800, which destroyed any prospect of an invasion from the south. William Wickham, his optimism brutally crushed, sent in a letter of resignation and retired, exhausted and depressed, to the Benedictine abbey of Kremsmünster. The regime there soon cheered him up – 'the best Hungary wine – delicious fish – and more delicious figs – and a theatre where we have heard Haydn's Creation performed by a band of above 40 musicians' – while Portland tried to cajole him out of his resignation:

> The King says you write very long letters, but that it is impossi-
> ble not to read every word of them, even of their inclosures, as
> well as the despatches. The Cabinet look for your communica-
> tions with equal impatience and anxiety, and there is nothing
> so difficult as getting your correspondence a second time from
> Lord Grenville.[34]

But for the moment, with the Austrians forced into an armistice, the plans for revolution in France were off. On 2 July Grenville wrote to Cadoudal to say that Marengo and the truce with Austria that followed had put a stop to British plans and that he should keep his people quiet. The genius of Bonaparte had defeated them.

However, the royalists did not abandon all hope. Artois

summoned Pichegru from the Rhineland and Hyde returned to London on 8 July. The talented engineer Charles-Léon Tinseau, who had served at Toulon, in Corsica, and under the Russian general Suvorov in Italy, was also summoned to London and was led to believe in August that he was to take part in a secret expedition to France.[35] Tinseau was one of the inner circle, familiar with Drake, Wickham, Fauche, Pichegru, Flint and Wright; he and Pichegru dined with Windham on 12 July. On 21 July Cadoudal arrived in London, having crossed in a fast cutter from the prince de Bouillon's Jersey flotilla, and he saw much of Pichegru over the next fortnight.[36] With the main players gathered in London discussions took place that led to the adoption of a plan for a 'coup' in Paris with or without Austrian aid.

6

The Infernal Machine

I f the problem was one man rather than a nation, assassination was a logical solution. With military options failing, this was the conclusion that royalist leaders had been coming to, and in the weeks after Marengo it became a firm plan, formed some weeks before Bonaparte wrote to Louis on 7 September 1800, finally closing off any possibility of a Bourbon restoration: 'You must not wish to return to France, it could only be over 500,000 dead bodies'.[1] Assassination was regarded as a shocking crime that needed special pleading to excuse it, and that was why versions of the pamphlet *Killing No Murder* were repeatedly circulated whenever assassination was contemplated. Even then, nobody wanted it made public that they had been a party to an assassination plot, and those concerned usually denied their involvement. These denials are not always credible. The royalists kept up a pretence of a design to kidnap Bonaparte rather than kill him – the prince de Bouillon was even said to be preparing rooms in Mont Orgueil castle for the reception of his prisoner – but this would have been very difficult to achieve and it is very difficult to believe that it was ever seriously contemplated.

In reality the royalist leadership was ruthless and the *chouans* selected to execute the plot were brutal killers. The French police came to believe that the comte de la Chaussée, a former artillery officer, and the chevalier Tinseau, a distinguished engineer, were directing proceedings from London and that these two explosives experts had resolved on a bomb as the means to kill the First Consul.[2]

On 31 July Georges Cadoudal met William Windham, the secretary at war, and told him that a couple of days earlier he and General Pichegru had had a meeting with William Pitt, the prime minister. A fortnight later Windham again

> saw General Georges, who . . . predicts that Buonaparte will be cut off before two months are over; though he professes not to know specifically of any such intention. Seems to think such course of proceeding legitimate, and had thrown out the idea to Pitt, as he had done before to me. Not necessary to say that no countenance was given to it.[3]

Pichegru dined with Canning on 28 August, Canning being by now an old friend.[4] Windham had a third meeting with Georges on 16 September: 'He talked of the designs to cut off Buonaparte by Assassination; second of the general instability of his government to which latter opinion I felt inclined to assent. On the other having before expressed my opinion I did not now say anything.' Three days later Windham saw Charles-François de Rivière, aide de camp to the comte d'Artois, who had just returned from France via Holland. Rivière also produced 'wild proposals of carrying off or cutting off Buonaparte which I [Windham] pointedly declared a Brit. Ministry could give no countenance to', even though the Frenchman did his best to persuade Windham, stressing Bonaparte's 'hatred against the English whom he considers his personal enemies', his 'determination to make the attempt at Invasion' of England, and the cruelty Bonaparte had shown at

Toulon seven years earlier 'in firing upon the Inhabitants after the Evacuation' of the city by British forces.[5]

Bonaparte further isolated the Bourbons and their loyal followers in October by lifting the exile imposed on forty-eight thousand of the hundred thousand *émigrés* who were still banned from France, and most of them chose to return; for them patriotism, and political stability under a charismatic leader, were enough to draw them back to France where they could more easily earn a living. On 31 October Windham reported the arrival of more peace proposals from him, but the plot went ahead.[6]

However shocked Windham may have been by the wild Bourbon assassination plans, the Royal Navy provided transport for Rivière and Hyde to return to Paris via Biville, the hamlet on the cliffs near Le Tréport which afterwards became a regular secret landing point for royalists; and when the wind failed Cadoudal the prince de Bouillon's cutter was sent to pick him up from Weymouth to minimise delay. Georges wrote to Windham from Portsmouth on 18 September to report that he and his lieutenant, François Prigent, were sailing from Weymouth in one of Bouillon's cutters, and Bouillon reported on 15 October that Georges had just left Jersey. Georges left for France with £12–14,000.[7] Windham may well really have told the royalists that the British could give 'no countenance' to their plan – meaning that they could not be seen to be backing it and would deny that they had done so – but there was no withdrawal of resources or facilities, as might have happened had Windham or Grenville or Pitt found the idea of assassination so truly abhorrent that they wished to prevent it happening. The British leaders sought deniability; but rather than forbidding the planned assassination, they funded and promoted its execution.

Meanwhile, Fouché, with some help from Bourmont, was hot on the trail of Hyde and his fellow conspirators, and on 29 October the police arrested Margadel in Ratel's sister's house; he was shot on Fouché's order on 19 November. Rivière escaped and Hyde went into hiding in the safe house of the perfumer Antoine Caron in the rue Four-Saint-Germain.[8] At this time the police also caught the scent of the Boulogne network and arrested a wine merchant named Louis Lefevre, whose Boulogne shop was the depot for packages bound to and from England. His papers led them to Ratel's mistress Julienne, and she spent a short period in prison in Paris, while Lefevre was released after a year. They also searched the houses of Rosalie le Camus, a local sympathiser, and the baron d'Ordre, who fled to Holland.[9] To prevent communication with England, Boulogne fishermen were forbidden to go further than six miles from the port and were guarded by two boats filled with armed men who could order the fishermen to return to port at any time.[10]

The arrests were a setback, but Cadoudal despatched a replacement for Margadel. Pierre Robinault de Saint-Régent, a former officer in the highly trained marine artillery who commanded a legion in Cadoudal's Breton army, arrived in Paris to take over as chief assassin. According to one of Cadoudal's officers Saint-Régent pulled rank to have the honour of going to Paris to execute the *coup essentiel*.[11] Another of Cadoudal's officers, Joseph Picot de Limoëlan, had come to Paris after the armistice earlier in the year and frequented various fashionable salons. On 3 December he wrote to Fouché to explain that he was only in Paris for leisure's sake, but in reality he had arrived early to set up accommodation for the others. As an assistant he was given François-Jean Carbon, a Parisian, who had previously been confidential servant to another *chouan* leader from Maine. When the armistice with Austria expired in November, four more of Cadoudal's senior officers secretly travelled to Paris – his aide Aimé-Augustin-Alexis Joyaux, known as Villeneuve, Coster de Saint-Victor, Edouard de la Haye Saint-Hilaire, and Michel Roger. The British replaced their captured agent Dupérou with another seasoned hand, Antoine Omer

Talon, who was appointed by Fouché to a position in the *haute police* on 22 November 1800, and Julien Leclerc was appointed to pick up the threads of the correspondence in Paris, along with Louis Bayard. On 9 December Hyde wrote to Artois to tell him that they were ready to strike their blow at the new one-man government.[12]

But Fouché already had eyes on them: an undercover police agent had infiltrated the group. He was able to report the arrival of Saint-Régent, after which he, Limoëlan and Joyaux went to buy arms and tried them out in the Bois de Boulogne. The agent thought they were waiting for the arrival of Rivière before robbing the Charenton mail coach, but the Charenton mail went unscathed. The agent's next news was more menacing: on 2 December the group met to discuss how they were going to do away with the First Consul, their first plan being to shoot him at the theatre with air rifles. Saint-Régent then received the order from Cadoudal to act and called another meeting to finalise their plans. Desperate to report this urgent news as quickly as possible, the undercover policeman made the mistake of turning up at headquarters in broad daylight: the *chouans* presumably suspected him and had him trailed, for after leaving the Ministry of Police he disappeared without trace, doubtless murdered by the group. Fouché was suddenly blind and anxious. On 6 December he tried to arrest all the *chouans*, but they too had disappeared.[13]

They were, however, still in Paris. It was claimed later that Saint-Régent alone was responsible for the choice of a bomb as a method of killing Bonaparte. He (or those who may really have made this decision) were possibly inspired by the bomb recently made by a Jacobin plotter whose plan had been discovered before it could be executed.[14] A gang of Jacobins including an explosives expert developed a bomb with which to assassinate Bonaparte. They tested it for power in mid-October at the Salpêtrière in Paris but the experiment attracted Fouché's attention and he tracked them down in November. As a naval artilleryman, Saint-Régent was trained in the use of explosives and competent to make a similar device, and the plan had the advantage that from its likeness to the earlier attempt it would probably be blamed on the Jacobins, not only causing them harm but also throwing out a false scent that might help give the royalists time to escape.

Cadoudal certainly knew that an assassination was planned, and had announced his intention soon to go to Paris. Roger left Paris for Rennes. He later said that he had disagreed with Saint-Régent over the choice of a bomb, but it is more likely that once the plan was in place he took up his prearranged post in charge of a depot for correspondence between Paris and Brittany.[15] On 17 December Carbon bought a little cart and a very old horse, which he took to a previously rented mews near Saint-Lazare. He also bought a barrel and had it specially hooped with iron for their bomb. The other conspirators remained as invisible as possible, and it was not until they collected the cart that any of them were seen by the witnesses who might identify Carbon.

On 24 December the *chouans* waited for the First Consul's coach to approach. There is a lot that remains unknown about what happened next. There is no evidence that Carbon was present in the rue Saint-Nicaise, although he might have been needed to help make the pile of stones that they unloaded near the corner to obstruct entry to the rue Saint-Nicaise from the place du Carrousel, perhaps posing as road-menders. It is also uncertain whether or not Joyaux and others may have been in the vicinity. The police never succeeded in tracing the driver of the cab that had formed part of the obstruction to Bonaparte's coach: it may have been there by accident, but given how fast the driver disappeared it is likely that it was part of the plan, and it is possible that Carbon or another conspirator was driving it, or had stopped it. The bomb was much more likely to succeed in killing Bonaparte if his coach was halted by a solid barrier than if it had to be timed to go off as his coach sped by. Just why the bomb went off too late is also unclear; in his explanation to Cadoudal, Saint-Régent blamed the powder, but it was almost certainly the case that he lit the fuse too late, and he probably didn't really know how long it would take to burn.[16] It is likely that he expected the obstruction to cause a longer delay, and the horse grenadier's intervention may have been crucial in saving Bonaparte's life, together with César's decision to push through the traffic at the first opportunity.

The explosion could be heard all over Paris. It had been an anti-personnel bomb, packed with shards to maximise its potential to kill and maim. The tally of killed and wounded varies from account to account, the number of killed rising as the badly wounded subsequently died. A number of people lost limbs or were hideously disfigured. One man lost both legs, a kitchen boy an arm. A woman identified the body of her husband by a piece of his trousers, his face unrecognisable as that of a man.[17] Houses were badly damaged, and two years later the whole area was demolished and cleared, either because the buildings were unsafe, or to erase the memory, or both.

When he came to his senses, Saint-Régent staggered eastward by a roundabout route to his lodging in the rue des Prouvaires, dumping his blue smock in the Seine. Around nine o'clock he hauled himself up the stairs and collapsed on his bed. An hour later Limoëlan arrived and told the landlady that his friend had been trampled by a horse, and that he was going in search of a confessor. He returned at eleven with his uncle, who confessed Saint-Régent, and a second *chouan* sought out a Breton doctor, who treated him. Next day Saint-Régent was well enough to move and changed lodging twice. Limoëlan went in search of Carbon, who had taken refuge in his sister's apartment in the rue Saint-Martin; he persuaded him that this was far too obvious a hiding place, and took him to the relative safety of the isolated convent of Notre Dame des Champs on the southern fringe of the city.

Fouché and his friend Pierre Réal left their wives at the concert and rushed to the scene, where policemen were holding back the crowd. The houses near the bomb had been reduced to rubble. Nothing like this had ever happened before, and there was no sign of the culprits. Even though the Consul had survived, Fouché's head was on the block. He had issued orders to his deputy, Pierre Desmarest, and the police were already at work. With the help of a vet, the local commissioner was trying to reassemble the scattered pieces of the horse that had drawn the cart. Réal noticed that the horse had been freshly shod and placed a guard over its remains.[18] Fouché gave orders to take the remains of the horse and cart to the Prefecture, circulate the description of the horse and find the blacksmith. An appeal was published in the newspapers next day.

At the Tuileries, with magnificent sangfroid, Fouché announced to the crowd of counsellors gathered there that in his opinion the crime was due to English gold: 'It's their game to pay people here to kill the first consul. I do the same thing with the men from the Vendée. When I want to have a man killed, I say to one of my people: here's 200 or 300 louis, bring me such and such a head. Why shouldn't the English do the same?'[19]

Bonaparte was convinced that he was wrong and that Fouché's own Jacobin faction was behind it. People thought that they had been behind at least two recent attempts on his life, and one, uncompleted, plot had involved a bomb. Fouché's final report on the case made it look as if he and his police had been in control of the situation the whole time but for one minor glitch, but the police were nothing like as efficient as Fouché liked to paint them.

He was helped by the shock that the bomb produced, the popularity of the Consul and the repugnance felt towards those who had not only tried to kill Bonaparte, but had not scrupled to murder and maim innocent people as well. On 27 December a grain merchant and a farrier turned up at the Prefecture of Police: the merchant had sold a horse and cart to someone he didn't know on 20 December and the farrier had always shod his mare. They both recognised the remains of the horse and the cart and gave a detailed description of the man who had bought them together with a bushel each of peas and lentils. Two days later someone came forward to say that he thought the bomb had been made in his workshop; he recognised the mare and gave an identical description of its owner. His wife also described two men who had come along and gone off with the third in the cart. The men who had sold the barrel and bound it with iron also turned up, as did those who had supplied the blue workmen's overalls.

Between 1 and 3 January 1801 the police paraded 123 republican suspects in front of these witnesses without them recognising a single one. This might suggest that royalists were behind the plot, and for a moment Fouché thought he had found the answer: the description given by the witnesses seemed to fit a royalist suspect in the files called 'Petit François'. He wanted to connect this man with the officers from Georges's army that he had been tracking earlier, but there was no link; 'Petit François' belonged to another *chouan* band. He asked for a search anyway for six named *chouans* including Limoëlan, Saint-Régent, Joyaux and Saint-Hilaire, who were the people the police had been tracking earlier on, but he was uncertain of their names and didn't have descriptions; and then he found other descriptions on file that matched those provided by the witnesses and lost confidence in his identification of 'Petit François'. On 5 January he offered a reward for Georges Cadoudal, dead or alive, with a letter of credit to back it up, and four days later he ordered the arrest of Coster de Saint-Victor, Roger, Charles d'Hozier and another, believing them to be in charge of correspondence between Paris and Cadoudal, and hoping to get some clue to what was going on.[20]

Limoëlan sent a note to Carbon to tell him to trust nobody but him and on no account to leave the convent, but for now Fouché was stumped. With no evidence against royalists he could not prevent Bonaparte and his allies blaming republican extremists, which was the popular view. Bonaparte made a hasty and ill-judged decision to purge their ranks without any proper legal process: he deported seventy Jacobins and placed fifty-two more under surveillance; those who were already in prison for attempts on Bonaparte's life were executed.[21] All this was done before Fouché gained any real evidence of who was genuinely responsible for the crime.

During this period it would not have been hard for Saint-Régent to have left Paris, but he stayed. It is true that his failure to kill Bonaparte, having adopted a strikingly odious method, had not made him overly popular with his friends as well as his enemies, but there are indications that he was committed to a second attempt for which he had asked for further funds. On 16 January Cadoudal wrote to la Chaussée in coded terms that probably imply that he expected Saint-Régent to make a second attempt to kill the Consul.[22]

The crucial breakthrough for the police seems to have come from somebody in Bourmont's circle who told Fouché or Desmarest who 'Petit François' really was, confirmed by the record of the issue of a passport. Armed with a name – Corbon or Charbon – and an old address for his sister in the rue Saint-Martin, on 13 January 1801 Fouché instructed the prefect of police to find the man and arrest him. The prefect was Louis Nicolas Dubois, a man chosen by Fouché and his friend Pierre Réal because he seemed to be obsequious and compliant, but who was turning out, encouraged by Bonaparte, to have ambitions of his own, and a certain jealousy was developing between the top policemen. By making local inquiries his detectives unearthed Carbon's sister's married name and her present address on the sixth floor of a building in a different part of the street. In her flat on the sixth floor of no. 310 they made the crucial discovery of peas and lentils that she admitted had been given to her by her brother, as well as blue overalls and some gunpowder. Carbon's sister and her daughters were arrested on 17 January and, after a little of the persuasion in which Dubois's policemen were adept, her daughters revealed their uncle's new hiding place – four days after Limoëlan had told him not to, he had been stupid enough to visit his sister and tell her his new address. Bourmont thought that his cooperation with Fouché had made him immune, but he was arrested on 17 January and confined in the citadel of Besançon until he escaped in August 1804. Fouché thought Frotté's successor the chevalier de Bruslart was staying with him, but Bruslart escaped.[23]

The following day the police appeared at the convent and arrested Carbon. Interrogated by Dubois, at first he denied everything, but he was recognised by all the witnesses. In the hope of buying his life he explained his subordinate role in the plot and identified the main players as Limoëlan and Saint-Régent, but he denied having gone with them as far as the rue Saint-Nicaise or knowing what they intended to do. He betrayed Saint-Régent's refuge, but by the time the police got there Saint-Régent had fled, warned by Coster de Saint-Victor or Saint-Hilaire. The British plant in the police, Omer Talon, was presumably able to issue some warnings, even in these circumstances of tight security, and Joyaux must quickly have learned what had happened to Carbon.

On 18 January the local prefect tried to arrest the agents for Cadoudal's correspondence at the theatre in Rennes, but an actress helped d'Hozier escape, and Roger was ill and hadn't gone. By now Fouché had learned, apparently from people in Bourmont's circle, who Carbon's employers had been, and he launched searches for Limoëlan and his uncle, Saint-Régent, Hyde, Ratel (whom he called 'the chief executive with a long-standing commission from England for the assassination of the first Consul'), Joyaux, Coster de Saint-Victor and Saint-Hilaire.[24] All police agents were told to turn up at Bertrand's office at five in the morning of 18 January, and between 18 and 20 January Fouché arrested eighty royalists.[25] Three hundred infantry and twenty-five cavalrymen were ordered to support the police in making their arrests on 19 January. In his report Fouché claimed that one of Cadoudal's *chouans* unwittingly betrayed Saint-Régent, but that does not seem to have been true: rather, Saint-Régent was betrayed by someone who gave him papers in a false name and a supposedly safe refuge at the Hôtel de Mayenne – the inn used by people from Bourmont's region – where Desmarest sent Bertrand to arrest him on 27 January. They took him to the Prefecture, but he gave little away and refused to implicate Cadoudal.

The trial began on 1 April 1801, and the two captured conspirators, Carbon and Saint-Régent, were condemned to death and guillotined on 20 April. Limoëlan, Joyaux, Saint-Hilaire and Coster de Saint-Victor were condemned to death in their absence. Limoëlan escaped to the United States, where he became a priest. Joyaux, Saint-Hilaire and Coster de Saint-Victor also escaped, eventually joining Cadoudal in Britain.

The disastrous defeat inflicted by General Jean Victor Moreau on the Austrians at Hohenlinden on 2 December 1800 forced them out of the war, and they made a separate peace at Lunéville on 9 February 1801, which handed Belgium to France – the very event to prevent which Britain had originally gone to war. Military disasters were compounded in Britain by domestic unrest. The failure of successive harvests in 1799 and 1800 tripled the price of wheat and the poor were starving; a fifth of the population was in receipt of Poor Rate relief; mortality rates rose; there were widespread riots – six successive days of clamour for bread in London in September – and in many places local militia and volunteers refused to act against the rioters. Twice in 1800 people took potshots at the King.[26]

Left without allies, Pitt felt that the only way forward was to make peace. One of his more Francophile agents was bold enough to write to Grenville's brother, the Marquis of Buckingham: 'we cannot deny that the difficulty has been drawn on us by ourselves, and that this spirit of revenge has been provoked by our wild and imperious attempts to restore the old government and by our folly in subsidising almost the whole of Europe for that more than criminal purpose.'[27] Pitt resigned on 16 February, ostensibly over the King's refusal to grant the rights to Irish Catholics that Pitt had promised in order to get their agreement to the Act of Union. It was widely suspected that there was more to Pitt's resignation than met the eye, and that the King's obstinate refusal to accept Catholic Emancipation was a convenient pretext, as the diplomat Lord Malmesbury confirmed in his remarks on a conversation between Lord Pelham and Pitt's bosom friend Henry Dundas:

> And after all, said Dundas, very unadvisedly, probably unintentionally, if *these new ministers stay in and make Peace*, it will *only smooth matters the more for us afterwards*. This betrayed a *great deal*, and stuck in Pelham's mind, as it did mine when he told it me, that from the beginning there has been ever some second and back view in all this; that really what appears in the French papers, and in ours, has some degree of truth, viz., that Pitt went out because he felt himself incapable either of carrying on the war, or of making peace.[28]

Malmesbury understood by this that Pitt's real reason for resignation was that he couldn't make peace in any comfort while attached to Grenville and Windham, but he sensed that the independent MPs who backed him, and public opinion more generally, would not tolerate further prolonging the war. However, behind Dundas's remark lay the further implication that if Addington made peace on unsatisfactory terms, and if Bonaparte was then suitably provoked into hostile posturing, it might prove possible to return to lead a more united country. It is interesting that such a shrewd observer as Malmesbury suspected that this was what Dundas and Pitt had calculated.

Grenville and Windham believed that to make peace with Bonaparte was in some sense to recognise the legitimacy of his government, and they felt obliged to resign rather than take any part in such a course. The King was thrown into madness by the crisis, so ministers who had resigned were unable to hand over and a very confused situation prevailed for nearly a month; but the King recovered the moment there was a threat that his son might take over as Regent, and Pitt was able to hand over to his close friend Henry Addington on 14 March. George III was very much opposed to making peace and described it as 'a fearful experiment', afterwards referring to it habitually as a truce; but he liked Addington, who was less high-handed and distant than Pitt, and he was quite glad to see the back of the bullying Grenville, despite sharing his views on the object of the war.[29]

7

The Character of Bonaparte

After Bonaparte became First Consul, claiming to have brought the revolution to completion and offering peace to his enemies, divining his true nature became an urgent priority and interpreting it a literary battlefield. Different parties wrote about him in markedly varying fashion. Staunch anti-Jacobin journalists, supporting Windham and the Grenville clan, saw the 'usurper' as a hypocritical opportunist, a Jacobin in disguise, seeking to perpetuate all the dire innovations of the revolution. Liberals were often sympathetic to Bonaparte, but when they criticised him it was for the opposite reason, for behaving as a dictator, seizing power, suppressing debate and ignoring republican institutions.

Canning's relatively moderate newspaper, the *Anti-Jacobin*, closed in summer 1798 but it was quickly succeeded by a periodical with a similar name but a more hardline agenda, the *Anti-Jacobin Review*. The new magazine had a different tone and expressed the views of the crusading wing of British ministerial thought and of the high end of the Church of England. John Gifford edited the magazine and John Bowles was an important contributor who played a major part in setting it up.[1] Dissenters were almost as much a target for its clerical reviewers as 'Jacobins' and the journal tended to assume that their goals were similar, but it shared the essential aim of the *Anti-Jacobin* in combating Jacobinism and it reminded readers early on that Jacobinism remained an ever-present threat:

> It will, we trust, be amply sufficient for our purpose, to remind our readers that the doctrines and principles in question had for their object, not merely the revolution of France, but that of the whole world – That the usurping rulers of France have laboured, with unremitting assiduity for the accomplishment of this object – That the war was entered into with the Emperor in order to complete the overthrow of the French monarchy, according to the well-known declaration of Brissot, 'It was the abolition of royalty I had in view in causing the war to be declared!' – That hostilities were afterwards extended to other countries in pursuance of the impious design, announced by the declaration of fraternity, of affording military assistance to the disaffected of all countries – And that in furtherance of the same scheme of universal revolution, France has had her emissaries in every state, to inculcate her doctrines and to incite the people to insurrection.[2]

To the *Anti-Jacobin Review* Bonaparte's coup changed nothing. They had been determined to undermine the optimistic liberal view of him from the first: he was not, as he was to liberal admirers, an art-collector, but a 'Gallic plunderer' who 'mingles the most impudent falsehoods with the most atrocious blasphemy'.[3] With studied irony it described how the French attempts to 'enlighten the minds' of the Milanese were not going as well as that 'general liberator of oppressed patriots Buonaparte' had hoped. It launched attacks on Englishmen who spoke up for him, such as the Unitarian Gilbert Wakefield, the eulogist of the 'great and glorious Buonaparte' who was imprisoned for seditious libel in

1799 after opposing the war in print, and died of fever shortly after his release in 1801. Similarly it had fingered Benjamin Flower of the *Cambridge Intelligencer*, who was subsequently prosecuted by Grenville. Dissenters in general came under assault for such crimes as 'calling the King a fool and a blockhead' and 'adorning their parlours with portraits of Buonaparte'.[4]

After Sidney Smith thwarted Bonaparte's progress at Acre, the *Review* contrasted the Corsican's 'audacious calumnies and atrocious falsehoods' with the behaviour of the gallant Sir Sidney. Bonaparte was 'haughty, insolent, rapacious and cruel in prosperity; abusive, vulgar, malignant and false, in adversity; he unites with the courage of a partisan, the sentiments of a pirate'.[5] After his coup the *Anti-Jacobin Review* spoke of his 'vague overtures for a peace ... unaccompanied by any renunciation of aggressive principles'. It was shocked that the 'insolent upstart' had suggested that England had been the aggressor and that he 'presumes to address our Sovereign on a footing of *equality*'. It listed his crimes so far as marrying 'the cast-off mistress of his protector as the condition of his promotion', burning, massacring and plundering in Italy, selling prisoners, 'combining the malignity of a fiend with the despotism of a tyrant', 'professing a respect for the Catholic religion but persecuting its ministers and deposing its chief', and then in Egypt massacring the inhabitants of Alexandria, before issuing 'an open renunciation of the blessed Saviour of the world'. But the writer, probably Bowles or Gifford, was most worried that the Treasury-owned *True Briton* was making conciliatory noises.[6] The *Anti-Jacobin Review* was now certainly employing the propaganda technique of repeating allegations and insults until they lodged in the public mind, 'prodigal in blood, treacherous and cruel', a 'detestable hypocrite' to be contrasted with 'our amiable sovereign' (a man who had not generally been considered amiable until a campaign on his behalf was launched at about this time).[7]

In order to secure French-language sympathy for the British

government, the *émigré* journalist Jean-Gabriel Peltier was taken onto the Treasury payroll in 1798 and thenceforth took orders from George Canning.[8] Tall and thin and wearing the powdered hair of a vehement royalist, Peltier had volunteered his services to Reeves in 1792, to William Windham in 1794 and to Pitt in 1796, and the first documented secret service payments to him for translations date from that year. Peltier was educated at the Oratory school in Nantes (where he was a contemporary of Fouché) before embarking on a financial career in Paris, but by 1789 his banking house had collapsed and on 14 July he took part in the march on the Bastille.[9] He published a series of anti-aristocratic pamphlets between August and October 1789, but he disapproved of the transfer of the royal family to Paris, and when he launched his satirical journal, *Les Actes des Apôtres*, on 2 November, he was aligned with monarchists and moderate counter-revolutionaries. After the overthrow of the monarchy he went into hiding and then fled to London, where he launched *Le Dernier Tableau de Paris* (1792–3), which gave eyewitness accounts of the September massacres, was translated into English and sold several editions, helping to harden British opinion against the revolution. Other publications culminated in the founding of *Paris pendant l'année* (1795–1802). At the same time he worked for the Alien Office, endeavouring to discover spies and revolutionaries among the *émigrés*.

Initially, as I explained earlier, Peltier expressed cautious admiration for Bonaparte, although early in 1797 he did print a letter supposedly written in January by a French officer.[10] This, one of the earliest virulent slurs against Napoleon, claimed that he aspired to the throne, had enriched himself on the plunder of Italy, wished to create an independent kingdom for himself out of Corsica, Sardinia and Sicily, liked to murder the wounded in hospitals and combined 'the vanity of a child with the atrocity of a demon'. The article drew a sharp rejoinder from a correspondent of the

Hamburg-based *Spectateur du Nord*, who, from his tone, might well have been one of Bonaparte's own team of publicists. Peltier did not reprint the letter to the *Spectateur du Nord*, but he did mention its contradiction of his own piece, and apologised, explaining that nearly all his pieces were lifted from the French press and that he was not responsible for what was said.[11] However, after Bonaparte's definitive refusal to engineer a Bourbon restoration in 1800 his language hardened to the point where it resembled that of John Gifford's *Anti-Jacobin Review*.

Two more French-language newspapers published in London projected news to the Continent with a sympathetic reading of British policy. The *Courier de Londres* was edited from 1797 by François-Dominique-Reynaud de Montlosier, a moderate constitutional royalist, but in Paris in March 1801, after Bonaparte's amnesty allowed him to return, he decided that the First Consul was an acceptable substitute for a constitutional monarch, returned to Britain, and edited the *Courier* with a pro-Bonaparte bias until he was ejected as editor on 20 June 1802.[12] He then returned to Paris and edited the violently anti-English *Bulletin de Paris*.

Jacques Mallet du Pan was a Genevan exile, distantly related by marriage to Wickham, with whom he had been associated in Switzerland; he was critical of the inflexibility of the princes and favoured constitutional monarchy, earning the hatred in London of the French 'ultras' while commanding the respect of his British audience. In September 1798 he founded the *Mercure britannique*, published in English as the *British Mercury* and also translated into Italian and Portuguese, which he edited until shortly before his death in May 1800.[13] Several royal dukes and most ministers subscribed and the Foreign Office took twenty-five copies; his *Essay on the Destruction of the Helvetic Confederacy*, which occupied the first three numbers, was influential in persuading liberals to reject Helen Maria Williams's republican view of the Swiss conflict.

An important new recruit was Friedrich Gentz, the son of

the future director of the Prussian Royal Mint. A good-looking, smooth-talking disciple of Kant, Gentz was converted from initial enthusiasm for the revolution by his reading of Burke. He married in 1793, but it did not turn out well, for he was a womaniser and gambler and, despite a decent income, in persistent financial trouble. In 1795 he published a translation of François d'Ivernois's British-sponsored study of republican finance, causing Pitt to urge him to continue his work. In 1799 he presented Grenville with an essay about Pitt's financial system, and on 1 June 1800 a gift of £500 from Grenville arrived on his doorstep. In November 1800 he sent two papers to London, one describing the adverse state of continental opinion on Britain, the other offering his services as a publicist. His offer was accepted – Grenville recommended a regular pension of '£150. or £200. per annum'.[14] His diary relished the consequences. In February 1801: 'Very remarkable that on the one side, Lord Carysfort [the Envoy to Berlin] charged me with the translation into French of the published "English Notes against Prussia," and shortly afterwards Count Haugwitz [the Prussian foreign minister] with the translation into German of the "Prussian Notes against England"'; on 5 April 1802, penniless: 'The most urgent, the most acute of my miseries, was the impossibility of making a present to Christel [an actress], who had her benefit today. And on the same day fate wafts to the wretch who could write this down a remittance of a thousand pounds from England.'[15]

As German opinion tended to regard British policy as selfish and exploitative, Gentz's efforts were valuable, but one other vehicle promoted sympathetic understanding of England through the influence of English caricature. In 1798 a Weimar publisher launched the periodical *London und Paris*, which was edited by Karl August Böttiger. Böttiger was a man with liberal views and a keen interest in British politics: he wrote that most of his 1300 subscribers preferred Fox's opposition to Pitt's ministry and were disappointed that with Gillray serving the ministry, opposition views were so poorly represented in caricature.[16] This mattered because his journal analysed small copies of prints from London or Paris, chiefly caricatures. Prints bought in London were folded up and sent over to Weimar with a description of the subject matter written on the back to help Böttiger explain the prints, and through his descriptions of caricatures a large and influential German-speaking audience was given a sympathetic understanding of the range of British political views, favouring those of the liberal opposition to Pitt.[17]

Despite the efforts of government publicists, liberals in Britain were still keen to see Bonaparte in a favourable light. He still seemed infinitely preferable to the Bourbons, and to some a good deal more attractive than Pitt. His seizure of power in November 1799 dented his image as a hero of liberty and in the anti-ministerial *Morning Post* Coleridge was sceptical, seeing Bonaparte setting himself up as an all-powerful military tyrant with vast patronage and dressing his democratic image with mere rags of pretence. But William Burdon, a Newcastle coalmine owner who had until recently been a fellow of Emmanuel College, Cambridge, defended Bonaparte, asserting that he sought no more than to 'reconcile all parties, to conciliate all his enemies, and to dissolve all opposition' and that not 'a single instance of cruelty, injustice, or tyranny' could be attributed to him.[18] John Aikin in the *Monthly Magazine*, though dubious about the new French constitution, remained positive about the 'clemency and moderation' with which Bonaparte had so far used his powers.[19]

The life of 'General Buonaparte' in the second, 1799, edition of *Biographical Anecdotes* added a note condemning military executions that Bonaparte was said to have ordered at Macegata and other villages on 8 March 1797; the 'indiscriminate butchery of the many on account of the supposed crimes of a few, reflects infinite dishonour on this great warrior.' It added details of the Treaty of Campo Formio, an account of Bonaparte's address to the army of England and of how he first saw England from Calais; then of the gathering of the largest fleet since the crusades in Marseille, Toulon, Genoa and Civita Vecchia, and of how it set sail, and how Bonaparte took Malta, seized Alexandria and Cairo, but had his war fleet destroyed by Nelson. It described the huge celebration in Egypt of the seventh anniversary of the republic, but wondered whether Napoleon had made a serious mistake in going there. On the whole, however, the account remained very positive.

In the Commons Richard Brinsley Sheridan directly challenged the anti-Jacobin version of Bonaparte's character:

> we have seen religion obtain a tolerant exemption in her favour under the government of this atheist; we have seen the faith of treaties observed under the government of this perfidious adventurer; the arts and sciences find protection under this plunderer; the sufferings of humanity have been alleviated under this ferocious usurper ... Such is the portrait of the man, with whom his Majesty's ministers have refused to treat![20]

Writing in the *Morning Post*, Coleridge was very level-headed about Bonaparte's Christmas 1799 proposal of peace, correctly calculating just how well the offer served the First Consul, as well as delighting in the discomfiture of the British government, for Bonaparte's proposal was 'extremely embarrassing to them, who wish to continue the war, with the grace of being desirous of peace'. Coleridge thought they would have to negotiate, but expected no result because the government was committed to the Bourbons: 'peace and the restoration of monarchy in France are wishes that do not exist separate in the minds of the English ministry. A peace concluded with the present government of France would tend to confirm its power, would render the cause of monarchy more hopeless than ever ...'[21]

He mocked ministerial support for the *chouans*, suggesting that to the French they served usefully as decoy birds for the supply of 'arms, ammunition and large sums of money from England, to which they return continual supplies of hope to our secretary of war and his young associates, towards their projected march to Paris'. In February he again wrote in support of Fox and peace:

> Mr. Pitt railed most bitterly at the character of Bonaparte … But the truth is Mr. Pitt knows Bonaparte to be sincere, and, therefore, will not negotiate, because that negotiation would lead to a peace, which peace would baffle that idle hope of restoring the French monarchy, which, spite of the document sent to Petersburgh, is and has been the real object of Ministers, both in beginning and continuing the war.[22]

The government published a third volume of *Intercepted Letters* early in 1800 to bolster the campaign to justify Britain's refusal to accept Bonaparte's offer of peace, and this volume provoked most controversy: the *Critical Review* denounced the crude introduction, in which Bonaparte was said to be 'famous for cruelties, blasphemies and frauds – a fugitive and traitor – the object of the fear and hatred of mankind'. In return, the *Anti-Jacobin Review* denounced the *Critical Review*, which as usual 'displays the Spirit of Jacobinism in all its naked deformity'.[23] In the Commons on 3 February the opposition MP Samuel Whitbread reflected bitterly that:

> Every topic that can revile, and every art that can blacken, has been resorted to, for purposes of political slander; and I am very sorry to see that the Intercepted Correspondence from Egypt, strengthened, and embellished with notes, and perhaps, too, garbled, has made its appearance to prejudice the country against the chief consul, and thereby to set at a distance every hope of a negotiation for peace.[24]

Coleridge questioned the authenticity of the *Intercepted Letters*, citing great imprecision about their source, the government's previous record of fraud, and a couple of devious manoeuvres by the editor to cover what could all too plausibly be seen as mistakes by the *émigrés* that Coleridge suggested might have been employed to fake some of the material. He pointed out (undoubtedly correctly) that four months earlier a fake letter had been printed in the *Sun* in a mendacious attempt to blame the assassination of the French envoys to Rastatt on a plot by one of them to murder the other two.[25]

It was in the context of the controversial rejection of peace that the harshest to date of Gillray's caricatures of Bonaparte appeared. *The Apples and the Horse-Turds* (24 February 1800) was a fable about legitimacy in the wake of the French ruler's over-familiar fraternal letter to George III, depicting Bonaparte as a horse turd floating among royal apples, but considering himself an apple. Gillray continued in this vein. *Democracy; – or – a Sketch of the Life of Buonaparte* (12 May 1800) has some claim to be the earliest black life of Napoleon, fixing him as a levelling democrat. Composed of eight little pictures of episodes from his past, it proposed a legend that owed little to what solid information was available, but became the core of the standard British narrative. Beginning as a ragged and impoverished 'free booter', the King's bounty got Buonaparte to the artillery school (no hint yet of his mother's adultery; in this print she is ugly); next he led the 'Regicide Banditti' who dethroned the monarch; he turned Turk at Cairo; he deserted his army to flee from the Turks; he overthrew the republic that had employed him; he received the 'adulations of Jacobin Sycophants & Parasites', and then dreamed of the murdered and of the assassins' daggers that threatened his usurpation.

By the time this caricature was published the royalist plot to assassinate the First Consul was fully developed but supposedly secret, and no others had yet taken place, so this precocious

The explosion in the rue Saint-Nicaise on Christmas Eve 1800. Bonaparte's coach, having turned the corner, was shielded from the blast

Louis Boilly's portrait of Napoleon Bonaparte as First Consul – thoughtful, melancholy and almost emaciated

The HOPES of the PARTY, prior to July 14. _____ "From such wicked CROWN & ANCHOR Dreams, good Lord deliver us."

Gillray's nightmare vision of a British revolution in 1791: opposition leader Charles James Fox is about to execute a confused and babbling George III

Library of Congress

Political prisoners in Newgate, 1793. William Holland, the printseller, smoking front left, talking with Joseph Gerrald; the booksellers James Ridgway (in blue, holding pipe) and Henry Symonds (holding tankard) seated right; Charles Pigott in green behind Ridgway

THE CONTRAST
1792

BRITISH LIBERTY.

FRENCH LIBERTY.

RELIGION.   MORALITY.
LOYALTY OBEDIENCE TO THE LAWS
INDEPENDANCE PERSONAL SECURITY
JUSTICE INHERITANCE PROTECTION
PROPERTY. INDUSTRY. NATIONAL PROSPERITY
        HAPPINESS

ATHEISM   PERJURY
REBELLION TREASON ANARCHY MURDER
EQUALITY.MADNESS.CRUELTY. INJUSTICE
TREACHERY INGRATITUDE IDLENESS
FAMINE NATIONAL & PRIVATE RUIN.
        MISERY

WHICH IS BEST

The most influential design distributed by the Association for Preserving Liberty and Property against Republicans and Levellers, issued as a subsidised print, but also printed on mugs and songsheets to reach as many people as possible

James Gillray the caricaturist was persuaded by George Canning in 1797 to put his talent into the government's hearts and minds campaign against France

Charles, comte d'Artois, ruthless and uncompromising leader of the royalists in Britain

Lord Grenville, Foreign Secretary from 1791 to 1801, was determined to restore the Bourbon monarchy at any price

Jean-Charles Pichégru, the republican general who changed sides in 1795

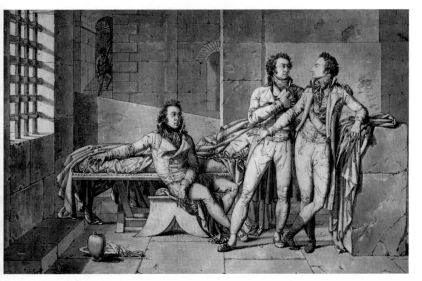

British spies Sir Sidney Smith (right), his assistant John Wright (centre) and the royalist soldier Jacques de Tromelin (seated, in disguise as Smith's servant 'John Bromley') in the Temple prison before their escape in 1798

Sir Evan Nepean was Britain's principal spymaster as well as a keen botanist – the model for Patrick O'Brian's Sir Joseph Blaine

Richard Newton's first caricature of the fearsome republican general
Napoleon Bonaparte (1797), with George III and ministers terrified that he
might visit England next

Bibliothèque nationale de France

Responses to the 'Gagging Acts' of 1795 that effectively banned adverse comment on the
government and Royal Family: John Bull's mouth is padlocked shut, while for farting on the
King's portrait he is threatened with a death sentence

Library of Congress

Detail from Gillray's print *New Morality*, issued with the *Anti-Jacobin Review*, showing the poets Samuel Taylor Coleridge and Robert Southey as asses

Gillray's *Democracy* shows eight episodes from the life of Bonaparte: his birth in poverty, his abuse of royal generosity, the massacre of Parisians, his conversion to Islam, deserting his troops to flee Egypt, overthrowing the government, becoming First Consul, and suffering nightmares over his murders and misdeeds

Thomas Girtin's 1801 watercolour showing, as he put it, 'Part of the Tuileries the palace where Buonaparte resides the house of Lucien Buonaparte and the ruins of the houses blown up by the infernal machine.' The damaged houses in the rue Saint-Nicaise were demolished and cleared and the Place du Carrousel enlarged reference to assassination is intriguing. It is unlikely to have been conceived by Gillray without a specific brief and forms part of a sustained campaign to unnerve Bonaparte with threats of assassination as well as to pursue genuine attempts on his life. In October 1800 Gillray promised Canning that 'any future work which J Gy may engage in, he will take ye liberty of submitting proposals before hand to Mr Canng ... very much wishing to publish only that which may give entire satisfaction.' Gillray may not always have been as good as his word, but it is probably true that much of what he produced henceforth passed under Canning's eye.[26]

In 1800 the ministry recruited another talented publicist with influence abroad. William Cobbett returned to England from America in July on a promise from the embassy in Philadelphia that he could have powerful friends if he wished, and within days of his arrival he was dining with William Windham, who offered him the editorship of a government daily newspaper, which he declined. Instead, his apparently independent *Porcupine* opened operations on 30 October 1800 with Windham's covert support, proclaiming itself anti-French, as his prospectus explained:

> The intrigues of the French, the servile, the insidious, the insinuating French, shall be the object of my constant attention. Whether at war or at peace with us, they still dread the power, envy the happiness, and thirst for the ruin of England. Collectively and individually, the whole and every one of them hate us. Had they the means, they would exterminate us to the last man ... while we retain one drop of true British blood in our veins, we shall never shake hands with this perfidious and sanguinary race, much less shall we make a compromise with their monkey-like manners and tiger-like principles.[27]

On 11 November an article appeared translating three letters from Fouché, 'this civil guardian of the Parisian police, the Runner, and

Watch-Dog, of the Corsican Usurper when he goes to rest', that had allegedly been printed in the *Moniteur* in 1793 and recently reprinted by Jean-Gabriel Peltier in *Paris pendant l'année*. One included the passage: 'The perfidious and ferocious English should be attacked on all sides; the volcanic Republic should overwhelm them with its destructive lava; and the infamous island which produced these monsters, who have no connection with humanity, should be sunk for ever, beneath the waves of the ocean'. Cobbett named John Gifford as the translator, and this illustrates how closely Cobbett, Gifford and Peltier collaborated.

There was always a realistic hope that Bonaparte would not last, however. In autumn 1800 the *Anti-Jacobin Review* was optimistic that 'his enemies are numerous; and the system of plots, and the science of assassination have been brought to such perfection in France, that the life of a foreign usurper cannot be worth many months purchase.'[28] It is unlikely that Gifford or Bowles knew any more than Gillray of specific Anglo-royalist plans; a plot by Italian Jacobins to shoot him at the theatre came to light in October, but these writers may have been given the same instruction as the caricaturist.

On 1 January 1801, soon after the bomb in the rue Saint-Nicaise, Louis Otto, the commissioner for French prisoners in London, drew Talleyrand's attention to articles in British newspapers that expressed the hope that the next assassination attempt would succeed.[29] For the most part the tone of the right-wing press was neutral, with a guarded welcome for the punishment of Jacobin terrorists, while the liberal press condemned the assassination attempt more forcefully but was shocked by Fouché's arbitrary punishment of its supposed left-wing perpetrators, which it saw as an act of tyranny: 'There is something so cruel, and at the same time so cowardly in assassination, that no situation and circumstances can divest it of its atrocity or palliate its enormity. But what does the French Minister of Police propose? To transport 130 individuals out of France instantly, without trial or defence.'[30] Nobody yet believed that the British government was really guilty, though the 12 January bulletin from Paris to the Alien Office was better informed: 'Before Christmas our cut throats were very cheerful, but since the failed coup, they are all in dismay.'[31] On 16 April Otto informed the new foreign secretary, Lord Hawkesbury, that he had evidence that the bomb plot had been masterminded by Dutheil in London and demanded his extradition. Hawkesbury refused but broke off direct contact with Dutheil, who was immediately replaced as intermediary between Artois and the British and effectively retired.[32]

Bonaparte's survival made the English loyalist press more vituperative in its vilification of the popular French leader. Gifford, reviewing John Bowles's *Reflections on the State of Society*, recommended his 'character of Bonaparte' (the 'foulest disgrace to human nature' was one of Bowles's choicer phrases) to those 'moderate and indulgent gentlemen who would fain exclude from our vocabulary, the unpolitic expressions, Atheist, Deist, Villain, Hypocrite, Thief, Adulterer, Assassin'.[33] (The *Critical Review* had found Bowles's reflections less stimulating: 'Buonaparte is a most horrible monster, &c &c &c. All civilised society will be destroyed by the French Revolution &c &c &c. This is the sum and substance of these reflections ... this work is the best sedative we have taken in our hands for some time ... It is impossible ... to read ten pages without falling asleep.')[34]

In 1801 the *Anti-Jacobin Review* printed in its entirety a pamphlet called *Le Grand Homme*, of which a copy had 'accidentally, fallen into our hands', written by 'a man of distinguished talents', later identified as the Austrian ambassador, Count von Starhemberg.[35] This pamphlet assumed that most people had a favourable impression of the 'Corsican adventurer', and sought to correct it by outlining his crimes. He had betrayed the king who gave him his start, had used grapeshot against the people of Paris, had got command on one shameful condition through Barras of an army of bandits of which he was chief brigand, and so on. It included one new personal slur: 'It is a fact that Madame Bonaparte's daughter is not her husband's daughter; it is also a fact that the hero knew that when he married Madame de Beauharnois his friend Barras was giving him a double present', implying that Bonaparte slept with both mother and daughter.[36]

Starhemberg taunted the 'little Corsican' with the notion that Nelson's victory at Aboukir was more spectacular than anything he had achieved; he accused him of massacring thousands of victims at Alexandria and Cairo, and of abandoning his army after being beaten by Sidney Smith. Starhemberg defended Grenville's reply to the insolent advances of the little crowned Corsican who, as other powers should see, was more dangerous than the republic he had annihilated. He insisted that England and Austria were fighting to halt the progress of anarchy and had made great sacrifices of men and money to that end, and that the accusations of self-aggrandisement levelled at Austria and of maritime tyranny at England were pretexts imagined by their enemies, which served the cause of France in counteracting the measures of those who still dared oppose the destructive colossus. Writing to Grenville in December 1801, Starhemberg referred to 'the Corsican monster', and described himself as 'the Anglo-Austrian, and above all Antigallican, inhabitant of Twickenham'.[37]

Despite the best efforts of the maverick Austrian anglophile and his loyalist allies, Bonaparte still had many British sympathisers at this date, chiefly as a result of what one liberal writer, Ralph Fell, a friend of William Godwin, called 'his sincere endeavours to restore peace to Europe'.[38] George Mackereth's *Historical Account of the Transactions of Napoleone Buonaparte* (1801) eulogised 'this astonishing man'. Helen Maria Williams's *Sketches of the State of Manners and Opinions in the French Republic* (1801), written in Paris with the authority of first-hand observation, was strongly supportive of the First Consul.

One extraordinary work savaged the British government as well as its continental allies: Lewis Goldsmith struggled to find a publisher willing to risk *The Crimes of Cabinets* (1801). Very little is known for certain about Goldsmith, but he was of Portuguese Jewish descent, had travelled widely on the Continent, and had been involved in British radical politics since the 1780s. Goldsmith praised 'that great man, Bonaparte, whose shining qualities in the field, and boundless talents in the cabinet; whose moderation and generosity in victory, stand unparalleled in the page of history', whose pacific overtures had been rejected by 'those *honourable* dealers in blood, Pitt, Thugut and Co.', who 'seem to have wished a little more of their commodity to be expended, for at least 150,000 men French and German, have perished, from the time of Bonaparte's offering to treat for peace, till the memorable battle of Maringo . . .'[39]

Goldsmith blamed the war squarely on the British administration: 'every man that has his intellects, must see, and be convinced, that all the blood that has been spilt since the confederacy began to be disjointed, is owing to its distracted councils.' He pointed to the collapse of trade, high taxes, high prices and scarcity of bread and then to William Windham's speech claiming happiness and prosperity under a fine constitution and praying: 'God avert a peace with a Jacobin republic!' To Goldsmith the constitution was not what it had been before 1792, now lacking the laws that had made it the envy of the world.[40]

After publishing *The Crimes of Cabinets* Goldsmith translated Hauterive's *State of the French Republic at the end of the Year* VIII (1801), an official French foreign office manifesto that, while promoting the French point of view at the expense of the English, nevertheless sought reconciliation between the nations. In December 1801 he crossed to Paris, returning in July 1802 to set up a pro-French newspaper in London, but very soon returned to Paris as the first editor of the English-language *Argus*, launched on 20 October 1802 with Talleyrand's support to counter the French-language propaganda generated from London. Its very limited circulation was investigated in November 1802 when the Post Office sent Home Secretary Lord Pelham a 'List of Persons to whom the English Paper the Argus publish'd at Paris is sent'.[41]

Before the Peace of Amiens Bonaparte was vilified in the anti-Jacobin press but writers lacked specific crimes to pin on him. Liberal writers feared that he might become a military dictator, but were willing to take a positive view of his attempts to drag France from chaos, and of the prospect for a lasting peace if Bonaparte could establish a settled government. Bonaparte seemed to be doing, and probably was doing, all he could to make himself acceptable to British public opinion. When Pitt resigned he felt that he could not continue the war with so many public voices ranged against him. If the country was again to wage war against Bonaparte with any chance of success this situation had to change – liberal opinion had to be brought round and the mass of the people had to believe that Bonaparte was an enemy with whom it was unsafe to make any compromise peace.

8

The Peace and the Press

The strange manoeuvres in British politics that preceded the Peace of Amiens and that occurred during it puzzled people at the time and remain difficult to explain. There is a considerable body of evidence to support the view that Bonaparte and his government had desired peace since 1800 and, having got peace in the winter of 1801, had no desire to go back to war in 1803. On the other hand, neither George III nor Pitt's ministry desired to make peace with Bonaparte at all, but in 1801 Pitt judged that he could no longer carry public opinion in Britain with him in pursuing a war that offered no prospect of victory. Having resigned, Pitt supported and secretly advised Addington's ministry in its negotiations for peace, endorsing the surrender of colonial conquests, to the consternation of Dundas for whom the main goal of the war had been their acquisition. In diametric opposition, Grenville and Windham resolutely opposed both the negotiations and their outcome. By making peace and by seeming to distance himself from Pitt, Addington was able to make an alliance with Richard Brinsley Sheridan and win the support of important liberal press proprietors.

Sheridan, formerly cast by caricaturists as Charles James Fox's

Jacobin chief henchman, had been trying to rebuild an image as a loyal patriot, and after October 1801, cautiously and gradually he and his friends swung behind Addington, becoming loudly patriotic and anti-Bonaparte from summer 1802, until by December 1802 Fox was the only major figure in favour of peace. By April 1803 the apparent tone of public opinion – it is difficult to judge by anything other than the press – had changed to such a remarkable degree that the return to war seemed, at least, to be backed by overwhelming public support. In diplomacy, both sides had made controversial moves, or failures to implement agreements, during the peace, but nothing so truly shocking had happened that it could justify a rupture. What happened was of decisive moment only in terms of the way in which it was interpreted so as to influence public opinion. To me, therefore, it seems that what was said in the press was often of greater importance than what was done, and in the following two chapters I try to shed some light on how the British public was instructed that it was vital to renew the struggle against a France led by Napoleon Bonaparte.

Had Britain made peace in 1800 there might have been far more chance of lasting success, but in 1801, in the immediate aftermath of a British-sponsored assassination attempt, Bonaparte had every reason to suspect British sincerity. He might have felt with some justification that he had done his best to answer each British objection to him as a leader of France as it arose. The new calendar went, religion was restored, exiles were welcomed back, stability was his watchword, but there was no sign from Britain that he was doing what they had asked for. As a pledge of sincerity and a clear sign that Britain had distanced itself from the Bourbons, he wanted Britain to abandon support for Cadoudal and his 'soldiers' and for pro-Bourbon journalists.

The new British foreign secretary, appointed in March 1801 to replace Grenville, was the thirty-year-old Robert Jenkinson, Lord

Hawkesbury, the son of one of Pitt's most faithful henchmen. He was a Christ Church contemporary of Canning and his chums but they didn't altogether like him. One wrote of Hawkesbury that:

> He was much ridiculed, seldom being addressed by any other name than 'Jenky', excepting always indeed by Lord Molyneux, who always called him either 'delightful' or 'beauteous fair one'; his manners were effeminate and cold, and were rendered still more unpleasing by an almost constant state of absence of mind either real or affected.

Mockery of the younger Jenkinson was not confined to Canning's circle. The elder brother of the future Duke of Wellington, similarly, could not respect 'young Jenky whom I have laughed at ever since I have known him and my habits of considering him as a ridiculous animal are so rooted, that I am afraid I cannot easily be brought to admire him as a minister.'[1] It was Hawkesbury who was chosen as the man who had to make peace. As soon as he took office in March 1801 he put out feelers and in late June the diplomat Anthony Merry went to France as counterpart to Louis-Guillaume Otto, like him, nominally as commissary for prisoners of war, but actually as peace negotiator.

While diplomacy was getting under way, military posturing continued. Napoleon prepared for an invasion of Britain, and Britain concentrated on resisting one. In August Admiral Nelson mounted a raid on Boulogne in an attempt to destroy the shipping there, but it failed in its objective and was beaten off. In late summer, however, peace was agreed.

The preliminaries were signed in London on the evening of 1 October 1801, bringing an end to hostilities, and the news became public over the following days. The unexpected armistice was greeted with wild joy in London and the stock exchange soared, but aristocrats such as the diarist and pamphleteer Lady Lucas, 'who own Peace to be necessary, yet dread its Consequences', greeted the news nervously, still afraid, like the King, that peace with France might bring on a revolution within Britain. She, the cousin of the new secretary at war, Charles Yorke, was astonished that, hearing that the French had ratified the peace, 'the Mob not only huzzad Buonaparte's Aid-de-Camp this Morning, but drew him & M: Otto along the Street, a Deviation from Old British Spirit which I never thought to have seen.'[2] London was illuminated (by people lighting candles at their windows) and thousands of people went into the streets to see the more spectacular illuminations of public buildings such as the Bank, the Mansion House and East India House. 'Joy appeared universal. Everybody in good humour', reported one witness on 10 October, before a tremendous thunderstorm cleared the streets.[3] The French negotiator Otto wrote to Talleyrand within the week to report that: 'There is not one man of leisure here who does not wish to see Paris, and above all the First Consul, and the portrait, painted by Boze, has created a great sensation.'[4]

Joseph Boze had brought his joint portrait of Bonaparte and General Berthier at Marengo to London and was exhibiting it to paying crowds. Printed pictures and lives of Napoleon were selling like hot cakes. A writer in Suffolk remarked that:

The peace is an event which has excited a tumult of joy which I never before saw equalled. The effect was the stronger as the event was totally unexpected – indeed, for two or three days preceding it was totally despaired of. The funds were falling and the expectation of an invasion was very general. ... Illuminations have been general throughout the kingdom and in London and some other places have been repeated several times. Last Friday we illuminated at Bury ... among the transparencies exhibited in London his portrait was shown, with the inscription: 'The Saviour of the World.' Indeed, it is curious to observe the change of style in the government newspapers. The 'Corsican Adventurer,' 'the atheistical usurper,' is now 'the august hero,' 'the restorer of public order,' &c. &c.; in fact, everything that is great or good. It reminds one of the transformation in a pantomime where a devil is suddenly converted into an angel.[5]

In a caricature published on 26 October, *The Child and Champion of Jacobinism, New Christened*, godfather Pitt, who had in February 1800 famously called Bonaparte the 'Child and Champion', now renamed him 'Deliverer of Europe & Pacificator of the World'. It is difficult to measure how many people saw Bonaparte as peace-delivering hero and Pitt as warmongering villain, but for a brief period Bonaparte enjoyed considerable popularity. The caricaturist Percy Roberts was brave enough to publish *John Bull's Prayer to Peace*, in which Bonaparte was hero, expelling Pitt, a belligerent gorgon armed with the daggers of an assassin. Around December 1801 Louis Dubroca's *Life of Bonaparte* was published in translation, reviewed by Gifford as a 'miserable attempt at unmixed panegyric'. Another *Histoire de Bonaparte* was dismissed as 'a tribute offered to the vanity of Bonaparte' and *La plus grande action de Bonaparte* as 'blasphemous adulation'.[6]

William Cobbett claimed that all of the press except his *Porcupine* and the *Anti-Jacobin Review* was united in support of the peace. He recalled how the *Morning Post*, the *Courier*, the *Times* and the *Sun* spoke of 'the "Chief Consul", "the Astonishing Person at the Head of the French Government", the "Wonderful Genius presiding over the affairs of France", numerous were the commendations bestowed upon him for the salutary change he had produced in that distracted country.' The newspapers approved of Josephine's taste for botany and English nurserymen, and of Bonaparte's preference for English carriages and of his gift of a book to the philosophical society.[7]

Cobbett himself, however, wrote to Windham on 7 October 1801 describing 'the despair into which I and my friend Gifford were plunged by the peace' and again, hysterically, half an hour after a mob had drawn Bonaparte's aide's carriage past his door in Pall Mall, 'it has sunk my heart within me and I look forward to a revolution with as much certainty as I do to Christmas'. He believed that the mob did it because the aide was one of those who have 'killed Kings and Queens and noblemen and have destroyed rank and property'.[8] He refused to light candles to celebrate the armistice had his unilluminated windows broken by a mob, and reported that:

> In many parts of the metropolis the language openly held, during the whole of Saturday and of Monday evenings, was infamously disloyal, not to say treasonable. At a printseller's in St. James's Street [this could only be the shop of Gillray's publisher Hannah Humphrey], where a considerable crowd were assembled, a man approached the window, and pointing to a portrait of a Great Person, not unknown to your Lordship [George III], first made the motion of stabbing, and then of ripping up, grinding his teeth at the same time, and exclaiming, 'Ah! that I would!' – Then turning to a portrait of Mr. Pitt, 'Ah!' said he, 'and that long fellow too,' repeating, at the same time, the gesticulations expressive of his bloody wishes. After this he pointed to a portrait of Bonaparte, and taking off his hat, gave three huzzas, in which he was joined by all those around him!!![9]

Cobbett was about to be silenced temporarily: in November John Gifford sold the *Porcupine* to the tamed former radical journalist Henry Redhead Yorke and a Mr Bateman, and Cobbett commented: 'I have every reason to believe that Yorke has an allowance from the Ministry'.[10]

At this date the *Times*, in which Hawkesbury sometimes wrote, was with Addington, as were the *Morning Post*, *Courier* and *Herald*. James Perry's *Morning Chronicle* remained loyal to Fox, while Heriot's papers, the *Sun* and *True Briton*, though essentially loyal to Pitt, took orders for the present from the Treasury and backed Addington. The warmongers were now inconvenient, and after Windham made a very eloquent speech against the peace on 4 November 1801 Heriot's papers turned on him. 'Those who know the influence under which Heriot acts', wrote Cobbett to Windham, 'must be assured that he has received his <u>instructions</u> for that purpose ... Gifford intends commenting on the article and I hope he will not spare them.'[11]

John Gifford's *Anti-Jacobin Review* and Jean-Gabriel Peltier's *Paris pendant l'année* continued to serve Grenville and Windham. Cobbett, who was on intimate terms with Gifford and Peltier, remained close to Windham, and with his backing and the stronger finances of the Grenville family he got a new newspaper, the *Weekly Political Register*, which commenced on 16 January 1802. Grenville wrote to Canning:

> It appeared to us that the undertaking was likely to prove of material public benefit, by giving circulation & currency to opinions & principles on which the only hope of safety for the country must, in our opinion, now more than ever depend. With this impression, and with a favourable opinion of Cobbetts principles and talents, an arrangement has been already made by which his pecuniary demand is fully answered.[12]

Grenville wanted Canning to write for the new publication, but Canning held back until he knew Pitt's opinion. Windham lost his seat at Norwich in the election of 1802 but was returned for a pocket Cornish borough by the Grenvilles.

Gillray almost ignored Bonaparte during this period. In November 1801 he appeared as a figure in Windham's nightmares in the double-edged *Political Dreamings*, and a year later he sat enthroned in *Introduction of Citizen Volpone and his Suite*, but neither of these was an image to which the Consul could take much exception. Gillray's work was directed at domestic politics, and several prints, including *Lilliputian Substitutes* in May 1801 and *Preliminaries of Peace* in October, mocked Addington's ministers to a degree that makes it plain that they could not have been paying him.

Coleridge, on the other hand, played a crucial role in winning over liberals to Addington and to a sceptical view of Bonaparte. In December 1801 his column in the *Morning Post* pointed out that the friendliness between Sheridan and the ministry was only possible because Pitt was no longer in charge. The numerous liberals who wished to see Fox lead the country but were prevented by the King's refusal to accept Fox would only support Addington if Pitt was nowhere to be seen. Coleridge's analysis, as usual, was compelling, and he took the opportunity to complain at length about the erosion of constitutional liberties under Pitt. He did not find Addington's administration a great improvement on Pitt's as far as civil liberty went, but France no longer compared favourably, as Bonaparte's government seemed to be 'an iron despotism'.

James Perry's *Morning Chronicle* was still defending Bonaparte wholeheartedly, arguing that he had every right to complain about his vilification by the *émigré* press. Fox was disgusted with the whole business, commenting in October:

> since there is to be no political liberty in the world I really believe Bonaparte is the fittest person to be master ... The truth is, I am gone something further in hate to the English Government than perhaps you and my friends are, and certainly further than can with prudence be avowed. The triumph of the French Government over the English does in fact afford me a great degree of pleasure which it is very difficult to disguise.[13]

While all this was going on, the manner in which Bonaparte sought to stabilise affairs in various neighbouring states was registered with alarm in Britain. On 5 February 1802 Lady Lucas noted in her diary: 'the principal News of this Week is that Buonaparte has declared himself president of the Italian Republic, which startles many People as a new mark of his aiming at the empire of all Europe.'[14] The existence of a powerful France with the borders sought in vain by Louis XIV and buffer states beyond them was enough to alarm any Briton, but there was no genuine reason to accept the assertions of the 'warmongers' that he aimed at the empire of all Europe.

Bonaparte made his first complaint against *émigré* journalism at the beginning of February. He was incensed by two passages published by Peltier in December and January that referred to his mother as 'so famous in the annals of Corsican gallantry' and described quarrels within his family that, like Starhemberg's earlier pamphlet, were particularly upsetting to Josephine and her daughter Hortense.[15] He instructed Talleyrand to tell Otto: 'Whatever the liberty of the press in England, the government always has means at its disposal to prevent or punish such disgusting abuses', and he asked his brother Joseph, who was leading the French negotiating team, to speak to the British peace negotiator Cornwallis 'about the abominable work that you find herewith and convince him how much it is contrary to the dignity of the two states to allow an émigré in London to print such rubbish, at a time when I am making special efforts to stifle everything offensive to decency that might be printed at Paris.'[16]

When Otto showed the offending paragraphs in *Paris pendant l'année* to Addington, the prime minister deplored them but regretted that English law did not allow him to clean up the press in the way that Bonaparte could in France. Otto reminded him that the Aliens Act allowed him to deport foreigners, but Addington replied that he could only deport those who were a threat to the security of the state. The French, of course, with people like Montlosier now working for them, knew perfectly well that the editor of the *Courier* had been prosecuted in 1799 for insulting the friendly monarch Paul 1. On 22 February Talleyrand instructed Otto to hint that if Peltier wasn't silenced the peace negotiations might be jeopardised, but in the event, when the formal treaty was signed on 27 March, the French failed to obtain an explicit clause about journalism.[17]

Bonaparte further reduced the list of political exiles to only 1000 in April 1802, and nearly all of those who were not banned returned home. This was alarming for the British secret service, as a number of people who knew too much about what had been going on returned to France, and they included Wickham's secretary (refused a pension by the Foreign Office) and Sidney Smith's assistant Jacques de Tromelin.[18]

On 23 April Otto requested permission to demand the extradition of journalists who attacked the French government, and Napoleon instructed Talleyrand to demand that the English press adopt the tone normally used for powers with which the country was at peace as a precondition for sending Antoine-François Andréossy as a full ambassador.[19] Pressure mounted on Peltier until he closed down *Paris pendant l'année* in June 1802; the comte d'Artois authorised Dutheil to reward him and to encourage him to write for the English newspapers.[20] At almost precisely that moment, however, the now pro-Bonaparte Montlosier was ejected from the editorship of the *Courier de Londres* and replaced by Jacques Regnier, who continued to publish the provocative anti-Bonaparte invective that had previously been delivered by Peltier. Regnier had been a contemporary of both Fouché and Peltier at the Oratory school at Nantes; he had worked with Peltier on *Les Actes des Apôtres* in 1792, then on a Jacobin magazine, before he fled to London in 1795 and eked out a marginal existence as a journalist and translator, before the owners of the *Courier de Londres* paid his debts and installed him as editor.[21]

On 5 June Bonaparte demanded the deportation of Georges Cadoudal and the removal of the Bourbon princes from London. Cadoudal had left Brittany at the end of 1801 after the new ministry had agreed to take around seventy of his officers into British pay and not to disband them. They made their way at first to Jersey. On 9 February 1802 Otto warned that they had asked to move to England but that Hawkesbury was thinking of sending them to Canada, an idea that Talleyrand approved. Instead, in March they were given permission to move to England and, with allowances fixed by Addington in May, they established a camp at Romsey, where they were commanded by Cadoudal's senior adjutant-general Pierre Guillemot, as Cadoudal himself remained in London.[22]

In July Napoleon, Talleyrand and Fouché all pressed Otto to urge Addington to suppress the libellers without recourse to a court case, but on 25 July Otto said the French government had authorised him to demand the punishment of Peltier. He noted the 'unfavourable impact' that Peltier, Regnier, Cobbett 'and other writers who resemble them' (meaning the *Anti-Jacobin Review*) were having on the cordial relations between the two countries; he complained that 'the perfidious and malevolent publications of these men are in open contradiction to the principles of peace', and hoped that in accordance with the principles of article one of the Treaty of Amiens and the law of nations, the government would punish Peltier. Hawkesbury's defence was that British ministers were subject to the same calumnies; he told Otto that he was seeking the attorney general's opinion on whether what Peltier had written was a libel, but warned of the difficulties of a trial. It seems likely that the immediate cause of this decision was the publication by Peltier of the first issues of a new journal, *L'Ambigu*; the earliest issues are undated but it seems plausible that it was its appearance that provoked Bonaparte to demand legal action.[23]

L'Ambigu, Variétés atroces et amusantes, Journal dans le genre égyptien was deliberately enigmatic. Even the title is difficult to translate – perhaps less 'The Ambiguous' than 'The Ambiguous One', because the headpiece was a portrait of Bonaparte as a sphinx. The first number of this 'Miscellany of the Atrocious and the Amusing, a Journal in the Egyptian genre' consisted of twenty-four pages. The portrait of Bonaparte as a sphinx wearing a crown was 'Found in the Valley of the Kings at Thebes and reprinted by Cox, Son & Baylis ...' Apart from various oblique recommendations that Bonaparte should be assassinated, the first volume contained a stream of quite amusing mockery of his style, his taste for Ossian, his fear of conspiracies, his short stature (given in one place as four foot two inches)[24], his *légion d'honneur*, his public building programme, all calculated to irritate.

On 8 August an angry article, thought to have been written by Napoleon, was published in the *Moniteur*:

> The *Times*, which is said to be under ministerial supervision, is constantly spreading invective against France. Every day two out of its four pages are employed to give credit to base calumnies. Everything that imagination can paint that is low, vile and wicked, this miserable organ attributes to the French government. What is its aim? Who pays for this? Who is it meant to convince?
>
> A French journal edited by some miserable *émigrés*, the most impure residue, vile scum, without homeland, without honour, soiled by so many crimes that no amnesty can wash them away, goes even further than the *Times*.

He complained that various bishops, led by Arras, were writing libels and that Jersey was full of brigands who had been condemned to death before the peace for murder and other serious crimes. The Treaty of Amiens made provision for the surrender of criminals, yet instead these brigands remained in Britain, were free to come and go in fishing boats, to land in France and commit murder and arson. The British government positively encouraged criminals:

> Georges wears his red sash openly in London, a reward for the machine infernale that destroyed a neighbourhood of Paris, and killed thirty women, children and peaceful citizens. Doesn't this special treatment make one wonder whether, had he succeeded, he would have been awarded the Order of the Garter?

Then Bonaparte wrote in general terms about the behaviour of friendly nations towards one another, suggesting that what was coming out of the English press was more characteristic of war to the death than of peace. He said that Richelieu was said to have helped to dethrone Charles 1, and that the British government was supposed to have contributed to the Terror, but did the two states really want to prolong this hostility that had caused so much trouble over the centuries? Would it not be better to support each other in protecting commerce, suppressing counterfeit coinage and refusing asylum to criminals? What did the English government hope to gain? Did it not realise that the French government was now more stable than it was?

> What will be the effect of this exchange of insults, this influence of insurrectionary committees, of the protection and encouragement given to various assassins? What will civilisation and the commerce and welfare of the two nations gain from it?
> Either the English government authorised and tolerates these public and private crimes, and in that case one could say that this conduct is not worthy of British generosity, civilisation and honour; or it can't prevent them, and then one might say that where there are no means to repress assassination, calumny and the European social order, there is no government.[25]

The Treasury secretary, Nicholas Vansittart, was told to threaten Heriot, who complained to Addington on 10 August; he had perhaps been picked on because the government knew that Bonaparte was aware that the *True Briton* was a Treasury newspaper – simply reading Cobbett told him that. Addington warned Heriot of the 'consequences produced by opprobrious observations, in papers of such established reputation as yours, on the proceedings of foreign governments, and on the characters of those at the head of them', after which Heriot dismissed Henry Redhead Yorke as editor of the *True Briton* and effectively apologised in print; Addington then explained to Otto that this had been done as a private favour.[26] Yorke, the son of the manager of the Codrington family's plantations and a West Indian slave, had been brought up as a gentleman from an early age, but went to France out of radical enthusiasm in 1792 and was imprisoned in Dorchester Castle as a Jacobin from 1796 to 1798. In gaol he had discovered an enthusiasm for Pitt's war policy that had eventually brought the reward of the editorship; his sacrifice for overzealous writing was purely temporary.

On 15 August Napoleon wrote to Fouché telling him to ban English newspapers from France, though he could admit *Bell's Weekly Messenger*, as Otto said it wrote with more moderation than the others.[27] Two days later Otto wrote to Hawkesbury in much stronger terms, reiterating what had been written in the *Moniteur*, complaining of Britain's support for French insurgents and of the abuse in the British press, especially the *émigré* press. This was not just a question of the odd paragraph but 'of a deep and continued system of defamation, directed not only against the chief of the French republic, but against all the constituted authorities of the republic'.

Hawkesbury told Anthony Merry that if the French could prove that the bishop of Arras was distributing papers along the French coast the government would expel him; he promised to remove *chouans* from Jersey and to consider Cadoudal's fate, but insisted that 'his majesty cannot and never will in consequence of any representation from a foreign power make any concession which can be in the smallest degree dangerous to the liberty of the press as secured by the constitution of this country'.[28] At the end of August some of Cadoudal's people were arrested and he protested their innocence to Windham.[29] The Duke of Portland was dissatisfied with the soft line taken by Addington's friends, writing to Pelham: 'I can not treat an Usurper with the same Civility that I would an old Government & more particularly when I am convinced that it is the interest not only of this Country but of all the Civilised World to use every possible means to hurl him from his Seat.' Pelham, his successor as Home Secretary, reassured Portland that he was 'determined not to remove Peltier or any other Alien for Libels against France', being 'unwilling to check the freest discussion of the demerits of the French Government & Constitution, as I consider such discussions very useful in satisfying the People of this country, that they cannot improve their situation by any attempts to follow the Example of France.'[30]

Lady Lucas noted in her diary that:

Our Newspapers have asserted this Week that all English Newspapers have been seiz'd in the Coffee-Houses in Paris, & that none are allow'd but a few for the Government. It has also been reported that Peltier's Ambigu (an abusive journal against Bonaparte) was to be prosecuted by the Attorney-General, & that Peltier had promised to desist; but however that may be the 4th. No. is come out.[31]

Indeed, Peltier continued to publish. His fifth number contained quite an amusingly imagined battle of the English and French newspapers. The sixth removed the crowned head from the sphinx woodcut beneath the title so that the sphinx was no longer a portrait of Bonaparte but a headless sphinx, insinuating that his magazine was no longer about Bonaparte, while simultaneously making a gesture of 'virtual' assassination. That issue discussed the anti-English *Lettres sur l'Angleterre* written by the journalist Joseph Fiévée, then working for Bonaparte, and reminded people of Napoleon's fear of assassination – 'he is in constant fear of the arrival from Jersey of a new infernal machine'.[32] He continued the *Ambigu* long enough to discuss Fox's visit to Bonaparte in late September, and it was not until 22 November 1802 that the newspaper finally closed down, pending Peltier's trial on the grounds that he had recommended the assassination of the First Consul. The ninth number was the last of the first, pre-trial, volume, and included a woodcut hieroglyph showing Bonaparte executing Peltier in anticipation of his fate after his trial.

In a first (and supposedly last) dated letter to the Consul, Peltier offered to make his peace with Bonaparte by telling him the truth about what people were saying about him in England – effectively that the annexation of Piedmont and his decrees to the Swiss had alienated all of his English admirers and that the country was uniting against him. Bonaparte, once so popular in England, would be hard put to muster fifty friends, and people were saying that he had gone slightly mad and was aiming at universal dominion. Peltier taunted him with what Cobbett and Regnier were writing and wondered maliciously just what his relationship was to the child to which Hortense had given birth on 10 October. He closed with an ambiguous warning about the character of *Bretons*: this, ambiguous as ever, was a pun, for it translates as Britons, but in French it might also mean people from Brittany, and Peltier was a Breton, as were Cadoudal and his assassins.[33]

Meanwhile, on 10 September Charles Whitworth had received his instructions as ambassador to France. According to Lady Lucas's diary he had 'landed at Calais on Wednesday Evening & was receiv'd with great Honors, & God Save the King was play'd! – yet it is Buonaparte's Aim to keep up as much National

Hatred as ever, & he allows an English Paper in the disaffected Style call'd the Argus to be publish'd at Paris, I suppose to retaliate on our Newspapers.'[34] Whitworth was a close friend of Lord Grenville, who was implacably opposed to the peace. A 'zealous anti-revolutionary', he regarded Bonaparte as a deranged tyrant, and in one letter of April 1803 described the First Consul's actions as 'a picture of despotism, violence and cruelty, at the contemplation of which humanity sickens'. As ambassador to Russia he had encouraged the assassination of the Tsar, and he, like Grenville, was imperious, insolent and quite uncompromising. The choice of Whitworth as ambassador is highly indicative of the attitude by this stage of the government to the peace and a clear indication of what was to come.[35]

The issue of the freedom of the press in Britain regarding its treatment of Bonaparte is an interesting one: there were such differences between the customs in Britain and France – and, indeed, most of continental Europe – that there were clear grounds for misunderstanding. But those differences were so well known abroad as to be almost notorious, and French knowledge of what was happening in the British press in 1802 was more sophisticated. They knew that certain papers were under ministerial control and that what they said usually responded to ministerial wishes – if they had any doubt, journalists like William Cobbett were constantly reminding them that this was the case, and of the influences under which other journalists acted. So French demands of the British government were not naive, even if ministers were correct in saying that their own control was not binding or legally enforceable.

But there was nothing like an attack on the freedom of the press to raise the hackles of liberal journalists. Writing in the *Morning Post* on 25 September 1802, Coleridge was talking only ambition and despotism. 'Many Englishmen were made merry, but none angry, by the article in the Moniteur of the 9th of

August;' he commented, 'because none of us have been led by it ever to suspect that Mr. Pitt and his colleagues "excited the massacres of September," or "encouraged the fabricator of the infernal machine".' One can only speculate on how Coleridge's view might have changed had he seen the evidence for the involvement of Pitt with the infernal machine, but he was principally concerned to defend the press, responsible for 'the awe, in which each government stands, of the opinions of its nation, and in which each nation stands of the opinion of its neighbours', as 'the most effectual guards and warrants of mutual freedom'. His despair at what seemed to be happening in France was bitterly expressed with the sentence: 'Formerly, when we spoke of Frenchmen, we used the words slavery and wooden shoes; now we say LIBERTY AND EQUALITY – and we mean the same things.'[36]

Coleridge now liked to think that in the past 'The Morning Post proved a far more useful ally to the government in its most important objects, in consequence of its being considered as moderately anti-ministerial, than if it had been the avowed eulogist of Mr. Pitt'. But now the Morning Post was no longer anti-ministerial. Cobbett wrote that it was 'notoriously under the immediate control of the ministers, of one of whom, indeed, it is well known to be, in part, at least, the property'; and Daniel Stuart, Coleridge's employer, wrote: 'I supported Addington against Bonaparte during the Peace of Amiens with all my power and in the summer of 1803 Mr Estcourt came to me with a message of thanks from the prime minister, Mr Addington, offering me anything I wished. I declined the offer.'[37] So one might be entitled to wonder whether even Coleridge was influenced in his opinions by the requirements of his employers and the need to fund his opium habit.

By October 1802, remarkably, he was arguing the benefits to be derived from the restoration of the Bourbon monarchy, and in November he published a critical examination of the conduct of Fox, which in its second part developed into an attack on him for courting Bonaparte and Talleyrand in Paris. 'Was it the First Consul's exploit at Jaffa, which has entitled him to the respect of the friend of humanity?' In a most un-Coleridgean manner we hear the language of the anti-Bonaparte publicists, of Mamelukes and 'certain detestable vices' of theirs, of a man 'who has availed himself of his military fame, bought for him by the soldiers of liberty with rivers of blood – who has availed himself of his own professions of republican enthusiasm – to institute a military despotism'.

Jean-Gabriel Peltier was finally brought to court in February 1803. It was a show trial and some circumstantial evidence suggests that some effort had been made to produce an obedient jury.[38] The former revolutionary enthusiast turned patriot James Mackintosh, supposedly acting for Peltier, took the opportunity to deliver a set-piece oration celebrating the liberty of the press in Britain, claiming that he considered this issue 'as the first of a long series of conflicts between the greatest power in the world and the only free press remaining in Europe'.[39] Cobbett reported to Windham that Mackintosh had betrayed Peltier and that Lord Chief Justice Ellenborough and the attorney general had told the jury that 'if they did not find him guilty, we should have war with France!!!' The judge instructed the jury to convict, which they duly did. On the very same day, with what was presumably choreographed symmetry, the United Irishman Edward Despard was executed for his supposed French-backed plot against the life of the King.

Despite Cobbett's fears, though convicted, Peltier was never brought to receive judgement, and by 1806 he enjoyed a government pension.[40] Mackintosh's speech was translated for international distribution and he was rewarded with a post in India. On the other hand Carlo Francesco Badini, the editor of *Bell's Weekly Messenger*, who had been working in London for twenty years as a journalist and writer of comic operas for the King's Theatre, was thrown out of England early in 1803 because his paper was deemed too favourable to Bonaparte. Nevertheless, the Peltier case made Bonaparte a reputation as an oversensitive enemy of free speech.

In March Whitworth wrote to Hawkesbury: 'I am persuaded that, if the First Consul has recourse to the desperate alternative of war, it must be attributed more to the irritation kept constantly alive by the public prints than to the nature of the questions at issue, however delicate.' Despite all provocation, Napoleon did not declare war, but the press attacks on him made him less willing to conciliate, and French writers felt that they were a key factor in the diplomatic breakdown. 'It is sad', wrote Louis Antoine Fauvelet de Bourrienne, at that time Napoleon's secretary, 'to think that an excessive sensitivity to the injuries contained in English newspapers and libels contributed certainly as much, and perhaps more, than the great political questions to the renewal of hostilities.' Talleyrand agreed that 'it will be wounded *amour propre* that decides war'.[41] Sheridan remarked: 'Among the provocations which our *atrocious* enemy has given us to renew the present war, I have considered his audacious attempt to bully our ministers into a surrender of the freedom of the British press to be the greatest'.[42]

The French remarks suggest that had Bonaparte made some dramatic concession at the end he might have prevented war, but this has to be doubtful, as I shall suggest in the next chapter. What remains puzzling is what prompted the change around summer 1802 from conciliation to criticism. Was it orchestrated? Did the British ever have any intention of keeping to the peace, or was the whole thing manipulated from the start? Clearly much has remained secret about this period, and it is not out of the question that Pitt and Addington were orchestrating things, using Grenville to stir up as much anti-French feeling as possible while simultaneously bringing Sheridan and those he influenced round to a bellicose stance.

The editor of the *Cambridge Intelligencer*, Benjamin Flower, was so disgusted with the declaration of war that after ten years of brave opposition he closed down his paper. 'The war in which we are now engaged is, on the part of this nation, a war of Injustice, and of course utterly indefensible on all those principles of Justice and Honour, which are professedly held by states as well as by individuals,' he announced. 'The war is far from being popular', he wrote, but fear 'prevents the expression of the public voice', 'lest in case of opposition to the measures of ministers, the system of terror should be revived'. Other newspapers were 'prostituted and servile, and with very few exceptions, are, either supporting the war, or disguising the sentiments of their Editors, who are well known to hold the war in abhorrence, but who dare not speak out to their readers.'[43]

The great achievement of the Addington administration during the Peace of Amiens was to bring round much liberal opinion to opposition to Bonaparte and to stifle the rest.

9

Rousing the Nation

The first clear moves to prepare the British public for the renewal of hostilities were made in the autumn of 1802, and the trigger was Switzerland. The French invasion of 1798 and the conversion of the Swiss Confederation into a puppet Helvetic Republic had been a shock to liberal opinion, as the mountain region with its sublime views and independent traditions had been viewed as a model of liberty. French troops had withdrawn from Switzerland in July 1802 in accordance with the Peace of Amiens. Soon afterwards counter-revolutionaries allied to peasants in central Switzerland who disliked the inefficient centralised system installed by France rose in revolt and drove the Helvetic troops from Bern and Zurich, the Helvetic government retreating on 18 September from Bern to Lausanne. Colonel Louis Pillichody led an attempt to recover the former Bernese territory of Vaud and this caused French troops to intervene against him. Napoleon summoned Swiss leaders to Paris to devise a new constitution.

While staying with Pitt at Walmer Castle in 1802, Lord Castlereagh wrote a memorandum for Addington recommending financial assistance to Switzerland, and arguing that any French invasion of Switzerland would be a violation of the Treaty of

Amiens and would justify Britain in retaining conquests that
had not been handed over, notably Malta.[1] Accordingly, Britain
claimed that the French intervention in the civil war was a breach
of the Peace of Amiens. That the revolt was led by aristocrats with
close connections to the exiled Bourbons and funded by British
money was kept as quiet as possible.

Britain had close connections with counter-revolutionaries
in aristocratic Bern from the days when Wickham had been
based there. Pillichody was a royalist with a commission from
Louis XVIII, and he was the nephew of Wickham's trusted agent
François-Louis Rusillon. Pillichody was among the royalist soldiers who gathered in Paris in September 1797, in 1798 he and
Rusillon had been imprisoned together in the Temple for their
counter-revolutionary activities, until Swiss pressure obtained their
release, and in 1802 Rusillon was living with Pichegru in London
as his aide.[2]

Bonaparte's eventual solution to the Swiss crisis was to dissolve
the Helvetic Republic and return to a federal system, but the
initial French armed intervention was presented by the British
in a quite different light, and played a major part in convincing
Britons of the need to resist continued French aggression by
returning to war. On 27 September Addington rescinded orders
to evacuate Malta, French Indian outposts and the Cape of Good
Hope, and on 18 October he confided to Dundas that 'a Renewal
of Hostilities is possible to say the least'.[3] Addington may not
yet have been sure, but a lot of preparations for war were put in
place that early. On 8 December the dramatist and former Foxite
Richard Brinsley Sheridan spoke in favour of the ministry and
its proposal of a high defence budget for the next year. Fox had
begged Sheridan not to abuse Bonaparte and to speak in favour of
peace, and accordingly Sheridan did advocate 'peace if possible',
but spoke of the need for vigilance and preparation in the face of
the boundless ambition of Bonaparte. He implied that the First

Consul's rule was dependent on an understanding with the French people that he would make them 'masters of the world if they will consent to be his slaves', and suggested that a war spirit was springing up in Britain.[4]

If the country was moving towards war, a strategy to forge national unity was important, and the answer was to focus all blame on Bonaparte. As the usurper he was the natural enemy of the monarchists, and as the tyrant who had destroyed the republic and replaced it with what looked increasingly like a military dictatorship he was the natural enemy of the liberals. The principal spy in Paris, Louis Bayard, had also suggested that to be seen to attack Bonaparte alone was the best way to get backing from the French.[5] For uniting opinion in Britain and deploying it against a French threat this strategy worked extremely well, although it was truly ironic that as Bonaparte sought to make himself acceptable by restoring order and taking a moderate position between the extremes of Jacobinism and royalism, his right-wing enemies labelled him a usurping upstart and his left-wing enemies a repressive tyrant. Cobbett himself seems to have been puzzled at the volte-face performed by the British press as liberals swung behind the ministry. He traced the change to Sheridan, who, he claimed in a letter to him, 'had long had the press, in all its branches, completely at your command'.[6]

In 1800, as noted earlier, William Burdon had asserted that not 'a single instance of cruelty, injustice, or tyranny' could be attributed to Bonaparte and until late 1802 there was little evidence to disprove his claim. However, conveniently, at the end of October 1802, Sir Robert Wilson's *History of the British Expedition to Egypt* produced two damning atrocities committed by Napoleon in Syria – the first serious crimes to come to light. Sir Robert Wilson was an unusual figure, 'a very slippery fellow', in the words of one of his biographers. Like Sir Sidney Smith, his upbringing brought him into intimate contact with the King, who was, he said, always his friend, and like Smith he had some flair for thrusting himself into the limelight. His book accused Napoleon of murdering 3800 Turkish prisoners and then of poisoning 580 of his own sick soldiers who had caught bubonic plague. The first incident occurred on 7 March 1799 at Jaffa after the city had been stormed by French troops. In Wilson's words:

Buonaparte, who had expressed much resentment at the compassion manifested by his troops, and determined to relieve himself from the maintenance and care of three thousand eight hundred prisoners, ordered them to be marched to a rising ground near Jaffa; where a division of French infantry formed against them. When the Turks had entered into their fatal alignment, and the mournful preparations were completed, the signal gun fired. Vollies of musquetry and grape instantly played against them; and Buonaparte, who had been regarding the scene through a telescope, when he saw the smoke ascending, could not restrain his joy, but broke into exclamations of approval.

The second event described by Wilson took place when Napoleon returned to Jaffa in late May and found a number of his soldiers stricken with the plague:

He entered into a long conversation with [a physician] respecting the danger of contagion, concluding at last with the remark, that something must be done to remedy the evil, and that the destruction of the sick at present in the hospital was the only measure which could be adopted . . . Opium at night was administered in gratifying food; the wretched unsuspecting victims banqueted and in a few hours 580 soldiers, who had suffered so much for their country, perished thus miserably by the orders of its idol.[7]

That these accusations had some basis in truth is not in doubt, but the numbers involved and the circumstances have never been definitively settled. Years later Napoleon explained that some North African mercenaries had been released after a previous siege on condition that they did not again serve against the French. When Jaffa was sacked, some defenders had been allowed to surrender, and among them were survivors of the force that had promised not to fight again. These, numbering five hundred, had indeed been shot, but by the rules of war their lives were already forfeit.[8] On the poisoning, Napoleon's story was that seven soldiers, expected to die soon, unable to move, and anticipating torture and worse, had asked to be killed before the Turks reached them. He had been inclined to agree but the physician, René Desgenettes, had refused to terminate their lives on the ground that as a physician his job was to preserve life, with which view Napoleon had acquiesced.

As so often with these things, it is very difficult to get to the bottom of claim and counterclaim. At Jaffa the number of people massacred was greater than Napoleon admitted, and there may have been other ugly incidents, but they do need to be viewed in a context of escalating brutality from both sides and lack of provisions and transport; some plague-afflicted soldiers may have been put out of their misery at Jaffa, but no more than forty or fifty, and for humanitarian reasons.[9] Napoleon was justifiably proud of his care for sick and injured soldiers, however many he may have sacrificed to his 'ambition'.

Wilson's journal reveals that he had been told the extenuating circumstances surrounding events at Jaffa and Acre by well-informed sources, but, being a patriot who believed Bonaparte to be both usurper and tyrant, he chose, nevertheless, to publish damning and exaggerated versions.[10] Napoleon assumed that he was motivated by money, and it is true that his book sold very well on the strength of the atrocity stories. However, the letter that he sent to the Emperor of Austria with a copy of his book makes it quite clear that he had propaganda in mind, and the instant presentation of copies to foreign rulers makes one suspect official backing (it must have occurred with Foreign Office approval). He wrote:

> as a friend to humanity I wished to make known to the civilised world the atrocious barbarity that has soiled and covered in infamy the commander in chief of a French army; as an enemy of all tyranny and all usurpation, I have wished to denounce actions that should unite in the same sentiment all the sovereigns and all the peoples of Europe.[11]

This is the language of a publicist, rather than of an historian, and Wilson's allegations were rapidly reprinted in Cobbett's *Political Register*, by Gifford in the *Anti-Jacobin Review*, in the *Times* on 18 January 1803, and eventually in any number of other publications, vastly increasing their circulation: there can have been nobody literate by the end of 1803 who was not aware of them.[12] And that was across most of Europe, for they were translated so rapidly as to raise further suspicion of prior collusion. A former interpreter for the French government called William Vincent Barré was employed to translate Wilson's book into French, for which, according to his obituary, he 'received a very handsome consideration from our Government'.[13]

The French ambassador Andréossy complained to Hawkesbury about Wilson's allegations, and according to the *Anti-Jacobin Review* he tried to get the government to prosecute Wilson.[14] Wilson wrote a reply to Andréossy, and received some backing for his allegation in William Wittman's *Travels in Turkey, Asia Minor and Syria*, although Wittman's evidence was flimsy and the *Edinburgh Review* cast doubt on its validity.[15]

The *Anti-Jacobin Review* was confidently painting an ever

darker picture of the regime in France. 'Revolutionary Portraits no. 1' – a portrait of Fouché – began with the now obligatory contrast between the enslaved press of France and the free press of Britain, which remained the terror of tyrants, and continued with a history of Fouché and his methods.[16] In amongst the usual wild exaggeration – alleging 320,000 registered and paid Parisian spies, for instance – were some accurate details of the resourceful Fouché's methods in creating a thriving power base in the police, of his sources of revenue, and how he made a considerable amount of money on top of what it took to run the department.[17] However, the article was somewhat unfair on 'the Corsican Usurper', since he had sacked Fouché and suppressed his Ministry of Police the previous September, partly in the forlorn hope of improving his image with British liberals.

In the *Anti-Jacobin Review* the portrait of Fouché's police state was followed by a continuation of the review of Wilson's *History* and then a review of Friedrich Gentz's recent book, *On the State of Europe, before and after the French Revolution; being an answer to the work entitled de l'État de la France à la fin de l'An* VIII. This was published in London in both French and English at the end of 1802, and its author, who had recently become an Austrian state counsellor, had decided to visit England in autumn 1802, remaining in London until just after Christmas, in part no doubt to see his book through the press. Gentz enjoyed himself, so zealously fêted that he was even introduced to the King and Queen. The book he attacked, written by Alexandre-Maurice Blanc d'Hauterive and produced in collaboration with Talleyrand, was a manifesto for Bonaparte's government, published in 1800. D'Hauterive had been rewarded with a post as Talleyrand's right hand at the Foreign Office. Gentz's riposte to his arguments included a hundred-page introduction by John Charles Herries, which explained the Navigation Acts of 1651–63 in an attempt to counter Hauterive's accusation of British tyranny of the seas.

The *Anti-Jacobin Review* appreciated the value of this defence of Britain by a German:

> To Mr. Gentz, then, Englishmen must feel particularly indebted, for standing forth in vindication of their character and principles, and for removing the film which France had laboured to cast over the eyes of foreigners in order to instil into their minds the most unfounded and unwarrantable prejudices against the government and people of Great Britain.[18]

In reality, Englishmen did not need to feel all that indebted to Gentz, since they were paying him very handsomely for his efforts to speak on their behalf.[19]

The caricaturist James Gillray, meanwhile, had returned to action with a fully-fledged cartoon Napoleon. 'Little Boney' made his debut in January 1803, and this caricature figure did most to convince the world that Napoleon was tiny rather than of average French height; the face was closely based on what was now known to be an accurate portrait of Napoleon by Louis Boilly.[20] Gillray's Napoleon had started life at the larger size, but he shrank during the winter of 1802–3. 'Little Boney' first appeared on 1 January in *German-Nonchalence; – or – the Vexation of little Boney*, a print about the ejection from France of Count von Starhemberg, the Austrian ambassador to Britain, because of his pamphlet of 1800, *Le Grand Homme*. The print showed the count taking snuff with haughty indifference to Boney, who, dwarfed by his bodyguard of chasseurs, hurled insults towards the Austrian's departing coach.

This raises the question of where the impetus was coming from. Starhemberg had a large and distinguished collection of Gillray's prints, certainly knew him and might have commissioned the print. As Gillray repeatedly mocked Addington – *Evacuation of Malta* of 9 February showed him shitting British conquests – it is unlikely that the ministry was paying him, but Canning might well have been. Those anti-Bonaparte images that did not simultaneously mock the ministry might have been inspired by sources within the administration, but more likely stem from Canning and Pitt's friends.

Cobbett claimed that 'this wretch's pension was stopped by Lord Sidmouth [Addington's later title], but it was again revived when the Whigs went out in 1807: and he was paid it to the end of his life'.[21] On the other hand the bookseller and radical journalist William Hone, under oath at his trial in 1817, claimed that he could prove that 'Mr. Gillray was pensioned by his Majesty's Ministers' in 1803 and that 'he had his information on this subject from the relations of that gentleman'.[22] Perhaps the truth lies somewhere between the two – that Gillray received money from government-linked sources in 1803 but not as a formal pension, or that those paying Gillray were among those friends of Pitt who remained in or close to Addington's administration.

On 8 March 1803 the King told Parliament that Britain must prepare for war. The Royal Navy always needed warning, as it took a long time for experienced sailors to be transferred (sometimes forcibly) from the merchant service into the King's ships. From March the country was committed financially to war and it became harder to go backward than forward. Although this could be presented as a warning, the practical implication was not lost on Bonaparte, who accosted Whitworth, the British ambassador, in what he considered inappropriate circumstances on 13 March, when British civilian bystanders were present, asking what the British thought they were doing, why treaty conditions were not being fulfilled, and announcing that if the British rearmed so would the French, but that it would be the fault of the British if war was renewed.

British accounts claimed that Bonaparte threw a tantrum. In reality the conversation was barely audible, as a British tourist confirmed, but those present quickly put together what snippets they had overheard. The tourist, on subsequently hearing that the Cape of Good Hope had not been handed over to the Dutch, as stipulated in the treaty, realised that: 'This step must have been taken, and the despatches sent from England by the end of November. What are we about? For hitherto it appears that we are the aggressors, and put our seal to a treaty which we presently resolved not to adhere to. This is rash work, and I hope may be well accounted for ... '[23]

On 21 March Whitworth's great fear was that 'this situation may last too long without coming to a crisis. We shall, it is true, remain in possession of Malta; but at the same time we shall be at the expense of a war establishment without the means of keeping alive the spirit of the country. Such an order of things would well suit the policy of the First Consul.'[24] From April all the principal caricaturists were publishing provocative images that lent support to the government's arguments. Even the 'Jacobin' William Holland was now willing to turn his hand to the loyalist cause, very probably following Sheridan's lead. *John Bull teazed by an Ear-wig!!* showed a diminutive Bonaparte disturbing Bull's tranquillity, while *An Attempt to swallow the World* supported the idea of Bonaparte's overweening ambition, as did Piercy Roberts's *A Stoppage to a Stride over the Globe*. Samuel Fores's *The Governor of Europe stoped* [sic] *in his Career*, a design much repeated on printed pottery, similarly illustrated John Bull's determination to halt Bonaparte's progress at the Channel. This tight cluster of publications was suspiciously on-message, and although evidence of official encouragement is lacking, it is not to be ruled out. Caricaturists, it should be remembered, were often paid to publish a particular design; they didn't always just make them up, as is often assumed.

Whitworth left Paris on 12 May, and three days later the King issued letters of marque to British privateers. In retaliation for the consequent British seizure of French ships that did not yet know they were at war, Napoleon arrested all the British tourists who had not yet left France, then invaded Hanover, taking the capital on 5 June. Officers of Elector George's army slipped away towards the coast, whence ships took them to Britain, where they formed the King's German Legion. During the year a recruitment organisation was established for the Legion, funded through the British envoy in Hamburg, George Rumbold. Whitworth told Malmesbury that 'the effects of war will soon be so severely felt in France as to produce great disgust and disaffection; that it will shake Buonaparte's power; that the army is not so much attached to him as it was. If he trusts an army to Moreau, he will risk it acting against him.'[25] Once again, British assessments of the mood in France were massively over-optimistic.

Gillray marked the declaration of war with *Armed-Heroes*, which showed a less than martial Addington facing Bonaparte across the Channel with brave words and private misgivings. Six days later Gillray published a much more complex and powerful image, *Maniac-Ravings*, supposedly depicting Bonaparte's behaviour to Ambassador Whitworth on 13 March. It showed 'Little Boney' dancing about, stamping his feet in rage, trampling underfoot the most provocative of the warmongering propaganda – 'Windham's speeches', 'Cobbett's Weekly Journal', 'Anti-Jacobin Review', Peltier, True Briton, and Wilson's Egypt. He curses 'the Liberty of the British Press' and 'English Blood hounds' and wails: 'Oh, I'm Murdered! I'm Assassinated!!' Napoleon also cries: 'Oh Sebastiani, Sebastiani, Oh!' Horace Sébastiani had been sent to Egypt to negotiate with the British over their promised evacuation according to the terms of the Treaty of Amiens, which they were very slow to honour. His report, published in the *Moniteur* on 30 January, had argued how easy it would be for the French to reconquer Egypt. British journalists interpreted this as evidence that Napoleon intended precisely that, and Sébastiani's 'threat' became a key reason for refusing to leave Malta and going back to war.

The chief publication in the government's campaign to unite the nation in backing its war was William Cobbett's (anonymous) *Important Considerations for the People of this Kingdom*, nominally 'printed by order of the Association for preserving liberty and property, &c.' and published on 25 July 1803, being 'an address to the people of the United Kingdom of Great Britain and Ireland, on the threatened invasion'. The supposed independence of John Reeves's Association is once more called into doubt by the evidence that this publication was 'circulated by government at a vast expence' and in such great quantities that 'the country was overwhelmed by them' (the words of Rachel Charlotte Biggs, a loyalist writer from Windham's kennel of 'bloodhounds' who had proofed Cobbett's text).[26]

Cobbett's message was that:

> the grounds of the war are, by no means ... to be sought for in
> a desire entertained by His Majesty to keep the Island of Malta
> contrary to the Treaty of Peace ... they are to be sought for in
> the ambition of the First Consul of France, and in his implaca-
> ble hatred of Britain, because in the power and valour of Britain
> alone, he finds a check to that ambition, which aims at nothing
> short of the conquest of the world.

For the benefit of anybody who might have suspected that His Majesty's desire for peace might not have been entirely whole-hearted, Cobbett explained that: 'His Majesty, ever anxious to procure for his people prosperity and ease, eagerly seized the first opportunity that offered itself for the restoration of Peace ... with the most sincere desire, that it might be durable ...' (We already know how sincere was Cobbett's desire for a dura-ble peace!) But Bonaparte immediately preyed on Piedmont, Holland and Switzerland, and then 'manifested his perfidious intentions, again to take possession of Egypt, whence we had driven him in disgrace, again to open a road to our possessions in India, there to destroy one of the principal sources of our wealth and greatness.'

He had done his best to damage British trade by 'shutting, as far as he was able, all the ports of other countries against us' and he had interfered in Britain's internal affairs. He:

> required us to violate our laws by banishing those subjects of the French Monarch, who had fled hither for shelter from his unjust and tyrannical government; demanded of us the suppression of the Liberty of Speech and of the Press; and, in a word, clearly demonstrated his resolution not to leave us a moment's tranquillity, till we had surrendered our constitution . . .

After this sober beginning, Cobbett proceeded to describe Bonaparte's 'forest of bayonets', his 'myriad of spies', and to retell the story of the unscrupulous Corsican's career of crime up to the present time. Just in case the labouring poor might be suffering under the delusion that they could fare no worse under Bonaparte, there was a dire warning of how his republican soldiery had behaved elsewhere:

> the lower orders of the people, the artizans and the labourers, were the objects of their direst malignity, against them was directed the sharpest bayonets; for their bodies the choicest torment, for their minds the keenest anguish was reserved; from one end of the country to the other, we trace the merciless ruffians through a scene of conflagration and blood; frequently we see them butchering whole families, and retiring by the light of their blazing habitations; but amongst the poor alone, do we find them deferring the murder of the parents for the purpose of compelling them to hear their children shriek amidst the flames!

This was propaganda for the masses on an unprecedented scale. Copies of these *Important Considerations* bearing the royal seal were sent to every parish to be distributed in the pews and aisles of every church, especially among the poor, on the Sunday following receipt. Broadsheet examples 'suitable for posting' were supplied to be displayed on the church door and in another public place in the parish. Inevitably, the tract was reprinted in *Cobbett's Weekly Political Register* for 30 July.[27]

In order to get their message across to people at a lower social level, the government resorted to placards that were pasted on walls. Gillray's *John Bull and the Alarmist* illustrates how every bit of spare wall space was taken up by such advertisements, so that they were constantly in the view of the widest literate public, 'stuck up on every dead wall, rotten post and dirty corner in the metropolis'.[28] One poster even warned the public to look out for disloyal people who sought to take them down or paste over them: 'Let Englishmen keep a watchful Eye upon French Spies, who are employed to pull down or deface all Loyal and Patriotic Papers'. The *British Critic* listed seventy-eight of these 'Posting-Bills and other cheap papers distributed for the present crisis' that 'have assisted very powerfully in exciting the Patriotic Spirit of Britons' in order 'to promote their further Circulation, and to preserve the memory of these laudable and useful Efforts'.[29]

Although all of the handbills were priced cheaply, the hope was 'that those who can afford it, will distribute these Papers among them who cannot', and for this purpose they might be bought by the hundred with a further discount. The bookseller James Asperne suggested that:

Noblemen, Magistrates, and Gentlemen would do well, by ordering a few Dozen of the above Tracts of their different Booksellers, and cause them to be stuck up in the respective Villages where they reside, that the Inhabitants may be convinced of the Perfidious Designs of Buonaparte against this Country; and expose his Malignant, Treacherous, and cruel Conduct, to the various Nations that have fallen beneath the Tyrannical Yoke of the Corsican Usurper.[30]

The fact that these efforts were channelled through a handful of booksellers is in itself indicative of central guidance. John Hatchard was a young man who had set up shop at 173 Piccadilly in 1797. He was George Canning's bookseller and published Canning's speeches before Canning appointed him Treasury bookseller (after Canning fell out with John Wright over the illustrated *Poetry of the Anti-Jacobin*), when he moved to 190 Piccadilly. John Ginger also set up as a bookseller in 1797, at 37 Old Bond Street. He took over Wright's shop at 169 Piccadilly and thrived, working closely with Hatchard, until he was appointed bookseller to the Prince of Wales, which bankrupted him because the prince never paid his bills. James Asperne was an older man, who during 1803 had taken over an established business that he had previously managed at the Bible, Crown and Constitution in Cornhill; he was one-third and finally sole proprietor of the loyalist *European Magazine*.

The authorities also launched three periodicals, the *Anti-Gallican*, the *Alarum Bell* and the *Loyalist*, which collected together 'the principal Papers, Tracts, Speeches, Poems and Songs that have been published on the threatened Invasion'. The *Anti-Gallican* was published in numbers fortnightly from July 1803 and the collected edition of 1804 was dedicated to the volunteers.

A number of booksellers (our own Publisher among the foremost) have undertaken the printing, and circulation at a cheap rate, of various popular tracts, poems, songs, &c. &c. tending at once to unmask the perfidious and cruel designs of the enemy, and to invigorate the people of this country who are arming in its defence. This loyal and laudable design has met with ample encouragement in every part of the United Kingdom. From a posting-sheet to a hand-bill, and from a page to a pamphlet, hundreds of thousands have been sold, and the present work printed in a magazine form, is intended to preserve them for futurity.[31]

The *Alarum Bell* and the *Loyalist* were both launched on 13 August, the first by Cox, Son and Baylis and the second from John Hatchard's shop in Piccadilly, and published every Saturday. The *Alarum Bell* was dropped in September, as it duplicated the *Loyalist*, which continued until December, sold by Hatchard, Robert Bickerstaff, Asperne and (a remarkable sign of national unity!) the former radical H. D. Symonds. The *Loyalist* was another compilation of loyal tracts. This publication was headed by Cobbett's *Important Considerations*, reprinted as 'Grounds of the contest in which we are now engaged', a contest, the *Loyalist* reminded its readers, 'which no less concerns the peasant in his cottage, than the prince on his throne':

> We are contending against an inveterate foe, who aims at the destruction of everything dear to you as Britons. We are threatened on our own shores and in our own houses. Our domestic, civil, and religious privileges are all at stake. The existence of our wives, our children, our relations, our friends, our family comforts, our freedom, our trade, and our property, may depend upon your immediate exertions.[32]

There were also copy-cat productions such as John Fairburn's *John Bull and Bonaparte, or important and interesting Dialogues, Speeches, Addresses, Declarations and Loyal Songs with a caricature frontispiece*. Two short-lived weekly newspapers, the *British Neptune* and the *British Press*, supported the effort as vehicles for ministerial propaganda.

The output of these loyal booksellers also included many songsheets, including work by famous names such as 'War Song for the
Edinburgh Cavalry Association' by Walter Scott, the 'Dumfries
Volunteers' by Robert Burns, Thomas Campbell's 'Soldier's Dream'
and 'Anticipation, a sonnet' by William Wordsworth. There was
a considerable number of songs by Charles Dibdin, who was
awarded a pension of £200, and his two sons Charles and Thomas.
Dibdin's 'British War Songs', taken especially from the popular
entertainment of *Britons Strike Home*, were 'equally calculated to
conciliate the minds of the Natives of the different quarters of the
United Kingdom, as to animate the general spirit against the proud
menaces of an invading Foe'.[33] Charles Dibdin sang his subsidised
collection of patriotic songs repeatedly in July 1803 at his Sans
Souci theatre in Leicester Square with the aid of a small military
band – they included 'The Song of Acre' and 'A Welcome to the
French' with the lines 'We're in Arms, Little Boney'. The songs,
like the prints, began to appear in April.[34]

The theatres contributed to the patriotic effort: Sheridan's
Pizarro (1799) was playing at Covent Garden with John Kemble as
Rolla, whose speech to the Peruvians (presented in placard form
as *Sheridan's Address to the People*) had become a clarion call to the
nation against the invader: 'They follow an *Adventurer* whom they
fear – and obey a Power which they hate – We serve a Monarch
whom we love, a *God* whom we Adore.' Shirley's *Edward the
Black Prince* and Shakespeare's *Henry V* inspired audiences at the
Haymarket, and at the end of August in an epilogue by George
Colman, Ben Block, a sailor, exclaimed: 'God! Must this mush-
room Despot of the hour / The spacious world encircle with his
power!' and exhorted his audience to 'hurl a tyrant from his upstart
throne'.[35] There was a 'Military Interlude' called *All Volunteers*, and
Thomas Dibdin wrote an opera, *The English Fleet in 1342*.

The outbreak of war triggered an avalanche of prints mocking and later vilifying Bonaparte, but a new feature of some

caricatures that appeared in June and July was the portrayal of George III in a favourable light. The positive images of George were the invention of two amateur artists. Thomas Bradyll, an immensely wealthy officer of the 2nd Foot Guards, whose father was groom to the bedchamber of the Prince of Wales, designed *The King of Brobdingnag and Gulliver* (one of Gillray's most famous images that was not, in fact, Gillray's idea at all), in which George, as the giant king in *Gulliver's Travels*, described the puny but belligerent Bonaparte/Gulliver as 'one of the most pernicious little odious reptiles that nature ever suffer'd to crawl upon the surface of the Earth!' It was probably Bradyll, in the interest of maximum distribution, who caused a second print of the subject to be published by Fores five days later. Meanwhile Temple West, another wealthy amateur caricaturist who was a distant relation of the Grenvilles, provided three similar designs with the King as hero for William Holland: *The Save-All and the Extinguisher*, *A British Chemist Analizing a Corsican Earthworm* and *Amusement after Dinner*. Eventually Gillray followed suit with *Death of the Corsican Fox*, cautiously showing the monarch in deniable back view.

Caricaturists had found it so easy to turn George into a figure of fun that until now publicists had avoided him as a liability, and only in French caricature had he been presented as a driving force behind the war. A beneficent monarch also emerged in songs and broadsheets. Hannah More's 'A King or a Consul?' was a prime example: 'No foreign usurper they hither shall bring, / We'll be rul'd by a native, our Father and King.'[36] George III's transformation into a heroic father of his people in both visual and verbal propaganda may owe something to the friendship between the King and Addington, for it had certainly not been a feature of propaganda under Pitt and Canning.

In July and August a series of prints showed the fate that would meet Bonaparte at the hands of the volunteers, should he dare to invade. Gillray's *Buonapartè. 48 Hours after Landing!* (26 July 1803) showed a peasant volunteer with Bonaparte's head on a fork; Fores's *After the Invasion* (6 August 1803) showed three volunteers with Bonaparte's head on a fork – another instance of Fores following Gillray with a subject that might have been commissioned by government; but Fores went further with *The Consequence of Invasion or the Hero's Reward* (1 August 1803), which showed a volunteer being mobbed by grateful women while bearing Bonaparte's head on a spear garnished with more severed heads. At least three other prints showed Bonaparte with a rope round his neck.

Although some caricatures may have been subsidised, the invasion prints seem to have proved to be a commercial success, with sales most probably sustained by the wave of patriotism and a collecting mania that allowed an enterprising publisher like William Holland to announce that 'Collections of all the Caricatures on the Invasion' could be 'made up at a day's notice'. By the end of November Holland could advertise:

> price 5s, The Funeral Procession of Bonaparte, a caricature, in two sheets, consisting of forty figures; likewise the late farce at Saint-Cloud; the Grand Flotilla; or Bonaparte really coming; John Bull viewing the preparations on the French coast; Mrs Bull viewing the same; John Bull sounding his bugle; and sixty other caricatures on the invasion, all at 2s each.[37]

There was no 'great terror' here: this was pure commercial opportunism from a caricaturist presented with a fertile theme on which he could design endless variations to serve a large and eager audience.

The commercial success of the 'invasion caricatures' and of any anti-Bonaparte propaganda that genuinely sold owed a great deal to Pitt's encouragement of volunteering. In 1798 Dundas had circulated the notion that: 'It is of much importance, to extend, as widely as possible, that feeling of confidence that will naturally result from men of every description being placed in a situation to take, in their respective stations, an active part in the defence of the country.'[38] In 1803 Pitt was full of the idea that mass participation in national defence would give everybody a stake in the patriotic effort and engage the whole nation against Bonaparte and France. Pitt 'transparently bullied Addington's government into legislating for a levée en masse', insisting that it was quite safe to arm the people in the face of French invasion.[39] Addington's ministers rightly considered volunteers to be militarily inefficient, but Pitt insisted that this was outweighed by the positive moral effect of mass volunteering on the patriotic spirit of the country. Before the end of autumn '342,000 men had enrolled themselves, were provided with arms, and were devoting their leisure hours to military exercises'.

One strident voice spoke out against all these slurs against Bonaparte, and oddly enough it belonged to William Cobbett. Ostensibly, he was highlighting what he took to be the arrant hypocrisy of Sheridan and his journalist followers, and the grounds of their opposition to Bonaparte – 'It is as a despot, not a demagogue that they rail against him; as a tyrant, not as an usurper'; but perhaps his *Letter to Sheridan* of 30 October 1803 was the first sign of a change of heart that turned him against Pitt's system and led him eventually to be stigmatised as a sympathiser with the French leader.

Cobbett expressed his disgust at the way the Whig and ministerial press had attacked French clerics and soldiers, who, effectively abandoned by the British at the peace, had accepted Bonaparte's amnesty, but especially he attacked the sudden and unprincipled change of opinion from hireling writers who, having heaped praise on Bonaparte only months before, now wrote attacks that were 'scandalously false and foul':

Now began the age of Placards, or 'Patriotic Handbills' and pictures, and scandalous indeed was the scene. The newspapers had led the way. They called Buonaparté 'a tyrant, a despot, a cut-throat, a murderer, an assassin, a poisoner, a monster, an infidel, an atheist, a blasphemer, a hypocrite, a demon, a devil, a robber, a wolf, an usurper, a thief, a savage, a tyger, a renegado, a liar, a braggart, a cuckold, a coward and a fool.'

What he objected to was that the very same writers, notably those of the *Morning Post*, had only recently 'applauded the ministers for making peace with him and reprobated, in the strongest terms, the conduct of all those, who ventured to doubt of his sincerity, or of the permanence and safety of the peace. They even extolled his character, talked continuously of his courage, his magnanimity, his wisdom, and even of his piety.' Newspapers, however, were too expensive: hence the 'placarding system', which, Cobbett felt, being crude and unprincipled, had:

> imprinted on the character of this nation a stain which will not easily be effaced. *Some* of the publications alluded to, contained *truths*, and truths very necessary for the public to be acquainted with; but, in the far greater part of them, the writers seemed to vie with each other, who should invent the most shameful, incredible, and ridiculous falsehoods, conveyed in the lowest and most foul and disgusting language. This was called 'writing to the level of the meanest capacity.'

After discussing examples, Cobbett went on to consider the contributions of the copper-plate publishers with their caricatures:

> There was, and yet is, to be seen the head of Buonaparté, severed from his body, and exhibited upon the pike of a *Volunteer*, with the blood dripping down upon the exulting crowd. In another

place you may see a volunteer, one of your favourite volunteers, having a score or two of ghastly and bleeding French heads tied by the hair around the handle of his pike, and hailed by a whole bevy of females, who vie with each other to reward him with their charms, all of them singing, 'none but the brave deserve the fair' ... shocking and disgraceful exhibitions, the tendency, and the sole tendency, of which is, to prepare the people for acts of cowardly barbarity. Buonaparté, the same Buonaparté, with whom we made a peace which these printers employed all their talents to celebrate; that same Buonaparté has been, and now is, exhibited by them as being in the pillory, at the whipping-post, on the gallows, at the gates of hell; and finally, the same window, nay the same pane of glass, which a few months ago, discovered him shaking hands with our king while the French and English flags united waved over their heads; that very identical pane of glass now shows the Consul no longer in company with King George III, but with the Devil, who has the little hero upon a toasting fork, writhing before the flames of hell! ... he certainly has been ten million times more abused, during the last six months, than ever he was before abused in the whole course of his life.[40]

Later Cobbett recalled the sudden volte-face from journalists who had referred to Bonaparte during the peace as 'the Wonderful Genius presiding over the affairs of France':

What have these writers not called him since the beginning of the war? Liar, Robber, Forger, Apostate, Assassin, Murderer, Poisoner, Hell-hound, Cut-throat, and Devil, are only a very small part of the terms they have applied to him; while their brothers of the pencil have represented him in every character, shape, act, and state of being that the mind can conceive capable of exciting, alternately, contempt, loathing, hatred, and horror;

their last effort, that has come under my eye, being to exhibit him as coming into the world by the ministry of the devil and from a mother much uglier than the devil himself! This exhibition is now to be seen in a window near the Sun newspaper office, in the Strand, in which very window, previous to the war, was first seen Buonaparté in the act of shaking hands with the King!

The broader issue that Cobbett was raising was that this unprincipled changing of opinion according to political instruction or circumstance damaged the credibility of the British free press. It is an issue that has not gone away.

– Now I ask, is this *lawful*? Are not these libels? Are we to be punished for satyrizing this man in time of peace; and are these scandalous effusions of hatred and malice against him to be tolerated in time of war? Are we thus to stand convicted before the world of being swayed in our writings with regard to foreign sovereigns, not by truth, nor by any moral or religious principle, but by our own selfish passions? Are we to be thus muzzled, and unmuzzled, as political circumstances may dictate? Is this the privilege of the much-talked-about British press?[41]

All of this abuse of Napoleon, he pointed out, was, after Peltier's case, libellous in peacetime, and he speculated that should there be another peace, the authors would have to execute another U-turn on Bonaparte's character: 'methinks I already see Mr. Gillray and his worthy fellow labourers transforming him from an infernal imp to an angel of light'.

Tory journalists had depicted Napoleon as the heir of atheist Jacobinism; Whigs saw him as the dictator who had betrayed the liberal aspirations of the revolution. The two strands fused in propaganda that was directed against Napoleon personally, inconsistent and all-embracing in its accusations, but effective in uniting Britons. The greater the threat from Bonaparte, the easier it was to unite people, so for the publicist a realistic threat of invasion was enormously helpful. Backed by the force of patriotism in the face of a traditional and powerful enemy nation, of which Bonaparte was an unusually successful and allegedly ruthless leader, the message put out by the publicists was plausibly compelling. It is very questionable whether such unity could have been achieved under Pitt, because by then he was so hated by the liberals, and it was a considerable achievement to unite opinion in this manner.

It was easy for the patriotic publicists to depict the invasion threat as a personal danger to the individual and to call for all to serve or assist the country. People were warned against the cruelty they could expect from invading French soldiers and especially from Napoleon himself, and as was later recalled, it felt, at least, as if Pitt's expectations had been realised:

> there soon was felt such a horror of Buonaparte in every glen and every valley, on every hill and every mountain, in every cottage and every cabin of the country, that the nation was roused to a man, and John Bull became invincible.[42]

10

Grand Conspiracy

Preparations began for another attempt on Bonaparte's life in 1802 while Britain and France were at peace. The 'Grand Conspiracy' picked up where the 'Infernal Machine' left off, with one significant change. As in 1800, the assassination of Bonaparte was to be accompanied by a military coup, but this time the coup would involve not just *pur* royalists but also constitutionalists and republicans. The plot had been hatching for quite some time, but the central idea was to engineer a rapprochement between General Jean Charles Pichegru and his former subordinate General Jean Moreau as a vehicle for a Bourbon restoration. One of the royalist Paris agents, Julien Leclerc, had first suggested this possibility when in London in 1800, and both he and Louis Bayard had connections with friends of Moreau.[1]

This idea was now being taken very seriously. After his crushing victory over the Austrians at Hohenlinden, Moreau had become a French national hero of almost equal stature to Bonaparte, with whom he was known to be disenchanted. The son of a lawyer from Brittany, Moreau had come to prominence fighting under Pichegru in the Netherlands and then on the Rhine frontier. He had been sympathetic to Pichegru's concerns about the Directory and had in 1797 captured correspondence that revealed Pichegru's treachery without passing it on to the government until Pichegru had already been exposed by Bonaparte. Even though he was supposed to be an ardent republican, there seemed to be hope that Moreau might join forces with the royalists to depose Bonaparte. Other erstwhile colleagues of General Pichegru in the army appeared to be equally disgruntled with the trend of Bonaparte's personal quest for power, and might be persuaded to help engineer the return of the Bourbon monarchy.

On 25 September 1801, while still at war, but with hostilities about to be suspended, Charles William Flint, then head of the Alien Office (in effect the central intelligence agency), had summoned Louis Fauche-Borel (the bookseller who had first contacted Pichegru on behalf of Condé in 1795) from Neuchâtel to liaise between Pichegru and Moreau. Fauche later recalled that when he arrived in London Flint told him that although the preliminaries of the peace had been signed, the government didn't expect peace to last, but were going through the motions as a sop to public opinion, 'a sacrifice made to public impatience'.[2]

While waiting for a mission, Fauche made a trip with Pitt's mentally unstable cousin Lord Camelford to Portsmouth to see Sir Sidney Smith and dined on board the *Tigre*. After conferring with Pichegru and the Bourbon princes Condé and Artois, he left for Paris on 5 June 1802. There he consulted Julien Leclerc, who introduced him to one of General Jacques Macdonald's former teachers who believed that Macdonald, the son of a Scottish Jacobite, could be turned. Fauche spoke to Macdonald and then had one meeting with Moreau, before being arrested and locked in the Temple prison on 1 July. In place of Fauche, another mutual friend, the abbé Pierre David, agreed to mediate between Pichegru and Moreau and the various French generals who were disgruntled at Bonaparte's rise. David was eventually arrested at Calais in November 1802 as he was about to board the Dover packet, and was taken to the Temple to join Fauche-Borel. His interrogation revealed royalist hopes that they might enlist certain discontented generals, but yielded no firm confirmation of the involvement in their plans of the British government.

Julien Leclerc had taken responsibility for maintaining the network in France after the departure in early 1802 of Justin Ratel and his mistress Julienne for London, where they settled in a suburban cottage in Fulham. About the time they left, police attention had again been drawn to the Boulogne area when in February 1802 two of Ratel's agents, the brothers Claudin and Joachim Poix, were arrested on the coast at two o'clock in the morning after a short gunfight, as a British boat was seen pulling away. Most of the band escaped, and Sub-prefect Amé Masclet of Boulogne, an anglophile *émigré* who had returned in 1800, ransacked the brothers' farm without finding anything, so they were soon released.

Bonaparte and his ministers felt a natural suspicion about what Artois and Cadoudal might be up to in London. That the British were maintaining Cadoudal and a large group of his men, several of whom had been in Paris at the time of the Infernal Machine plot, was bound to disturb them, and Bonaparte, Fouché and Talleyrand each separately sent over emissaries or instructed travellers to find out what they could about what might be afoot.

One such traveller was Michelle de Bonneuil, who visited Britain between mid-July and mid-November 1802, during which time she spoke both with Artois and with Pichegru, and was involved in discussions 'relative to a political intrigue planned by Lord Castlereagh to abduct Bonaparte in 1803', although Castlereagh didn't trust her.[3] She had been a royalist agent, she had acted as an agent for Talleyrand, and she was the mother-in-law of a key supporter of Bonaparte, Michel Regnaud de Saint-Jean-d'Angély. Nevertheless, on 15 November 1802 she went to Rotterdam and consulted Robert Liston, ambassador at The Hague, and between September 1803 and March 1804, as 'Mrs Smith', she was in correspondence with

George Rumbold, ambassador in Hamburg, using him as a means to communicate with Castlereagh to claim back £1000 that she said she had spent on his behalf on a plan that hadn't worked out. Another series of letters to Castlereagh relates to the same issue.[4] Her activities might possibly have been connected with the 'L. Smith' who was sent to Paris early in 1803 by Addington and Hawkesbury with private instructions to investigate various issues and 'carte blanche to act as I thought proper for the good of His Majesty's service'.[5]

On 7 September 1802 Windham, then in opposition, received a visit from Jean-Baptiste Coster de Saint-Victor, the *chouan* still wanted in Paris for his part in the Infernal Machine plot, and noted that he 'must try to get him something to enable him to go to France'.[6] Two Norman *chouans*, Jean Picot, formerly attached to Frotté, and Charles Lebourgeois, attached to Mallet, embarked at Southampton and landed at Le Havre on 8 January 1803. They also had left England with money supplied by Windham, who was conceivably acting as a free agent. Picot, 'the butcher of the Blues [republicans]', had on 2 August 1796 been interrogated by the authorities after being arrested, drunk and riotous, in Bayeux, in possession of £500 given to him by a mysterious 'Keith', presumably the British agent John Keith who later accompanied Sidney Smith to Egypt. Picot was implicated in an atrocity at Sap-en-Auge in Normandy in which the *juge de paix* had been burned alive in the town square and eight members of the municipal administration hacked to death with axes. His companion Lebourgeois was wanted for stagecoach robbery. They were arrested on 16 February at Pont Audemer en route to Paris and were taken to the Temple. In London they had attracted the attention of a French spy who had heard that they were boasting that they were on their way to end the days of the First Consul.[7]

Understandably, Bonaparte had been trying to eliminate Picot for some time, and letters from Mme Picot in London proved that he was being paid by Georges Cadoudal, who, it would seem, was again leading a plot to kill Bonaparte. This correspondence, intercepted after their arrest, led to complaints by Ambassador Andréossy to Foreign Secretary Hawkesbury on 28 March 1803. On 3 August 1803 Lebourgeois told Secret Police Chief Desmarest that Georges Cadoudal's plan was to intercept Bonaparte's coach with a group of royalists and fight it out hand to hand with Bonaparte's bodyguard, as he refused to undertake some base assassination. Assassination was regarded as so heinous a crime that you were not likely to admit to it unless you had already succeeded. It is conceivable that Cadoudal genuinely entertained some notion of killing Bonaparte in a fair fight, or even of capturing him, but as a hard-headed practical man he would have recognised the odds against success, and there is very little evidence that any such plan was really being prepared as anything other than a cover story, supported by a handful of fake uniforms.[8] Neither Picot nor Lebourgeois ever revealed the precise nature of their mission, but they were evidently there to pave the way for Cadoudal.[9]

They were taking orders and received Windham's money from Raoul Gaillard, formerly a senior aide to the Norman commander Mallet. Known to the French police for his expertise in robbing stagecoaches from a base at the edge of the Forest of Lyon near Rouen, Gaillard was fairly tall, with dark blond hair and blue eyes. He himself arrived in France early in 1803 via Hamburg, a free, neutral city that for some years had been a hotbed of espionage, with a brief to arrange a network of safe houses for Cadoudal and his men in Paris and along the route to the landing point at Biville near Le Tréport. In February he appeared at Aumale, north-east of Rouen on the route from Le Tréport to Paris, where two of his old soldiers got him a false passport to enable him to travel more safely.[10]

At Paris Gaillard met three young royalist noblemen. Charles d'Hozier and Athanase-Hyacinthe Bouvet de Lozier had been in the capital for some time, and d'Hozier had established a riding school and a coach business, situated latterly in the rue de la Vieille Temple. Louis de Sol de Grisolles had come to Paris from England early in 1803. Raoul Gaillard asked d'Hozier and Bouvet de Lozier to arrange accommodation in Paris, and d'Hozier engaged a builder he knew named Pierre-Antoine Spin to construct secret hiding places in three of the properties they rented. For the seaward end of the coastal route Gaillard was dependent on Michel Troche, the clockmaker from Eu, a town in which he was president of the board of trade. They established three separate chains of safe houses running from the lonely hamlet of Biville on the cliffs between Le Tréport and Dieppe, then fanning out through the Forest of Eu, which stretched almost to Aumale, and from there south, bypassing Beauvais through the woodland to the west, down to Saint-Leu la Forêt in the Forest of Montmorency and finally converging on the Porte Saint-Denis in Paris about a hundred miles away. By the time that Britain declared war on France in mid-May 1803 all Gaillard's preparations were already in place.

In January 1803, long before the King told Parliament that they must prepare for war, Lord Hobart, the secretary for war, informed Philippe d'Auvergne, prince de Bouillon, that his Channel Islands correspondence was to be reinstated, and on 16 March Bouillon reported: 'Our Communication with Brest has resumed.'[11] For the benefit of the newly installed politicians, Hobart and Secretary at War Charles Yorke, Bouillon had drawn up a memorandum stating just what his correspondence required. For the purpose of obtaining weekly intelligence from Brest and the coast and conveying packets and persons into the western departments of Brittany his needs included a resident in the arsenal at Brest – this was an agent known as 'l'Intelligent', 'a very intelligent person, who offered his services for Brest'; 'a confidential person in town who can occasionally bring packets'; eight women to carry packets across different stages of the journey; three safe houses on the road and one on the coast; one director of boats; and two boys to fetch packets and guide people. He drew Hobart's attention to a characteristic naval financial subterfuge: that 'two French boats crews are paid as Sailors on the strength of armed vessels in that service'.

For communication with the eastern districts of Brittany and Maine, Bouillon required one person in the bureau at St Malo; one pilot and director of the boats; one director of houses and chief of guides; two guides and carriers of packets; a resident at Granville for communication with Normandy; an armourer; and an adjutant to summon people, keep accounts etc. He noted that Georges Cadoudal had recommended two people should they need to communicate with Morbihan overland.[12]

Bouillon explained that nothing could be achieved without a naval squadron of small boats such as he had commanded in the previous war when in charge of the Channel Islands. The situation was complicated by the fact that Admiral Sir James Saumarez now commanded the Channel Islands station from Guernsey, but eventually Bouillon received the broad pennant of a local commodore, a suitably imposing aged flagship, and a number of fast brigs and cutters. In the autumn he was telling the undersecretary for war, John Sullivan, that he had a confidential printer near the French western army headquarters, if the government wanted to circulate propaganda, and that his contacts there were eager for copies of the *Courier de Londres*.[13]

On 12 March 1803 Sidney Smith was appointed to the fifty-gun *Antelope* with command of a similar small squadron of fast boats for service in the Channel. Smith introduced his assistant John Wesley Wright to Addington and Wright travelled to Paris, armed with letters from Hawkesworth saying how intelligent he was, intending to speak to old friends.[14] The Paris embassy was already full of suspicious people: the first secretary was Wickham's former assistant James Talbot, and the spy Antoine Viscovitch, who had helped to free Smith in 1798, was a frequent visitor. Evidence of just what was going on in the embassy is missing, however, for when Talbot eventually left Paris he was threatened with internment and burned those embassy papers that 'might convict any individual or contain any secret information'.[15]

It is possible that another member of the family, Lord Camelford, was also involved in secret plotting, although Camelford was so wayward that it is very plausible that he acted on his own initiative. In March 1803 Commissioner Mengaud arrested Camelford at Calais; he had travelled to France in a fishing boat, armed with pistols, and bearing a false passport in the name of Rushworth, an American merchant. Taken to Paris and locked in the Temple, Camelford was set free after Ambassador Whitworth's intercession, and was deported in the Dover packet on 11 April. With their preparations well under way for an attempt on the First Consul's life, the royalists stepped up their output of propaganda. A week after hostilities resumed they issued a caricature, *A Consular Attempt at a Crown*, which showed Napoleon climbing fortune's wheel and reaching for the crown with his sword. A dagger hangs by a thread from a heavenly cloud, poised above Bonaparte, and Death is about to cut the thread and kill him. The writing was partly in French and partly in English, but it appears to have been intended for distribution on the Continent and it carried a clear threat of impending death: '*La balance du destin vient de peser ton sort, / et tu trouv'ra ensemble la Couronne & la mort.*' The two examples that survive in the British Museum carry different letterpress translations. One of them reads: 'Your fate is weighed in the scales of destiny, / and you may find the crown and death together!'[16]

Soon after the outbreak of war Peltier relaunched the *Ambigu*. The third issue contained a translation of Cobbett's *Important Considerations*, of which he claimed more than a million copies had been distributed in every parish of the three kingdoms. He offered it for Bonaparte's perusal and promised him copies of the placards, caricatures and songs of which more and more were appearing each day.[17] Each issue of the second volume had a new hieroglyphic headpiece showing a pharaoh and his slaves, with the words 'Thou shalt rule them with a rod of iron and break them in pieces, like a potter's vessel', and beneath the design was the threatening near-anagram '*Révolution Française / Un Roi Corse tué à la Fin*', attributed to Nostradamus, which fits if you make a v equal a u.

Peltier commenced with a description of his own trial, claiming that he had stopped *Paris pendant l'année* when the definitive treaty was signed and only started the *Ambigu* when it became clear that France was not complying with the treaty. He then launched into a second letter to the First Consul, opening a series of them. He had promised to send over all the placards and caricatures on Bonaparte, but there were too many – enough to fill one of his invasion barges – and Britain was covered with them. Hatchard, Ginger, Asperne and the printers Cox, Son and Baylis (Peltier's own printers) were the worst culprits for libels, and they were not always even subsidised – sometimes these people attacked Bonaparte at their own expense (which, incidentally, confirms that normally they were subsidised). He said that if he had not so much faith in Bonaparte's good fortune he would say that he had troubles in store, so much was he hated and despised by all the people of Britain.

Moreover, these libels were beginning to circulate abroad – indignation was an electric current – and soon the whole of Europe would be one big England. He suggested that Bonaparte should quickly attack the root before it was too late. 'I will content myself by sending you today 17 new caricatures of which six show you hanged or decapitated – things have moved on since I suggested your apotheosis –

> now people show your decapitated head on the end of a fork – in truth, citizen Consul, you will agree with me on seeing this latest effusion of Gillray, that it is a 'cou monté'. And speaking

of 'coups montés', vague rumours are circulating of plots, royalist conspiracies, of conspiracies to kill a tyrant, to kill a Bonaparte, people talk of Donadieu, of Moreau, they accuse Tallien and Santerre; they even say that Talleyrand-Périgord has gone to take the waters at Bourbon l'Archambault just because you have discovered that he is at the head of a political plot. So many people are suspected that I don't know which ones to denounce especially ... [18]

In July Peltier proposed that the British government should buy a number of each issue of the *Ambigu* to send to their ambassadors abroad for local distribution in order to counteract the effects of French propaganda, and they were soon buying fifty of each issue, worth £254.[19] As early as May 1803 they had subscribed to 200 copies of the *Courier de Londres*.[20] Numbers xiv, xv and xvi closed with woodcuts of Egyptian scenes showing the massacre at Jaffa, the defeat at Acre and the poisoning of his own soldiers. Real or faked letters providing evidence were published with the pictures. The last of the volume taunted Bonaparte with scenes between his sister Pauline and his wife, and closed with a letter dated 30 September 1803.

Volume iii had a new hieroglyphic headpiece showing the French failing in an attempt at invading Britain. He reprinted the letter that he had printed in 1797 with its first hostile character of Bonaparte.[21] He continued to taunt him, dared him to cross the Channel in the fog, and warned how well prepared and motivated people were in England. He published a series of letters to Cobbett about the re-establishment of the French monarchy and describing Louis xviii. He gave a history of the sexual indiscretions of the young Pauline Buonaparte and in January 1804 invented a comic new Bayeux tapestry celebrating Napoleon's life.[22]

Other royalist propaganda included a *Lettre à Bonaparte* (translated as *A Letter to Napoleon Bonaparté*) by the engineer Tinseau, of which, so Tinseau told Windham, 1500 copies had been distributed in France. Its biography perpetuated the myth that Bonaparte was born in 1767, a year before the French occupation of Corsica (so that he was not French), described how in 1793 he had tried to deliver Corsica to the British, how he lived in hiding at Marseille until Toulon, where his massacres of French civilians got him promoted brigadier, and how he again hid as a terrorist until 13 *vendémiaire*, for which he was given the army of Italy. Tinseau contrasted the adventurer Bonaparte, 'this modern Attila', with Louis XVIII, the lawful monarch.[23] The British government published an *Adresse à Bonaparte*, answering the complaints that Bonaparte had made against Britain and explaining the British view of the causes of the war. Among other points it made plain that this was not a war against France, which had little place in Bonaparte's calculations, but specifically a war against the First Consul.

Meanwhile, Julien Leclerc got the Boulogne network ready for action. The former abbé Julien Leclerc de Boisvallon had been a member of the Institut Philanthropique and had worked for the royalist agency in Paris with Ratel. He was forty, five foot five and a half inches tall, with brown hair and blue eyes, and he lived in Paris on the rue du Bac. Leclerc was not a native of the Boulonnais, though he was not exactly a foreigner either, having grown up on the border of southern Normandy and Maine at Basoche in the Orne. A former teacher at the seminary of Saint-Marcel, he had abandoned his calling in 1792 and qualified as a lawyer in Paris. His role was to gather in and decode bulletins from Paris, Brest, Holland, and from various local underling spies based in Boulogne, Etaples, Ambleteuse, Calais and Dunkerque; from these he compiled a weekly report and sent it to Ratel in London. The secret sources in Paris were Louis Bayard, his two assistants and their contacts in the War Office and the Naval Ministry. When in the Boulonnais Leclerc took over Ratel's isolated house,

Godincthun, which was equipped with a *cachette* big enough for twelve people.[24]

Ratel had recruited the Boulogne network with the help of another priest, the abbé Louis Delaporte, codenamed Lacôte, who served the local Catholic community in secret, taking his orders from the exiled bishop Asseline of Boulogne. Leclerc moved from house to house in the area, but resided chiefly with Mme Duchâtelet, who nursed a 'sentimental attachment' to him, at her secluded manoir d'Escault at Offrethun, three miles north of Godincthun, and there he kept the network's accounts.

Leclerc's right-hand man was Pierre-Marie Poix, also known as 'La Rose', who went under various codenames that included 'la Besace', 'le Sourd' and 'Durieux'. He was one of a large family with many brothers and a sister. Two or three brothers remained with their father at their farm of l'Ecuelle-Trouée, just outside Saint-Martin-Boulogne, a couple of kilometres south of Godincthun. Joachim had served the correspondence until he was drafted into the army, but he was stationed locally at Calais. Claudin, aged thirty, Pierre-Marie's principal assistant, was a merchant with a shop on the main square in Boulogne, where his twenty-year-old sister Celestine also worked when she was not running errands for the network. The youngest brother, Antoine, also ran errands.

Pierre-Marie was a weather-beaten man in his thirties, with brown curly hair and a thick beard, Roman nose and brown eyes. He was Leclerc's fixer – he hired the hands and looked after them, undertook long journeys to fetch packets or make arrangements to do with the network, and tried to keep the fishermen, package recipients and other agents happy. As a cover, but also as part of his livelihood, Poix maintained a business as a *marchand-colporteur* – the businessman who supplied pedlars with their goods – which gave him the excuse for meeting his couriers and giving them things to carry. In November 1802 he had been in London, where, as befitted a *marchand-colporteur*, he had spent a considerable amount of money on textiles with Stirling & Co. of Bow Churchyard. The French police, who believed he had undertaken many more journeys to London that year, considered him cunning and resourceful. Leclerc thought he was careless, slapdash and content with a job half-done, but he valued his panache and bravery.

Pierre-Marie Poix had a second job as estate manager to Madeleine de Roussel de Bedoine, widow of a naval captain who died just before the revolution, who lived at the château of Bédouâtre, very close to l'Ecuelle-Trouée, below the massive hill called Mont-Lambert. Madeleine's daughter Nymphe, 'la Belle', received money from London in the form of bills of exchange sent from Rotterdam, organised payments to the members of the correspondence, and served as a long-distance courier. According to her cousin Jean-Baptiste-Antoine Dubuisson, vicomte de la Boulaye, whose surname she borrowed, she was remarkably beautiful, with the most charming eyes in the world. They were blue, her hair auburn, her chiselled nose aquiline. The police described her as usually wearing a straw hat with a ribbon in it and a loose dress, but she might also be found disguised as a man called Henry Dubuisson and sometimes dressed as a sailor boy. They said she was under five feet tall, but her cousin reckoned she had much the same build as himself; he was arrested because a gendarme took him for her in disguise as a man. Boulaye claimed that, standing on the ramparts of Boulogne, he had berated her about the morality of working for the British.[25] The police claimed that while on the run she spent four days in a room in a Calais inn with either Pierre-Marie or Claudin Poix without ever emerging for air. Her brother Godefroy, chevalier de Roussel de Préville, was also involved in the correspondence, but probably only as a host.

Two miles west of Mont-Lambert at the edge of the forest of Boulogne was another safe house, the spacious château of Macquinghen, home of the baron d'Ordre, who had evaded police inquiries in 1800; his château remained a royalist centre, but was too conspicuous and notorious to serve as an operational headquarters for the correspondence.[26]

To deliver its letters, the correspondence still used the same Boulogne fishermen it always had, with Louis Lefevre's wine shop on the main street in Boulogne as its depot. They had four predetermined points of communication, one near Cap Gris-Nez, one at Waldam north of Calais, one near the mouth of the river Canche leading to Montreuil, and one at Le Portel.

When war was declared in 1803 everything was prepared and all Leclerc was waiting for was the go-ahead from London to put things back in motion.

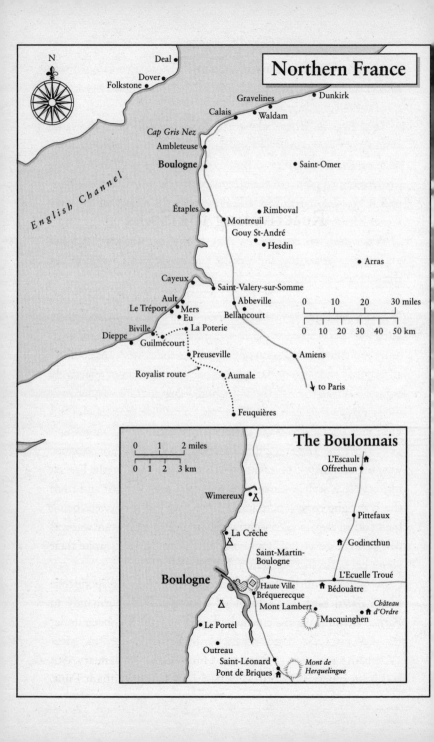

11

Reactivating the Spies

In the last three weeks before Britain declared war Bonaparte sold Louisiana to the United States for 80 million francs in order to finance an invasion of Britain. As the Americans couldn't afford to pay hard cash, Baring Brothers and the Hopes effectively bought Louisiana from the French and sold it to the Americans for 6 per cent bonds, paying Bonaparte 2 million francs a month.[1] He immediately set to work gathering and building barges and gunboats. The threat of imminent invasion called for advance warning of Bonaparte's intentions from the spies within the French ministries, as well as news from the naval port of Brest and from the Boulogne coast where ports and invasion barges were being built and an army was concentrating. Some months before war was declared the government and its French royalist allies woke their secret networks in France from hibernation.

Sir Sidney Smith was keen to reactivate the correspondence that he had established through Boulogne and Normandy to Paris. Relations with the principal spies at Paris had been under the control of the 'inner office' of the Alien Office, and after Wickham's resignation from the Home Office in January 1801 had been supervised until May 1802 by Charles William Flint.

But Flint had joined Wickham at the Irish Office as the joint Irish undersecretary based in London. His name does not occur in documents relating to events in France and Europe for this period, and it seems that his experience was reserved for Irish affairs. Responsibility for French espionage fell to George Hammond, as he told Sir Sidney Smith in early May 1803. Hammond was a highly experienced Foreign Office undersecretary, but had not previously had to deal with the special practicalities of spying, though Smith considered himself an expert. The network itself was to be run from London by the seasoned and capable Justin Ratel – now codenamed 'Le Moine', 'The Monk' – who by May was already receiving bulletins from Paris, although not yet on the British payroll.

On 14 May Smith had spoken to Ratel and had delivered Ratel's proposals to Hammond. Ratel wrote to Hammond to arrange a meeting somewhere more discreet than the Foreign Office, but he had not yet received a reply from Hammond when a week later he wrote to Smith to complain that he was still waiting for confirmation that the British wanted to proceed. In France Ratel had gone ahead and set things up on the assumption that the British would pay for his service, and he sent Smith his first bulletin from Paris, which contained a warning about a secret agent planted by Bonaparte in London named Martin Laubéypie.[2]

However, to his fury and frustration, having accepted command of the *Antelope*, and theoretically also a squadron of boats, Smith received orders to return to his ship. On 17 May he wrote to Hiley Addington, the prime minister's brother, to complain that once again his naval duties were conflicting with his secret service aspirations. He had decided 'when I quitted the *Tigre*, never again to [accept] ... a Captain's duty ... in addition to occupation of a superior sort' – the superior occupation being secret operations of an important and exciting nature. Now, when he needed to sort out 'our projected correspondence with the coast, ... and Pichegru's affairs', the idiots at the Admiralty had sent him to sea without his squadron. He told Addington:

> I have done my best to prevent it all falling to the ground by rendering my uncle au fait and connecting him in the affair as my representative, and I beg you will have the goodness to consider him as such, and request your brother to do the same in that or any other thing whereon he may have occasion to address you.[3]

Ten days after sorting out the prime minister, Smith wrote to the foreign secretary from his ship *Antelope* off Orfordness to get Hawkesbury's permission to give a positive answer to the Monk so as to get things moving, insisting to Hawkesbury that the later they left it, the harder increased French vigilance would make it; and he took the opportunity to complain that he did not yet have the squadron of cutters that he had been promised to support the operation.[4]

The correspondence through Boulogne to Ratel had been set in motion in April 1803, a few weeks before the outbreak of war. In late May Ratel was expecting the arrival of his agent Pierre-Marie Poix at any moment, but he could not introduce Poix to Hawkesbury without confirmation from Hammond. In fact Poix did not arrive in England until 21 June; he stayed at the inn at Deal and met Ratel, Wright and Colonel Smith, before travelling to London for more meetings – one of them, if codenames can be trusted, with Addington himself. Shortly afterwards Ratel's aide Lelièvre de Saint-Rémy visited Boulogne and the fishermen Lefort and Tuttelet were paid for three voyages to England to ferry the agents.[5]

Running a correspondence from Boulogne when it was the base for an army of invasion and watched closely by British cruisers was not easy, particularly when the operation was being kept secret from the Royal Navy as well as the French. Things had hardly begun when on the night of 23/24 June British cruisers off

Boulogne pounced on the Boulogne fishing fleet and took the fishermen prisoner. Unfortunately, one of the boats they captured was carrying the correspondence from Paris and was supposed to pick up Poix from Deal; Ratel learned of this setback when he found the package the fishermen were to deliver waiting for him after a meeting with Hammond, and wrote to Hawkesbury to ask him to stop the fishing boat being sold as lawful prize, since Colonel Smith had been unable to prevail on this point locally, being unable to explain himself. He enclosed a bulletin from Paris of 19 June. It may have offered useful intelligence, but it showed a clear tendency to feed the British (and perhaps Artois too) with information that the over-optimistic or self-deluding royalists wanted them to hear: it announced, for instance, that General Masséna was telling the Jacobins that he was unwilling to bring down Bonaparte in order to replace him with Moreau because he feared that Moreau would bring back the Bourbons, thus raising everybody's faith in Moreau.[6]

It turned out that the British had captured not just one but both of the boats that were working for them. Julien Leclerc wrote from Boulogne on 8 July to complain that 'our two correspondence boats have been taken with a lot of fishermen from this town nineteen days ago', which left him unable to send on several important reports from Paris. Leclerc had received no answer to his previous despatch, and was uncertain whether the captures were accidental or caused by some concern unknown to himself. He asked to have his agent Poix sent back and hoped for the release of the fishing captains Verlingues and Delpierre. On 18 July the Monk wrote to George Hammond to ask for a cutter to land Poix on the coast of France, as he had been stuck in England for a month, and for the release of the daring and loyal crew of the *Don de Dieu* with £265 compensation for the loss of their vessel and equipment. Far too late, Hammond issued orders to this effect, but this was clumsy, as by then it was obvious that one crew had been released specially, confirming suspicions in Boulogne that these particular fishermen were working for the British.[7]

George Hammond was not as good at this job as Charles William Flint had been, partly, perhaps, because he was massively overworked, and partly out of inexperience. Ratel, too, was a novice at this new job and had not presumably reintroduced the system of passports that had been in use in the previous war. The slip-up was a disaster for the correspondence, but it took place mainly because the Admiralty had not been told what was going on. So bent on secrecy was Henry Addington that, as far as possible, he wanted to keep the Admiralty in the dark, and so operations were directed by Evan Nepean, now conveniently serving as Admiralty secretary, following orders from the Foreign Office, without consulting his naval superiors.

It did not help that St Vincent, now First Lord of the Admiralty, did not like Sir Sidney Smith from previous experience, and Thomas Troubridge, another board member, could not stand him. As a result of his naval rank Smith was under the orders of Admiral Lord Keith, commanding the North Sea Fleet, and Keith couldn't stand him either. There was bad blood between the two from the time when Smith had negotiated the evacuation of the French army from Egypt and Lord Keith, under instruction from St Vincent, and then from the government, had been obliged to disown Smith's treaty and to refuse to allow the French to leave. Sir Sidney was the first to fall foul of the desire for total secrecy; he thought he was to control the correspondence from the Downs station, but instead Admiral Lord Keith put him in charge of the coast between Flushing and Ostend.[8] It served Smith right: speaking in Parliament on 2 December 1802, he had criticised St Vincent's naval economies and warned that a French invasion would come via the Low Countries. It is a moot point whether Addington noticed or cared that Smith was supporting the warmongering opposition, but the Admiralty certainly noticed. However, at this stage, Admiral Keith did not know that Smith was involved in a secret operation, and the government's plan was that he should not be told any more than he needed to know.

With Sidney Smith exiled to the Belgian coast, it fell to his uncle Edward and his elder brother Colonel Charles Douglas Smith, governor of Dover Castle, to run the operation. Their headquarters was Walmer Castle near Deal, home of ex-Prime Minister William Pitt, who, as Warden of the Cinque Ports, had taken charge of invasion defence in this most vulnerable area and was living in the castle for almost the entire period. It is hard to believe that Pitt was not actively involved in what was going forward, but if so, he took care to leave no evidence.[9] Colonel Smith lived with his aged father, John, in an extraordinary Gothic folly called 'The Cave' under the East Cliff at Dover that John had built in 1791. John Smith died on 25 February 1804, leaving The Cave to Sidney. Smith's other brother, Spencer, was, from 1802 to 1806, MP for Dover, and when in England was also based at The Cave.[10]

The role of supporting the spies and assassins was instead given to Smith's chief assistant, John Wesley Wright. Wright was essentially a spy, indoctrinated into the secret operations of the previous ministry and familiar to other initiates, such as Francis Drake and the chevalier Tinseau. He had been promoted commander in the navy after the successes of the *Tigre* in Egypt, but his naval rank covered his clandestine activities, and it is questionable whether his seamanship justified command of any vessel. Theoretically, Wright now commanded the *Favourite* sloop, but as she was still in dock for repair Smith loaned him his private yacht until the Admiralty came up with a solution. On 31 July Evan Nepean wrote to Rear-Admiral Robert Montagu at Deal, who had been given the Downs command that Smith coveted:

Captain Wright who will be the bearer of this letter being charged with the execution of a very important Service; I have received the commands of my lords Commissioners of the

Admiralty to signify their directions to you to furnish him with the best of the Hired Cutters or Luggers under your orders, and direct the Commanders to proceed with him to such place as he may fix upon and comply with any requisition he may make to them to enable him to execute the said Service.[11]

This was probably the letter that First Lord St Vincent recalled writing to Montagu, 'at the request of Lord Hawkesbury, signified to me by Mr. Hammond, desiring he would furnish one or more vessels to Captain Wright as occasion might require on a very urgent mission'.[12] At some point St Vincent wrote to Keith to instruct him that 'it is of the utmost importance that Captain Wright should be indulged in the fullest latitude', but offered no account of what Wright was doing, and Keith soon became suspicious of both Wright and Montagu.[13]

Once Bonaparte had visited Boulogne in late June and had chosen to make the town his headquarters, police scrutiny inevitably intensified. On 29 June Napoleon and Josephine arrived at Boulogne with Denis Decrès, minister of marine, Pierre Forfait, inspector-general of the flotilla, Vice-Admiral Eustace de Bruix, generals Soult, Lauriston and Marmont, and Josephine's son Eugène de Beauharnais. Napoleon worked late with Decrès, then watched the dawn from the ramparts, then inspected the harbour where 1500 labourers were digging new docks and building jetties. He inspected the coastal batteries and then the areas of farmland that had been recommended for camps. After a third day in Boulogne, the First Consul set off on a tour of the coast, reaching Calais in the late afternoon of 1 July, before continuing next day to Dunkirk, Ostend and Brussels. General Ney was to command a corps based at Montreuil, General Soult another with his headquarters at Saint-Omer, and General Davout commanded a third based on Bruges. Chief of Staff Berthier aimed to assemble seventy thousand men by the end of 1803.

Napoleon chose as his headquarters the château of Pont-de-Briques, two miles south of Boulogne, and as a forward headquarters had a pavilion built on the bluff overlooking the harbour, close to the site of the Roman lighthouse that cliff erosion had almost entirely demolished. His generals had pavilions nearby, and the senior officers of the Boulogne camp took up residence in smart houses in the very pretty Cluse valley, within a kilometre or two of the Poix family farm and no more than three from Godincthun.[14] The steady increase in numbers of troops, naval forces and workers at Boulogne cut both ways for the conspirators: there were more people to avoid, but there was also some confusion to exploit in a constantly evolving situation.

August proved to be a difficult month for the British spies around Boulogne: Poix's people were interrupted while trying to get Ratel's emissary Lelièvre de Saint-Rémy into a British boat at Waldam near Calais, and had to bury packets of correspondence in the sand which were subsequently discovered by Calais Police Commissioner Joseph Mengaud. Worse than this, several sets of police were on their trail, or, more specifically, on the very cold trail of Ratel and his mistress Julienne.[15]

On 8 August 1803 a highly dedicated and unscrupulous police-man, Chief Inspector Pierre Veyrat, arrived at Boulogne with a colleague and sent an undercover agent to Mme Tiraceau, a minor courier for the correspondence, with a message designed to make her cooperate. She agreed to a meeting at her house that evening when she admitted having dined with Mme Combremont, Ratel's housekeeper, at Godincthun two years ago, and having seven or eight months previously received a heavy package which was afterwards collected by Antoine Poix. Several more packets had arrived at other addresses soon after. She had asked after Julienne but had received ambiguous answers. She promised to go and ask whether Julienne was still at Godincthun next day, but returned saying that on the way she had met her lover, who had better

introductions to the royalist circle. The lover, who claimed to be
a veteran republican soldier, went first to Macquinghen and then
to Godincthun, claiming to be on the trail of Julienne but really,
as Veyrat afterwards realised, raising the alarm. However, Veyrat
scored one notable success: hidden at the back of a linen cupboard
at Mlle Duchâtelet's house, l'Escault, he discovered a red morocco
portfolio belonging to the abbé Delaporte, which contained some
of the accounts of the correspondence for that year and confirmed
the roles in the ring of numerous suspects.

On 25 August news of this spy ring reached the First Consul,
who was also troubled by reports of signals being made by rocket
from the Boulogne coast to British ships off shore. He ordered
Grand Judge Claude Ambroise Régnier to send a secret agent to
investigate the signals, and ordered General Moncey, head of the
gendarmerie, to send an extra three brigades of his men to patrol
the coast either side of Boulogne. With gendarmes, soldiers, customs officers and coast guards all patrolling simultaneously, it was
becoming extremely perilous to operate against the government
in this area.[16]

Régnier sent Justice of the Peace Pierre Fardel, who had investigated Hyde's network in 1800, north to Boulogne. Fardel arrived
on 1 September and interviewed Sub-prefect Masclet, who complained that of the suspected royalist agents only Mlle Duchâtelet
had been arrested, and that the police agents Veyrat and Daubenel
had gone off on 22 August with the material seized at her house, so
that it was not available to examine. There was some suspicion that
Amé Masclet might not have been as hard on the Anglo-royalists
as he should have been, and in September Bonaparte had him
transferred to a less sensitive post at Douai.

Fardel was ruthless: straight away he arrested Combremont,
Camus, Lefevre, Verlingues, two post office officials and a *juge
de paix*. Once his arrest warrants arrived next day, he also picked
up Celestine Poix, Louis Delpierre and Robert Lefort. Delpierre

and his crew had returned in an English cruiser on 30 August and Delpierre was put on shore just in time to fall into Fardel's hands. On local advice Fardel also arrested the fisherman Tuttelet. Verlingues, Lefort and Tuttelet were said to have helped the English before and after the peace, and Verlingues was suspected of signalling to British ships. Fardel sent the prisoners to Paris, the men to the Temple prison and the women to the Madelonnettes prison. After investigation he thought the officials not guilty, merely persecuted by the sub-prefect. Ratel and Julienne were agents of the English and the princes, and the others were fanatics. But Claudin and Pierre-Marie Poix, Préville, Laporte and Ordre could no longer be found. He blamed their escape on the earlier searches, made too noisily using lots of cavalry, so that in the general commotion the guilty could go to ground.[17]

Fardel could make no headway on the signal rockets: they had been launched chiefly from inland woods or from the foot of hills, and his men had been unable to locate the right place. He thought it possible that spies were being landed to inspect the work on Boulogne, but he couldn't be sure: Delaporte's papers did not reveal much about local spying, and so Fardel did not learn the full extent of the work carried out by Leclerc's network, nor did he know that Leclerc was involved. The people who were actually watching the camps and harbours were not even implicated. The one rocket that had been found didn't come from local stock: indeed, Poix had acquired a bundle of rockets in May from 'Captain Gilles'. Fardel judged that the city of Boulogne was loyal and well disposed to the consular regime, although the sub-prefect was generally disliked. He felt that the countryside was more fanatical in mindset, with more sympathy for the old ways, but that even there the only people who were actively disloyal were those who had been arrested and were now on their way to Montreuil.

The royalists thought that things had calmed down after the search at l'Escault, but the main players were on the alert and fled in time. Such a retreat had already been anticipated, as the dangers of Boulogne were obvious, and a fall-back position had already been agreed with Ratel, based on Abbeville and using the fishermen of Le Tréport to make contact with the British. Several trips to contacts in Abbeville in August, recorded in the accounts, suggest that plan B had been activated at the first sign of serious trouble in Boulogne, but arrangements took time to set up.

The little fishing town of Le Tréport, with its 1500 inhabitants, was much quieter than the city of Boulogne (population 12,000 without the soldiers). It was actually a cluster of three little ports – Le Tréport, Mers and Eu – and most people thought that was where its name came from; Leclerc often referred to it as 'Tripolis'. The drawback of using it for spying was that it meant sharing resources that had already been allocated to the top-secret mission involving Cadoudal and Pichegru, which might prejudice either operation. Though silent about it in their correspondence, Ratel and Leclerc certainly knew about the projected coup.

Le Tréport had been thoroughly suborned. The thirty-three-year-old schoolmaster responsible for naval signals, Jacques-Joseph Duponchel, sold them to the correspondence for 264 francs on 28 October. This meant that British ships approaching the shore could make the correct recognition signals in response to French challenges and pass for friendly vessels. Duponchel had been a member of the royalist group that had been ambushed in 1800, so he was deeply implicated in their activities. The commander of the battery at Mers had been paid to see nothing at all. The commander of the shore battery at Le Tréport, Jean-Louis Philippe, a young grocer who also ran a bar, was the chief royalist agent there, and packets coming from Boulogne or Abbeville were taken to his wife at her ramshackle cottage in the Cordiers, the fishermen's quarter down by the quay. Philippe was responsible for signalling to ships approaching the port, and British vessels could rely on never being hit by his battery. His wife Marie-Françoise Bachelier was the widow of one of the original 'friendly' fishing captains, who had disappeared in a storm in November 1800. It was she who had recruited many of the people, who had drawn the schoolteacher into the conspiracy, and she also served as a courier, taking urgent deliveries to Abbeville in person.[18]

Packages and letters that had been dropped at Mme Philippe's bar were taken to the shed at Jean Antoine Gallien's oyster park in the sheltered water of the harbour, where oysters were fattened and purified after having been fished from the sea, before being loaded onto coaches for Paris. It was natural enough for fishermen like the cross-eyed, bearded Jean Dieppois to go from the bar to the shed and from the shed, where their kit was kept, to their boats. Several of the Tréport fishing captains were in on the deal, which was lucrative enough, since the local conspirators now received 20 louis (roughly the same as 20 guineas) for each mission, having forced the price up from the 15 for which Leclerc had originally allowed. In early September 1803 Pierre-Marie Poix paid the people ashore at Le Tréport an advance of 480 francs to bring in by signal all the English vessels, with a little extra to keep a close eye on the sea, and a further bonus in case of success.

Poix then sailed for England, probably bringing with him the reports to the end of August, and went to London to sort out the new addresses to which to send correspondence. His return was delayed by bad weather, and after spending a fortnight in attempts to cross the Channel he landed at Morlaix in Brittany on 1 October and went to Paris to put the new arrangements in place. Lelièvre de Saint-Rémy travelled over to Helvetsluys near Rotterdam in Holland, where he arrived on 9 October and met Poix at Douai near the old Belgian border. Leclerc, meanwhile, met Wright, and they made arrangements for signals and meeting places, which Wright then took to Colonel Smith at Deal, together with the current French naval recognition signals that Leclerc had got from Duponchel at Le Tréport.

Colonel Smith passed the various signals to Admiral Montagu, but he refused to act without an official order, so on 19 October Ratel asked Hammond to get an Admiralty order to Montagu instantly so that Saint-Rémy could bring back the outstanding correspondence that had been building up for months. It does not look, from the Foreign Office files, as if they acted in time.[19] Sidney Smith was very much on top of current events, and on 4 September he wrote confidently to his friend the prime minister to put in his bid for

a diplomatic mission to any new government that may raise itself up in France on the ruins of this, it will necessarily be a military one and therefore fit for a military man ... Pichegru &c would be glad to have soldier, sailor and diplomatic man in one person with them as the medium of their correspondence with England. Pray think and act on this.

When Leclerc and Poix moved to Amiens they lodged at first with the curate Prosper Quennehen at Bellancourt until he found them a good house of their own. Poix drove Nymphe to her relations in Abbeville, the Flouets, in a cabriolet, dressed on this occasion not as a boy but as a woman in a straw hat, but it was not long before Bonaparte's police arrived to look for her there. Leclerc had anticipated this and had advised against her going there in the first place, but they got her out in time, dressed as a boy, and hid her with Quennehen in Bellancourt until Poix was able to take her to their safe house in Artois. Meanwhile, Leclerc was hiding the baron d'Ordre and others in a safe place that they called the 'dog house' – possibly the *cachette* at Godincthun – but eventually he smuggled the baron into Belgium, because the good old man was so frightened that Leclerc felt that he might accidentally betray them all.

The weather in December was so bad that at first the naval

cutters and the fishermen were unable to make contact. Ratel told Leclerc that he now had a cutter for his own exclusive use, but it had tried five times to make contact at Le Tréport, and on the sixth attempt on the night of 15–16 December it had spent four hours in the bay but had seen only one light in the town. Leclerc eventually explained that this had happened because a British cruiser had been making such a nuisance of itself off the port during the day that the fishermen had been banned from putting to sea in the evening or remaining at sea at night. Leclerc was furious that the British captain was too cowardly to go to the agreed spot, right in the heart of Le Tréport between the forts, while for his part the British captain was reluctant to put faith in the assurance that one fort had been bribed to become blind while the other was run by the 'Trocherie'. Finding that the British would not come to the shed in the oyster park on the right bank of the river, the fishermen shifted to a spot on the left bank that was more accessible by boat.

Wright, who was merely anxious to keep Biville clear for his own use, had offered Leclerc to take over the handling of Ratel's correspondence so long as it was kept separate from Cadoudal's affairs, and he had suggested that an inland postbox between Le Tréport and Eu would work much better than the hazardous spot that they had been trying to use on the shore. Sidney Smith also offered Ratel his own agents and boats as an alternative channel for communication via Rotterdam.

Everyone was tense and tempers were short because they were approaching the climax of Cadoudal's operation, and it was during this episode that Ratel deduced that his old friend Raoul Gaillard was in charge of Cadoudal's arrangements.

However, Ratel's captain set out again on 21 December intending to return four or five days later, and this time he was successful, going ashore himself and receiving the package at the oyster shed by hand. Wright also finally managed to land at Biville on 23 December, having been trying for a fortnight. In January 1804

Leclerc wrote that the first three deliveries through Le Tréport had all gone perfectly; the last had again been on shore, hand to hand. He pointed out, though, that the British boat had arrived an hour after the deadline expired, and would they please see to it that they were early rather than late, because waiting around on shore put his fishermen in jeopardy. Also, would the British please make sure never to signal towards the coast during the daytime when Bonaparte's sentinels could see what was going on.

Leclerc reported that he and Poix now had a variety of very safe houses at their disposal (though he grumbled light-heartedly that for people who were used to living in cities and châteaux these cottages, isolated farms and little townhouses meant rather a fall in lifestyle). They had one horse between the two of them, but riding Blondine they could cover many miles when they needed to; usually they went out on foot, and only ventured out at night.

What really worried Leclerc was that because of the lapse in communication he was carrying far too much incriminating stuff around with him, especially the accounts for the previous nine months. He begged to have these passed on quickly so that he could destroy his own copy, as they clearly demonstrated his counter-revolutionary activities and might be interpreted as show-ing him to be a spy for England. His house, which was fine in most respects, had no proper hiding places, and their Abbeville friends were not sure enough of the local workmen to trust them to install any. Poix wanted to call in his own trusted builder from Boulogne, but that was risky too. Even Poix was nervous, and would no longer go out in the evening to see his friends; he had gone round the house tapping every brick and plank for a suitable void, but the best they had managed was between ceiling and floor, which was an obvious hiding place, far too common.

Leclerc reported that Poix had hired more people to watch and report on troop movements through Saint-Omer and Montreuil as detachments came and went. His spies around Boulogne, though supposedly soldiers, were not very good at these observations. There had been an inquiry into signals seen off Le Tréport, but it had been conducted by Duponchel, who was in their pay, and he had reported that they were distress signals from British boats struggling with storms. The fishermen said that in reality the signals came from either their cutter, or Wright's, signalling to its boat to guide it, and he asked Ratel to tell the British that this was a stupid thing to do. He would soon get copies of the *Moniteur*, *Argus*, *Publiciste* and *Journal des Débats* delivered to Colonel Smith, but pointed out that if they were only going to be able to arrange one post per week, regular newspapers would be difficult, because they were too bulky for their fishermen to carry. Indeed, everything was now ten times more difficult than in the past because of the increased level of surveillance.

12

Atrocities of the Corsican Demon

> As to Buonaparté himself, there is every feature in
> his character, every circumstance in his conduct, to
> render it certain that no species of fortune, mental
> and bodily, no sort of infamy, which a malignant
> spirit, a depraved imagination, and a heart black
> with crimes of the deepest dye, can possibly suggest,
> or a hand, still reeking with the blood of murdered
> innocence and stimulated by the most insatiable
> thirst of vengeance, can inflict, which will not be
> exhausted upon the conquered inhabitants of the
> British empire.[1]

The campaign to vilify 'the Corsican Usurper' was extraordinary. It was hardly unprecedented – William Pitt knew what it was to be picked on, as did George III – but it is difficult to think of anybody in the entire history of the world that had ever previously suffered quite such an intense, extensive and unscrupulously mendacious attack.

At the end of 1803, two major scurrilous lives of Napoleon appeared. William Vincent Barré's *History of the French Consulate, under Napoleon Buonaparte* came out in November.[2] Barré had been employed as an interpreter to the French government and claimed that his account was based on recent experience and first-hand knowledge. In January 1803 he had written to Windham, claiming that he had interesting information about Bonaparte and volunteering his services.[3] He translated Robert Wilson's *History of the British Expedition to Egypt* into French (April 1803), 'for which he received a very handsome consideration from our government', and translated a pamphlet called *Answer from M. Méhée to M. Garat*, which accused Bonaparte of tyranny, into English.[4] His history of the Consulate shows signs of having been written very rapidly and is full of mistakes, especially in the parts he knew nothing about. What it lacked in accuracy, however, it made up for in hatred.

The other major life of Bonaparte was printed in a two-volume book called *The Revolutionary Plutarch*. This was a parody of *Plutarch's Lives*, the collection of classical Greek and Roman biographies that was said to be Bonaparte's favourite reading matter. It also parodied the *Biographical Anecdotes of the Founders of the French Republic* published by Richard Phillips, a collection of more factually accurate, but sympathetic, lives.

The introduction gave some information about the anonymous author, who claimed personal acquaintance with many of his subjects 'either from his travels, residence, or imprisonments in France', and to be 'but a literary recruit, though an officer of long standing'. In one footnote the writer claimed to have met Phélippeaux in February 1798 while he (the author) was in prison, and in his later life of Talleyrand, where he referred to himself as 'the compiler', he claimed to have visited Talleyrand's mistress at her villa at Montmorency between two spells in prison in the Temple. He also claimed that anti-revolutionary articles that he had written in 1792 in England were shown to him in the Temple in 1799.[5] But the credentials of the supposed author changed in other parts of the book, and it is highly likely that there was more than one author, with contributions from *émigré* generals and journalists, employing their various stores of knowledge and expertise.

An additional third volume of *The Revolutionary Plutarch*, published in autumn 1804 as part of a second enlarged edition, contained material that can only have come from sources within the government – official documents, published in justification, that were not available to outsiders.[6] This implies strongly that all the volumes were produced with the support of ministers, and, by analogy, argues that the earlier deployment of the same sources also had government backing. The books do not seem to have been translated into French, which indicates that they were intended for a British and American audience, and they do seem genuinely to have sold well, having gone through four editions by 1805. The arrangement of *The Revolutionary Plutarch* was changed for the second and subsequent editions. In the first edition long and detailed lives of Moreau and Pichegru were both in the first volume, together with those of Fouché, Talleyrand and the other politicians, while the second volume consisted of the generals of the army of England, the Bonaparte family and *Killing No Murder*. In the second edition, published in autumn 1804, the arrangement changed so that the first volume began with the life of Moreau and the second with Pichegru, his place in the first volume being filled with the generals. The pamphlet *Killing No Murder* was suppressed, excluded from this and subsequent editions.[7]

The Revolutionary Plutarch supported its narrative with footnotes naming French sources that looked authoritative but, for the most part, either never existed or were factually unreliable works of royalist propaganda. Even the *Anti-Jacobin Review* admitted that its authors had never seen *La Sainte Famille* (a pamphlet about the Bonapartes), or *Annales du Terrorisme*, or *Les Crimes des Républicains en Italie*, or *Nouvelles à la Main*, or the *Livre Rouge de Bourrienne* (*The Red Book of Bourrienne*), so that it was impossible to vouch for their authenticity (and, had they existed, surely Gifford and

Bowles would have seen them?).[8] On the other hand, one or two of the sources used certainly did exist, even if they were profoundly biased royalist sources published by the British government: it is possible to consult the exiled French royalist General Danican's *Les Brigands démasqués* (London, 1796) for the story of 13 *vendémiaire*, and for the calculation that reckoned casualties of the civil war in the Vendée at 800,000, blamed chiefly on 'Attila Buonaparte'. *The Dictionnaire des Jacobins Vivans* by 'Quelqu'un', bearing the imprint Hamburg 1799, was also a real book, if of questionable value as a reliable source.

A substantial part of the material in the life of 'Buonaparte' in *The Revolutionary Plutarch* had already been published earlier in 1803. A wonderful potted version of the central allegations was serialised in the new weekly newspaper the *British Neptune*, ending on 23 October 1803, and extracted in a sixteen-page pamphlet sold by John Ginger, *The Important History of the Atrocious Life and Actions of Napoleon Buonaparte*. This was very similar to the *Summary View of the Life and Actions of Napoleon Buonaparte alias Bonaparte (at present) First Consul of France* in the *Anti-Gallican*, although there were slight differences – where the *Summary View* cited eight thousand people massacred on 13 *vendémiaire*, the *Important History* gave eighty thousand. A broadside issued by Peltier's printers, Cox, Son and Baylis, *A Full, True and Particular Account of the Birth, Parentage, Education, Life, Character, and Behaviour, and Notorious Conduct of Napoleone Buonaparte, the Corsican Monster, alias the Poisoner, who is shortly expected to arrive in England, where he means to massacre, assassinate, burn, sink, and destroy. With a short Description of the various Murders, Poisonings, and Assassinations committed by him and his Gang in Foreign Parts*, where the title tells the story, was very similar in content, although it contained interesting exaggerations along the lines of Gillray's caricature life, and introduced such promising characters as Sukey Badharness, Bonaparte's wife.[9] All the key atrocities recounted in

The Revolutionary Plutarch, including those of Napoleon's child-hood, were also reiterated, this time at length, in a short book, *The Atrocities of the Corsican Demon, or a glance at Buonaparté*, and in *The Life of Napoleone Buonaparte, containing an account of his parentage, Education, Military Expeditions, Assassinations, and Avowed Intention of Invasions; the greater part from the original infor-mation of a gentleman resident at Paris*, published in Manchester for circulation in the dubiously loyal northern industrial towns in 1803 and closely based on *The Revolutionary Plutarch*. The poster *Such is Buonaparte!* was abstracted from *Atrocities of the Corsican Demon*. Cox, Son and Baylis published a large sheet, *The History of Buonaparte*, adorned with a portrait and three woodcut scenes from his life, which sold for 6d. and was recommended to be 'stuck up in Public Houses, and all Places of Resort'. They were said also to have published '30,000 copies of Buonaparte's Life, in a very popular form, and distributed the whole impression gratuitously. 70,000 more copies have been reprinted in other parts of the British dominions, and sold or given away by different persons.'[10]

The Revolutionary Plutarch's life of Napoleone Buonaparte began with an attack on usurpers in general, which discussed a number of historical examples and attempted to insinuate that the First Consul of the Republic had usurped the throne of the rightful dynasty. There followed a parallel between Maximilien Robespierre and Napoleone Buonaparte that sought to establish Bonaparte as the direct heir of the arch-terrorist Jacobin tyrant. The selfsame text was published in the *Anti-Gallican* and as a broadside.[11]

The central effort of the life went into establishing the idea that Bonaparte had been guilty of multiple atrocities, and here the effort was cunningly extended back beyond his own life to encompass the examples afforded by his villainous Corsican ancestors. The first appearance of murderous antecedents had been in *Cobbett's Weekly Political Register* for 9 July, which lifted details from 'a pamphlet much circulated in France in 1800, called The Genealogy of the Corsican Successor to the French Bourbons, written in La Vendée and printed in the Temple by a Chouan', elsewhere presented as 'The Genealogy of Brutus, Aly, Napoleone Bonaparté'. From this spurious-sounding source we learn that Bonaparte's father was a lawyer, his grandfather Joseph Buona a butcher, and his great-grandfather Carlo a tavern keeper who was convicted of robbery and murder and condemned to the galleys in Genoa; his great-grandmother Birba ended up in the house of correction there (or Geneva in the cheaper reprints). The same text was printed in the Anti-Gallican, reprinted in The Revolutionary Plutarch, in the Anti-Jacobin's review of Plutarch, and in abbreviated form in the British Neptune and in Ginger's Important History.[12]

As far as Napoleon's own birth went, The Revolutionary Plutarch suggested that there might have been more to the relationship between his mother Letizia and the French governor of Corsica than mere friendship. She was, after all, hardly a paragon of virtue, having when fifteen 'made a faux-pas with a friar' before quickly marrying Carlo. Some of Napoleon's traits could be traced to his mother, who 'was accused of blending the Italian cunning with the Corsican duplicity, prudery with wantonness; and to cover all fashionable vices with religious hypocrisy ...'[13]

Barré went further. His account of Napoleon's birth was one notch more suggestive:

Buonaparte, was a poor lawyer; and his mother, Letitia Raniolini, was handsome enough to have attracted the attention of the French commander, the Count de Marboeuf who, it is even asserted, was the real father of our hero. This is in no ways improbable, as it is well known that the French troops landed Corsica in the year 1768, and that Napoléon was born in the eighth month of the year following.

But, be what it may about his being a legitimate son, or a

bastard, it is a well-known fact, that the Count de Marboeuf paid his assiduous addresses to his mother; and that he honoured the whole family of Buonaparte with a parental care.

Ginger's *Important History* said plainly that Letizia was Marboeuf's mistress.[14]

For Napoleon's youth *The Revolutionary Plutarch* claimed that its chief source was the royalist engineer Antoine de Phélippeaux, who had rescued Sidney Smith from the Temple and then accompanied him to Acre, where he died after masterminding the defence. Phélippeaux had been a contemporary of Napoleon at the military academy at Brienne and was named as the eyewitness authority for stories of Napoleon nailing a pet dog to his door and getting the daughter of a washerwoman pregnant, before poisoning her and then courting her sister. Phélippeaux had also revealed that in youth Bonaparte's favourite amusement had been 'to frequent the public hospitals when any dreadful or disgusting operations were to be performed, and to regard the pains and agonies of the sufferer, and of the dying'. Before he was fifteen he had seen 544 operations or amputations and 160 agonies or deaths.[15]

Having been trained at the artillery school at the King's expense, the story continues, Napoleon became an officer and found himself in charge of a battery at Ajaccio in Corsica. He tried to betray the town to the British and was cashiered. Reappearing at Toulon, he, the Jacobin Louis Fréron and Barras rounded up 1500 men, women and children and mowed them down with grapeshot, tricking any that were still alive after the first volleys to show themselves in order to make sure they were all killed. In reality Bonaparte played no part in this purge carried out by the all-powerful representatives-on-mission, which had been opposed by officers of the regular army, and he could not in truth be held responsible for their actions. However, 'proof' that Bonaparte personally had carried out the massacre was presented in a letter that was referred to by Cobbett in an article in the *Weekly Political Register* of 9 July and printed in the *Loyalist* as copied from the *Annales du Terrorisme*, a publication that as stated above was, if not spurious, so rare that it has proved impossible to find:

> To Citizens Barras, Freron, and Robespierre, jun. Representatives of the People. Toulon, 29 Frimaire, Year 2 (December 4)
>
> Citizens Representatives, Upon the field of glory, my feet inundated with the blood of traitors, I announce to you, with a heart beating with joy, that your orders are executed, and France revenged; neither sex nor age have been spared; those who escaped, or were only mutilated by the discharges of our republican cannon, were despatched by the swords of liberty and the bayonets of equality!!!
>
> Health and Admiration. Brutus Buonaparte. Citizen Sansculotte.

This letter begins as quite a good parody of terrorist-speak, for in truth the representatives themselves genuinely wrote: 'The national vengeance has been unfurled. The shooting is constant. All the naval officers have been exterminated.' But its seriousness is undermined by the signatures (could Bonaparte conceivably have signed off in this manner?) and one wonders if its deniability was supposed to lie in its being obviously a comic forgery.[16]

The fictional episode in the life of Bonaparte that was the massacre at Toulon was given authority by a print. Both the *Anti-Gallican* and Ginger's *Important History* carry the note: 'This dreadful transaction has furnished Mr R. K. Porter with a subject for one of the four interesting and truly seasonable prints, which have been published by Hatchard &c., representing the crimes of Bonaparte, and which, for patriotic purposes, are sold at a price so much beneath their value.' The *Loyalist*, which, like Robert Ker Porter's prints, was published by Hatchard, recommended the designs to the public as 'well calculated to further the views of the Loyalist' and they were advertised on the poster *Buonaparte's Confession of the Massacre at Jaffa*. Porter's *Buonaparte Massacring Fifteen Hundred Persons at Toulon*, published by Hatchard on 12 August 1803, centred on a woman and a child who are about to be finished off. It made a set of four with the later 'atrocities', *Buonaparte Massacring Three Thousand Eight Hundred Men at Jaffa*, *Buonaparte sends a flag of truce & at the same instant commences an assault on Acre* and *Buonaparte ordering five hundred & eighty of his wounded soldiers to be poisoned at Jaffa*.[17]

According to *The Revolutionary Plutarch* and its precursors, the Toulon massacre made Bonaparte a favourite of Robespierre, but after Robespierre's fall Bonaparte was arrested as a terrorist and imprisoned at Nice. He was released by an amnesty and went to Paris, where he was selected by Barras to fight for him. *The Revolutionary Plutarch* gave a detailed account of the events leading to 13 *vendémiaire* 1795 based on that of the royalist general involved in the rising, Danican, in his pamphlet *Les Brigands démasqués*, and ended with 'eight thousand mutilated carcasses of both sexes, and of all ages' as the fruits of Bonaparte's first victory. The cheaper versions, giving the date as 1794, have Bonaparte imposing Barras's will on the Parisians by spraying the streets near the Pont Neuf with grapeshot, so that he 'covered the steps of the church of St. Roch with heaps of slaughtered bodies and massacred in the whole about eight thousand persons' or, in the version printed by Ginger, 'about eighty thousand persons'. The real casualty figure was about three hundred.[18]

So satisfied with this had Barras felt that he gave Bonaparte his mistress as a wife and appointed him commander of the army in Italy. *The Revolutionary Plutarch* included a life of the enlightened libertine Josephine de Beauharnais. Before the revolution she and her husband had taken pride in 'their mutual infidelities, and with their equal refinement in vice and debauchery'. Since his death on the guillotine she had spent her time enjoying herself with Madame Tallien; they liked to 'change lovers, as they changed their clothes; and to exhibit at the theatres, in the public walks and assemblies, their new and motley suitors, as impudently as their more than half naked persons'. A note explained the origin of the 'naked fashion' as pioneered by the topless Tallien and Beauharnais in the baring of women's shoulders for the guillotine.[19]

On this issue William Barré improved on the *Plutarch*, for he believed that Bonaparte was only interested in Josephine's money: in this light Barras's 'mistress, the Countess de Beauharnais, a rich widow, with several children ... although about twenty years older than Buonaparte, was a very valuable acquisition to a young man without any fortune.' (In reality she was six years older than him.) She might have been damaged goods – 'the reputation of the Countess de Beauharnais was well established even before the revolution' – but Buonaparte wasn't going to 'find fault with a woman presented to him by Barras'. Then came Barré's stunning revelation: 'Besides, the Corsican hero is not remarkably fond of the fair sex; his affections are of another kind, and such as Cambacérès is a great admirer of.' It was notorious that the 'depraved and vicious' Jean-Jacques Régis de Cambacérès was a homosexual – and this explained his friendship with Bonaparte! Barré returned to this theme later when 'Buonaparte was affected with a troublesome disorder, which bad tongues ascribed to his benevolent friendship for a young Mamelouk'.[20]

According to *The Revolutionary Plutarch* Buonaparte's progress through Italy had seen a series of massacres and pillaging; at Venice he stole a diamond necklace for his wife. He marched from victory to victory owing to the inferiority of the Austrians, who fielded poor soldiers and poor generals, including the wonderfully named Vuckassowich. He invaded neutral countries and plundered them. *The Revolutionary Plutarch* reprinted a denunciation supposedly written by a disenchanted French officer that had first been published by Peltier in no. 101 of *Paris pendant l'année 1797*. This already well-exposed letter claimed that on one occasion Bonaparte made sure that any badly wounded French soldier was 'thrown into a waggon appointed to remove the dead bodies to the grave and is generally strangled or smothered!' and on another he gave orders that 'not only the dead, but the dying and wounded should be buried!' Another 'source' (*Les Crimes des Républicains en Italie*, Verona 1797) stated with great precision that during the course of the Italian campaign 'Five thousand and forty-two virgins were ravished, and fourteen thousand six hundred and twenty-six married women were violated.'[21]

At this point *The Revolutionary Plutarch* summarised his character:

> A revolutionist by constitution, a conqueror by subordination, cruel and unjust by instinct, insulting in victory, mercenary in his patronage; an inexorable plunderer and murderer, purchased by the victims whose credulity he betrays, as terrible by his artifices as by his arms, dishonouring valour with ferocity, and by the studied abuse of public faith, crowning immorality with the palms of philosophy, tyranny and atheism with the cloak of religion, and oppression with the cap of liberty.[22]

He now showed his wickedness and hypocrisy by invading Egypt, the land of his ally Turkey. On the way he seized Malta and forced into the fleet 110 young Maltese knights, the sons or relatives of *émigrés* serving with Condé, of whom twenty-two were blown up in *L'Orient* during the battle of the Nile. Wilson was quoted on the massacre, and the poisoning and other familiar Egyptian stories of lies, hypocrisy, convenient adoption of different religions, and stories of further massacres at Alexandria and Cairo were again rolled out. These atrocity stories were at the heart of the vilification of Napoleon, and publicists really knew how to twist the knife where it hurt in developing the Jaffa hospital poisoning, there being little by which Bonaparte set greater store than his treatment of his wounded soldiers: 'Among the perfidious deeds of Napoleone Buonaparte, none has excited greater indignation than his treacherous conduct towards the unfortunate Frenchmen who have been mutilated, or fallen sick in his own service ...'[23]

In *The Revolutionary Plutarch* Napoleon's escape from Egypt was glossed over, although Barré commented: 'It is rather astonishing that the British cruisers had kept such a bad look-out as to enable both French frigates to make their escape. But, according to Dr. Wittman, a Turkish admiral was beheaded on that account.' Before leaving his army in the lurch the Corsican deserter ordered General Jacques-François de Menou to have Kléber assassinated. His distress at his wife's infidelity was reiterated, using the *Intercepted Letters* and *La Sainte Famille*, which supposedly contained a *bon mot* from Thérèse Tallien who said when upbraided by a messenger from Josephine: 'Tell your mistress, that if all Paris knows that I had two children during Tallien's absence in Egypt for near four years, her miscarriage during General Buonaparte's absence of only sixteen months, has been admired by all Paris as the last efforts of nature in an old woman.'[24]

The Corsican Cromwell had always aimed at usurping the crown, and now seized his opportunity with the help of some unprincipled friends. Barré explained how 'The crafty Sieyes, the unprincipled Talleyrand and the hypocrite Roederer, set up the insolent Corsican as a bugbear wherewith to frighten fools, that the revolutionary thieves and robbers might enjoy, undisturbed, the fruits of their plunder.'[25] *The Revolutionary Plutarch* clearly saw why Bonaparte and his henchmen instantly clamped down on press freedom:

> It is difficult, if not impossible, to find in the pages of history, three guilty characters, such as Buonaparte, Talleyrand, and Fouché, who had more to apprehend from a liberty of the press,

which might alike expose the crimes of the barbarous poisoner, of the crafty unfeeling intriguer, and of the ferocious terrorist drowner and plunderer.

It was therefore no surprise that they were determined to fetter the presses of all countries, not just their own.

Bonaparte's presumptuous and cheekily offensive offer of peace, made as if he were the equal of George III rather than an upstart usurper, and ignoring all diplomatic protocol, was totally unacceptable. *The Revolutionary Plutarch* denounced Frotté's murder in the article devoted to Fouché.[26] Bonaparte then employed a fabricated narrative (something these writers took pride in) to pin the Christmas 1800 bomb attack – the assassination attempt by an infernal machine – on the British government.[27] During the peace he had behaved treacherously to Toussaint, the black leader, and had used the climate and circumstances of Saint-Domingue to wipe out most of the soldiers who were loyal to his rival generals Moreau and Pichegru. Saint-Domingue, previously the richest place in the world and France's prize colony, had revolted under the leadership of François-Dominique Toussaint Louverture. It became Haiti.

The pamphlet version of the life in *The Revolutionary Plutarch*, the *Important History*, explained the renewal of conflict after a peace that Bonaparte had only negotiated so that he could bully lesser nations like Switzerland with impunity:

Had the British submitted to the dominion of Buonaparte, and would they never resist his will, they might have had Peace, and they might promise it themselves for the future. But to preserve their Constitution, their Laws, their Wealth, their Liberty, and their Independence, they wage with Buonaparte one of the most just Wars that ever called forth the energies of a People.[28]

The Revolutionary Plutarch also included lives of Bonaparte's wife and family. The *Red Book of Bourrienne* was cited as evidence for court finances: this had supposedly been printed after Bonaparte dismissed his school friend and private secretary Louis Antoine Fauvelet de Bourrienne, but all but three copies had been seized and the author and printer had been sent to the Temple (an episode absent from Bourrienne's memoirs). The government printed this account of court expenditure on 13 August 1803 in the *British Press* and the *Globe*, but in a review the *Anti-Jacobin Review* said it had had it in manuscript for months but had not published because (almost unbelievably) it suspected its authenticity.[29] From this we learn that vast sums had been lavished on Napoleon's family – chiefly his wife: Josephine's mechanised baths cost hundreds of thousands of francs. If Josephine was spendthrift and sexually promiscuous, her son was also violent: 'Eugenius is a brutal, ill-looking, debauched young man ... At the age of twenty-two, he modestly prides himself on keeping no more than six mistresses: one of them, Mademoiselle Chameroy, an actress at the opera, was killed last year by his brutality, when in a state of pregnancy.' On the other hand *The Revolutionary Plutarch* could find little to say against her daughter Hortense, who was said to be in love with a royalist.

Napoleon's family was uniformly villainous. His brother Lucien was

bound apprentice to a petty retail grocer in Bastia: for some pilferings he was turned away and joined the Marseillois Brigands, who, on the 10th of August, 1792, took and plundered the Castle of the Thuilleries, and murdered the Swiss Guards ... he married a strumpet of the corps called the *Furies of the Guillotine* ... he possessed the means to gratify all his degrading and cruel passions. Not a woman, whom chance exposed to his view, or caprice to his fancy, and whom money, power, violence, or intrigue, could procure, but was seduced, dishonoured, and ruined by him ...

The youngest brother Jérôme had gone with the fleet to Saint-Domingue. 'At his arrival, his virtuous sister, Madame Le Clerc, had presented him with a beautiful mulatto-woman, for a mistress ... in a fit of jealousy Jerome ordered her to be devoured alive by some famished blood-hounds'.[30] Napoleon's sister Caroline had left Marseille with an actor from Paris with whom she had two children. Another sister was simply a model of sexual depravity:

> at the age of fourteen, the Princess Borghese, then Pauline Buonaparte, ran away from her mother's house with a Sardinian corporal and deserter, Cervoni ... until Napoleon's usurpation, in 1799, when she, according to the pamphlet *La Sainte Famille*, was found covered with rags and disease, in a house of ill-fame in the rüe St. Honoré ... [31]

The life of Talleyrand, which closed the first volume, was chiefly devoted to a memorandum of 14 December 1802 that had been sent from France by a spy, recommending peace with Britain 'for ten or fifteen years' at all costs on the grounds that France could then build up the means to invade and conquer Britain. This had been printed in August as a separate publication and in the *Loyalist*. Talleyrand had been trying to persuade Bonaparte to keep the peace, and his argument that if Bonaparte wished to punish the English he would do better to wait was made in that context. Ministers were perfectly well aware of Talleyrand's sincere desire for a settlement, and so to publicise this gambit was another proof of their uncompromising belligerence.[32]

Other episodes of the life of Talleyrand in *The Revolutionary Plutarch* were lifted from the fuller life that had been published in the May–August issue of the *Anti-Jacobin Review* as 'Revolutionary Portraits No. 11'. As a stylistic sample, one might offer its ingenious explanation of how Talleyrand acquired his (congenital) limp:

When a young man, in company with some of his debauched associates of his own age at a public brothel, Talleyrand being involved in a quarrel, refused to give his adversary the satisfaction demanded, the consequence of which was, he was thrown from a two pair of stairs window into the street, and both his legs were broken by the fall, the fracture produced a lameness from which he has never recovered.

Talleyrand, it explained, became wealthy: his income as a priest was upwards of 100,000 *livres*, 'but large as this sum is, it was far from being sufficient to supply his extravagance in gambling and women'. Having established him as an immoral spendthrift, Gifford's journal was intent on dispelling any recollection of Talleyrand's anglophilia; instead, he was 'a man whose hatred to England is proverbial' and his appointment to the head of the foreign office was in itself enough to prove the insincerity of the peace proposals of 1797.[33]

The life of Fouché was written at much greater length than the piece on Fouché in the *Anti-Jacobin Review*, but the central description of the police was almost identical, which might suggest that they were written by the same person – indeed, both articles contain near-identical versions of the passage: 'The author of this work called, in 1801, sixty-two times at Fouché's office, and was obliged, in the end, to pay fifty Louis d'ors for the release of his friend, Mr. P. an American, arrested by mistake, as an accomplice in the escape of Sir Sidney Smith from the Temple in 1798'.[34] Elsewhere in both pieces, the author claimed to have been drummed out of the exchange at Marseille.[35]

Whereas the passage in the *Review* focused closely on corrupt police and the suppression of press freedom in France, the *Plutarch* allowed more space to revel in Fouché's past terrorist atrocities. The volumes also included lives of the politicians the abbé Sieyès, Paul Barras, Pierre Louis Roederer, Constantin Volney, Honoré

Riouffe, the painter David, and the admirals and generals of the French army of England. These were all treated to crudely rancorous calumny. General Pierre Augereau, we read,

> for one night put sixteen young nuns into requisition for himself and his staff; the tears of youth, the pangs of conscience and the prayers of virtue availed nothing; they were, by a drunken soldiery, carried away almost lifeless, from the retreat and cells of religion, to the infamous beds of vice; to endure the horrid and disgusting embraces of cruel crime in power. Four of these devoted victims to the lust of republicans afterwards destroyed themselves, six lost their reason; and the six others, their health.[36]

Nevertheless, for liberal opinion, which continued to be a principal target, tyranny was key. Thus *Buonaparteana* (1804), dedicated to Sheridan, aimed 'to eradicate the minutest particle of partiality by such as may have been dazzled by the ill-gotten victories and atchievements [*sic*] of a man, whose career commenced in blood, was continued with treachery, and now concatenated by the combination of corruption, cruelty and crime'.[37] Bonaparte was a Tiberius or a Nero presiding over a police state with twenty thousand spies employed in the metropolis alone.

The exceptions to the general rule of calumny were the lives of generals Pichegru and Moreau. These two were treated with great sympathy in order to prepare the public for their prominent situations in France after the planned coup to which, as propaganda, these volumes were intrinsically linked. William Barré's book also lavished praise on Pichegru, citing his superiority to Bonaparte as the reason for his exclusion from the amnesty offered to royalist *émigrés*, but allowing that 'Pichegru has no claims to have murdered and poisoned Frenchmen, nor even to have massacred prisoners of war; and in those kinds of exploits he is certainly inferior to the Corsican Buonaparte.'[38] Barré encouraged the idea that the overthrow of Bonaparte would be easy to achieve by deploying Moreau or Pichegru as a rival claimant to the leadership of France.

They were unstained by crimes that were reduced to a sort of catechism in *Buonaparte's True Character*:

> An obscure Corsican, that began his Murderous Career by turning his Artillery upon the Citizens of Paris – who boasted in his Public Letter from Pavia of having shot the whole Municipality – who put the helpless, innocent and unoffending inhabitants of Alexandria, Man, Woman and Child, to the Sword till Slaughter was tired of its Work – who, against all the Laws of War, put near 4000 Turks to Death in cold Blood, after their Surrender – who destroyed his own comrades by Poison.[39]

Bonaparte's height was still a subject for debate. He was known to be 'Little Boney', but how little? The modest five foot four of the penny broadsheet *Twenty Thousand Pounds Reward* was little less than his real height of five foot six and a half, but in June 1804 Jean Peltier went much further, calling him 'a little green monkey of four foot two inches'.[40]

This illusion was sustained by Gillray's caricatures, which became more savage in the autumn of 1803. The *Hand-Writing upon the Wall*, published at almost the time that the assassin Georges Cadoudal was landed in France, was a threat that shared with *A Consular attempt at a Crown* the idea that Bonaparte had been weighed in the balance against the rightful French king and found wanting. It also provoked: Napoleon's three sisters stand bare-breasted behind an obese and bloated Josephine who guzzles wine. *The Corsican Carcase-Butcher's Reckoning Day* similarly implied a threat, and like *The Arms of France*, which emphasised continuity from Robespierre to Bonaparte, was certainly commissioned, being published by Ginger and Hatchard as well as Humphrey. Gillray's single most offensive image, *The Corsican-Pest; – or – Beelzebub going to Supper*, showed Bonaparte defecating while being toasted before a fire on a fork held by the devil.

Six of Gillray's attacks on Bonaparte in 1803 received further continental exposure when Karl August Böttiger published copies and descriptions of them in his influential Saxon journal *London und Paris*: he chose *Armed-Heroes, French Invasion, The King of Brobdingnag and Gulliver, Maniac-Ravings, John Bull and the Alarmist* and *The Corsican-Pest*. Aware of Napoleon's campaign against personal attacks on him in England, Böttiger had his engraver tone down Gillray's two most abusive caricatures, so that *Maniac-Ravings* became *The Flying Sword run mad*, with the raving little Boney transformed into a winged sword, while *The Corsican-Pest* became *The Kitchen below*, with Napoleon replaced by a Gallic cock on the devil's toasting fork.[41]

Tame reviewers gave glowing endorsements to *The Revolutionary Plutarch* at the end of the year. The *European Magazine* considered that:

The contents of these volumes are interesting in a remarkable degree; as detailing, either from personal knowledge, or from accredited works of other writers, the lives, conduct, and crimes, of every person distinguished as a relative, a courtier, a favourite, a tool, an accomplice, or a rival of the Corsican Upstart, who has hitherto with impunity oppressed, and plundered the continent of Europe; and as exhibiting at the same time a clear display of the extraordinary kind of police by which Paris is now regulated. Such a mass of moral turpitude as is here displayed, yet in a form that leaves little room to suspect its authenticity, makes us blush for our species.[42]

The *Anti-Jacobin Review* thought that everybody in the country should read *The Revolutionary Plutarch*:

> It were much to be wished that these volumes could find their way into every house, and into every cottage in the united kingdom. The perusal of them could scarcely fail to excite abhorrence of the wretches who now threaten to convert *our* country into the same scene of blood, desolation, and vice, as they have converted all other countries into, in which their intrigues or their arms have secured them a footing.

On the other hand, in a combined review of Barré's *History of the French Consulate* and *The Revolutionary Plutarch* the reviewer for Arthur Aikin's *Annual Review and History of Literature* merely wrote:

> Fear is always cruel ... In the late war and in the present the British Ministry has been loudly accused of participating in, and encouraging those plans of assassination, which have been directed against the person of the chief magistrate of France. Let the ministry, if they can with truth, vindicate themselves from so black a charge by a solemn and authentic disavowal; and let the British public show the high honour and intrepid courage, for which they have long been renowned, by consigning to merited contempt and abhorrence all works, together with their authors, whose direct tendency is to degrade the generous and high-spirited patriot into the lurking assassin.[43]

Aikin's reviewer made the assumption that these works were approved by the British ministry, and his suspicion that the French accusation against them of encouraging assassination might be just had been aroused especially by the appendix to volume II of *The Revolutionary Plutarch*. This struck a very serious note that contrasted with the near-comedy of the atrocious black lives with a reprinting of *Killing No Murder*, the famous appeal for the overthrow of Oliver Cromwell, that was an unconcealed threat to Bonaparte as well as an attempt to justify violent regime change:

It has been considered an appropriate Appendage to this Work, to republish the celebrated Pamphlet of 'Killing no Murder,' one of the most singular controversial pieces the political literature of our country has to boast; one of those happy productions which are perpetually valuable, and which, whenever an Usurper reigns, appears as if written at the moment, and points with equal force at a Protector – or a Consul.

It recommended and justified assassination.

13

Landing the Assassins

M any people now thought that a terrible struggle between Britain and France 'must last as long as the life of Bonaparte'.[1] The final preparations for a second attempt to cut this period short by assassination were completed in July 1803. Georges Cadoudal's aide Jean-Marie Hermilly had landed in Normandy in late spring to finalise arrangements with those responsible for landing, guiding and housing the royalist hitmen, and Julien Leclerc arranged lodgings for him and Michel Roger at Amiens. Hermilly returned to England in July in a Tréport fishing boat with Gaston Troche, son of the clockmaker, who was to serve as Cadoudal's guide.[2]

An accommodation between generals Pichegru and Moreau was looking promising. As his latest go-between Pichegru had turned to General Frédéric Lajolais, who had fought under him on the Rhine and may then have been involved in his plotting. Lajolais was an ugly, balding man, whose pretty and clever wife Catherine had for many years been Pichegru's mistress, and Pichegru was the real father of her son. Armed with a letter of recommendation from Pichegru, her complaisant husband had made contact with General Moreau and reported that Moreau would welcome a meeting with Pichegru and wanted Bonaparte overthrown.

Captain Wright was given the mission of taking Georges Cadoudal and some chosen followers across the Channel and landing them secretly in France. As we have seen, on 31 July Admiralty Secretary Evan Nepean ordered Admiral Montagu at Deal to give Captain Wright the best of his hired cutters or luggers and to tell their commanders to follow Wright's orders. Just how and when they landed remains slightly mysterious: French police investigations concluded that Cadoudal landed in France in the early hours of 21 August, but there is no particular reason to suppose that the police learned the truth. The logs and musters of Montagu's cutters and luggers, in the form in which they survive in the National Archives, reveal almost nothing of any secret operations and do not match what is said of their activities in letters from the spymasters, but this was possibly because the documents were falsified in order to hide what had really been happening from the Admiralty.[3]

Towards the end of 1803 First Lord St Vincent tried to find out what had been going on at Deal behind his back and what the vessels based there had been doing: 'It is absolutely necessary that the whole of this dark business should be cleared up,' he wrote to Captain John Markham on 3 December. Admiral Keith's inquiries proved fruitless, and so on 28 December, in frustration, he demanded the journals of all Wright's vessels.[4] I think that it is likely that the logs were rewritten for Keith's benefit, in order to conceal the truth, and that it is these doctored versions that survive in the National Archives.

Keith learned from the logs that the gun brig *Basilisk*, while off the French coast in early August, had had her boat stolen by nine French prisoners and then on 9 August was attacked by French gunboats. This is indeed how Commander William Shepheard's journal in the National Archives reads. However, *Basilisk*'s muster book gives additional information. Captain Wright had come aboard on 'secret service' on 3 August and left to join the *Augusta* cutter on 10 August. In between, on 6 August, the muster book records, nine French prisoners 'took away the boat in the night off the coast of France on Secret Service'.[5] It is possible that this record in the muster book correctly dates the landing of the first party of *chouans* in France. But it is equally possible that *Basilisk*'s muster book was as false as her log, or the episode was pure fiction, or that it was falsely dated, though the incident with the gunboats is confirmed by Thomas Troubridge's report to Keith of Wright's complaints to the Admiralty.[6] Keith eventually learned that Wright's activities were concerned with espionage. Much later he learned that: 'It was the five men brought by Captain Wright from London, I am told, who kept the Basilisk's boat and sent the vessels to the rendezvous to fall upon her.'[7]

After this flurry of activity in *Basilisk* the next reference to Wright was on 6 September, when Keith ordered Lieutenant Carpenter to take Wright on board the cutter *Speculator* and follow his instructions.[8] So Admiralty records do not provide any detail to support a landing on 21 August, and, if anything, hint at an earlier date; but at some point in August Wright landed Cadoudal at Biville, probably from *Basilisk*.

The choice of landing place was extraordinary: the sheer chalk cliffs of the 'Alabaster Coast' between Dieppe and Le Tréport are the highest in Europe, and anybody hoping to advance inland had to climb them. At two points near Biville deep valleys reduce their height from over three hundred feet to about half that, but the drop to the sea remains terrifying in the extreme. Where the eastern valley now called 'Parfondval' comes out, a crevice makes it possible to scramble down to where, early in the twentieth century, as a postcard of the period reveals, steps were cut leading down along a precarious, projecting ridge. During the Second World War the Germans built a concrete staircase here, but there are few remains of this now, as it has been washed away. The cliffs suffer constant erosion, and it is not clear whether there was any aid to an ascent in 1803: but if there were any easy route, it would have been guarded. In the western valley nearer Biville the drop to the sea is greater and more sheer. Here there was an '*estamperche*', a long cord fixed to wooden stakes, generally used by mussel gatherers and sometimes by smugglers, down which people could slide, and up which they could climb.

It is a very isolated spot, and nobody could possibly have suspected that this route would be used to bring assassins into France. It needed to be isolated because Bonaparte was strengthening the forces on guard on the coast, especially in places known to have been used by Anglo-royalist agents. On 28 July he had ordered Berthier to base a squadron of the 20th Chasseurs at Le Tréport and Eu with posts as far as Cayeux and a permanent picket of twenty-five men at the batteries guarding the mouth of the bay of the Somme, and to base another battalion or squadron at Dieppe.[9] They were on the lookout: the watchtower at Penly had spotted two fishing boats in contact with a British cruiser on the night of 13/14 August and the two captains were investigated next day.

On the exposed, windswept cliffs near Biville an old sailor named Etienne Horné, a woman called Marianne Mons and a boy from Penly named Pageot scanned the sea when the tide was right for British vessels. When Horné picked out a boat at sea, Mons flashed a lantern three times and an answering light came from offshore. Horné slid down the rope to the rocky undercliff while the cutter ran in to the cliff and lowered a boat.[10]

The ascent from the beach was intimidating, and to haul oneself up the rope to the top of the cliff required considerable strength, agility and courage. Cadoudal carried a lot of weight, but he was built like a bull, had enormously strong arms and certainly did not lack courage. In the party with him was the guide Gaston Troche, together with Raoul Gaillard and Jean-Marie Hermilly, who had set up the Norman network. Cadoudal brought his Breton servant Louis Picot and his aide Aimé-Augustin-Alexis Joyaux, who had organised the 3 *nivôse* plot. With them were two more *chouan* soldiers, Pierre Querelle, a former naval surgeon whose medical skills might be useful, and a man named as Breche, also called Labonté.

The seven *chouans* and Troche refreshed themselves after the climb with a meal at Horné's cottage, half a mile from the cliff, and then Troche and the boy guided them to their first overnight stop at Guilmécourt, about three miles away. The next night they travelled through deep valleys and woods to the isolated half-timbered farm of La Poterie, near Saint-Pierre-en-Val, right up against the edge of the forest of Eu, owned by a cousin of the Troches. After resting at La Poterie, Cadoudal rode a black horse on a long fifteen-mile leg through the forest to a farm at Preuseville. There they were met by one of Gaillard's old soldiers, Louis Ducorps, who guided them on another long ride through the forest to his lodging at Aumale, a former convent of Dominican nuns, home of a royalist schoolmaster called Pierre Monnier. From there Ducorps took them on twelve miles to Feuquières.

They passed the next day at the farm of Monceaux in Saint-Omer-en-Chaussée, and at night the farmer's son guided them round the city of Beauvais to Auteuil, and the next night to a farm in the isolated hamlet of Saint-Lubin. The farmer, Jean-Baptiste Massignon, passed them on to his brother Nicolas at Jouy-le-Peuple, who helped them to cross the river Oise, using the ferry at Méry, and guided them to the wood of La Muette, where they were met by a vinedresser from Saint-Leu Taverny. He took them to a rendezvous with the *chouan* officers de Sol de Grisolles and Charles d'Hozier, who took Joyaux and Georges into Paris in their coaches. Two rode in on the horses and three waited for the public coach into town. D'Hozier, who was formerly a page to the King, drove Georges to the Hôtel de Bordeaux in the rue de Grenelle-Saint-Honoré where Raoul Gaillard was staying.

Georges left in the evening to sleep at the Cloche d'Or at the corner of the rue du Bac and the rue de Varenne, where he was joined by Louis Picot. The Cloche d'Or was a sort of headquarters for the conspirators; the proprietor, Jean-Baptiste Denand, a wine merchant, came from upper Normandy, and he had sheltered Jean-Baptiste Coster de Saint-Victor above his wine bar after the 3 *nivôse* explosion. His wife Sophie owned a portrait of Coster de Saint-Victor. The conspirators gathered in a room on the first floor, coming in by a back door from an alley to avoid the shop, and Denand rented a stables in the rue du Bac for the horses belonging to his guests.

After six days at the Cloche d'Or Georges took possession of an isolated house by the Seine in the village of Chaillot just outside Paris (now roughly opposite the Eiffel Tower). Bouvet de Lozier had rented the house for his mistress, Mme Costard de Saint-Léger; it had two apartments of three rooms, fashionably furnished, with a large garden running down to the Seine. After a short stay Georges moved in late September to 21 rue Carême-Prenant (now Bichat) in the Faubourg du Temple. D'Hozier had rented a mezzanine there, and had engaged the builder Spin to fashion a secret hiding place in it. Spin made a concealed trapdoor, with a stair to the ground floor and an exit through an unoccupied shop whose door opened under the porch of the house.

Just what Cadoudal did in Paris is not known, but presumably, beyond checking the arrangements that had been made, he conducted some sort of reconnaissance. Philippe de Ségur, recently appointed commander of the First Consul's bodyguard, recalled reported sightings of Cadoudal in the grounds of the palace of Saint-Cloud; he thought that he might once have seen him himself.[11] In November, Georges's aide Joyaux met Moreau's secretary Fresnières to sound him out; they were old acquaintances from Brittany and Fresnières had been to school with Georges.[12] At the end of September Cadoudal and three of his officers left Paris to meet the vinedresser at Saint-Leu. They returned along the chain of safe houses to Eu, where Michel

Troche the clockmaker had found Cadoudal an isolated lodge in the woods outside the nearby hamlet of Mancheville, and it seems that he may have spent most of the autumn hidden there rather than at Paris.

Meanwhile, other *chouan* emissaries were at work. Georges had given orders to some of his officers to precede him and others to follow, with orders to go to different destinations.[13] Michel Roger disembarked in Brittany in early summer and made contact with various old comrades before travelling to Paris in December. Admiral Cornwallis arranged for a senior officer of Cadoudal's, Joseph-Laurent Even, to be landed in Brittany in October, and he also recruited former officers and despatched them to Paris to join an ever-growing secret force of *chouan* soldiers.

In late summer the royalist officer Etienne-François Rochelle went over to Paris with money and passports to enable General Lajolais to travel to London for discussions with Pichegru. Lajolais went via Hamburg and Denmark, travelling as a merchant under a false name. His arrival at Harwich was expected and he reached London in December, spending three weeks at Brompton with Pichegru. At least one of the meetings was attended by the royalist military commander, the comte d'Artois. Lajolais assured Pichegru and his friends that Moreau was unhappy with the government of the First Consul and was prepared to do all in his power to help them overturn it.[14] Peltier later wrote that Moreau had demanded the assassination of Bonaparte first, and Artois had agreed that Moreau should then be First Consul until he appeared a few weeks later, and if this had any truth the common notion that the coup would be triggered by the arrival of a Bourbon prince was not the main strand of thinking in December 1803. The blow was expected to fall on or around 15 February 1804.[15]

During the autumn there was at least one further landing of royalists at Biville. The trial records, full of denials, are not conclusive, but in the period from September to early December the royalists were reinforced by a number of other senior officers from Cadoudal's 'army'. The Foreign Office file contains a list of sixteen of Cadoudal's officers who were ready to leave London at this time, and Jean-Marie Hermilly served as pilot and guide for all who came and went.[16] On 21 November Wright asked Admiral Montagu for the *Lively* revenue cutter 'to procure me the means of executing a particular and delicate service of very high importance to the interests of this country', and this may have been the service.[17] On the other hand he may have been delayed by the autumn's persistent bad weather: on 7 December he landed at Biville but the snow was too thick for the landsmen to come to him for fear of betraying themselves by their tracks. There is evidence that Armand de Polignac landed at Parfondval in thick fog on 18 December, was met by Cadoudal, and spent the night at the farm called Neuvillette.[18]

It was at this time that Admiral Keith was getting very vexed about what his cutters were doing, as the navy never had enough small boats. As a result of complaints to the Admiralty, St Vincent wrote to Markham on 3 December:

> My head is too bad to write to Sir E. Nepean, but I will thank you to desire he will send me a copy of all the directions he has given to Rear-Admiral Montagu tomorrow. I wrote one letter to the rear-admiral at the request of Lord Hawkesbury, signified to me by Mr. Hammond, desiring he would furnish one or more vessels to Captain Wright as occasion might require on a very urgent mission.

On 13 December 'that Prince of Intrigues' Robert Montagu was replaced.[19] It was then that Keith demanded to see the journals of the cutters under Montagu's command. He sought an explanation for their activities, and was told it had to do with espionage. 'Your expression respecting Captain Wright and others being intended as spies, surprises me,' he wrote to Markham. 'By whom are they sent?'

Eventually, he learned that the Foreign Office was the controlling power, but he remained grumpy, partly because subordinates were acting outside his control while he was being kept in the dark, but also because he was being excluded from intelligence relevant to his mission of preventing invasion: 'On the subject of Cutters employed by the Secretary of State, there is no reason why I should be let into the secrets they contain, but it seems decent that I should be acquainted with the vessels so employed, and not be told by my inferiors such vessels are about.' He blamed the underhand operations that were going on within his command on the Smiths and the 'ex-party' – by which he meant former ministers allied to Grenville and Pitt.[20]

Meanwhile, Sir Sidney Smith continued to campaign for an appointment to the Downs with Wright as his assistant, as Lord Keith confided to Markham, his friend on the Admiralty board, quietly threatening resignation:

> if I can discover that any branch of the government have not confidence in me I shall request to make way for the man they may prefer. Such times require the ablest men that can be got. I am not uninformed that Sir S. S. wants the Downs command independent, with a captain; his uncle told me nearly to this effect.

The problem was that Smith's uncle General Edward Smith, one of the last surviving veterans of Wolfe's 1759 victory at Quebec, could not tell Keith why Smith wanted the role because Keith was not in on the secret, thus reinforcing his paranoia.

Markham explained that: 'The ex-party are in strict intimacy as you know with all the Smiths, and it is on their part alone that I consider any espionage can be expected. I hope I have made myself understood, and that you can't have a doubt of this Board.'[21] He continued in conciliatory manner:

A wish has been expressed to-day by Lord Hawkesbury to have two cutters with intelligent men employed on secret service, and as it is the desire of the Board that these officers should be immediately under your orders and control and all pass through you, Lord St. V – intends to express that desire to Lord H – tomorrow. Perhaps Lt Shepard in the Mitchell cutter would be well for one, and Lt. Stewart for another. However, you will judge of this.

John Markham did not take to Wright when he met him:

I never saw a man with more pretensions than Captain Wright, and he talks it very well; but I should suppose that to be the extent of his abilities in our line. He has all the passions of the family at Deal.[22]

Keith had by now traced the centre of Captain Wright's secret operations to Walmer Castle, but remained very sceptical as to their value. On 5 January 1804 he wrote to John Markham: 'Captain Wright went off yesterday in the Hound. He talks of sixty officers at Southampton. He wants a 20-gun ship to be sent for.' Wright was bound for Le Tréport in order to land Ratel's assistant Lelièvre de Saint-Rémy, because the correspondence's regular cutter had been sent away on other duty. Two days later Keith told Markham:

Wright thinks France is ripe for insurrection, or pretends to think so. You know he came from town with a lot of loyalists, and got the Basilisk to carry them over. They got into her boat after appointing a rendezvous, settling signals, &c., with all the mummery, and off they went; but kept the boat, and they sent out five of the gun-boats from Boulogne, which attempted to surprise and ram the *Basilisk*. This I know to be a fact.[23]

Despite his qualms and his irritation Keith had come to appreciate that he was to support an important secret operation that was about to reach its climax, and that the current ministry was directing operations, not simply the 'ex-party'. On 9 January Nepean wrote Keith the very formal instruction:

> It has been judged advisable that an officer of rank and consid-
> eration should be landed in France as soon as possible, and as it
> is of great importance to His Majesty's Service that he should
> not be placed in a situation to be likely to fall into the hands
> of an Enemy, they are pleased to direct that you should order
> a Frigate or large Sloop to receive him on board with orders to
> her Commander to land the Person above described, and any
> other Persons who may accompany him, on such part of the
> coast he may point out.[24]

Keith told Markham: 'The person shall be attended to as soon as I am informed where he is.' He was still keen to control things himself: 'This [East Cliff, Ramsgate] is the best place, as he may embark from my door without ever entering the town or being seen by any but my own family ... I gave Captain Wright the *Admiral Mitchell* and *Hound* cutters, but can afford him no more. The *Vincejo* is at a stand for want of officers, Admiral Rowley writes me.'[25] Three days later he discovered that he had been bypassed once again, Wright having 'come to Deal in the night and called on Admiral Patton for two cutters (*Speculator* and *Flirt*), with which vessels he has set off. Thus he has the *Admiral Mitchell*, *Hound*, and *Griffin* doing he only knows what, whilst I have only two small vessels of all those belonging to the Downs station to watch the coast from Ostend to Calais.' He wrote Wright a stiff letter telling him to give back the two cutters he had taken, still complaining to Markham that 'If Captain Wright would be open he would get what he wanted, but that does not belong to the House. Mystery is the word.'[26]

Pichegru left London on 10 January with Wright, Frédéric Lajolais and François-Louis Rusillon, in a post-chaise for Deal, and they probably embarked for France in *Speculator* with important royalists including Jules de Polignac and Charles-François de Rivière. Wright's other boats were presumably deployed in such a way as to ensure that the landing was safe and uninterrupted. They sailed on 11 January but bad winds prevented them landing until 16 January. Georges and Armand de Polignac met this distinguished aristocratic party at Biville. The group split after La Poterie, Pichegru and Rusillon travelling with Georges Cadoudal and Picot, while the courtiers of the comte d'Artois, Rivière and the Polignacs went separately. On 23 January Georges and Pichegru entered the Porte Saint-Denis in a gig. Raoul Gaillard lodged Pichegru with an employee of the finance department whose wife was an old friend, in the second floor of a house in the quiet rue du Puits-de-l'Ermite close to the Jardin des Plantes, in what an English traveller called 'quite the most remote quarter of Paris'. They stayed there three days.

Frédéric Lajolais had travelled separately and went straight to Moreau on 24 January to tell him that Pichegru was in Paris and would like to meet him, and they fixed a rendezvous for that night on the western edge of Paris in the boulevard de la Madeleine not far from Moreau's house in the rue d'Anjou.[27] Pichegru and Moreau met in an alley at the corner of the rue des Capucines because there was less moonlight there. Lajolais also made contact with Henri Rolland, a senior figure in military transport, and an old colleague from Pichegru's days on the Rhine front.

In London the plot seemed to be moving on smoothly, with the conspirators having all reached Paris successfully. In a letter of 26 December Ratel had told Leclerc that Spencer Smith was going as ambassador to Stuttgart to take on the role formerly performed by Wickham, coordinating efforts towards regime change in France, and Smith had asked what they could tell him about François Charles Luce Didelot, recently appointed Bonaparte's minister to the court of Württemberg. Leclerc must have passed this request on to Paris, for his bulletin of 31 January 1804 reported that Didelot was young and rich; as prefect of Finisterre he had been hostile to royalists and he had been made prefect of the Palace, but Bonaparte didn't like him and had sent him to Stuttgart. He learned of his new post when one day he turned up at the Tuileries to be greeted by the First Consul with 'Bonjour M. l'ambassadeur de Württemberg', leaving him thoroughly disconcerted.[28] Leclerc noted that the newspapers said that Spencer Smith had arrived at his post and asked Ratel to instruct him whether he should at once make arrangements to send Smith the Paris bulletins.

Preparations on the propaganda side were also far advanced. A new version of the most famous apology for assassination, *Killing No Murder*, came out in *The Revolutionary Plutarch* in time to be reviewed in January 1804. The pamphlet, originally published in 1657, had been republished to encourage counter-revolutionaries in 1689, 1715 and 1745, and was playing the same role now. From 6 January it was serialised in French in the *Courier de Londres* as *Tuer n'est pas Assassiner*.[29] It was issued independently as a pamphlet in both English and French editions, and the *Lettre d'un Anglais à Bonaparte* that, as we shall see, Francis Drake, the British minister in Munich, got printed in November 1803, and distributed in France, was the same pamphlet, addressed to 'Monsieur Consul' and explaining that to kill a ferocious beast or a tyrant like Cromwell or Bonaparte was not assassination.[30]

Reviews of *The Revolutionary Plutarch* repeated the message: James Asperne's *European Magazine* said simply that 'though actually levelled at Cromwell, the arguments will suit any other usurping tyrant as well as him', while the *Anti-Jacobin Review* found *Killing No Murder* 'strikingly applicable to the present usurper, and to the present times'.[31] The letter published on 18 January in the *Star*, in a series written by Henry Redhead Yorke as 'Galgacus', quoted *Killing No Murder* to urge 'every man ... to endeavour, by all rational means, to free the world of this pest'.[32] It is possible that this was some kind of signal to the conspirators that it was time to act. Even the *Morning Chronicle* published articles predicting that the death of Bonaparte and the restoration of Louis XVIII were imminent.[33]

That trusty and discreet retired diplomat the Earl of Malmesbury noted that at the beginning of February 1804:

the measures concerted by Pichegru, Moreau &c were confided to me. They were represented as *immanquable*. The idea was the restoration of the monarchy under a Bourbon prince. Their plans were extensive, and, as they thought, well and secretly arranged. Pichegru left England about the middle of January. As soon as anything like a successful step had taken place, and whenever the event became certain, and the moment arrived that a more conspicuous character was necessary, Lord Hertford was to appear in the double character of making peace, and restoring the old Dynasty. The Duc d'Angoulême was to have gone to France, on due notice being given him.[34]

14

Méhée de la Touche

Méhée is about thirty-six years of age, and one of the handsomest men in Paris. He is rather more than six feet high, well proportioned, has a round face, fair hair, and a smiling and prepossessing countenance. From what we have said of him, it is easy to guess that he is a well-informed, steady republican and a resolute and active patriot, but at the same time, a man of immoderate ambition, and of a turbulent and dangerous character. (*Biographical Anecdotes*, 1798)

Méhée de la Touche is near forty-two years of age, but does not appear to be thirty-six. He is a very handsome man, six feet two inches high, well-proportioned, has a round face, fair hair, and a smiling, prepossessing countenance. Besides French, he speaks some Italian, English, Polish and German. His intelligence and insinuating manners, his savoir vivre, and his hypocritical though enthusiastic praise of virtue and liberty, make him, with his other personal qualities, to the good and unsuspicious, one of the most dangerous and unprincipled men who have weltered in the mire of the French Revolution. (*Revolutionary Plutarch*, 1804)[1]

While the British government viewed the progress of the plot involving Pichegru, Cadoudal and General Moreau with considerable satisfaction, they also had another pot on the fire, and that too was bubbling away nicely.

This project had begun with the arrival in Guernsey in January 1803 of an author named Jean-Claude Méhée de la Touche, and with a letter that he wrote introducing himself to the government. In this he announced himself as a well-known republican whose enemies had traduced him with a calumny that Bonaparte had chosen to repeat in his official newspaper. Méhée had sued, but he had been arrested and exiled to the Isle of Oléron off Rochefort, from where he had recently escaped. He was aware that he had irritated Bonaparte by refusing to take the editorial line that the tyrant wanted after the government had taken over his *Journal des Hommes Libres* and by writing a pamphlet in reply to the obsequious praise heaped on the usurper by one of his favourite senators.

Over the years, he explained, his republican idealism had leaked away as he watched unscrupulous opportunists take advantage of the revolution to feather their nests and ruin the project. He had come to believe that monarchy was better, and that if the royalists would promise not to punish the republicans but to treat them as partners, republicans would come flocking to overturn the tyrant. He explained that he himself came from an Irish family that had gone into exile with James II, so he had no great loyalty to France and wished to settle in Ireland. He had connections with the French ministry for foreign affairs, enclosed some documents revealing Bonaparte's thoughts on Egypt, and could provide more. If the government was interested, he had a plan to restore the Bourbon monarchy.[2]

Some weeks went by, during which time he had charmed the governor of Guernsey, General Doyle, and the inspector of militia, Thomas Saumarez, who invited him to dinner, and, so he said, convinced them to pay for a journey to London by telling them about Bonaparte's current projects for fomenting a rebellion in Ireland. On 3 February Méhée wrote a memorial for Doyle to forward to the British government, saying that his plan was to create a republican group in France whose leaders would be secret royalist agents in order that royalists and republicans could combine to beat the Corsican. He again claimed that his family came from Ireland, that he was a repentant republican who, after two years' thought in exile and in prison, had decided to support the British government. He would use his literary connections to support the English cause in Brussels, to help Englishmen infiltrate influential groups, to convert the Indians of Louisiana to the British cause and to convince republicans of the genuinely beneficent motives of the British government.

Although some of his plans (notably for the natives of Louisiana) sounded far-fetched, Méhée convinced Doyle of his ability and sincerity, and on 6 February 1803 Doyle sent his memorial to London, with covering letters to Home Secretary Lord Pelham and Foreign Secretary Lord Hawkesbury, telling them that he had given Méhée a passport to go to London. He told Pelham that although he had been sceptical about Méhée at first, he now had 'every reason to believe he may be trusted'.[3] Five weeks later Doyle forwarded to George Hammond, undersecretary at the Foreign Office, a box of out-of-date French Foreign Office papers that had been addressed to Méhée. 'The Plot thickens very fast,' he wrote excitedly.[4]

Méhée claimed that Saumarez gave him exactly the price of the journey to London, so that he had only 18 shillings to his name when he arrived at the Union Coffee House in Parliament Street, the hostelry where the government placed immigrants whom they might find useful. He was soon introduced to Hammond, whom he later described as a little, pockmarked, very ugly man, when in reality Hammond was tall and portly. Hammond explained that, being still at peace with France, Foreign Secretary Hawkesbury could not employ him for the present, although circumstances might change. Hawkesbury wrote to Doyle to tell him that the government could have nothing to do with Méhée de la Touche's propositions, and to warn him rather pompously to have nothing to do with the man's connections in France, the strong implication being that Hawkesbury thought Méhée might be a spy.[5] Nevertheless, what Hammond told Méhée was enough to persuade him that he had good reason to stay.

Stuck in London without income, Méhée ingratiated himself with Bertrand de Moleville, now owner of a flourishing patisserie, a man for whom he had worked in Paris when Moleville had been first minister of marine and then in charge of a royalist secret police, and whom, by providing a passport, Méhée had helped escape to England in 1792.[6] But not everybody was sympathetic. Cobbett subsequently wrote: 'every person that I was acquainted with, and that talked about Méhée, openly declared him to be sent over by Buonaparté. Méhée did me the honour of a visit. He came several times to repeat it; but, he never could get at me a second time, though he offered to communicate much secret political information.'[7] Peltier publicly denounced Méhée as a Jacobin terrorist, as did others.[8]

According to Peltier's recollections the following year, which were almost certainly intended to damn Méhée in the eyes of Bonaparte, Méhée was full of stories of how in the 1790s he had been one of the many lovers of Madame Bonaparte. The translator and author William Vincent Barré also wrote that Josephine was one of Méhée's mistresses in the 1790s at a time when Méhée claimed to have been subsidising the then 'needy Corsican' shilling by shilling.[9]

Worried that he was running into debt, Méhée wrote to Pelham, asking him to pay the bill for his lodgings while he waited to learn whether the government would employ him.[10] Unfortunately, the letter went to the Alien Office, where it was not only delayed but also linked to an anonymous letter of 12 April that denounced

Méhée as one of the most sanguinary Jacobins at the sack of the Tuileries, a leading advocate of the execution of the King, and the man who paid for the September massacres and had promised to be the first to kill any new king that arrived in France. The Alien Office thought it would be a good idea to pay Méhée's hotel bill and then deport him, but government departments then became involved in a long internal wrangle over which of them should pay the £4 bill, Hawkesbury refusing to pay it at all.[11] Méhée wrote a memorial for Lord Pelham, defending himself against these allegations of terrorism.[12] This altercation lasted long enough for Méhée to have been arrested for debt before it was settled, but by then war had broken out.

Not wishing to meet Méhée personally, Pelham asked Bertrand de Moleville to find out what he had to propose.[13] Méhée now came up with a much more precise and plausible plan for uniting royalists and republicans against the tyrant, and Moleville, who was impressed, recommended it to Pelham. If uniting royalists and republicans should seem unlikely, one should remember that the British government had just succeeded in uniting the left wing of British public opinion with the right in an alliance of enthusiastic hatred against the tyrannical usurper.

In his proposal Méhée explained that he was a member of a republican committee that was dedicated to the downfall of Bonaparte and that, although some members of the committee were determined republicans, most, like him, saw the best future for France to be the restoration of the Bourbon monarchy. The committee was in correspondence with almost every department of the army all over France. Britain, therefore, had a powerful ally within France. Britain had realised that its existence was incompatible with Bonaparte reigning in France (a point underlined in the manuscript by Pelham or Hawkesbury in pencil). Toleration of usurpation put Britain's existence in peril. The Bourbons were incapable of replicating either Bonaparte's gigantic plans or his unquenchable hatred for Britain. Méhée's plan was that whenever the British government gave the signal, his Jacobins would create a revolt in the east where they had much support, while the royalists raised Brittany and the Vendée. Republicans would seize Dôle, Dijon and Auxonne and create a camp at Auxonne as a rallying point for the enemies of the First Consul. Their emissaries would raise Switzerland and cut off the Army of Italy. If the plan was accepted he proposed to go to Hamburg and then to the Rhine under a Swedish, Danish or Polish name. There, under the direction of the British commissioner, he would distribute pamphlets to manipulate public opinion and would put the commissioner in touch with republican malcontents.[14]

Méhée's plan was so similar to the royalist schemes that were already being pursued as to make them even more credible and to recommend itself for support. The two plans were mutually supportive, and one was a fail-safe for the other. Malmesbury's diary for 4 June 1803 reveals that Lord Pelham had received 'a very good memorial from a Frenchman of the name of La Touche, with a plan of attacking and molesting France, but that Addington had paid no attention to it'.[15] Addington took care to seem to pay no attention to it, but the plan was given the go-ahead, Moleville was told to perfect it in consultation with Méhée, and preparations were put in train to chime with the existing plan to bring down the tyrant.

After a short delay, Moleville extracted Méhée from his sponging house, paid the £4, gave him £50 and told him that the British government would pay him 10 guineas per month and would soon give him a mission.[16] In the meanwhile, Méhée wrote anti-Bonaparte pieces for the English press. He had old friends in liberal circles and was well enough known to have been included in the *Biographical Anecdotes* published by Richard Phillips.[17] Indeed, notoriously, the government had used the Alien Bill to deport him from England in 1792, though nobody seemed to remember that now.[18] Ministers tried to proceed cautiously though. Méhée was sounded out and tested by both General Willot and the constitutionalist Pierre Henry-Larivière, before being taken to see the bishop of Arras, head of the royalist council, who gave him somewhat shabby reassurances on amnesty for republicans and national property.

Méhée had a respectable background: he was born in 1762 in Meaux, the son of a distinguished military surgeon and anatomist, Jean Méhée, known for his *Traité des lésions à la tête, par contre-coups* (1773) and *Traité des plaies d'armes à feu, dans lequel on démontre l'inutilité de l'amputation des membres* (1799), who was professor at the military hospital of the Val-de-Grâce. Méhée studied at the Collège Royale de Mazarin in Paris, but his father died when he was young. It was what happened after that that was worrying, because the accusation received by the Alien Office conveyed what was commonly believed in France – that Méhée had been one of the most bloodthirsty of terrorists, and was these days protected by Fouché and his journalist friend Pierre Réal. Méhée told royalists that he was working for Moleville's royalist secret police as an agent in 1792, in the dangerous job of infiltrating the Jacobin Club, taking part in the attack on the Tuileries in August and signing the orders for the September massacres. The one man who could defend Méhée was Moleville, who supported Méhée's story that during the Terror he had been a double agent and had been secretly working for him on behalf of Louis XVI. As Moleville trusted Méhée, there must have been some truth in the story, but Méhée was probably also working for the other side. It is as difficult now as it was then to get to the truth. It seems, from what happened afterwards, that Méhée was not a secret royalist in 1804, but he was plausible and persuasive.

Standing thus under the spotlight, Méhée persuaded many people. As well as Moleville, he convinced Barré, who translated his *Réponse au Cen. Garat, par le Cen. Méhée*, and used him in his history of the Consulate to prove Bonaparte's treachery to his erstwhile republican friends:

> In order to prove to some republicans, infatuated with the *republicanism* of Buonaparte, that the Corsican tyrant spares nobody, let it be here observed, that a French republican is now in London, after having escaped from the Island of Oléron, whither he had been transported, previous, no doubt, to a further transportation, only because he wrote an historical disquisition concerning the usurpation of Caesar ...
>
> The Corsican despot thought himself Caesar and banished the republican historian, who fled to the only free and hospitable country in Europe.[19]

Barré was completely taken in and introduced Méhée to the government French-language printer William Spilsbury, with a view to taking on the editorship of the *Mercure britannique*. In order to prove his commitment to the cause of unseating Bonaparte, according to Barré, Méhée even wrote a preface for a translation of *Killing No Murder*, applying it to Bonaparte.[20] Barré made this allegation a year later when he was trying to discredit Méhée with Bonaparte, so he might have been lying, but the idea was not implausible as Méhée had already written a similar preface in 1792 in order to make the pamphlet applicable to Louis XVI and might reasonably have volunteered a preface or been asked to write one.[21] Stylistically, the text that Barré reproduced resembled Méhée's work and it was probably this preface that introduced the *Lettre d'un Anglais à Bonaparte*, the version of *Killing No Murder* that was designed for distribution in France, of which no example is known to survive. It was different to the preface published in the *Courier de Londres* or to that in the *Revolutionary Plutarch*. The version recorded by Barré ran:

Citizen General, This small pamphlet, the sixth edition of which I have the honour to dedicate to you, was directed against Cromwell; and it is asserted that its effect was such, that this great man was frightened to death some time after. You know how much his loss was regretted, and you have, no doubt, perceived in the esteem attached to his memory, how grateful our posterity will be to you. Cromwell saw in this small pamphlet a provocation to murder his person . . . The principle stated in the pamphlet has never been questioned by any man. It is generally admitted as an axiom: - 'That it is allowed to kill a tyrant.'[22]

Barré further alleged that Méhée wrote a song called 'Napolisson', sung to the tune of 'La Carmagnole', explaining that '*Polisson* means *blackguard*', and that he also wrote:

an address to the French soldiers, entitled *La Ramée*, being a place near the Invalids Hospital in Paris, much frequented by soldiers, who go there to drink. It is impossible to write better to the feelings of soldiers, in order to seduce and excite them to revolt; and every Frenchman to whom M. Méhée de Latouche read his *Ramée*, remained fully persuaded that such an address being distributed among the French soldiers could not fail to excite the French party against the Corsican rabble and cause their immediate destruction.

This was another pamphlet destined for distribution in France, specifically aimed at republicans in the army, and Barré claimed to have watched Méhée writing it.

On 9 September 1803 Hawkesbury agreed to send Méhée to Ambassador Drake in Bavaria, now Britain's most experienced spymaster. He was given £200 for travel and expenses, £500 to finance his Jacobin committee, and £50 per month as a stipend. The decision was top-secret: 'I wish the Draft to Mr Drake to be put into Cypher by the most <u>confidential</u> Person in the Office & then sent to me for my signature', Hawkesbury wrote.[23] He told Drake on 23 September that it was hoped that the Jacobins might prove useful allies against the tyrant and that much might be learned from them, but that working with the Jacobins was an experiment and Drake must treat it as such. Drake must only give them money when it was clear that the results justified it, and Méhée's increased allowance of £50 per month was only to be paid if Drake sent a favourable report. But nowhere was Drake warned specifically to beware in case Méhée should prove to be a spy. Méhée was travelling under an alias and had a bottle of 'Sympathetic Ink, but he neither knows how it is made, nor the manner in which it is rendered legible; both these requisites you are informed of by the inclosed paper'.[24] The sympathetic-ink issue caused anxiety, John King, undersecretary at the Home Office, wrote to Hammond:

Write a note to Drake, or send this, desiring him not to let la Touche use his *own*, but *our* sympathetic ink – *Ours* will never appear, without the necessary application. But his will, after it has been written for some time. Altho Drake may give him our ink to use, he need not give him the receipt [recipe] for making it appear.[25]

Moleville invented a patriotic society of *émigrés* and Englishmen as cover for the enterprise, and told Méhée 'to concert with his friends measures for overthrowing the existing government in France, in order that the nation might have an opportunity of choosing the form of government the most calculated to ensure its happiness and tranquillity'. He also gave Méhée pamphlets and songs to print and distribute in France, especially amongst the army, almost certainly including *Lettre d'un Anglais à Bonaparte* and *Lettre de La Ramée à ses camarades de l'armée*.

Méhée was told that Francis Drake would give him more

detailed instructions. He set out for Germany on 22 September
with two passports, one in the name of Count Stanislaus Jablonski,
a Pole travelling for amusement, and the other as Méhée, expelled
from Britain as a Jacobin. Two days later he embarked at Harwich
for Husum in Danish Schleswig-Holstein, a voyage of six days. At
Altona he met the French consul and sent off to Paris an account
of his mission, adding a letter to Talleyrand, explaining his visit to
Drake and asking for a passport to enter France. He then travelled
to Munich, learning en route that Louis Otto had arrived a few
days earlier as French ambassador. He took an inn close to Drake's
residence, wrote to him the following morning, and received an
immediate reply inviting him to meet and stay for dinner. Drake
sounded Méhée out cautiously, refusing on the first day to discuss
serious business; he showed Méhée two bulletins from Paris and
introduced him to his family as Count Jablonski, an old friend from
Poland. They discussed a journalist in Ratisbon, Paoli de Chagny,
who Drake said was happy to write anything against Bonaparte.
Méhée took careful note and warned the French authorities.

Méhée pretended, as an excuse to leave, that he wanted to go
to an opera by Mozart that was being performed that evening,
but instead wrote a note for Otto, and, after walking randomly
about Munich until he was sure he was not being followed, he
took the note to Otto's house, leaving it with the concierge, who
said that she would give it to Otto as soon as he returned from the
theatre. When he got back to the inn Méhée used invisible ink
to write down all that he remembered of his conversation with
Drake. He returned to Drake's house at nine next morning and,
having successfully deflected Drake's inquiries about the opera,
read some newspapers while Drake dealt with his correspondence;
then Drake showed him his private office and they worked all day
on Méhée's plans.

On Sunday they worked on Méhée's instructions from Moleville.
Drake retained Moleville's cipher on the grounds that it was not

safe to try to take it into France; on the same grounds he objected to Méhée's briefcase – its English manufacture would attract attention at the border. Méhée looked on in horror as Drake picked it up and proceeded to leaf through its contents on the pretext of pointing out to Méhée that the documents inside, printed on English paper, could also betray him to the French authorities. Drake was, of course, discreetly checking what the contents were, and Méhée, trying not to betray his anxiety, was desperately racking his brains to remember whether or not it still contained the French consul's receipt for the report he had sent to Paris from Altona, and if so, how he could prevent Drake from discovering it without betraying his guilt. He was extremely relieved when it turned out not to be there, as he happened to have taken it out. They spent the rest of the day determining Méhée's additional instructions and settling methods for their correspondence.

On Monday Méhée made contact with Otto, but the result was disturbing: Otto had no passport for him, appeared hostile, and Méhée wondered what was going on. He spent Monday with Drake, revising the instructions, which Drake had copied, and going through the pamphlets, songs and caricatures that Méhée had brought from London. Drake gave him a course in chemistry, so that they each understood how they would use invisible ink, and how to place a blot to indicate where invisible writing started. Invisible ink was straightforward enough to make – two ounces of salt of Saturn, which is lead (II) acetate, dissolved in a large glass of water. The liquid required to render the ink visible was more complicated to make and more unstable: you mixed two ounces of quicklime, two ounces of orpiment or arsenic, two ounces of lead monoxide, and a good third of a bottle of water; you sealed the container hermetically, shook it well, left it to rest, then opened it carefully, dipped a brush in and passed it over the paper.

Méhée asked Drake for a passport to Strasbourg and another to get into France, hoping to discover how the British smuggled in their agents, and all through Sunday Drake hoped his friend the Russian ambassador would provide him with a passport, but finally he refused. Drake said that he had to give a dinner because his closed doors were causing gossip and told Méhée to return at nine o'clock in the evening. He gave him his apparently blank notebooks and a passport for Strasbourg in the name of Müller, including visas for a journey from London so that it didn't look brand-new, and provided him with a letter of introduction from the bishop of Châlons to de Mussey, the agent of the comte de Lille (Louis XVIII) at Offenburg, ten miles from Strasbourg.

Méhée was now in a position to expose two major royalist agents and to entrap a British diplomatic spymaster, but his advances to the French ambassador were being ignored. Failing again to make contact with Otto, Méhée wrote to Henri Shée, the prefect of the Bas-Rhin department at Strasbourg, explaining his mission, with a letter from Drake and Châlons's letter as proof; then he set off for Offenburg.[26] There, de Mussey told him how to get a fake passport, which inn to use at Strasbourg, and the place where anti-Bonaparte pamphlets were printed. He learned in effect that the royalist committee at Offenburg still existed, that it still met at the home of the baroness de Reich (niece of the Austrian general Klinglin, whose papers, captured by Moreau, had revealed Pichegru's treason), and that it was responsible for passing pamphlets printed in Germany into France. Méhée duly went to the Ville de Lyon inn at Strasbourg, obtained a fake passport, and wrote to Shée, who met him that evening. Together they used Méhée's recipe for making invisible ink visible in order to read his instructions from Drake, and on this evidence Shée sent Méhée on to Grand Judge Régnier at Paris, escorted by his secretary, Forest.[27] Méhée wrote on 24 October to Drake telling him of his safe passage and instructing him to direct post for him to M. Obreskow at Kehl on the eastern bank of the Rhine opposite Strasbourg. He then reported his safe arrival at Paris on 3 November.

Grand Judge Régnier had already passed Mehée's reports to Bonaparte, who had read them with considerable interest. On 1 November the First Consul wrote to Régnier, instructing him to have Méhée write to Drake to say that he had access to the usher of Bonaparte's secret office at Saint-Cloud, who was willing to steal documents written by Bonaparte for the small consideration of £100,000. Napoleon also wanted to know whether Méhée had witnessed the same sense of military urgency in England that there had been in France in 1790. The same day he wrote to Talleyrand, ordering him to get the *Mercure de Ratisbonne* closed down because the author was in English pay, as Méhée had told him.[28] Three weeks later Bonaparte urged Régnier to keep up the correspondence, as he couldn't supervise it personally as closely as he would wish.

Méhée duly followed Napoleon's instructions, and claimed to Drake to have bought two presses in order to print pamphlets and handbills. At the beginning of December Drake asked who was on his committee. He could not commit himself over the usher who promised leaks from Bonaparte's office until he knew what the usher could produce and was prepared only to pay according to the value of the usher's services. Méhée in turn raised the spectre of a second royalist–Jacobin committee supported by an English agent, tried to find out when Drake expected the royalists who were supposed to raise a revolt in the west to act, and pretended to be worried about his own safety in Paris. Drake denied knowing anything about a second committee, but urged cooperation with it, as it mattered very little by whom the beast was brought to the ground, so long as everybody was ready to join in the chase.[29]

In early December Méhée proposed setting up a correspondence with Jersey with the aim of discovering d'Auvergne's organisation, as well as throwing out various other lines in the hope of exposing people suspected of being British agents. He told Drake that his committee consisted of two former generals, a lawyer from the *parlement*, two ex-conventionals, a *chouan* leader who was very good at pretending to be a convert, and himself. Their general was aged twenty-eight (and not, therefore, Moreau, who was forty), tall, distinguished, very brave and very ambitious and totally trusted by republicans. He painted a much more enticing picture of the portfolio that the usher hoped to raid. Drake sent money and wanted to know more about the usher.

On 3 January 1804 Drake expressed his satisfaction with bulletin no. 8 and with the progress of their correspondence. An emissary of the French government had been making inquiries about Drake, but Drake assured Méhée that there was no suspicion of their correspondence – what had caused the inquiry was the appearance in almost every department of France of the pamphlet *Lettre d'un Anglais à Bonaparte*, and the suspicion that Drake was behind its distribution. Drake was indeed behind it: his accounts show that his main expense in this period was Father Horn's bill, paid on 22 November 1803, for printing and circulating the 'Letter to Buonaparte' (239 Florins, 53 Kreuzer, with a further 40 Florins for paper and for making up the sheets) and Teissonet's expenses, paid on 29 March 1804, for circulating the 'Letter to Buonaparte' in France (149 Florins, 53 Kreutzer).[30] This was clearly the *Lettre d'un Anglais à Bonaparte*, brought over by Méhée, which was, as we have seen, a version of *Killing No Murder*, a pamphlet explaining that tyrants might be killed lawfully like wild beasts. Father Horn was Alexander Horn, a Benedictine monk and British secret agent at the Scots monastery at Regensburg. 'Teissonet' was almost certainly Jacques-Marie de Tessonet, a former agent of Wickham and aide to Condé, based at Lons-le-Saunier in France.

Drake said that he had been told that Bonaparte was embarrassed by his preparations for invasion because, for all his fine words, he was afraid to embark, and that his increasingly extravagant tyranny presaged a crisis, and asked Méhée to address these issues. In his next letter Méhée announced that the committee was going to print the *Lettre de La Ramée à ses camarades de l'armée* ahead of the pamphlet that Drake was going to send, *Bonaparte à un Anglais*, because it was likely to be more appropriate to their republican audience.[31] On 31 March 1804 Drake paid Father Horn for printing 'Buonaparte's Answer'.

Drake reported to Hawkesbury Méhée's various snide comments on the unreliability of Willot, Moleville and Arras ('your Lordship will observe some very singular Remarks with relation to General Willot and his Associates'), but he was generally excited: 'I am glad that the Correspondence is now becoming more and more interesting. ... The footing upon which my correspondence is established leaves me no reason to apprehend a discovery of it.'[32]

In the next bulletin Méhée sent the result of the committee's inquiries into the invasion:

At the War Office I saw an officer who had just arrived from Boulogne who told me that they were going to employ some fearsome modes of attack against the English which they would only reveal when the order was given to raise the anchor. A naval officer was supposed to have found a means of attacking a first rate man of war successfully with gunboats ...

I had a conversation with the secretary of [ ] on the Invasion, and the reasons for the abrupt departure of the First Consul. His self-esteem, he said, his reputation, the glory he has acquired, demand that this Invasion Project must be attempted. The preparations that have been made, the enormous sums that they have cost cannot just be written off ...

The invasion would go ahead, and he had also discovered that armourers had secretly made a bulletproof cuirass for the First Consul.

The game of tennis continued, with Méhée generally scoring more points: Méhée asked whether Drake could get a fake newspaper tax stamp engraved for him in Germany and Drake replied that it could only be done in London. Méhée was being paid very well at £1200 a year but he was always in search of more money – though not on the scale of Napoleon, who had demanded the extravagant fee of £100,000 for leaking his own plans, hoping to score the double triumph of cheating the British of their money while exposing to the public gaze the corrupt uses to which the British government put the gold extracted with such pain and hardship from poor old John Bull.

Méhée was now working with and for Napoleon and had re-established himself in the First Consul's good graces. This had certainly been one object, and perhaps the principal object, of Méhée's journey to England, if you believe the account that he wrote afterwards, in which he claimed to have gone to England on his own initiative in order to restore himself to favour through 'some signal service'. But his escape from Oléron and the journey to Guernsey via Paris is suspicious: could he really have done it without help? Some thought so. Astonishingly enough, Bertrand de Moleville continued to believe that Méhée was a royalist, and as late as 1810 he argued that the plan only failed because Drake in his enthusiasm had 'dispatched him to Paris where he could not appear without being known immediately, and of course without being obliged to betray the secret of his mission'.[33] The double agent's life is tricky, and a French spy in London had also believed that Méhée really was working for the British and had denounced him to Prefect of Police Dubois for plotting there against the First Consul. But Méhée's correspondence with Henri Shée proves that Moleville was deluded and that Méhée was working for Bonaparte's France. But just who was he working for? His initial rejection by the French authorities suggests that he had not been sent to England on an official mission with Foreign Office and police knowledge and support, and that the denunciation by the French spy in London may have been taken seriously by the French authorities.[34]

Lewis Goldsmith, writing in 1810 after his conversion to the

British cause, and so with every reason to lie, but writing of a time when he had been working for Talleyrand, said that he had met Méhée fresh from Oléron, in the theatre at Paris, and had heard Méhée say that he had Pierre Réal, the republican counsellor and friend of Fouché, to thank for his liberation and that he was about to leave for Britain on a government mission. We may be sceptical about the government mission, because Goldsmith was writing to support the British line that Bonaparte had invented and directed the entire plot in order to discredit the British, but Réal rings true, as he had always been Méhée's friend and patron.

When Méhée was imprisoned briefly after the 3 *nivôse* assassination attempt, Pierre Réal remonstrated with Bonaparte because he wanted to employ Méhée, whereas the First Consul had intended to deport him. 'He's a man who won't assassinate me, I do believe that,' Bonaparte admitted, 'but he finds and he says that I'm a tyrant, and he would have approved if I had been assassinated. But he's not a man who ought to be deported. And it wasn't me, it was the police who arrested him.'[35] He escaped deportation on that occasion, but was banished to Dijon early in 1801 for his pamphlet *Réponse au Cen. Garat, par le Cen. Méhée*, before his attacks on Catholic religion and the clergy in his journal *L'Antidote* at the time of the Concordat caused him to be imprisoned in November 1801 for a longer period on the Isle of Oléron. Introducing himself to Shée in 1804, Méhée claimed that he had been exiled owing to an intrigue of Fouché's, had escaped to England before the war, and that while he was in England his wife had petitioned Grand Judge Régnier, who had said that he could only return after shedding some light on hostile English projects. It is possible that there was an element of truth in this version, too.[36] At all events, it seems that Méhée's subplot started as an unofficial republican initiative, intended to restore Bonaparte's faith in republican patriotism, rather than an official Bonapartist mission, and that Bonaparte only directed its progress after Méhée's return to Paris.

But during January 1804 the main plot was drawing close to the moment of consummation, and Bonaparte was about to discover that he was not quite as much in control of events as he had thought.

15

Paris in Panic

Bonaparte had every reason to suspect that his enemies were plotting against his life, but in January 1804 he had no idea that Cadoudal was in Paris, much less that Pichegru was also in the capital, holding discussions with Moreau. Grand Judge Régnier's police had only the vaguest indications of any *chouan* activity – the identification of a few adherents of Cadoudal in the capital, signs of unrest in royalist areas, a few purchases of gunpowder.[1] Bonaparte's aide, the twenty-nine-year-old General Savary, claimed to have issued the alarm that first triggered action: a former *chouan* chief alerted him to stirrings in his part of the Vendée, and when Savary went there to investigate he found that a band of *chouans*, led by two men who had recently landed on the coast, was going about 'announcing a speedy change in affairs' and telling people to hold themselves in readiness for this moment. There was a rumour that Cadoudal was coming. On receiving Savary's report, Bonaparte asked for the list of *chouans* who had been detained on suspicion, and found that three, Jean Picot, Charles Lebourgeois and Pierre Querelle, had come from London.[2]

On 21 January Bonaparte ordered the military trial of these three, and of two other *chouans* associated with Cadoudal, Piogé the Pitiless and Louis de Sol de Grisolles. 'I have secret information that makes me believe that Querelle only came here to murder. Sans-Pitié and Desol were here with the same design,' Bonaparte wrote to Régnier.[3] It is likely that this secret information came from Fouché, who had already been called in to give private advice and guidance to Bonaparte, and that that was how Bonaparte was sometimes one step ahead of his policemen. Savary found Bonaparte and Fouché closeted together and overheard their conversation. 'You still do police work then, Fouché?' inquired the First Consul. 'Yes, I have kept a few friends, who keep me up to date,' replied the ex-minister quizzically.[4]

Before the police ministry was suppressed in September 1802 Fouché had sent spies into London to infiltrate Anglo-royalist networks, and it was one of these who had reported that Picot and Lebourgeois had said they were going to Paris to kill the First Consul. Fouché still kept his finger on the pulse of police work and he may well have had a hand in sponsoring Méhée's mission to London. It has been suggested that Bonaparte also had his own independent channels – specifically, there is some circumstantial evidence that Michelle de Bonneuil and her son-in-law Regnaud may have had some knowledge of Cadoudal's project through her infiltration of royalist circles in London in 1802 and their familiarity with the royalist quartermaster, Athanase-Hyacinthe Bouvet de Lozier.[5] There may have been something in this, but the signs are that Bonaparte did not know much. Secret Police Chief Pierre Desmarest certainly had no secret information. He recalled a sense that they were walking in a minefield, but that they had no evidence of where the danger lay. He had nothing against de Sol de Grisolles except that he was suspected of having been involved in the Infernal Machine conspiracy three years earlier.

Picot and Lebourgeois were interrogated, tortured, condemned by a military tribunal and shot, having revealed very little. Querelle, denounced by the same London spy and arrested in October, cracked after his condemnation and on 27 January begged to be heard. When Joachim Murat, then governor of Paris, announced that Querelle was prepared to talk, Bonaparte sent Pierre Réal to question him; for the purpose he appointed Réal assistant to the Grand Judge, with special responsibility for state security and this operation. Having persuaded Querelle that he was not necessarily about to die, the revelations poured out: he was part of a conspiracy led by Cadoudal, he had landed with Cadoudal five months ago at Biville and had travelled with him to Paris, where some seventy conspirators were hidden and more had been supposed to follow. According to Réal, this news took both him and Bonaparte completely by surprise. Their reaction was electric: security in the capital was immediately stepped up massively, everybody going through the customs barriers was checked, and sentinels were placed to make sure that nobody could climb over the walls.[6] The commander of Napoleon's bodyguard was woken during the night and told to change his passwords and carry out all guard duties as if in the presence of the enemy; instantly, he increased the number and scope of patrols.[7]

A first step was to ask Méhée to fish for information about Cadoudal from Drake.[8] On 30 January Méhée wrote to Drake that a member of his committee had denounced him as either useless or a traitor because, as an English agent, he should have known about the two agents of Georges who had just been shot and that the royalists planned to act in the first half of February. He had replied that it was perfectly reasonable that he should have been told nothing about what was happening in the Vendée and that his correspondent might not learn until later about orders given to agents sent from England, and that in any case this mission of Georges's agents could just have been the crackpot scheme of some partisan with no link at all to any great political plans. He was hoping that Drake would reveal something about what was going on. On 31 January Bonaparte angrily criticised Desmarest's interrogation of de Sol, and ordered the arrest of a man who,

Desmarest revealed, had in September bought twenty kilograms of gunpowder, and the solitary confinement and interrogation of Ambroise d'Hozier (brother of Charles), who had received and stored the gunpowder. Throughout this crisis Bonaparte behaved like a man in sudden danger, not like an assured manipulator.[9]

Some details of these discoveries were published, alarming the conspirators. The *Moniteur* of 30 January reported the execution of the two killers from London and related mysteriously but ominously that if what Querelle had told the police was as important as he said it was, he might have earned a pardon.[10] Meanwhile, the Alien Office bulletin from Paris of 1 February warned that the police were saying that Querelle came from London and that his revelations were mostly about Cadoudal, who the police now thought might be in Paris.[11]

Meanwhile, at this very time, discussions were taking place between Moreau, Pichegru and Cadoudal, but they were not going altogether smoothly. On 26 January, two days after the encounter in the shadows off the boulevard de la Madeleine, they met at Moreau's house in the rue d'Anjou. Pichegru introduced Georges and explained his plans for Bonaparte's overthrow; Moreau was profoundly suspicious of Georges, took exception to some aspects of their plan, and seemed distinctly grumpy, being reluctant to express his own views in front of Georges. A third meeting took place at the house in Chaillot, to which Georges and Pichegru had returned as a discreet venue not far from Moreau's home in the faubourg Saint-Honoré. With Georges again present, Moreau was cold and silent. He admitted the need to topple Bonaparte but suggested that it should be up to the Senate to decide what happened next, and seemed to favour the idea that he might be made dictator while the Senate prepared for a return of monarchy.

Pichegru then consulted General Macdonald, another friend, who promised to bring Moreau round to a more reasonable attitude. They held a fourth meeting without Georges, to whom Moreau evidently objected, and at this meeting at his own house Moreau agreed that the downfall of the tyrant should be followed by the proclamation of the monarchy. Moreau still wanted guarantees from the royalists that sales of national property would not be reversed and that army officers would keep their ranks. Lajolais and Victor Couchery waited in the salon while Moreau and Pichegru hammered things out in the library. Victor Couchery was the brother of Jean-Baptiste, a politician and journalist who lodged with Pichegru in London and was a close friend; Victor now worked in the office of General Moncey, the head of the gendarmerie, and had been brought into the circle because he was well placed to give early warning of trouble. At a fifth meeting the details of the plot were settled, and it was decided that if the blow had to be struck before the prince arrived, a provisional government consisting of Moreau, Pichegru and Macdonald should rule France.[12]

Whether this happy resolution, whose source is an unsigned report that from its place in the British Foreign Office file was probably written by one of Napoleon's spies, was ever really achieved is open to doubt. Pichegru's aide Louis Rusillon later admitted that he had heard the Polignac brothers say to each other that everything was going badly, the leading conspirators couldn't agree, that Moreau was not keeping his word, that he had his own aims and that they had been deceived – but what Rusillon admitted to his interrogators is no more trustworthy than what the spy said, for the spy was trying to convince the British that he was on their side, did not know how much they knew, and had to produce an account that was close enough to the truth to be convincing.[13]

Leclerc reported that the conspirators had already managed to get into the interior of the Tuileries through the mediation of a young woman who was related to Josephine and in her entourage:

> This young lady and her brother, a former Chouan, were arrested, and their arrest gave credence to the idea that it

was they who had succeeded in getting one of the conspirators admitted as a wood-porter, who was discovered when
he dropped a pair of pistols in delivering wood to one of the
apartments of the château.

This conspirator had been living there for four months. According
to Leclerc, the conspirators were only waiting for Napoleon to go
to Boulogne in order to launch Moreau's coup, and the people who
went ahead of him to set up his palace were already on the coast on
8 February when they were abruptly recalled.[14] Whether this was
true, and Cadoudal and Pichegru were about to act, with a date
set for 15 February, or whether they were really about to attempt to
pull out of a deteriorating situation, it soon became clear that the
police were following clues that led in their direction.

Promising him his life if his information was sufficiently
important, Réal made Querelle re-enact his nocturnal journeys,
leaving Paris by the Porte Saint-Denis on 3 February and heading
for l'Ile-Adam.[15] On the third day Querelle recognised the house
of the vinedresser. He named the person who had brought the
conspirators to him, who pointed the police to his brother, and so
the network unravelled. Julien Leclerc reported that it was at one
of these safe houses that by chance the police surprised and caught
Gaston Troche eight leagues from Paris carrying correspondence
to Georges from the coast. Other accounts, following the *Moniteur*,
state that they picked up the Troches in Eu on 2 February, but
Leclerc probably knew the truth, and he dated his own problems
from that event.[16] Leclerc's account rings true, because Réal's
police instantly learned that another landing was imminent, and
that is what spurred Bonaparte to send Savary with Troche at
top speed in the direction of Biville, followed by a wagonload of
Gendarmes d'Elite.[17]

It was perhaps Querelle who led the police on 8 February to
search the Cloche d'Or, the Golden Bell, Denand's wine shop in

the rue du Bac, but it was an established royalist haunt and might well have been under routine suspicion. Two of Cadoudal's men, Yves Lagrimaudière and Jean Mérille, were in the wine shop at the time, and Louis Picot happened to turn up at Denand's door just as the police were searching the place: Lagrimaudière rapped on the counter to warn him, Picot saw that he was about to be arrested and, in an attempt either to get away or to alert those who were behind him, he fired a pistol. Raoul Gaillard and Joyaux were following him, but, warned by Picot's pistol shot, they disappeared into the crowd.[18] Picot was taken to the Prefecture of Police and questioned by Dubois and his more violent colleagues. When bribery failed to move him he was tortured and came out with a mixture of truth and fantasy.[19]

Meanwhile, the piece in the *Moniteur* about Querelle's disclosures had inspired an anonymous letter to Consul Lebrun informing him that a gentleman named Bouvet de Lozier was receiving various suspicious and locally unfamiliar visitors at his house, giving the address of his mistress in the rue Saint-Sauveur. The police were busy ransacking the place for papers on 9 February when Bouvet himself came in, so they arrested him, and they had only just removed him when a woman arrived with a note inviting Bouvet to a secret rendezvous in the rue Saintonge. The police went instead and arrested Coster de Saint-Victor and the bomb-maker Michel Roger.[20]

Cadoudal had moved back to the rue du Puits-de-l'Ermite, from where Raoul sent his old friend and hostess Catherine Osvalt, with a message for Bouvet de Lozier signed Saint-Vincent, inviting him to a meeting. Once again, the police were waiting in ambush, and she was arrested the moment she entered. After waiting some hours for her to return the conspirators fled from her house in the night.

Twenty-four hours after leaving Paris, Savary arrived at Dieppe, where the coast guards told him that an enemy cutter was hovering off Le Tréport in very rough seas. Savary banned vessels from leaving the ports of Dieppe and Le Tréport to try to prevent anybody warning the British that he was waiting for it.[21] Gaston Troche explained that the cutter was trying to hold a position from which she could reach the foot of the cliff in a single tack, and so Savary and his gendarmes set out for Biville in disguise, from where Troche guided them to the cottage where parties that had been landed first refreshed themselves.

Troche, so he claimed, had only just learned that he had been working for potential assassins, and was doing his best to atone for his capital crime by helping Savary. From the garden Savary peered through the cottage window and saw wine and pies laid out on a table, but Troche cautioned him that the tide was about to ebb and if the conspirators did not arrive soon they could not come that day, because the rock could only be approached at high tide when enough water covered the reefs. Savary spoke to the sailor's wife, who took him for a royalist, and then strode with Troche through snow towards the cliff with a bitter wind driving into their faces across the open fields. They heard someone coming, but when the gendarmes were poised to leap out from hiding, they saw only the boy Pageot coming from the cliff. He told Troche and Savary that the surf was running too high for the boat to come in, and the crew had said they would return next day; they had been trying to land for the past three nights but the sea had always been too rough.

Savary spent the night at the cottage and walked with Troche through the snow down to the cliff's edge next morning. The cutter bore away before dawn but returned at dusk, taking its station from a signal tower on the height above the deep valley at the end of which hung the rope for scaling the cliff. For the next week Savary's gendarmes lay in ambush on the coast from Biville to Tocqueville waiting for a landing, but the sea continued to run too high. Some of them spent more than thirty hours on the track of a fat curate and a thin estate manager in the belief that they were Georges and Joyaux.[22]

Since landing Pichegru on 16 January John Wesley Wright had been agitated, and angrily demanding vessels from Admiral Keith who still did not know what he wanted them for and resented being kept in the dark. 'Here is Captain Wright returned', Keith wrote to Markham; 'he seems not satisfied, and writes in a style not to be understood. As his correspondence is of a private nature, I send it to Lord St. V – he is a cabinet minister and can act while knowing I am ready to do anything Wright wants short of placing the whole squadron at his disposal.' On 23 January Keith added:

> Captain Wright has two of the largest cutters and seems content, but he wanted a power to direct any ships or vessels on the station at pleasure. He shall want for nothing if he will ask, but he cadgels [a Scottish dialect word meaning 'is closely involved with' in the sense of 'conspires'] with General Smith and the colonel at Deal, added to the old father at Dover; they are all mad with vanity, and hold no terms in their abuse of all such as do not hold up their nonsense, to call it by no worse name.[23]

Soon after this Wright's new brig *Vincejo* was ready for sea and he set out with the sloop *Bonetta* in company. The muster book of the *Vincejo* does not survive, but *Bonetta*'s reveals that she was carrying twenty-three French officer supernumeraries who came aboard from the *Fox* cutter on 11 February and were discharged at Guernsey on 20 March. These must have been more of Cadoudal's officers from the camp at Romsey, although the names were false and it is impossible to know whether a Bourbon prince had embarked. It does seem certain, however, that a large reinforcement to Georges's band was meant to have landed in early February, and this implies that the '*coup essentiel*' was imminent. The *Moniteur* of 29 February reported that on the 25th the British luggers commanded by Wright had approached the cliff at Biville but in the evening a frigate joined them and signalled them to come away, which may have been true. On 4 March Pierre-Marie Poix made the signal of 'no further hope' to the British cruiser off Le Tréport and she promptly disappeared from sight. The same night, according to police agents, rockets had been set off in the Bresle valley and travellers had been reported moving by night through the forests of Eu.[24]

On 6 March Keith wrote:

> I have been obliged to write Lord St. Vincent to-day, as Captain Wright's correspondence is all a cabinet secret ... after being five weeks in the Downs, he has discovered all the vessels attached to that service are unfit, and goes about Deal and Dover threatening me with the secretary of state and signifying the admiralty must do as he pleases ... If his services are indeed necessary I wish the secretary of state would take up some vessels for him, for he is my torment.[25]

The same day the Admiralty instructed Admiral Patton at Deal that as soon as either *Bonetta* or *Vincejo*, the sloops with the French officers on board, appeared in the Downs, he was to send Captain Wright to London for further orders, and this message probably indicates the moment when the British learned that Biville and Le Tréport were no longer safe.[26]

Savary, however, had moved quickly on to Le Tréport and, as Leclerc subsequently reported, made many arrests, 'notably of the signals officer who delivered the coastal signals to us and of the proprietor of the oyster park whose cabin was our point of communication in the bay of Tréport'. Leclerc and Poix, the agents for the correspondence, were not unduly alarmed, as 'we had very few connections with the Troches and thought the arrests were purely to do with the conspiracy', as indeed they were. The 'signals officer' (in reality an employee of the inspector of signals – Jacques-Joseph Duponchel, who also worked as a schoolmaster) and the oyster park guardian, Jean Antoine Gallien, were released and their three principal sailors had not been troubled. 'On 13 February two of these sailors told us at Abbeville all that had been going on,' Leclerc wrote. 'Their conduct raised no suspicions especially as they had served us faithfully in the same capacity during the last war.'[27]

Leclerc later suspected that the fishermen had betrayed him, but they may have been followed. It seems that it was the schoolmaster who had sold the naval signals who was the first to crack; through him Savary captured three undelivered packages in the hands of the fishermen, who admitted having previously delivered one package to an English boat, others having been burned; and he sought to track down the two returned *émigrés* who had sent the packages to the fishermen.[28] At three o'clock in the morning of 15 February his gendarmes surrounded the house in Abbeville in which Leclerc and Poix were sleeping and two neighbouring ones. 'We were on our guard and noticed immediately,' wrote Leclerc. They climbed over a series of garden walls – one forty feet high – to another part of the town and managed to get into the street unnoticed. A neighbour pointed out their ladder to the police next day. They left town by the Rouen gate 'the keeper of which was on our side', and went to a village where they had trusty friends.

From there next morning Leclerc sent Poix to Abbeville to discover the extent of their problems. He learned that an hour after their escape the door of their house had been forced and their hosts, intimidated and maltreated, had been feeble enough to reveal the place where their papers were hidden, with ciphers, codenames and funds.

In reality, Savary's gendarmes had announced to André Dumont, the deeply republican sub-prefect of Abbeville, at two o'clock in the morning that they were about to make arrests, and then returned at five to report their failure. Dumont then took over, but ran into considerable difficulty locating the documents;

it was only after long interrogations, fruitless searches and the application of threats and tricks that Leclerc's landlady Catherine Denis remembered that her servant had once told her of hearing hammering upstairs, and that Leclerc had then prevented her from entering the attic. Even then, it took time to locate the hiding place Leclerc had made under the floorboards in which Dumont eventually found Leclerc's correspondence, accounts, money, letters of exchange, signals, codes and bottles of nitric acid. After spending the night of 16 February reading the correspondence, he sent the papers to Savary, who had already told Bonaparte that he was after the key to the cipher in which the documents he had captured were written. Dumont's discovery of the key to the codes was gold dust; he sent it off to Paris with the heaps of papers, and from these the government eventually learned a great deal.

Poix was told that the sailors had served as guides to the gendarmes, and he assumed, therefore, that they must have also handed over the despatches that had been accumulating for three weeks at Le Tréport, because of the bad weather that had prevented Captain Wright from sending people to look for them. Floored by this terrible news, Leclerc decided that they could not carry on where they were and should get out as soon as possible, so they left that night for a safe house in Saint-Omer.

There, Leclerc decided to 'send for the good Benoit to get me to England by the roundabout routes that he had so often used and to get my friend into a safe house in the Département du Nord from where he could help the afflicted and gather news on happenings in Picardy and the Boulonnais'. Poix promised that if, against all expectation, Bonaparte really tried to launch an invasion, he would go in person to the Mont d'Herquelingue south of Mont Lambert, and send off four rockets to give warning to the British cruisers.[29] At some point, he got Nymphe de Préville away from the safe house in Artois and out of the country. As she is next heard of in Münster with Delaporte, Poix probably took her to Benoit Laisné, an expert in getting people out of France, and she may even have accompanied Delaporte to Rotterdam in mid-December, where he took over the provision of finance from Lelièvre de Saint-Rémy, before being forced to flee from the police.[30]

On 19 February Dumont sealed Abbeville, rounded up everybody without a passport, and ransacked the houses connected with the fugitives. They found more or less nothing except Poix's horse at a house in Bellancourt. Dumont gave orders to intercept post to suspect addresses and picked up a letter written in invisible ink. The curate Quennehen suggested that Poix might have taken refuge at the house of Rosalie le Camus near Boulogne, and there a gendarme arrested what he took to be a girl disguised as a boy, but was in fact Préville's cousin, the real Dubuisson. Dumont traced the flight of Leclerc and Poix as far as the isolated farm of the Fontaine family at Gouy, which they surrounded with national guards, but the fugitives were long gone, or at least so he concluded at the time.[31] In fact Poix was still very much around, engaged as best he could in a solo campaign of damage limitation.

While the net was closing in around Cadoudal and the Boulogne–Abbeville spy network had been broken by Savary through a stroke of fortune, the police still had no idea of Pichegru's presence in Paris, or so they said. But on the night of 13–14 February Bouvet de Lozier declared his willingness to confess, or determined to bring down Moreau along with the royalist cause that he believed Moreau had betrayed.[32] Before or after he confessed to Pierre Réal, Bouvet either tried to kill himself or was tortured, depending whether you choose to believe Bonapartists or royalists. It is difficult to work out which interpretation might have been true, but perhaps Réal lulled the young nobleman into talking too freely and he then tried to kill himself in a fit of despairing remorse.[33] In any case, Bouvet revealed Lajolais's visit to London, Pichegru's presence in Paris, and the conspiracy between him and Moreau.

Bonaparte acted at once: on 15 February General Moncey, his top military policeman, arrested General Moreau on the bridge at Charenton as he returned from his château at Grosbois to Paris and escorted him to the Temple; Lajolais and Rolland were also arrested. Victor Couchery had been with Lajolais on the day of his arrest and knew that he had a rendezvous with Moreau's secretary Fresnières, so Couchery turned up instead and Fresnières told him what had happened to Moreau. Together with Moreau's chief of staff, General Victor Lahorie, who was also deeply implicated, Fresnières immediately fled and they escaped to Swabia.

However, it is certain that the police knew more about Pichegru's network than they admitted: what is not clear is how much and when. One Désiré Joliclerc, a childhood friend of Victor Couchery and a former colleague when they had both been teachers, was a spy for Bonaparte. He had been sent to London during the peace along with Martin Laubéypie in order to infiltrate royalist circles, and there made friends with Victor Couchery's brother Jean-Baptiste, who lodged with Pichegru, and with the royalist Etienne-François Rochelle. He left London during the peace, carrying letters from Rochelle to his mother, but it does not appear that he knew then about the plot; he was, however, very well placed to infiltrate it later when the plotters needed contacts and lodgings, and as he remained undiscovered he was able to continue to betray Couchery and Rochelle.[34]

Towards the end of February the French newspapers began to publish material that they found in London newspapers indicating that London knew about a plot in Paris. On 22 February the English-language *Argus*, then edited by Carlo Francesco Badini, editor of *Bell's Weekly Messenger* until deported in 1803, reported the printing in the *Courier de Londres* of 6–10 January of a letter to Bonaparte that included *Killing No Murder* with a dedication addressed to Bonaparte and the message that a tyrant was a ferocious beast and that it might be imprudent to kill a tyrant but it was always legal. The same edition published a letter from an Englishman supposed to have escaped from Fontainebleau which announced that Paris was in turmoil, and commented that had the Englishman only waited he might not have needed to leave France. Three days later the *Argus* noted that from what was written in the *Morning Chronicle* it was clear that the assassination of the First Consul was expected in London at any moment – that people discussed the possibility publicly at the Royal Exchange, and that Georges, Pichegru and Moreau were said to be the conspirators.[35]

On 10 February, a week before any public announcement was made, Méhée revealed the discovery of Georges's plot to Drake, saying that they had arrested a lot of people who had orders either to spark off a revolt in the Vendée or to help to assassinate Bonaparte. Counsellor of State Réal had been put in charge of investigations. Méhée claimed that the authorities had known for a long while that Georges was in Paris, because he drank too much and was better at hiding than keeping his plans secret. The police had infiltrated *chouan* circles but had allowed the plot to develop while arresting some suspects, such as Querelle, in order to get information out of them. This makes no sense: if the authorities really knew what was going on they hardly needed to interrogate Querelle to find out. Rather, the claim was thrown Drake's way in order to sow seeds of doubt and distrust between the British and their royalist allies. Méhée announced that Querelle had betrayed all their friends in Dieppe, Le Tréport, Aumale, l'Ile-Adam and Brittany, and warned Drake that anyone trying to escape by the normal route would be caught, though he might be in a position to help people escape from the Temple or the Madelonnettes. There was no hope of getting anywhere with the patriotic Réal, but it might be possible to introduce a sympathetic *commis* into his office.

On 13 February Méhée announced more arrests and a search of his own lodging outside Paris, as well as the arrest of Jean-Baptiste Dossonville (Régnier's deputy, who was another British agent planted in the police).

These two letters, which he received simultaneously on 21 February, struck Drake like thunderbolts. He instantly reported to Hawkesbury the

> account of Georges' Projects being discovered and of several of his principal Agents being seized. It is possible that your Lordship may be apprized of this most unfortunate event, but as it is probable that the French Police may have intercepted the direct communication which Georges may have had with England I cannot hesitate sending this by *estafette* [mounted courier] to Mr Jackson at Berlin requesting him to forward it to Huysum [Husum, a neutral Danish port] by an equally expeditious conveyance.[36]

On 25 February Drake instructed Méhée to come to Offenburg and from there to Munich. He told him that he had sent the information stolen from Bonaparte straight to London and wondered how much the usher would cost. He denied knowing anything about any other agencies, or about Georges, but told Méhée that if it was possible to rescue any of Georges's people he should do so and that he should print a pamphlet urging the army to free Moreau. Drake then wrote to Hawkesbury, informing him that

> J. [Jablonski *i.e.* Méhée] feels somewhat hurt that he should be kept in such profound ignorance of the Projects of the Royalists. There certainly could be no occasion to entrust him with the knowledge of these Projects but if Monsieur Bertrand had been informed of them a diversion might possibly have been created by means of Jablonowsky [*sic*] and his Associates which might

have served to occupy the first Consul's Attention in a very different direction.

Drake gave his opinion that the police had known nothing about Georges's project until they learned of it from those first arrested.

After the meetings with Moreau, Pichegru went to lodge with his old friend Henri Rolland in the rue de la Loi, but he only spent two days with Rolland because he judged the place unsafe, and indeed the presence of a guest was reported. From there he went to stay with Lajolais, but amid various arrests he didn't feel safe there either and asked Victor Couchery to look for an alternative. It was through Couchery and through the need for lodgings that the spy Désiré Joliclerc infiltrated the circle, as Couchery consulted him on the matter and he prepared lodgings for Pichegru, most of which, he said, were eventually only used by Couchery.[37] Pichegru found sanctuary for four days in the rue des Noyers as a bankrupt hiding from his creditors, but on the second day Couchery brought the alarming news that Lajolais and Moreau were in custody. On 17 February Régnier addressed the Corps Legislatif on the plot and his report on it was published. His landlady, made aware who Pichegru really was, asked him to leave, and for ten days he disappeared from view.[38] In the evening he would come out of hiding to talk to Victor Couchery or Charles-François de Rivière – once, Rivière told Desmarest, he spoke of blowing his brains out with a pistol, so disgusted was he with skulking about in hiding.[39] Finally, he took refuge with a woman he had known in Alsace and her husband, who was a businessman. Their apartment proved unsuitable, so they introduced Pichegru to their friend Leblanc, another businessman from Savoie, with a flat in the rue du Chabanais. He, unfortunately, was a 'mouchard', an informer, and once he had Pichegru safely locked in his house, he went straight to Murat to claim the 100,000-franc reward for capturing him. Whether

Joliclerc arranged this, or whether Leblanc beat Joliclerc to the prey, is impossible to know.

Leblanc returned to 39 rue du Chabanais at three o'clock in the morning of 28 February with an inspector and six policemen who pushed back the chest of drawers Pichegru had wedged against the door and threw themselves on the general before he could point his pistol. Pichegru leaped naked from his bed and pushed two of his assailants against the chimney so hard that he almost knocked them out and punched a third in the stomach so hard that he coughed blood for days. He cut his hand in warding off a knife but a gendarme finally got a pistol against his head and forced him to surrender or, according to another account, the fight was ended by 'violent pressure on the most tender part of his body, causing him to become unconscious'.[40] Wrapped in a blanket and bound, Pichegru was carried down the stairs and thrown into a cab from which he was deposited on the floor of Réal's office. After ineffectually interrogating the bundle, Réal allowed him to get dressed, and had him escorted to the Temple.

Joliclerc was now on the trail: the safe houses (or possibly the other safe houses) he had arranged for Pichegru were used by Victor Couchery, who was probably allowed to remain free until Joliclerc had located Rusillon, the Polignacs and Rivière. Armand de Polignac was captured on 29 February in the rue Saint-Denis along with Rochelle's sister; on 4 March Rivière was arrested at 8 rue des Quatre-Fils with Jules de Polignac, and on 6 March Louis Rusillon and Rochelle were arrested at their lodging.

Meanwhile, Georges Cadoudal had disappeared. Descriptions of him were pasted on the walls of Paris and prints showing the supposed appearance of the chief of the assassins in British pay were on sale and on display at all the print shops. On 29 February Prefect of Police Dubois announced that 'Georges' was still in Paris and reminded citizens that to harbour him or his accomplices was a capital crime. They were to report any suspicious persons, and he promised a reward to those who helped the police.[41] Marie Hizay, the daughter of the builder Spin's quantity surveyor, had rented a shop and a flat above it in the rue de la Montagne Sainte-Geneviève. She had installed a florist in the shop, and the room above was meant for d'Hozier but was instead given to Cadoudal, Aimé Joyaux and Louis Burban, another of his men. She also slept there and ran errands for the conspirators, to whom she was thoroughly devoted.

They stayed there from 17 February until 9 March, without going out, but the flat was small and cramped for so many and it lacked good escape routes. Eventually, Joyaux went to meet Louis Léridant, the relatively unsuspected Parisian brother of a *chouan*, to arrange for him to take them to the house of the perfumer Antoine Caron in the rue du Four. Caron was a militant royalist who had sheltered Hyde de Neuville for several weeks. His house had been used as a safe house for years and was well provided with secret hiding places. Léridant agreed to come in a cab at seven o'clock the next evening to take Georges the short distance to the rue du Four. But Léridant was being followed, and his tail, a policeman named Petit, recognised Joyaux from the wanted posters now liberally spread over the walls of Paris.

Petit followed Joyaux to the place Maubert, and, suspecting that Georges was not far away, posted officers in the place du Panthéon, and in the narrow streets around it; then he took his post outside Léridant's address in the Corderie behind the old Jacobin Club. Petit discovered next day that Léridant's fellow lodger had hired a cab for the whole of the next day; he went to the Prefecture for reinforcements and posted more inspectors in the place Maubert, where the main streets in the area converged. If cab no. 53 had been hired for Georges, as Petit guessed, they might trap him at that point. The police were told to let it pass and follow with extreme caution.

It was not until after dark, around seven o'clock, that the cab appeared in the place Maubert from the rue Galande. The police, waiting in the shadows, recognised the coachman as Léridant and noticed that only one lamp on the cab was lit. It climbed slowly up the steep rue de la Montagne Sainte-Geneviève with Petit and Destavigny, officers of the peace, and three police agents fairly close behind, hoping to arrest Georges where it stopped. Instead of stopping, the cab turned right into the rue des Amandiers. Avoiding the bright lantern light, the policemen watched Léridant climb down from the cab and disappear into a house for nearly a quarter of an hour. Then he came out, turned the cab round and mounted up again. As Léridant turned right towards the Panthéon, agent Jean-François Calliole kept close behind.

The cab crossed the place Saint-Etienne-du-Mont; then, at the corner of the rue des Sept-Voies, four figures stepped out of the shadows and one swung himself into the moving vehicle, which sped away downhill. Calliole broke into a run and, throwing aside Joyaux, Burban and Raoul Gaillard, who tried to block his path, chased the cab into the rue Saint-Etienne-des-Grès. As it entered the passage des Jacobins, policemen running in pursuit were yelling 'Stop!'

Léridant had to slow down for the sharp turn left into the rue de la Harpe, onto the place Saint-Michel, and sharp right into the rue des Fosses-Monsieur-le-Prince. He accelerated towards the rue du Four, hoping to outdistance the detectives and arrive at Caron's while out of their sight. Through the cab window Georges could see several sweating figures running as hard after them as they could and shouting. For a moment, they seemed as if they were losing the pursuit, but as Léridant drove wildly along rue des Fosses, another group of policemen ran towards him, scattering passers-by.

At the top of the rue Voltaire the fit and sprinting Calliole threw himself forward, grabbed hold of the horse's bridle, and, allowing himself to be dragged along the street, mastered the horse, which stopped, exhausted. A policeman called Etienne Rebuffet caught up with the cab just as Georges jumped out into the street. Rebuffet took one step towards Georges and the *chouan* shot him dead with one of his pistols; with the other he seriously wounded Calliole. As another policeman ran after Léridant, Georges dropped the pistols and tried to disappear into the crowd, walking up rue Voltaire to the Odéon. The rumour had spread that the quarry was Georges and crowds had gathered to watch the chase. When Petit and Destavigny ran up, panting, they thought they had lost him, but then Destavigny spotted him standing calmly in the shadows, ignored by those around him. Georges was about to slip round the corner and disappear when Petit grabbed him, but Georges still had a knife and it was only with the help of three or four civilians that the policemen eventually overpowered him, threw him to the ground and tied him up.[42]

The policemen marched Cadoudal, bound with cords, to the Prefecture off the Quai des Orfèvres. The party was surrounded by an ever-increasing, jostling, excited mob, as the rumour spread that Georges had been captured. In this once sumptuous building, fallen into decay, a place of narrow corridors and many staircases, Dubois, Desmarest and Judge Jacques-Alexis Thuriot questioned Cadoudal in an all-night session. Desmarest was surprised and impressed by Cadoudal's calm demeanour and gentle expression. He remained firm and said little, but what he said was pithy. When Thuriot reproached him for killing a married policeman with children, Cadoudal replied drily: 'You should have had me arrested by bachelors.' Failing to get much out of him, they put Cadoudal in a cell on the ground floor of the tower of the Temple. Pichegru was imprisoned opposite, separated by an antechamber in which three gendarmes stood guard night and day.

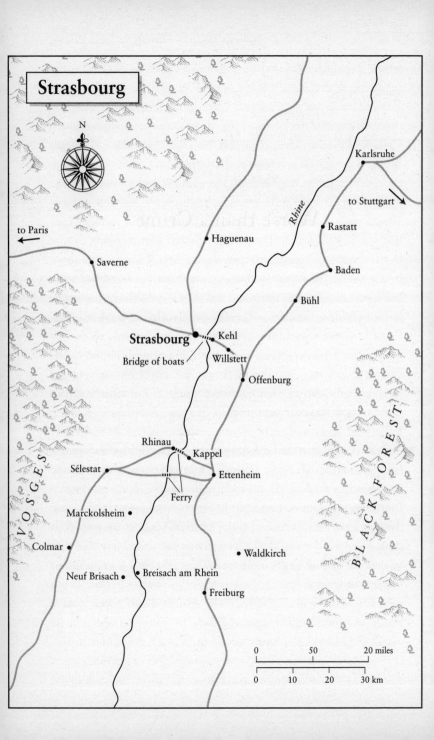

Strasbourg

N

to Paris

Saverne

Haguenau

Rhine

Karlsruhe

to Stuttgart

Rastatt

Baden

Bühl

Strasbourg   Kehl

Bridge of boats

Willstett

Offenburg

Rhinau   Kappel

Sélestat

Ettenheim

Ferry

Marckolsheim

V O S G E S

Colmar

Waldkirch

B L A C K F O R E S T

Neuf Brisach   Breisach am Rhein

Freiburg

0	50	20 miles

0	10	20	30 km

16

Worse than a Crime

The conspirators spoke of a Bourbon prince who would become the figurehead of the coup. But which prince? It was never likely to be the man then known as the comte de Lille, or 'Louis XVIII', then living at Warsaw. It could have been his younger brother the comte d'Artois, who had moved from Edinburgh to London, and was at the centre of Anglo-royalist plotting, but hitherto he had shown little appetite for personal involvement. He had two sons in their twenties: the dukes of Angoulême and Berry, both possible candidates, although Angoulême was in Warsaw. Or there was Artois's cousin the prince de Condé, descendant of Louis XIV's greatest general, but he was old and his son the duc de Bourbon had been bypassed as the family warrior by his grandson Louis-Antoine-Henri, duc d'Enghien, who was thirty-one and an experienced soldier, having fought for years in his grandfather Condé's army.

If Cadoudal and Pichegru really expected the support of a Bourbon prince from England it was probably Artois, and he might even have been hovering off the French coast in a British cruiser at the time that Savary went to ambush the royalist party that was said to be about to land. However, various indications led towards Enghien, who was popular and highly regarded by those many royalists who thought Louis XVIII too feeble and Artois too extreme and inflexible.[1]

Enghien was living in Baden, because, and probably purely because, he wanted to be close to his lover – to whom he may well have been secretly married – the princesse de Rohan-Rochefort, who happened to live very close to the French border at Ettenheim, her father's seat in the German part of his diocese as bishop of Strasbourg, in congenial hunting country.[2] After the declaration of war in May 1803 there had been rumours among royalists in England that Enghien had visited France and was willing to come to terms with the First Consul. Enghien denied this forcefully and wrote that it was his duty to prove his recognition of his debt to the British government – as it gave him his living it was only fair that he should serve it, and he offered to go to England and fight if invasion seemed imminent.[3] On the other hand, he dreamed of leading a force into France, and speculated that were Bonaparte toppled the royalists would have to act fast and he would be a rallying point:

> There are not many months when I don't receive questions from our old comrades in arms on the left bank in or out of employment who are just waiting for the point of assembly and the order to come to me and bring me their friends. I am told there is a large number of them, but I am obliged to reply that I am waiting, hoping, but I know nothing.[4]

When the Grand Conspiracy was discovered, Enghien's grandfather the prince de Condé wrote to him to assure him that he had known nothing about it.

> Probably, they judged that what has just happened wasn't my kind of thing any more than it was yours, for I was no more trusted with knowledge of the great project that has

From a design by Mr R.K. Porter.

BUONAPARTE

Massacreing Fifteen Hundred Persons at
TOULON.

This print of 1803, from a set of four showing atrocities perpetrated by Bonaparte, depicts the massacre of royalists after the siege of Toulon. In reality, Bonaparte had no part in it

The woodcut headpiece to Jean Peltier's journal, *l'Ambigu*, depicted Bonaparte as a sphinx surrounded by threatening hieroglyphs. The owls stood for *chouan* assassins and the axes beside them hinted at a death threat

Author's collection

William Cobbett in his days as francophobe patriot and loyalist, engraving by Bartolozzi, after the painting by John Raphael Smith

Mary Evans Picture Library

Samuel Taylor Coleridge in 1805. The influential republican journalist reversed his earlier pro-Bonaparte stance when the proprietor of the *Morning Post* decided to back Addington's ministry

© National Portrait Gallery, London

Gillray's *Maniac-Ravings* depicts Bonaparte's supposed tantrums at the taunts of the British press; while, according to *The Hand-Writing upon the Wall*, the First Consul had been weighed in the balance and found wanting; at almost the moment it was published the Royal Navy was landing assassins in France

Armand de Polignac was one of the royalist conspirators: his watercolour shows the interior of the farm where they spent their first night in France

Pitted against the conspirators were Joseph Fouché, soon to be reappointed Minister of Police, and his friend Pierre Réal, appointed special investigator to penetrate the 'Grand Conspiracy'

Armand de Polignac's drawing of a British boat landing the royalists at the foot of the cliffs below Biville near Le Tréport

The postcard shows the real appearance of the sheer, three-hundred-foot cliffs, with the two possible routes up from the beach with the aid of ropes marked

A Full, True and Particular Account of the Birth, Parentage, Education, Life, Character, and Behaviour, and Notorious Conduct of NAPOLEONE BUONAPARTE, the CORSICAN MONSTER, *alias* the POISONER, who is shortly expected to arrive in England, where he means to massacre, assassinate, burn, sink, and destroy. With a short Description of the various Murders, Poisonings, and Assassinations committed by him and his Gang in other Parts.

NAPOLEONE BUONAPARTE was born not only of very poor, but of very notorious Parents in the Island of Corsica; who not having wherewithal to educate their Children, having a large Family, very little Business, and no Credit, were obliged to inhabit Part of the Year upon Chesnuts and other Fruits, the common Produce of that Island. When little Bony was Twelve Years of Age, by great good Luck got into a Charity School; shortly after he was recommended to, and brought up at, one of the French King's Free Schools, at Autun, from whence he was removed to Brienne, and from thence to Paris. In return for the King's Kindness towards him in bringing him up, he being of a very vile Disposition, and given to ungodly Company, most traitorously joined and assisted Robespierre in murdering his good Benefactor. After which he gave himself up entirely to him, and received a Reward in murdering 1500 Gentlemen, Merchants, and Tradesmen, at the Town of Toulon, just after Lord Hood left that Place, and of all Days in the Year, on Christmas Day, 1793; he had them brought into the open Streets, and fired Grape Shot upon them from the Cannon's Mouth; he was so diabolically cruel, that he desired those who survived to get up and go home, which they no sooner did, than he gave Orders to have them stabbed and cut to Pieces, with Pikes, Swords, and Bayonets, in which he assisted himself. Some Time after, on the Execution of his Master, Robespierre, he was committed to the Jail at Nice, for Murder, from whence he was released by one of his Associates, named Barras, who having got into Power, engaged him to murder the People of Paris (who began to be tired of the Revolution) telling him, he would make him a General, and give him beside his cast-off Mistress, one Sukey Badharness, if he succeeded; which he did so effectually, that on the 4th of October, 1794, he slaughtered 6000 of the Citizens of Paris, firing Grape Shot on the principal Streets. All the Shops of Paris were shut for 8 Days after. After this Exploit he was made General of the Army of Italy, where he burnt several Towns to Ashes, first robbing the Inhabitants, and most dreadfully ill-using the poor defenceless Women, and all because they would not let his Gang have their Desires of them. At the Town of Lugo he cut to Pieces 1000 of the Inhabitants, and when they had even surrendered, he gave the Town to Pillage. He massacred the People of Pavia, because they would not suffer their Churches to be robbed of the Ornaments of Gold and Silver, and fine Pictures, which he afterwards took away, and sent to Paris. At Benasco he massacred 800 of the Inhabitants, and then burnt the Town to Ashes; first robbing every Body, nay, he was so cruel as to rob all the different Charities, and force the poor little Children belonging to them away. This he did in May, 1796. At Verona he stole a beautiful Diamond Necklace for his Woman Sukey Badharness, a Million of Money, several Ships of the Line, every Thing in the Arsenals, and all the naval Stores he could find, all the Pictures he could lay his Hands on, telling the Inhabitants he was their Friend, that he came to make them happy, and then he sold the Town to the best Bidder. In short, it would fill at least Ten Volumes of the Book of Martyrs to mention all the Robberies and Murders committed by him and his Gang in that unfortunate Country in the Years 1796 and 1797. On the 20th of May, 1798, he set off for Egypt, and the first place he landed at, the Town of Alexandria, he gave another Specimen of his Atrocity. He told the poor Egyptians that he came as their Friend, to relieve them from their Tyrants, and then ordered a general Massacre for Four Hours together. The poor unfortunate People flew to their mosques (the same as our Churches) but the Men, Women, old, young, Children at the Breast, all were murdered. This Monster said, after that, "there was

" no Necessity for doing this, as too men could eat " fly have taken the Town; but it was necessary," said he, "to strike Terror amongst them." This happened on the 14th Day of July, 1797. He then told the People, that he was a good Mahometan, that he had done all in his Power to destroy the Christian Religion. He had the Blasphemy to tell them that he did every Thing in the Name of their Almighty, and that he was the Envoy of God; that he had destroyed the People of Malta, because they were Christians. Some Time after he went to the Town of Jaffa, where, because they would not believe the impious and horrid Faith he uttered to them, he committed, if possible, a more hellish Transaction than he had yet done: for he desired Four Thousand Eight Hundred of the Inhabitants which he called his Prisoners, to be brought upon a Hill at a little distance from the Town, and then ordered his savage Officers and Men to fire upon them with Grape Shot, and stab them with their Bayonets till they were all killed, whilst he surveyed them at a distance through a Spy Glass, laughing and smiling all the Time.—Many of these poor loyal Turkish People were between 60 and 70 Years of Age, and had served their Sovereign many Years.—In the very same Town he poisoned 580 of his own Soldiers with Opium, only because they were ill in Bed, and could not be of any farther Use to him.—He afterwards wanted to stab our gallant Countryman Sir Sidney Smith, for having with only a handful of British Sailors and a Thousand Turks thrashed him and Ten Thousand of his Murderers for Sixty Days together, obliging them to run away from the Town of Acre, only Thirty-seven Miles from the holy City of Jerusalem (which he likewise wanted to destroy). Thanks be to God he failed, and that Heart of Oak lives to give him another good thrashing. He was so mad that he failed in stabbing Sir Sydney Smith, that he set fire to all the Corn Fields just ready for Harvest, for many Miles together, and he has threatened to do the same in Old England, if John Bull is silly enough to let him—for since he has been so mauled he cannot bear the British Nation, so he says he could murder unmolested all Mankind if it were not for them. The name of Lord Nelson drives him mad, because he took his Ships from him.—After committing numberless other massacres, particularly at Demanhour, where he gave the town to pillage, the women to his soldiers for violation, and killing 1500 of the inhabitants, he was obliged to make his escape from Egypt, in the Middle of the Night, covered with Bloody Spots; he has never been able to wash himself Clean since that Time.—He afterwards went to Paris, banished his friend Barras, and by means of fresh Murders has got himself placed in his good King's situation, whom he helped to murder, and is the most despotic, incestuous, bloody-minded Tyrant that ever disgraced Human Nature; and now quite forgets that he once lived upon chesnuts;—*a Beggar on Horseback, and he will ride to the Devil.* He raves Night and Day against Old England, because he says, we are well off, and have plenty of Trade: he is of such an envious Nature that he cannot bear to see any Body happy. He says, we exploit him and his Bandits to the whole World—that he will not let us talk about him—that he will have no Liberty of the Press, and that our Parliament Men shall not even utter a Word concerning him, for as he is haunted to death by Night and by Day with a guilty Conscience, he cannot bear that any Body should speak about him. He wants our good Old King (God bless him!) to be his Lackey, and the honest people of John Bull to be his slaves, and he threatens to murder us all, even our aged Fathers and Mothers, our Wives, and our blessed little Children, yea, even those sucking at the Breast —he says, he will assassinate us for his Amusement, as he did at many other Places, and that he will rob and plunder us from one end of the Country to the other: and to convince us that he will, he has already begun in Hanover, only because it is Part of the King's Dominions, to violate the poor Women, rob the People burn Villages and Towns, and murder the Inhabitants. Therefore let us get ready; let us stick by one another like a band of brothers: let us be preparing for the very worst, for he cometh like a Thief in the Night, seeking whom he may devour.

OLD ENGLAND FOR EVER

[footnote:] * Bony being a Great Grandfather, kept a Wine House for Porters (like our Gin-shops), and being convicted of Murder and Robbery, he died a Galley Slave at Genoa in 1786; his Wife was likewise an Accomplice, and she died in the House of Correction at Genoa in 1776—His Grandfather was a Butcher of Ajaccio, and his Grand-mother Daughter of a Journeyman Tanner at Bastia—His Father was a pettifogging Lawyer, who served and betrayed his Country by turns, during the Civil Wars. After France conquered Corsica, he was a Spy to the French Governor, and his Mother their Tool.—*What is bred in the Bone will not come out of the Flesh.*

Cox, Son, and Baylis, Printers, No. 75, Great Queen Street, Lincoln's-Inn Fields, London.—In order that Bony's Character may be known in every city, town, village, and remotest cottage in the United Dominions, Gentlemen, are requested to have copies printed in their respective places of residence, and have them well circulated, particularly on market days.

This broadsheet is one of the more outrageously mendacious examples of British propaganda designed to stir up patriotic feeling and to persuade the labouring classes that it was in their interest to oppose a French invasion

Georges Cadoudal, leader of the band that was to assassinate Bonaparte

Cadoudal's aide, Aimé-Augustin-Alexis Joyaux, organiser of the Infernal Machine plot

Charles-François de Rivière, aide to the comte d'Artois

Jean Moreau, the popular republican general, who was to persuade the army to support the coup

SIR Francis DRAKE, *fuyant de Munich, et retournant à Londres,*
avec ses Cartons, sa Correspondance, ses Encres sympathiques et ses Clefs.

(1) Aquila non Capit muscas!!!　　　NON......*Mr Drake n'est point un Gobe Mouche!!!*

just foundered than you were. But even though I wasn't in on
the secret, I can't complain about the people who undertook,
advised, commanded or permitted it. I only knew what was
made public about the departure of the actors; their object
wasn't difficult to work out, but I only knew of it positively
through the newspapers.

The comte d'Artois similarly denied involvement to his brother
Louis on 9 March. 'I have seen in the public papers the report
of the Grand Judge on the new conspiracy that the French government claims to have discovered,' he wrote, and then claimed
that most of it was fabrication by Bonaparte. 'Knowing absolutely
nothing more about anything to do with that business, I can't tell
you anything about it.'

But both of them were lying. The proof that Condé knew what
was going on can be found in a letter written to him on 14 August
1803 by the comte de Botherel, an *émigré* soldier in Britain:

All the fears of which I told your Serene Highness about
the method that would be followed in attempting a counter-
revolution were but too well-founded: it is assassination and
chouanery that have prevailed. Georges has gone off to raise the
army he claims to have, and to go and assassinate Bonaparte if
he can. I believe that it will be M. Coster who will play the role
that M. de Saint-Régent played on 3 *nivôse* with the explosion
of the *machine infernale*. He is leaving this week for Brittany. A
lot of the self-styled royalist officers have already gone there to
cooperate with his acts which they regard as meritorious.[5]

The fact was that both Condé and Enghien were ready and eager
to exploit any opportunity produced by the Grand Conspiracy,
even if they genuinely disapproved of assassination as a solution
to their problems.

Bonaparte was alerted to Enghien's presence in Baden by his now trusted spy Méhée, who had arrived at Strasbourg on 24 February in order to concert measures for the next stage of his operation to uncover Anglo-royalist machinations with Henri Shée, prefect of the Lower Rhine. Shée proposed a candidate for the role of fictional aide to the fictional Jacobin general who Méhée had convinced the British minister Drake was about to launch his own coup against Bonaparte. On 27 February Méhée went with this candidate to Offenburg in Baden, just across the Rhine from Strasbourg. He learned that various English-pensioned generals and officers from the Condé army were gathering in that town and at Freiburg; they were in contact with the duc d'Enghien, who was nearby, and were waiting for instructions from England. On return to Strasbourg he pronounced Shée's first candidate for the role of fictional aide not astute enough to fool Drake, and they settled on a second, Captain Rosey, adjutant of the 9th Line Infantry. Having reported his discoveries to the government, Méhée and Rosey left for Basel on 1 March, in order to discover the routes used by the English agents there, whose identity he had just discovered, to get people into France.[6]

Bonaparte soon discovered that the alarming news from Méhée about Condé's officers gathering on the border was true. An official in Alsace had also reported an unusual concentration of *émigrés* on the Rhine, and General Leval estimated their number at six or seven hundred. He was right: on 15 January all the Condé officers in British pay had been ordered to gather on the Rhine; the colonels of three of the four regiments of the Condé army were at Offenburg and the colonel of Enghien's regiment was with Drake at Munich. Colonel Grunstein travelled from London to instruct Enghien to concert measures with the officers at Offenburg, and to hold himself in readiness for an invasion of France at the earliest opportunity. But Enghien was not officially told about Georges's plot, for obvious reasons.[7]

Meanwhile, other indicators were pointing towards Enghien as a source of danger. On the Rhine frontier troops were loyal primarily to Moreau and Pichegru, and there had always been friction between their armies and Bonaparte's Army of Italy. The plot that had persuaded Pichegru to change sides had operated through the Austrian General Klinglin and his niece the baronne de Reich, who was based at Offenburg, seventeen miles from Strasbourg on the east side of the Rhine. The wife of General Lajolais, who was Pichegru's lover, was at Strasbourg. When Bonaparte mentioned his doubts about Enghien to Pierre Réal, now in charge of security, Réal recalled that in 1791, when the Condé family hoped to take Strasbourg and race to Paris to rescue Louis XVI, they had been based at Ettenheim, twenty miles south of Offenburg. Intercepted correspondence from the Viennese ambassador announced that Enghien was about to travel in Germany, but the cipher clerk wrote France instead of Germany. The Austrians were moving troops and the French expected a declaration of war.

Réal wrote to Shée, ordering him to find out whether the duc d'Enghien was still at Ettenheim. He sent orders to all the French ministers in Germany to redouble their vigilance, and especially to Ambassador Didelot at Stuttgart to keep a close eye on Spencer Smith and discover whether he had with him a royalist agent called Péricault. This alarm derived from the captured correspondence of the Boulogne agents to whom Ratel had announced that Smith was on his way to Stuttgart to play the role that Wickham had played in the last war – that is, as spymaster, paymaster for the Condé army, and coordinator of insurrection within France. Attention focused closely on Smith, who was likely to be organising whatever efforts were being made for a strike from the east.

Shée received Réal's order to find out whether Enghien was really at Ettenheim on 4 March and, having selected an intelligent sergeant of the gendarmerie, maréchal de logis Lamothe, sent him that very evening over the Rhine to that town, where he lodged at the Rising Sun, before returning next day to file his report. At Kehl the postmaster told him that Enghien was indeed at Ettenheim with the ex-General Dumouriez and a Colonel Grunstein, recently arrived from London. A while ago it had seemed likely that Enghien would go to England, but that was no longer on the cards. At Ettenheim Lamothe confirmed the presence of these three. He was also told of a Lieutenant Schmidt who had arrived even more recently from London. He learned that the duke often went hunting, that he had a French secretary, that he was popular in the locality and that he had recently had a lot of post from Offenburg and Freiburg.

Having fulfilled his mission Lamothe left in the early morning for Offenburg, where he learned of the presence of a large number of *émigré* officers who were said to be in British pay. The inhabitants of Baden were eager for news from France but looked forward to a change of government there, which they expected soon, and seemed to be attached to the interests of the duc d'Enghien. Most of Lamothe's report was very accurate, but either he or his informants had unfortunately misheard the name General de Thumery (lieutenant-colonel of Enghien's regiment in his grandfather Condé's army) as General Dumouriez (Charles François Dumouriez being another exiled former republican general who had changed sides and was in London advising the British government).[8]

The innkeeper warned the prince's secretary of the visit of a spy and the secretary warned the prince, but he was unmoved. Enghien was not worried about being spied on, or about having his post opened and read, because such measures would only reveal, he wrote on 9 March, his 'consistent disapprobation for underhand measures that were unworthy of the cause we serve, and had already done so much harm'. He hoped that the arrests in Paris would 'rid the cause of a heap of semi-converts who could only do great harm', which shows what the 'ultras' thought of Pichegru and Moreau.[9]

However, Bonaparte was now under the impression that General Dumouriez was at Ettenheim along with Spencer Smith, whose name had been confused with that of Enghien's companion, Lieutenant Schmidt. A report from Ambassador Didelot in Stuttgart planted this possibility in Bonaparte's mind: not only was Smith accompanied in Württemberg by the abbé Péricault, as a document captured by Savary had indicated, but he was making journeys into Baden to concert arrangements with the *émigrés*. Lamothe's report was sent on 5 March and received four days later. Bonaparte and his advisers took Dumouriez to be one of the generals that Lebourgeois and Picot had said would arrive in France and found his presence at Ettenheim thoroughly alarming. Dumouriez had commanded the French army intended to invade Britain in 1778, and it was known in France that he had recently provided the British with a history of French invasion plans for Britain; he and Pichegru were thought to be the senior royalist generals in Britain and it was expected that he would be sent to France. So, finding him reportedly at Ettenheim, Bonaparte assumed that he had come to advise Enghien and take command of the royalist forces on the eastern border. The commander of the military district and the police commissioner had also reported *émigré* soldiers gathering on the Strasbourg border. Bonaparte ordered further espionage and the arrest of the aged royalist agent, the baronne de Reich. He told off Réal and Talleyrand for not warning him that Dumouriez had moved from London to Ettenheim and that troops had been converging on Offenburg and Ettenheim.

It was on that very day, 9 March, that Georges Cadoudal was finally captured. One of the few things he said during his initial interrogation that night was that he was waiting, before taking action, for the arrival of a Bourbon prince and that prince had not yet arrived. The interrogation of other conspirators had confirmed that the trigger for the coup would be the arrival at Paris of a Bourbon prince. Most indications suggested that the conspirators expected the prince to be Artois, but apart from the fact that Artois's previous behaviour suggested that he lacked the nerve for such a bold move, the passage from England had become very difficult since the discovery of the prepared route. It was more than possible that Artois had been replaced in royalist plans by the more popular and intrepid duc d'Enghien.

Bonaparte was incensed by the latest Bourbon plans to assassinate him. Both Fouché and Talleyrand were strongly in favour of taking action; both were desperate to conserve their own positions and prevent a Bourbon restoration, and Fouché in particular was keen for Bonaparte to have royal blood on his hands.[10] 'The Bourbons believe they can spill my blood like that of animals. I shall return the terror they want to inspire in me. If I am going to have to pardon Moreau for his weakness and a kind of jealousy, I shall have the first of these princes who falls into my hands shot without pity. I shall teach them what sort of man they are dealing with.'[11]

He was backed by widespread ill-feeling against the Bourbons who, having failed to overturn the republican government through invasion or civil war, and finding power consolidated under one strong man, had resorted to assassination. There was very little sympathy for them or for the old feudal system. Bonaparte held a family council at which most were in favour of sacrificing a prince, at least if he was captured on French territory. On 10 March he held a council at the Tuileries with his fellow consuls Cambacérès and Lebrun, Réal, Murat, Régnier, Talleyrand and Fouché. Régnier explained the plot and Talleyrand, just as alarmed as Fouché at the prospect of a Bourbon restoration, proposed seizing Enghien; he said that the margrave of Baden would cooperate because he wanted the rights of the children of his second marriage recognised and had promised that *émigrés* would not be allowed to be active in his territory. Cambacérès and Régnier argued moderation, that it would be better to seize Enghien in France and then to let the law take its course. Talleyrand, backed by Fouché, pointed out that it was unlikely that Enghien would now repeat his rumoured trips across the border and that an example must be made. Cambacérès argued that it would be better to hold Enghien hostage than to kill him, and warned Bonaparte that to kill him would be to implicate himself in the crimes of the revolution, joining himself with those revolutionaries who had royal blood on their hands; but Napoleon maintained that the world would see the death of Enghien as a just reprisal for the attempts on his life, and that 'it was necessary to teach the House of Bourbon that the blows it aims at others can fall on them themselves'. He told Talleyrand to demand the expulsion of all *émigrés* from Baden: as those remaining in exile were obviously hostile to France, their expulsion was in accord with the Treaty of Lunéville.[12]

Bonaparte put Michel Ordener, commander of the horse grenadiers of the Consular Guard, in charge of the main operation to seize Enghien, Dumouriez and the Englishman with them. On Talleyrand's advice he consigned the diplomatic part of this sensitive mission to his aide Armand de Caulaincourt, by birth a nobleman whose mother had been a lady in waiting to the countess of Artois; Caulaincourt had narrowly survived the Terror and then distinguished himself in both military and diplomatic roles. Three hundred troopers of the 26th Dragoons, thirty-one gendarmes and fifteen pontoon engineers, led by Ordener, would cross the river Rhine using the ferry and five boats at Rhinau, go to Ettenheim, seize Enghien and the English emissaries, and return to Strasbourg with their prisoners. Caulaincourt with thirty gendarmes and two hundred of the 26th Dragoons was to seize the baronne de Reich and the other English spies identified by Méhée, sending patrols toward Ettenheim. Three hundred cavalry and four light guns would cross the Rhine from Strasbourg to Kehl and establish an outpost at Wilstett, while one hundred men and two guns crossed from Neuf-Brisach to ensure access to Fribourg.

At Strasbourg Caulaincourt was to seek guidance from the prefect Henri Shée and from Méhée as well as from Captain Rosey, who was to brief him on the English plots against the safety of the state and of the First Consul.[13]

On 11 March Shée received the order to seize the baronne de Reich and her papers, but he discovered that she had left Strasbourg the day after the arrest of Catherine Lajolais, so he asked the French representative in Baden to request her deportation and the magistrate at Offenburg to detain her in the meanwhile. She was arrested later that day and, after authorisation arrived from the margrave, taken to Strasbourg. Enghien learned of this, but thought he was not a target and so he went hunting, as he did every day. Before setting out that morning he sent Grunstein to find out what had happened at Offenburg, and after his return he ordered Grunstein to stay that night.

Ordener left Paris during the night of 10/11 March and reached Strasbourg on the night of 12/13 March. He consulted with Shée and others and early on 14 March they sent two German-speakers to watch Enghien's residence in order to establish his habits and identify potential problems. Enghien's servants noticed two men watching the house from the shadows and correctly identified one of them as a gendarme from Strasbourg. Louis XVIII's agent at Rhinau warned Enghien that all the boats on the left bank had been chartered and that he had seen alarming troop movements. Grunstein reported nothing untoward on the German bank and so Enghien went to sup with Charlotte de Rohan-Rochefort, who had also received warnings of inquiries about him.

On the night of 14/15 March troops seized the roads from the bridges at Kehl and Marckolsheim and the ferry at Rhinau. Schmidt and Grunstein woke at four o'clock to find the courtyard full of soldiers. According to Schmidt, the prince couldn't find the key to a secret exit, and by the time he did find it the exit had been covered; the prince and his servant Canone then went to the windows armed with double-barrelled hunting rifles ready to defend themselves. Accounts of Enghien's capture differ from each other markedly, but it was clear that resistance was futile and Enghien did not believe that he had committed any significant crime. Ordener arrested Charlotte, who was in tears, watching the scene from the window of a neighbouring house. When asked by an aide to identify the prince, she responded with more tears and told a French officer that they were taking away what she held most dear in the world.[14] Ordener arrested the marquis de Thumery, immediately appreciating the likely confusion of his name with that of Dumouriez, together with Colonel Grunstein, Lieutenant Schmidt, two former assistants of the archbishop of Strasbourg who worked with the baronne de Reich, and four of Enghien's servants. He then tried to calm agitated citizens by saying that the arrests had been agreed with their sovereign, saying the same to the margrave's Grand Huntsman, Baron Schilling.

The French seized Enghien's documents and took the prisoners to a mill outside the gates, where the mayor identified them and from where Enghien sent back for some clothes. The prince was taken to Kappel in a wagon and there crossed the river in a boat with General Ordener, who evaded his attempts to ascertain the reasons for his arrest. The prince's dog Mohiloff, a present from Charlotte, swam after them, having been kicked away from the boat.

On 15 March at Malmaison Bonaparte received a letter telling him that the operation had taken place, and the next day he assembled a military commission for a trial; he still believed that he had captured Dumouriez. Between 17 and 20 March he learned that Enghien's papers contained no proof of complicity in any plot against his life and that the person they had thought was Dumouriez was in fact de Thumery. On the other hand, Enghien's papers did show that he had offered to serve in the British army, was receiving large amounts of money from London, was using this British money to pay other *émigrés* and was hoping to march into France.[15] Josephine told her *dame du palais* Madame de Rémusat that she was in despair because Bonaparte was determined to punish Enghien, being set on taking decisive action in order to quell further conspiracies.[16] That night Enghien reached the château de Vincennes, having been moved on alone.

Urged on by Claire de Rémusat, Josephine repeatedly pleaded for clemency on the grounds that the execution would be seen in a worse light by royalists than Bonaparte realised. But realising there was little chance that he would change his mind Josephine spent much of the day in her garden planting a cedar in a newly-designed area. Napoleon's brother Joseph also argued against an execution and later claimed that Bonaparte's attitude softened. Bonaparte supplied Réal with a draft interrogation and then spent the evening calmly playing chess. Réal went to bed giving orders not to be disturbed, with the intention of starting the interrogation in the morning.[17]

Enghien was greeted at Vincennes by the *commandant d'armes*, an old Jacobin, like all the others involved in passing judgement on him. The soldiers for the execution squad were in place at midnight. It had been a foggy day, and it was now raining lightly and icy cold. Before the commission appointed to try Enghien met, Pierre Dutancourt, adjutant-major of the Gendarmes d'Élite, conducted his interrogation, during which Enghien effectively told the story of his life. He freely admitted being in English pay and that that was his sole means of subsistence. He pointed out that Ettenheim had formerly been a part of the archbishopric of Strasbourg, the territory of the cardinal de Rohan, and that was why Charlotte de Rohan was there, which was why he was there. He still thought some mistake had been made, since he was not compromised and asked for an audience with Bonaparte.

His judges sat round a long table by the fireplace with an armchair for the president; the room was dimly lit by candle sconces on the walls. The judges were the colonels of the regiments comprising the garrison of Paris. The president, Pierre-Augustin Hulin, was an old professional who had been in and out of the army for sixteen years before the revolution. He had taken part in the storming of the Bastille, went to Versailles on 6 October 1789 to fetch the King to Paris, and took part in the assault on the Tuileries on 10 August 1792; he was commander of the Foot Guards in Bonaparte's Army of Italy. Aimé Guiton, colonel of the 1st Cuirassiers, had also been in the Consular Guard; Colonel Barrois of the 96th Infantry, the son of a baker, was noted for his bravery at Marengo; Colonel Rance had also fought in the armies of Bonaparte, including the battle of the Pyramids. Napoleon's aide Savary was colonel of the Gendarmes d'Élite, then also part of the garrison, according to his own account. But he was also an aide to Bonaparte and probably saw himself (or was seen) as an enforcer, to push the affair through.[18] Dutancourt read out his examination. The commission was uncertain about the technicalities of their job and Hulin later claimed that he had wanted at least to notify Bonaparte of Enghien's request for an interview before executing him, but that Savary, who did not have much of an imagination, was in a hurry.

The commission unanimously declared Enghien guilty and condemned him to death. Being uncertain as to which laws had been broken, the commissioners didn't even fill in the blanks of the document. According to the *Moniteur*'s subsequent account, they found him guilty of carrying arms against the republic; of offering his services to the English; of having received and aided English agents; of putting himself at the head of a force of *émigrés* in English pay; of conducting correspondence in the Strasbourg area tending towards a diversionary rising favourable to the English cause; and of being involved in the conspiracy against the life of the First Consul, and preparing to enter France in case of success.

An execution squad of sixteen men marched into the castle's dry moat. For half an hour they waited, shivering in the cold, wet, dark night, before being told that a conspirator would be brought to them, who had been justly condemned to death. They complained that they couldn't see to shoot.

Until he was escorted down to the ditch Enghien remained unworried – he had not realised that his interview had ended with his condemnation. At about two o'clock in the morning of 21 March, however, a group of gendarmes led by Lieutenant Noirot and Harel, commandant of the castle of Vincennes, hurried him down the stairs of the entrance tower on the side facing the park. They halted five paces from the firing squad in front of a freshly dug grave, the gendarmes backed off quickly, and Enghien realised what was happening. Adjutant Pélé, commanding the execution squad, read the accusation and the sentence; the prince asked if he could not see and speak to Bonaparte. He was told that this had been refused. The prince asked for a priest but they told him that there was no priest either in the castle or the village. He cut a lock from his hair that Noirot promised to give to his lover Charlotte. Enghien said how dreadful it was to die at the hands of Frenchmen, Adjutant Pélé made a signal, eight men shot and the prince fell dead. The gendarmes refused to touch his clothes, which would normally have been a perk.[19]

According to Savary, who made his report in the morning, Bonaparte was astonished that the execution had already taken place, before the important interrogation by Réal that he had ordered. Réal claimed also to be thunderstruck to find that Enghien was already dead when he turned up next morning to interrogate him. It is difficult to know who was lying here. Bonaparte may have deliberately rushed the execution through, wishing to make an example of Enghien – he certainly did wish to do that, and could be impetuous, but he usually erred on the side of mercy, whatever his detractors might say. Others, such as Savary, may have thought that Bonaparte wanted Enghien executed quickly; Talleyrand or Fouché might have played a hidden role;

or it may genuinely all have been the result of miscommunication and misunderstanding.

The famous phrase, 'It was worse than a crime, it was a mistake!' is sometimes given to Fouché and sometimes to Talleyrand, but both had argued in favour of Enghien's seizure and execution. Fouché, indeed, had been particularly anxious to push it through. He fed Bonaparte's fears and exaggerated the evidence against Enghien, assuring Bonaparte that he would find compromising evidence in his papers. He wanted Bonaparte to have Bourbon blood on his hands to get him out of the hands of the 'royalists' at his court, to make sure that there was absolutely no chance that he could ever play the role of Monck and reintroduce the 'legitimate' royal family.[20]

However it came about, Bonaparte had taken the decisive action that he hoped would put a final end to all conspiracies by showing the Bourbons that if they thought they could kill him, he could also kill them. He had sent out a signal and it worked: the death of Enghien put an end to Bourbon plotting against Bonaparte's life.[21]

At first, British propaganda made very little of the 'murder' of the duc d'Enghien, and it was not until early June that a single caricature appeared; published by Samuel Fores, it showed Enghien tied to a tree by night with Bonaparte stabbing him to death. At about the same time the government paid for the printing of the abbé Bouven's *Eloge funèbre de S. A. S. Mr le duc d'Enghien*, of which some copies reached France.[22] In later years Enghien's death became one of the central crimes of Napoleon's black legend, but at the time of his execution the publicists and their paymasters were perhaps too shocked at the multiple disasters unfolding around them to be sure of the right strategy for counter-attack.

17

The Eagle Does Not Catch Flies

The same document that led Bonaparte into the mistaken belief that Spencer Smith was at Ettenheim plotting with Enghien, also gave the British government the first hint that some of its secret communications might have been exposed. In a letter of 26 December 1803 Justin Ratel had told Julien Leclerc that Spencer Smith was going to Stuttgart to take on the role formerly performed by Wickham, coordinating efforts towards regime change in France. This document having been captured by Savary and decoded, the *Moniteur* published on 23 February 1804 a denunciation of Smith as a spymaster in succession to Wickham:

> Mr Spencer Smith, who was English Minister at Constantinople, has been named minister of His Britannic Majesty at Stuttgart. This promotion would seem to be a strange fall if one didn't know that the mission of Mr Spencer Smith extended further than the relations of Great Britain with the Elector. It is entirely related to operations of spying, corruption and plots. Mr Spencer Smith has thus replaced Mr Wickham. England could not find a man more worthy of its confidence for such services. Nature has equipped him with the feelings and

disposition necessary for such a shameful mission. However, the First Consul might ask one day whether the rights of man permit England to maintain in a political guise at Munich and Stuttgart, agents of espionage, corruption and plotting.

On 8 March Jean Peltier wrote to the Foreign Office enclosing this extract from the *Moniteur*. The fact that Drake at Munich was also mentioned might have rung alarm bells in the Foreign Office had they not been reeling from successive revelations of the discovery of conspirators at Paris, and the arrest of Moreau and Pichegru.[1]

In Munich Francis Drake still remained blissfully unaware that he had any problem to contend with. Méhée avoided his summons to see him by pretending that he had been sent by his committee on a mission to Holland and promised that he would instead send to Drake the aide de camp of their tame general in order to concert plans for their insurrection. His emissary, Captain Rosey of the Strasbourg garrison, was given his instructions (to appear suitably Jacobinical) and arrived at Munich on 7 March, as Drake announced to Hawkesbury next morning, saying that if, on reflection, this still seemed to him to be one of those cases foreseen in his instructions where he should act on his own authority

I shall employ all the Means which are within my Power to enable the Royalist Party in France to avail themselves of this favourable conjuncture for liberating their Adherents and prosecuting their own Plans, and Your Lordship may perhaps think fit to apprize their Friends in England of the Circumstances in order that they may be prepared to take Advantage of it for which purpose I shall forward this by Estafette to Berlin that no time may be lost.

At the same time Drake warned Hawkesbury that his Russian colleagues had told him that they believed that 'the French

Government obtained a knowledge of the late Conspiracy through the Means of the Counter Police established in London by M. Talleyrand'. On receipt in London this warning about counter-police was taken seriously – annotated in pencil 'it is very important to set about discovering if this really exists'.[2]

Next day Rosey met Drake and put forward his plan: Besançon, Auxonne, Dijon, Macon and the surrounding territory as far as Auxerre would be seized by the general, and the sections would rise in Paris and free Moreau, who was not guilty but was being persecuted by Bonaparte. After asking some questions and thinking for a moment, Drake got out a map to find the town in Germany best suited to provide support. He spoke of Pichegru but insisted that neither he nor Cadoudal was in Paris, and eventually offered his warm support now that he had a clear idea of the plan and the general's eagerness for action, urging them to take Huningue and the citadel of Strasbourg. He gave Rosey a long letter of instruction and advice, written in invisible ink. Drake was satisfied that the emissary had been duped and would fall in with the plan to turn Jacobin measures to the benefit of the royalists, telling Hawkesbury: 'the Emissary sent to me is a violent Republican: but though he is thoroughly informed of the preliminary Measures which are intended to be pursued he is not in possession of the real Secret of the Committee, nor has he the remotest suspicion of the ultimate and final object of the Plan.' Drake was only disappointed that he had been able to give Rosey (known to him as Lefevre) so little money – 'Mr. Lefevre took back with him about five Hundred Pounds: I could have wished to have sent about Three Thousand, but it was impossible to procure here Bills on Paris for more than Five Hundred.'[3]

On the very same day that Drake wrote this to Hawkesbury, 11 March, Napoleon in Paris had just read the last letter that Drake had sent to Méhée and sent a note to Régnier, instructing him to pass Drake's last letter to Hugues-Bernard Maret, the journalist turned statesman who now supervised the *Moniteur*, so that he could print it with the rest of Drake's correspondence, suggesting that he added notes to the effect that the aide was an officer from the Strasbourg garrison and the usher was an invention, there being no such person.

In England the King fell ill in February – according to the *Moniteur* on the very day that Bonaparte would have been assassinated had not things gone wrong – and from 9 March Addington's ministry was under great strain as the opposition minority grew (under Grenville, Windham and Fox). William Cobbett first considered the conspiracy at Paris in his *Weekly Political Register* for 3 to 10 March, hoping for evidence that would 'see his country and its government stand clearly acquitted of the charge of having either directly or indirectly stimulated any persons whatsoever to commit an act as atrocious as assassination'. His first thought was that if they could prove that Pichegru was in England on 15 February they were in the clear. He pointed out that it was well known on the Continent as well as in England that Pichegru was paid a salary by the government, and though he might have gone to Paris without their knowledge it would be well to prove that he was in London. For someone who had remained constantly loyal to the French monarch to kill Bonaparte might be viewed as a duty, but for Pichegru or Moreau to do it would clearly be murder.

As to us, or our government, God forbid that we, to all our other disgrace, should add that of having, in anywise, aided in the perpetration of such a deed. We have a right to kill the French, and the Consul, of course, in war, if we can: we have a right to engage Frenchmen in our cause, and to employ them in descents upon the coast, or as spies in the camps, the garrisons, or any part of the territories of the enemy: we have a right even, by the means of money or otherwise, to incite insurrections or

civil war in their country, particularly if our object be to produce, by these means, the restoration of the rightful heir to the
throne: after, however, having made peace with the Consul, and
thereby solemnly, though tacitly, acknowledged the legitimacy
of his authority, the motive of restoration adds, perhaps, little or
nothing to our rights, in this respect. At any rate, here *our* rights
end. *We* have no right to commit, or to abet, any act of violence
upon the Consul, any more than we formerly should have had
to commit, or abet, such an act upon a king of France; and,
therefore, as we are, in the French official paper, and in official
documents emanating from the government; as we are thus in
the face of the world, distinctly charged with this most base and
perfidious deed, let us hope, that his Majesty's ministers possess
both the means and the inclination to make out our justification,
for we may be assured that our silence will not be construed as
our contempt of the charge, but, as a proof of our guilt.[4]

He noted, ominously, that it had been stated in some of the
London newspapers that Pichegru was in London on the day that
the French documents declared him to have been at Paris, and that
if that was true it was easy to prove.

By the time that Cobbett's next number came out Pichegru had
been captured and it seemed clear that the ministry had known
about the plot and had possibly consented to it and encouraged
the plotters; but it was not proven that the aim of the plot was
assassination, rather than merely exciting revolt with the aim of
overturning the Consul. He was scornful of sympathy for Moreau
and of the idea that he was too honourable to be concerned in an
assassination plot. 'I have heard of an attempt to justify this plotting on the ground that Buonaparté is a troubler of the world, and
that it is impossible ever to live in peace with him. This may be
true, and I believe it is; but it forms no justification for our using
foul means against him.'[5]

On 21 March from the opposite political wing the *Morning Chronicle* demanded assurances from government that there had been no plan to assassinate Bonaparte; it waited to see what proof the French could produce.[6] Cobbett published the French official documents as they appeared, and on 24 March he repeated his demand for a clear refutation from the ministry. He pointed out that the French were claiming that bills of exchange for huge sums drawn on London had been captured on the conspirators, and that

> if this be true, the circumstance, though by no means decisive as to the fact of intended assassination, will most certainly be regarded as a proof of the participation of the British government in the conspiracy; and, unless ministers come forward with a satisfactory explanation, the intention to assassinate, will in the opinions of mankind in general, forever make part of the charge against us.

Other damning factors were that the assassination of Bonaparte had 'but a few weeks before discovery of the conspiracy, been predicted in a hand-bill posted all over London'; that 'the accomplishment of that deed' had 'been rumoured upon the Exchange' and had 'even caused a rise in the price of funds (detestable traffic!)'; and that Peltier, having been tried and convicted of 'making publications calculated to excite the people of France to assassinate the Consul', had since the rupture gone unpunished, so an 'official explanation' was needed without delay. How far the government 'after having solemnly recognised the legality of his power' might be justified in exciting insurrection against Bonaparte might be a matter of opinion, but 'with respect to assassination the unanimous voice of mankind has pronounced'.[7]

Pitt, who was in London through this period, saw the King on 7 April, exploring the possibility of a ministry that included Fox, to whom Grenville and Spencer were pledged, but found that the King refused point-blank. He left for Walmer on 11 April and returned five days later. On 19 April the Princess of Wales told Canning that the King had made up his mind to part with Addington; in a debate on 23 April the government majority was only fifty-two and on 26 April it was down to thirty-seven.

On 16 March Leclerc, who with help from the specialist escape guide Benoit had reached Varel an der Jade in neutral Oldenburg on the coast north of Holland, wrote to Julie Dupuis, who was receiving correspondence for Poix, to inform him of his safe arrival, and to Ratel in London, employing the sort of emergency code that was commonly adopted in cases where neither cipher nor invisible ink could be used, writing as an international business-man to a colleague abroad with a serious warning:

> the failure of Mr. Bouchardon & Co of which you are no doubt informed, and which unfortunately appears to be of the most deplorable extent, has also precipitated the failure of the house of Paget & Sourdet; despite the bankruptcy of the former, the latter retain the hope of keeping up their credit and continu-ing to do business. It would even seem that their hopes would not have been dashed had not some of their employees been so unworthy as to have revealed to their creditors the critical situation in which the disasters suffered by M. Bouchardon had placed them. These employees, namely Messrs Philippe and Jean of Tréport even pushed their wickedness so far as to plot the total loss of Messrs Pageret et Sourdet [*sic*] who only escaped the trap by a stroke of the greatest good fortune that it had ever pleased Divine Providence to grace them with.[8]

Nevertheless, he had to report that their whole fortune had fallen into the hands of their creditors, or rather, had been handed over to them by those with whom it had been deposited. Sourdet had left his native land while Paget had retired into the country hoping to recover some part of his fortune to enable him to continue. He wrote that he had resolved to leave Germany in order to report in person and in detail about all these failures, which could have dire consequences for the credit of Ratel's own house if prompt measures were not taken to stop the evil spreading. High tide, snow and ice had delayed him and he appealed for help in crossing to England because neutrals were presently unwilling to take Frenchmen with no papers. The Royal Navy probably sent somebody to pick him up; at any rate, he was safely in London by 23 April when he wrote full reports on what had happened.

Meanwhile efforts were launched to rescue anybody who could be rescued. On 6 March William Marsden (the new secretary of the Admiralty) instructed 'commanders of any small Cruizers ... to stand in as close to the Coast of France as may be consistent with their safety, in order to favour the escape of Generals Pichegru and Georges, or other Persons who have lately escaped from Paris'.[9] John Wright had finally been given the brig *Vincejo* and, with the Norman network in tatters, he sailed for Quiberon Bay on 10 March, taking with him his nephew and Jean-Marie Hermilly, in the hope of rescuing the conspirators. The bad weather was not helpful and on 7 April Admiral Keith wrote sarcastically: 'Here is my friend Wright run the *Vincejo* on shore and knocked her up.' Bouillon launched similar missions from Jersey, reporting on 20 March the successful landing two days earlier of a 'M Stevenot' in Normandy with a guide on a mission to help surviving conspirators out of France. Police surveillance was so intense that Stevenot found it difficult to cross France and did not reach Paris until 10 April, having made arrangements with Bouillon that he should be back at the coast between 4 and 15 April. He quickly realised that the prisoners were far too well guarded for him to have any chance of rescuing anybody and he left Paris on 4 May. When he finally reached the coast he failed to make any contact with Jersey cruisers and stayed in France until the end of the year, hiding in Brittany but visiting Paris for Napoleon's coronation. He finally succeeded in getting back to Jersey.[10]

But in Paris the arrests had continued. The perfumer Caron had provided a refuge for Burban and Joyaux until his arrest on 20 March while he was visiting someone in order to ask for the address of Bouvet de Lozier's sister. On 25 March Joyaux and two others were captured in one of Spin's hiding places in the house of the fan-painter Pierre Dubuisson. Inspector Pâques – regarded by Prefect of Police Dubois as 'my best mastiff' – approached the house at the head of a posse of policemen. Dubuisson locked the door and refused to open it while his guests hid. Pâques called a locksmith and, once inside, the police discovered items that evidently didn't belong to Dubuisson. He eventually admitted that he was lodging one individual who had gone out. Pâques thought that people were hidden in his house but could not find them.

The police were about to leave when, in order to place a sentinel, they moved a washbasin that was leaning against a wall and found that the board under it was loose. Pâques had soon exposed a hole of 30 × 15 inches; he reached in and felt an arm. Peering down he saw not only an arm but a pistol, and quickly pulled back his head; a gendarme took a stab at the arm and they fired several shots into the void without apparently injuring anyone. Pâques summoned reinforcements but more shooting did no good; he then had the brainwave of announcing to the fugitives that he had summoned the firemen in order to flood the hole. At that, the three *chouans* surrendered and climbed out. The police recovered two large loaves of bread, four bottles of wine, two roast chickens and a ham, money and English letters of exchange; Joyaux was carrying a passport signed by Lord Pelham, giving him free passage in and out of Britain.[11]

On the Sunday before Easter the authorities opened the barriers into Paris again and some of the conspirators seized the opportunity to slip away. Having caught seven *chouans* in a shoot-out near

Fougères, Bonaparte urged Régnier to discover the line of safe houses – '*gîtes*' – used by royalists travelling between Paris and Rennes and to pursue various other leads; he was taking a very personal interest in the destruction of the Anglo-royalist networks. Of the *chouans* remaining in town, they arrested the builder Spin, found hiding in a secret room in his own house, and on 31 March they finally caught Charles d'Hozier in lodgings he had occupied for two months on the third floor of no. 60 rue Saint-Martin.[12]

The Gaillard brothers and their friend Victor Deville, another Norman *chouan*, had slipped through the Porte Saint-Denis and with their *gîtes* in enemy hands they had spent a night in the forest of Montmorency. The only physical barrier between them and escape to Normandy was the river Oise. A peasant working his field near the wood of La Muette, which had been a hand-over point on the route, saw four suspicious men who claimed to be deserters looking for ways to cross the river inconspicuously. Eventually, they tried to cross by the ferry at Méry, but a gendarme demanded their papers and when they admitted they had none, put them into the ferry house, where they demanded eau-de-vie and the ferryman, citizen Eloi, who knew them, they claimed.

After trying in vain to persuade the gendarmes to let them either go on or back they escaped through the back door; a gendarme grabbed one by the collar but they drew pistols and ran into the forest. Shouting '*Au voleur*' and '*À l'assassin*' the gendarmes pursued and a number of locals joined in the chase. Shots were exchanged and Raoul, hit several times, was captured along with Armand, who went back to help him. Some accounts stated that Raoul Gaillard tried to blow his brains out, but if so, he failed; he was taken to the hospital at Pontoise where he died on 3 April. Victor Deville escaped and was given shelter by a local resident, but his presence was reported next morning and he was picked up by a patrol. If, as some accounts state, there was a fourth, he must have escaped. Bonaparte ordered Régnier to give the 11,000 francs found on Raoul and Armand Gaillard to the citizens of Mériel. A 12,000-franc reward was given to the gendarme who found d'Hozier.[13]

Méhée wrote to Drake in his guise of the general, reckoning that the time was now ripe for a rising, that Burgundy and the Jura were sure to revolt, and demanding 200,000 *livres* to get started. Méhée was now worried about timing, as he knew that Talleyrand was preparing a circular letter revealing Drake's activities to all diplomats (dated 24 March) and that Drake's correspondence was about to be published in the *Moniteur* (28 March), but he hoped (correctly as it turned out) that his emissary would get away from Munich before Drake found out what was going on. He told Drake that he had sent back his aide to deliver the plan for insurrection and collect the necessary funds, and on 25 March Rosey, 'the general's aide', returned to Munich, arriving in the evening and staying at Drake's house. Drake gave his advice, approved the aide's measures, and sent him off with 14,976 *livres* in gold to Stuttgart, promising that Spencer Smith could provide him with a much larger sum. Drake wrote to Smith next morning:

I write to you <u>by Estafette</u> to apprize you that a Person will set out from here tomorrow (Tuesday) Evening about 8 o'clock on his return to Paris by way of Stuttgard, who will make himself known to you by delivering a copy of this letter. It is to this person that I request you to deliver whatever sums you can procure from Madam Kaula, either in Louis d'Or, Ducats or draughts on Paris, <u>payable immediately</u> ... The total sum wanted is 200,000 French livres, but I shall be able to procure a part of it here. Madam Kaula's son is now making enquiries upon this point, ... I will thank you to take receipts from the Person for the Sum you may deliver to him. This person is directed to arrive at Stuttgard in the night, or at least after dark, and it will be extremely expedient that everything should be ready for him at the very moment of his Arrival that he may continue his Journey without a moment's loss of time.[14]

In a postscript Drake told Smith that the person in question was called 'Lefebre', and added: 'permit me earnestly to recommend to you the utmost Secrecy and Precautions in this Business'. Spencer Smith had been deciphering despatches just brought by King's Messenger Sylvester when 'Lefebre' arrived on 28 March in the guise of another British government courier. According to Captain Rosey, Smith greeted him coldly until he presented his credentials, and Smith then explained that he didn't feel safe in Stuttgart and only greeted strangers with his pistol in his hand. He told Rosey that he had been disconcerted by the arrest of Enghien and was most upset by the misfortune of Pichegru; he had known him, had been in on the plans, and it was his brother's lieutenant who had landed him on the coast of France. He had hoped that he would escape, but sadly it now appeared certain that he had been arrested. He asked Rosey to try to find out how Henriette de Tromelin was, as he had known her husband at Constantinople.[15] If Rosey's account can be believed, and there is plausible detail in it, this was an unimpressive display of candour from a diplomat. Smith then 'scraped together all my own ready money, all that those about me possessed; and all that my credit (employed with the utmost circumspection) could realise'.

Shée wrote to Paris saying that Rosey

has returned here and reports that Mr Drake appears demented, and still duped by the fraud employed in his regard. He has given Rozey a last reply written in sympathetic ink ... has added to this a sum of 14,976 francs in gold. Mr Smith added four Lettres de Change on Frankfort, together making a total of 128,426 Livres Tournois. This was destined for the Général supposé, who must act on England's account.[16]

Spencer Smith had been having a tough time ever since his arrival at Stuttgart. The Elector, he reported to Jackson at Berlin, seemed generally hostile, saying of Moreau: '<u>I hope the rascal will recover to carry his head under a Guillotine</u>. I know him well and shall rejoice to hear he has paid the forfeit of his crimes.'[17] In the Rhineland the Anglo-royalists found little sympathy: an *émigré* officer of the Condé army called Leinhart had written saying that he had suffered insults for being part of the conspiracy, was fearful of being seized, and wanted a passport to escape from Baden. According to Rosey, Captain Leinhart turned up at Smith's house while he was there; in fact Leinhart provided a very accurate account of what happened at Ettenheim, including the fact that the French thought they had captured General Dumouriez and Spencer Smith. Smith sent him on, writing to the British minister Brook Taylor at Cassel that he had given Captain Leinhart a passport and hoped that the courier 'Lefebre' had reached Cassel safely and expeditiously.

He wrote to Hawkesbury while still raising money for Rosey that:

I hope to be able to complete the needful twenty four hours more, and I have the Messenger Sylvester in waiting to convey the Results of my Operations to Mr Drake. I am shocked to say that the Duke d'Enghien has been doomed to death by a Court Martial. I have reason to believe that the Elector rec'd a Letter from the First Consul yesterday.

Then he told Drake:

I am going to send a trusty Person [his secretary, abbé Péricault] to Salzburg to fetch Mrs Smith and I shall direct him to call upon you coming and going. We do not feel quite safe here. I am condensing my <u>Archives</u> into the most compact form and at

the same time the most <u>innocent</u> ... and recommend the same
Precautions to your Consideration.

On 3 April he informed the court of Württemberg that news
of his wife's illness had caused him to leave that very day, but at
Augsburg he learned that Drake had left Munich and wrote to
Hawkesbury worried that 'if as is reported he has retired from his
post, I conceive the passage of a British subject thro' that country
may become unsafe'. In cipher he noted that he had left cipher N
in safe hands at Stuttgart and was about to destroy cipher O.[18]

In Munich until the very end of March, Drake was still unaware
of his impending doom. He wrote to Hawkesbury on behalf of his
journalist friend Paoli de Chagny, who had been in great distress
since his newspaper, the *Mercure de Ratisbonne*, had been closed
down by the authorities. Paoli was hoping to set up a new journal
in Altona, which, indeed, he did. Drake still did not realise that
the reason for Paoli's misfortune was that he had told Méhée that
Paoli was a tame editor in British pay and that Méhée had then
told Napoleon.

In his report to Hawkesbury, Drake explained his motives for
giving his support to Méhée's Jacobin committee: given that an
invasion or a continental war was likely and that the exemplary
punishment of the conspirators would consolidate the power of
Bonaparte, he had felt that he must help the committee to liberate Moreau, Pichegru and Cadoudal. The aide de camp (Rosey)
had explained that support for Bonaparte was exaggerated, the
congratulations to him had been cooked up under duress, he was
not really popular, there was much disaffection in the army, and
Bonaparte had few real friends. Drake

could not reasonably hope or expect to receive an answer from
your Lordship in less than eight or Ten Weeks; and it was
more than probable that, before the Expiration of that Period,

Moreau would perish or be transported; thus one great Resource upon which we relied would have been entirely cutt off, and all the Chiefs (at least) of the Royalist Party in France (upon whom we depend so much for the accomplishment of the final End which we have in View) would have perished with him.

Moreover, news of George III's illness might make Bonaparte attempt an invasion since it was so desirable to provide a distraction for him at home.

He reminded Hawkesbury 'Your Lordship is aware that the Movement will in the first Instance be (in appearance at least) Republican, and that it will wear this Mask until the grand object – the Destruction of Buonaparte's Government – is effected' before laying out the reasoning that had informed his judgement:

> The leading Principle of my Conduct and which I have all along had in View is – That no Government in France could be more hostile to us than the present, any change whatever would afford a chance at least of being favourable to the Interests of England; for even upon the supposition that such a change may not be exactly what we might wish, any change must necessarily bring with it Distractions and Divisions which cannot but weaken the Efforts of France in the present War ... – The most desirable Effect of the present Measures for the Tranquillity of Europe would doubtless be the Re-Establishment of the Bourbons Family on the Throne of France; but if this should be unattainable, any and every other Species of Government would be less dangerous than the present, because no new Government, intent as it must be in its Origin, on securing its own Existence, could display equally formidable means of aggressions.

Essentially, as no government could be worse for Britain than Bonaparte's, any change had to be for the better, however it might turn out – and, he repeated, even if the revolt got under way but ultimately failed it would have the benefit of creating civil war in France. (This was precisely the callous line of reasoning of which the French accused the British, although Drake had said nothing so explicit in his letters to his French correspondents.) The cost of this patriotic achievement would be 200,000 *livres* each week, and Drake believed that his machinations were still veiled by total secrecy, as was the Jacobin committee: 'There is every reason to conclude that the First Consul has not [the] slightest Suspicion of its Existence.'[19]

Then, on 31 March, the Elector of Bavaria's minister Montgelas sent Drake the report of the Grand Judge – a printed copy of his own letters – and told him he was no longer welcome at court.[20] Drake realised with horror and humiliation that he had been conned. He wrote to Hawkesbury attempting to shift some of the blame – 'I cannot well describe the Sensations which I felt on discovering that La Touche [Méhée] has shewn himself so utterly unworthy of the Confidence which had been placed in him upon the Suggestion and strong Recommendations of Mr Bertrand de Molleville' – and hoping that it would be possible to claim that the letters were forgeries; he didn't think that the letters could be proved to be his, as only one, and that an invitation to dinner, might have been in his hand.[21]

The Elector required him to depart and he went to Salzburg but found that he was not welcome there either. On 8 April he generously suggested to Hawkesbury that 'it may possibly be thought to be highly desirable and expedient for the interest of His Majesty's Service that the whole of my conduct in this affair should be entirely disavowed, and that it may appear that I have acted throughout wholly without any degree of authority, or sanction of my superiors.' He admitted that: 'There is one expression in one of my Letters to Prince Jablonowsky which has given me considerable uneasiness since I find that it is by some people construed into a provocation to <u>assassinate</u> the first Consul. The expression I allude to is – terrasser.' He blamed the clerk, explaining that what he wrote was 'deterrer' and that the word was wrongly copied: 'it would be absurd to say join in the chase of an animal that is ter-rassé as the very word itself implies that he already is taken'.[22] It is difficult to take this seriously, but there is evidence that Drake's proof-reading was not faultless: he was not even consistent with the codename of his 'perfidious and treacherous' correspondent, which was sometimes written 'Jablonski' and sometimes 'Jablonowski'.

The report of the Grand Judge, reinforced by Talleyrand's cir-cular letter to diplomats, was having a positive effect; almost all diplomats had responded with sympathy for Bonaparte.[23] Spencer Smith was soon also in retreat following a protest from the Elector of Württemberg and a request for his recall. Smith looked for Drake but found that he had disappeared, and, joined by Paget, went to Carlsbad in Bohemia. He sent his remaining papers to Jackson at Berlin, explaining that he had 'found it necessary to destroy all my Cyphers. I am only in possession of one, (O) which has been lent to me by Mr Wyndham.'[24]

On top of this came an anonymous pamphlet sarcastically entitled *Alliance des Jacobins de France avec le Ministère Anglais*, printed by the Imprimerie de la République in April 1804, and written in the first person by Méhée, designed to lay bare 'the despicable resorts of a political system which seems to feed on the tears and blood in which it has deluged the world since our neighbours adopted it'. Keep your gold and stop trying to buy Frenchmen, Méhée advised the British government, larding his work with moderate remarks to placate open-minded Britons and Europeans, as well as with comic observations on the English to amuse Frenchmen. Incidentally, the pamphlet demonstrated how someone like Méhée, forced by past circumstances to express unacceptable views, could be reintegrated into Bonaparte's France, in contrast to those obstinate *émigré* traitors who plotted from London to betray their native land. Méhée concluded with a resounding condemnation of the British government:

This was not just a few vile agents who can be disavowed when necessary; this was the whole British cabinet, caught red-handed, commissioning and subscribing to assassination, revolt, explosions of powder stores with the very same hand with which it caresses our friends and allies in whose homes it builds its workshop of destruction.

Passports, instructions, correspondence and money: what more do you need as a body of proof to stain this government as a barbarian nation.[25]

Méhée's account was given detailed documentary support by the two reports of Grand Judge Régnier, the second dated 11 April, which analysed what had been going on and included the full text of the correspondence.

In the House of Commons on 16 April Lord Morpeth, falling in with the line of ministerial journalists that the French allegations were trumped up and designed to divert attention away from the atrocity committed against Enghien, set up an invitation to Addington to issue an official denial, and with carefully chosen weasel words he duly denied the serious and calumnious accusations of one of the most evil and tyrannical governments ever to be established against the King, his government and the people.

Cobbett, however, remarked pointedly that Addington had not said that the letters were forgeries. Addington did, Cobbett said,

utter some very big words about the atrocious calumnies published against us by the French government; he did, in most delightful bombast, pledge his honour, and not only his honour, but that of all his colleagues, that they had neither done, nor sanctioned any thing not strictly consistent with the laws and usages of modern Europe; though he did positively declare, that ministers were not, either directly or indirectly, implicated in the transaction alluded to by Lord Morpeth (Mr. Drake's

correspondence) and they had not given instructions or authority to any one human creature for the purpose of carrying on
such a negotiation; and, though he did promise, that he would
take the strongest means of convincing the world of the purity of
the intentions of himself and the rest of his Majesty's ministers;
though the Doctor came out with all this, he did, nevertheless,
not think it prudent to deny or call in question, the *authenticity*
of Mr. Drake's letters; on the contrary, he evidently evaded that
point ... [26]

Cobbett recommended that until Addington proved that Méhée
had not been sent to Drake by Hawkesbury, and that no instructions had been given to him, people should be hesitant about
imputing blame to Drake.

At one time, British government discomfiture would have
excited caricaturists, but in the face of this government embarrassment British caricaturists were as silent as their paymasters and
minders, and for once more reticent than their French colleagues.
The French issued at least three caricatures of Drake. Two of them
formed a pair: the first depicted Drake running from Munich so
fast that his servants couldn't catch him, carrying his portfolio and
his invisible ink, and the second showed his arrival in London,
greeted by Smith, Whitworth, Pitt, Addington and the Duke
of Cambridge (recently ejected from Hanover). The other, which
was almost certainly a government commission, distributed by
the principal Paris printsellers, was a more detailed composition
in which the principal joke centred on Drake's genuine motto,
Aquila non capit muscas: The eagle does not catch flies. In French
the word for flycatcher, 'gobe-mouche', also means a fool or gull.
It was entitled *Sir Francis Drake, fleeing from Munich, and returning
to London, with his boxes, his correspondence, his invisible ink, and his
keys*; flies buzzed around Drake's mouth as he boasted, 'L'Aigle ne
prend pas les mouches; the eagle does not feed on flies', confirmed

below with the inscription, 'No, Mr Drake is not a gobe-mouche!!!'
A copy of this print was published as a frontispiece to the German
translation of Méhée's *Alliance des Jacobins*.

The British silence was not quite complete, though: the former
'Jacobin' printseller William Holland could not resist showing his
enjoyment of the affair with a couple of caricatures of which the
most revealing, published on 16 April, was *Mr Drake's Reply to his
Calumniators!!*: 'Quack! Quack!'

18

Trials and Executions

After Benoit Laisné had guided the Anglo-royalist agent Julien Leclerc on his way to Oldenburg, his lieutenant Pierre-Marie Poix returned to the Boulonnais to warn friends of the danger. There were many arrests, but only of those who had lodged Leclerc, Poix, Nymphe de Préville and Louis Delaporte. Although he had a price on his head and although Delaporte's sister and her family helped the police (at least, André Dumont, sub-prefect of Abbeville, thought they were on his side) Poix was not betrayed, and he stayed hidden near Montreuil until the end of May, gathering the reports of the agents in Boulogne, Etaples, Ambleteuse, Calais and Dunkerque, helping those who had been detained and waiting for news or help from Ratel, Leclerc or Delaporte.

However, the police investigation was gradually closing in on him. At the house of Lucie Dusouliers, a cousin of Nymphe de Préville, Dumont discovered receipts for sums paid for painting copies of the naval signals as well as paints and brushes belonging to her brother the curate Prosper Quennehen, who became a more important suspect. On 28 February Dumont interrogated the Flouets, trying to discover where the beautiful Nymphe de Préville was hiding, and found M. Flouet prepared to cooperate.

Savary required Dumont to send Quennehen and the Tréportians Philippe and Dieppois to Paris for interrogation there, and Murat ordered Dumont himself to report. He returned with copies of some of the correspondence and learned that Mme Duchâtelet rented one of her farms to Delaporte's sister, Françoise Vidor, and her husband. He summoned the family of Delaporte's sister to Abbeville for questioning and her husband Jacques Vidor, daughter Françoise and son-in-law Louis Leblond all seemed eager to help.

On 22 March, thanks to a tip-off from Leblond, Dumont intercepted a letter addressed to Julie Dupuis at Lille in the hand of Leclerc, that Poix had recently posted. Thinking that this 'Julie Dupuis' was in reality Nymphe, Dumont sent Flouet with a disguised gendarme to arrest her, but they came back with Julie Dupuis. Dumont also arrested Antoine Poix, and a little violent persuasion led to the discovery at the family farm of papers in a pot hidden under the oven and others in a straw mattress. He also had to torture Julie Dupuis before she would finally admit that she had received a letter announcing that the correspondence would in future come to her and that she had received a letter signed Seraphine Blondeau from Leclerc dated from Varel on 16 March and posted at Bremen which proved that Leclerc had left France. Julie admitted that she had known La Rose well since the time of the Terror, that he visited her occasionally, and that it was at the house of her sister Françoise Dupuis at Rimboval that Poix and Leclerc had concerted their plans.

With the treacherous help of the Vidors Dumont was now close on the heels of Pierre-Marie and Claudin Poix, but whenever he sent Leblond and disguised gendarmes to arrest them, as on 31 March at Herly, and later at Gouy and Rimboval, they had already fled. He came close at Rimboval after threats and trickery had wrung the truth from the son of Françoise Duval after his parents had remained obstinately silent, and Mme Hanot of Herly eventually admitted that Poix had actually been in her house when

Leblond led the gendarmes there to arrest him but he had fled through the barn. This would have alerted Poix to the treachery of the Vidors (even if Leblond was not playing a double game and contrived to warn him). If his own story is to be believed, Poix remained in the area for another month, setting up another recipient for the correspondence, before leaving the country. For some time, no money had come in. The police in Holland tried to arrest an agent called Boquet who had taken over from Lelièvre de Saint-Rémy as the finance man at Rotterdam, but he left his inn just before they arrived.[1]

In the Temple prison the interrogations continued, led by the regicide judge Thuriot, whom Georges Cadoudal persistently misnamed 'Tue-roi', and usually attended by Pierre Réal, who also had private conversations with Pichegru. On the morning of 6 April Pichegru was found dead in his cell with a black silk cravat tightened round his neck with a piece of firewood; he had garrotted himself, and beside him a book that he had borrowed from Réal the day before was open at a page where Seneca described the suicide of Cato. Although royalist reporters instantly accused Bonaparte of his murder, there was never any evidence to support the theory and it was not in Bonaparte's interest that he should die before the trial, despite Peltier's arguments in the *Ambigu* to the effect that Bonaparte had put paid to the highly respected general because he had no evidence against him except that he had come to Paris from London. Peltier used a very crude but effective rhetorical technique of repeating over and over in the French text the English phrase 'Pichegru was murdered'. Peltier anticipated that Moreau would meet with the same fate. Of course, this sidestepped the fact that the French already possessed the Anglo-Austrian documents that demonstrated unequivocally Pichegru's treachery on the Rhine front, never mind more recent evidence of Anglo-royalist attempts to combine the talents of Pichegru and Moreau.[2] Réal's first reaction to the news of Pichegru's death was that it had deprived Bonaparte of his 'most important piece of evidence against Moreau'.[3] William Barré simply reversed this argument and asserted that although the gendarmes who arrested him had orders to preserve Pichegru alive, the 'Corsican assassin' had afterwards realised his mistake and 'deemed it expedient to assassinate him, as the surest means to prevent him from speaking'. The method of suicide that the French report cited was obviously impossible, but Buonaparte no longer cared to take the trouble even to be plausible.[4] But if Pichegru was murdered, it is more likely that some royalist agent murdered him than that Bonaparte did. It is unlikely that Pichegru was looking forward to the trial, and this was the second time that he had led a conspiracy to the point of consummation and then vacillated, only to be discovered and thwarted by decisive action from the opposition.

Ratel and Leclerc were anxious to get the correspondence with Paris re-established, doubtless partly to justify their salaries, but also in order to find out what was going on in the French capital. Leclerc reported on 23 April that he thought it impossible to re-establish a direct coast-to-coast correspondence with northern France; it had been difficult enough before the conspiracy, given the winter weather and the obstructive navy, but since the recent catastrophe the existing watch of coast guards and gendarmes had been strengthened by patrols of regular soldiers of all arms and the countryside was infested with spies, so that you were highly likely to be betrayed by one of your minor couriers – and Holland was more or less the same. However, none of the informants in Paris or on the coast had so far been compromised, so that it should be possible to get the normal reports on Brest, Paris and the Boulonnais to a frontier town for transmission via Germany. Reports could be written in invisible ink in papers or new books for rapid transmission to the frontier in the new Velocifers (lightly built carriages which had reduced the twenty-eight-hour journey from Rouen to Paris to a mere twelve).[5] Leclerc suggested that he could place himself in Varel or somewhere similar and, as long as there was a Foreign Office postal service to and from Heligoland (a Danish island forty-three miles off the mouth of the Elbe that the British used as a base and smuggling centre even before it surrendered to them in 1807), he could get despatches there by boat, and it might be possible to use the Danish ports of Husum or Tonningen (Tönning) in summer. Leclerc reckoned that by staying longer in London he was wasting precious time and that he ought to pick up the threads of the correspondence and try to help his friends. The Monk gave him £500 of secret service money on 1 May to set the correspondence up again; by 14 July he was at Westerstede in the Duchy of Oldenburg and was soon sending back reports, having adopted the name Hachmayer. The Monk also sent £200 to sustain Delaporte and Nymphe de Préville in Münster.[6]

At the beginning of May Hawkesbury issued a circular letter, provoked by the responses of European diplomats to Talleyrand's, which Barré described as 'the scandalous and shameful conduct of the distinguished diplomatic body at Paris, or rather at the Corsican Court'.[7] Basically, European diplomats, shocked at British behaviour (or, as the British maintained, terrified by Bonaparte), had come down in favour of France. Hawkesbury denied assassination, suggested that the Drake publication had been cooked up to distract attention from the murder of the duc d'Enghien, and asserted the right of the British government to assist the French in liberating their country. The obedient *Courier* and *Times* weighed in on 1 May with condemnation of the murder of the duc, the daily crimes of the Corsican tyrant, and a reign of terror unprecedented even in the days of Robespierre.[8] Cobbett subjected the 'vulgar sophistry and commonplace recrimination' of this letter from the 'solid young minister' to merciless analysis, cheering himself with the thought that there was 'now some reason to hope, that no other state-paper will ever come from the same pen'. Five days later Addington resigned and Pitt returned to office.[9]

At about this time the *Anti-Jacobin Review* gave a summary of the events of the previous few months as it saw them: France was, as it had been for the previous hundred years at least, grasping at universal empire, and had been violating the laws of nations to an unprecedented degree. Neutral Hanover had been 'invaded, plundered, desolated, and ruined by the Corsican Usurper, under the stupid pretext that the elector was sovereign of England'. It was on the Corsican, of course, that invective was heaped: 'the Usurper has proceeded, with increased rapidity, in his career of ambition, scarcely deigning to veil his ultimate designs beneath any specious or plausive pretexts.' Knowing that Britain remained a wise and resolute enemy and might make other states realise the danger they faced, 'all his efforts have been directed to render her odious to every other state, and to create a general distrust of her object, her views, and designs', using 'every mean and pitiable art, which envy, hatred, and malice, combined with falsehood, perfidy, and fraud could devise'.

The chief 'instrument employed by this adept in the use of revolutionary weapons has been the plot ascribed to the British cabinet of not only fomenting a civil war in France, but of conspiring to assassinate the First Consul'. John Gifford was not arguing that there was no plot 'for the desirable purpose of hurling this bloody Usurper from his throne' – after all, inciting civil war in France was entirely allowed by international law – and 'it would be consummate hypocrisy in us to profess feelings which our heart disavowed, to deprecate the death of a man sinking beneath the weight of crimes, unparalleled in number and atrocity, or to say that if some loyal Frenchman were to rid the world of such a monster, we should *lament* the deed.' He admitted that a plot might have existed, 'but most certain it is, and the truth should be proclaimed to the whole world, that the British government had not the smallest participation in it, nor even any knowledge of its existence.' Gifford was not surprised that the fearful ambassadors fell in with the Consul's accusations, though he took exception, as Cobbett and Barré did, to the endorsement of the American ambassador. From a 'cursory view of the letters ascribed to Mr Drake' Gifford felt 'strongly disposed to doubt their authenticity'; they were merely being used as a pretext for another foul and atrocious deed, the murder of the duc d'Enghien, 'butchered by an Italian banditti'.[10]

Of the suspects listed by Grand Judge Régnier early in March as connected with the assassination plot, at least two dozen were still at large, and there were others abroad that he did not know about. Peltier reported on 30 March that some were beyond the reach of the Consul's claws, while eight senior officers sent to France by Cadoudal were named as still at large at the end of the year.[11] Quite a number of Cadoudal's officers, including la Haye Saint-Hilaire, did succeed in escaping to Britain. The Royal Navy was ordered to try to rescue fugitives: on 24 April Admiral Keith wrote to John Markham, 'I am going to put a gang of hands into a fast revenue cutter and try and pick up this Dieppe fellow', while St Vincent wrote that *Vincejo*'s mission was 'to rescue the valuable characters in France from the fangs of the First Consul'.[12]

On the dark and windy evening of 7 May 1804 Captain Wright and his surgeon, John Lawmont, went on shore on the Island of Houat in Quiberon Bay, off Vannes in the heartland of Georges Cadoudal's territory, where they were landing Jean-Marie Hermilly and two other royalists; one of them may have been Pierre Guillemot, one of Cadoudal's top-ranking officers, who crossed to France from England in May on a mission to try to rescue Cadoudal from prison.[13] After returning to the *Vincejo*, Wright steered with the cutter *Fox* in company towards Port-Navalo at the mouth of the Golfe du Morbihan. To the consternation of those on board the British ships, the wind fell away completely. At daylight the French spotted the two boats becalmed, and seventeen (or by French accounts five) gunboats rowed out towards them. Wright's men launched boats to tow *Vincejo* out of danger, and used oars from her sides to row her, but the crew was weak and the boat was leaky, having previously been damaged running aground, and they were caught in the flood tide which pulled them back towards the bay; they were forced to drop anchor to avoid drifting onto the Teignouse rock. His officers urged Wright to row to the faster *Fox* cutter, which was escaping, but Wright refused to leave his own vessel.

When the tide slackened, Wright tried to escape by the Teignouse passage, but the French were gaining on them, so Wright turned his broadside on the gunboats. *Vincejo* was armed only with eighteen-pounder carronades, and when the French realised how short their range was they pounded *Vincejo* from a distance with their heavier and more accurate long twenty-four-pounders until after two hours, during which time they caused many casualties, they had brought down *Vincejo*'s yards and rigging onto the carronades, dismounting three and making most others unworkable. Wright, who had himself been wounded with a grapeshot in the groin, had no choice but to surrender.

The prisoners were taken by boat to Auray, where they were kindly treated, and then by cart to Vannes. At Vannes General Julien, prefect of the Morbihan, recognised Wright as the man Sidney Smith had sent to negotiate with the French in Egypt (or in the British version he had once been a prisoner on board the *Tigre* in Syria).[14] Julien sent Wright to Paris, where he returned to the Temple to be confronted on 20 May with Querelle, Troche and Rusillon, who recognised him as the captain who had carried them to France, although when questioned at trial on 2 June Cadoudal, Rivière and others denied knowing him. Wright refused to answer any questions at all, claiming that he had been acting on the orders of his government. His 'nephew', aged thirteen, was also questioned and eventually the other officers of the *Vincejo* were also taken to Paris for interrogation, including the two other thirteen-year-old gentlemen, George Smith, nephew of Sir Sidney, and Mr Mansel, son of the Pittite Master of Trinity College, Cambridge.

Meanwhile, the trials went ahead. The trial of Cadoudal and Moreau was preceded in point of time by the trial of William Cobbett for seditious libel. Addington's government had already had enough of Cobbett's efforts on behalf of Windham and Grenville and had prosecuted him for libellous comments on their policy in Ireland the previous November and December, when he had referred to Lord Hardwicke, the Lord Lieutenant, as 'a very eminent sheep-feeder from Cambridgeshire' with 'a wooden head' and Baron Redesdale as 'a very able and strong-built chancery pleader from Lincoln's Inn'. When brought to trial on 24 May 1804 each of these phrases cost him £500, with another £500 damages awarded to another lawyer he had supposedly injured. Lord Chief Justice Ellenborough, summing up, advised the jurors that 'no man has a right to render the person or abilities of another ridiculous'. 'It has been observed', he continued, 'that it is the right of the British subject to exhibit the folly or the imbecility of the members of the government. But, gentlemen, we must confine ourselves within limits', and if in so doing 'individual feelings are violated' then 'the offence becomes the subject of *penal visitation*'. This was effectively a death-knell to the kind of caricature and satire that had flourished in the previous two decades.

But Cobbett's trial was a minor affair compared with that of Moreau, Cadoudal and the other conspirators against the life of the First Consul. This took place amid fevered excitement. A list of the brigands in British pay was posted all over Paris and many cheap portrait prints of the accused were being sold outside the court. A pamphlet war raged between Bonapartists and supporters of Moreau, who had a lot of followers, his many friends reinforced by disgruntled republicans horrified by the proclamation of the Empire, who seized on Moreau as a figurehead. It was a war in which the British were interested: on 24 March a faked letter appeared in the *Times*; supposedly sent from Moreau to Bonaparte, it invited the Consul to kill him, and add him to the pile of murdered bodies, because he would never beg for mercy or come to terms. When the French eventually published Moreau's letter of 1 March, explaining his actions to Bonaparte and asking for a rapprochement, the *Times* was somewhat embarrassed, and was forced to suggest that the letter published by the French must be a fake.[15]

During the early hours of 26 May the prisoners were transferred to the cells of the Conciergerie, close to the Palais de Justice. On 28 May the trial of Moreau, Cadoudal and forty-five others began at ten o'clock in the morning. A watercolour drawing by Armand de Polignac showed a neoclassical room, the small public galleries filled, the public floor thronged with spectators, robed lawyers in the open court, the prisoners in four rows each seated between two gendarmes. Some of Moreau's supporters were inside the court, and others outside hoped to stir up the crowd, but six thousand troops were stationed around the Palais de Justice to keep order. Ten judges replaced the jury the defendants would normally have been allowed.

First the forty-seven defendants were identified and then the charges were read, which took five hours. The questioning began next day. Cadoudal proudly proclaimed his royalism and that the goal of his mission in Paris had been to restore the Bourbons, but he responded to questioning laconically, giving nothing away; some of the others were more forthcoming; at one point General Lecourbe appeared with Moreau's four-year-old child in a bid to win sympathy for him.

The British government had ordered the agent they knew as 'L.

Smith' to try to persuade Moreau to join his partisans, break out of prison, and lead a coup against Bonaparte. Smith thought there was every chance of success: 'there was an explosion of the public mind such as had not been seen in Paris since the beginning of the Revolution' and soldiers were shouting 'Vive Moreau' as the general went from prison to the court. But he found that 'Moreau, brave in the field, is without ambition & chicken-hearted in scenes of civil contention' and would not take action. Smith sent a full report to ministers by 'a lady who risked her life to carry the voluminous account', but due to an imprudent letter written in London about the sending of Paris newspapers to George Hammond, Smith was arrested in Paris while she was in London, remained in the Temple until she got him out in 1805, and in prison in France until 1810.[16]

Observing from London, Cobbett had no sympathy for Moreau but plenty for Georges Cadoudal, whom his patrons Windham and Grenville had held in high regard. 'There is no proof that Georges and his companions meant to assassinate; and if there were, some allowance is to be made for their long state of irritation; for the sufferings they have undergone.' Bouvet de Lozier, he explained, had seven brothers, all of whom had been murdered by republicans (in reality he had one).

When the conspirators were sentenced on 10 June Georges and twenty conspirators were condemned to death. Jules de Polignac, Léridant, Rolland, the Hizay girl and Moreau were given only two years in prison, and the others were acquitted. Napoleon had realised that the evidence against Moreau was slim and had recommended clemency, but was furious that his sentence was so light, as he had no idea what to do with him. Murat (apparently) and the women of the Bonaparte family recommended leniency and Josephine and the women begged for the lives of the well-born and got them grace: Bouvet de Lozier, Armand Gaillard, Armand de Polignac, Charles-François de Rivière, Charles d'Hozier, Etienne-François Rochelle, Louis Rusillon and Frédéric Lajolais all escaped with their lives and had their sentences commuted to lengthy prison terms. Fouché advised Madame Moreau to ask permission to go to the United States, and permission was granted. Moreau left the Temple immediately, with an escort of gendarmes for Barcelona, where he embarked for America.[17]

After three days those condemned to death were taken from the Conciergerie to the Bicêtre, where they spent nearly a fortnight. Georges Cadoudal was said to have been offered a pardon by Napoleon, or at least the opportunity to ask for one with some prospect of success, but refused it, preferring to die with his followers. They returned to the Conciergerie for execution on 25 June, breakfasted on cold meat, and were confessed. In the eyes of the authorities these were hardened criminals: Joyaux, Coster de Saint-Victor and Michel Roger were all also wanted for the 3 *nivôse* bomb; eight low-born *chouans* were executed with them. They were taken off at eleven o'clock in three carts each containing four prisoners and four priests to the place de Grève in front of the Hôtel de Ville, where a guillotine had been raised on a platform at the top of wooden steps to allow a good view. Cadoudal, who insisted on being executed first, is said to have quipped: 'We wanted a king, we have made an emperor.' Their effects were sold at auction.[18]

Having set up the means for the correspondence to continue in his absence, but needing guidance and money, Pierre-Marie Poix set off for England to consult the Monk. He travelled through France and Belgium, crossed the frontier into Holland, and on 9 June was at an inn in Amersfoort when he was denounced by a servant and arrested by four soldiers. His passport was not in order, so he was imprisoned until instructions arrived from headquarters at Utrecht, the site of one of the huge invasion camps where General Marmont had built a pyramid topped by an eighteen-metre obelisk in honour of Bonaparte. Poix had not been searched, so he destroyed his compromising papers. He was taken to Utrecht, where the commanding officer accused him of being a spy and confined him in irons, hands and feet, before reporting to Paris and Boulogne, where the police recognised who Poix really was.

After he had spent forty-seven days in a cell an order arrived to send Poix to Paris. Escorted by a captain of gendarmerie and two chasseurs, he set out on 23 July. They stopped to sleep at Rotterdam, where Poix was lodged on the fourth floor of a prison by the side of the Meuse. At ten o'clock at night he was left alone and promptly used the planks of his bed and a bench to remove the bars from the window; he made his shirts and trousers into a cord and dropped from the bottom of it into a boat that formed part of the public baths. Availing himself of some work clothes, he lit his pipe and emerged on the quay disguised as a workman from the baths, passed the prison guards, and made off into town. He hid during the night in a sewer and left Rotterdam after the gates had opened, dressed as a labourer in a linen smock, smoking his pipe, with his clothes in a bag.

Having hidden in a cornfield, he begged a farmer to put him up in his barn; he told the farmer's wife that he was a conscript who had deserted from the hospital at Delft, and on the offer of some gold coins she let him stay for a fortnight, working on the farm to avoid suspicion. He asked whether anyone knew of a priest who spoke French and was directed to the curate of Vlaardingen on the Meuse. Taken to the priest, Poix asked him to hear his confession, and revealed the truth to him and all the danger he was in. The priest promised to help him and put him in a safe house in his parish. There Poix fell dangerously ill, and would have died but for the help of the priest, a doctor the priest had found, and fifty *louis* that Poix had hidden in his clothes so well that they had survived two searches by prison guards. As soon as he was fit enough to travel the priest sent him with a reliable guide to Emden, where he arrived on 14 September, and three days later he embarked in a ship bound for Hull. Thanks to adverse winds the voyage took twenty-four days and his fever returned even worse than in Holland. He gave his last two *louis d'or* to the captain.

He disembarked at Hull on 13 October, dressed in rags, seriously ill, and penniless; the customs officers and mayor thought him suspicious and locked him in a cell with common criminals. Rather than reveal who he really was, he put up with this in silence, convinced that the Monk would not leave him to suffer for long. Justin Ratel arrived five days later to release him, but his fever had grown much worse and he was delirious when he finally reached London on 22 October. By 5 November Poix was well enough to write a report of what he could remember and to make a list of those who had been detained or were in flight. Four days earlier Poix had been condemned to death in his absence by a military tribunal at Rouen, along with Julien Leclerc and Nymphe de Préville. Philippe the fixer, Duponchel the schoolmaster and Dieppois the fisherman were executed the next day.[19]

19

The Emperor Napoleon

The possibility of turning Bonaparte into the Emperor Napoleon was first discussed at a council meeting at Saint-Cloud on 13 April 1804. The idea evolved from a power struggle within Napoleon's entourage in which figures such as the counsellor of state Michel Regnaud de Saint-Jean-d'Angély were in favour of a form of hereditary constitutional monarchy, while hard-line republicans like Fouché were bitterly opposed to such a development. Despite his conviction that he alone could drive forward the recovery of France, Bonaparte himself took some convincing that becoming emperor was a good idea, but by 1804 the constitutionalists had persuaded him that this was the best way of creating a durable political system. The hereditary empire was not created to satisfy Bonaparte's political ambition or his supposedly insatiable desire for power, though Bonaparte certainly did like power, and it really did produce a constitutional monarchy of sorts, even if it contained the seeds of an autocratic system.

In the Council of State, after long and impassioned discussion, twenty counsellors voted for an Empire and seven against. The new dynasty was to be a barrier against factions and against the return of the Bourbons. In the Tribunate, where the question was also debated, tribune after tribune argued that the Empire was in accord with the principles of 1789. The Senate had in a sense been bought by the regime, but that does not mean that its desire to cement the revolution of 1789, and to institute certain safeguards to preserve what it called the 'social pact' achieved by the revolution in order to establish permanently a middle way between absolutism and chaos, was not entirely genuine.[1]

The middle way between absolutism and chaos was the settlement that the British had welcomed so wholeheartedly in 1789, and it is a sad, almost tragic, irony that at the moment that the French voted to cement a constitutional monarchy, the British rejected their initiative totally, the British government painting it as the achievement of the unbridled ambition of a tyrant and holding out for the restoration of the 'legitimate' Bourbons. 'Legitimacy' was now held to be all-important.

The Senate passed the measure overwhelmingly on 18 May 1804, voting to recognise Bonaparte not as Emperor of France, which would have meant that he owned the territory, but as Emperor of the French, which meant that the French owned the territory and he acted as their military protector, in the way that Roman emperors acted for the Senate and People of Rome. From that moment Bonaparte became Napoleon.

The title Emperor was chosen to be different from that of King, but it also carried many classical associations. The move was the direct result of the attempt to kill him, as he was the sole guarantee of the safety of the republic, and a hereditary successor was needed just in case another attempt to assassinate him succeeded. Only Britain, Sweden and Russia refused to recognise Napoleon as Emperor; Austria did so in exchange for French recognition of Francis as Emperor of Austria. Friedrich Gentz wrote that to recognise Napoleon was to 'sanction the revolution and all its doctrines', and Jean Peltier was bitterly ironic: 'Finally the farce is consummated. And on 18 May, France has proclaimed, through the organ of its senate, a little green monkey of four foot two inches, its hereditary emperor.' William Cobbett, however, admitted that 'it will certainly tend to the internal tranquillity of France, and will induce foreigners to have greater confidence in any transactions with that country,' but this was not a good thing as far as he was concerned, for although he was developing a reluctant and very qualified admiration for Napoleon, and had a high regard for loyal and principled Frenchmen such as he took Georges Cadoudal to be, he continued to regard the French in general as implacable and inveterate enemies.[2]

A huge number of petitions and letters from all over France congratulated Napoleon on his escape from the assassins and his elevation to Emperor; in what was almost a mirror image of the British loyalism of 1792–3, Fouché played the part of John Reeves in getting the ball rolling and triggering official congratulatory letters, but there were so many unofficial letters expressing horror at the idea of losing Bonaparte to a British plot that they cannot be discounted as merely organised by a few people in his entourage. New symbols had to be found for the new regime: the eagle was chosen for its imperial associations with Rome and Charlemagne thanks to Napoleon's art adviser Vivant Denon – Napoleon had preferred a lion, his instinct reflected in a piece written by Montgaillard in March 1804 about the struggle between the lion and the whale. As a personal symbol, Cambacérès proposed the bee, which was then thought to be associated with the Merovingians and Charlemagne, as well as having positive associations with hard work and ceaseless activity for the common good. In June a partly rigged plebiscite with a 35 per cent turnout ratified the Senate's measures.

On 19 July Napoleon finally made the visit to Boulogne that had been postponed because of the threatened coup. From the suburb of Saint Léonard onward the road was lined with soldiers and sailors and a cheering multitude welcomed him. He passed under twelve triumphal arches along the rue de Bréquerecque, which was hung with flags and banners, and the houses were decked; three triumphal arches represented the bridge of Lodi, one was topped with musicians and girls who threw flowers onto the Emperor as he passed; on the quay stood an obelisk with an inscription invoking the liberty of the seas; from the forts and the warships, which were decked with flags, came a nine hundred gun salute. Napoleon rode along the beach with the ministers of war and the navy, Admiral Bruix and the camp commanders, then boarded a boat and inspected the forts of l'Heurt, du Musoir, l'Expédition (the wooden one in the harbour mouth), and La Crèche, ordering their guns to be fired in order for him to assess their range. The barges performed evolutions in sight of the British squadron off-shore, which began to aim guns at the imperial staff; as Napoleon landed at La Crèche shots threw up a shower of sand quite near him but, unperturbed, he mounted his horse and trotted up to the Tour d'Odre, where the headquarters pavilions had been built.

Early the next morning he was directing the manoeuvres of the fleet and then he inspected the harbour works; that night there was a violent storm, two small boats were wrecked and one of the larger ones narrowly escaped destruction. He remained at Boulogne until 5 August, inspecting the four divisions camped around the town at Wicardenne, Outreau, Ambleteuse and Wimereux, culminating with a review on the plateau de l'Odre followed by a reception at his pavilion.[3] On 6 August he left Boulogne to inspect the coast between Etaples and Dunkirk and the camps at Montreuil and Saint-Omer. He then made a trip to Ostend before returning to Boulogne for a grand ceremony at which he was to distribute two thousand crosses of the legion of honour. On 16 August, the day after his thirty-fifth birthday, close to Boulogne in a natural amphitheatre opening towards the cliffs, sixty regiments and twenty squadrons were drawn up in ranks in a semicircle around a platform on which stood the bronze throne of Dagobert the Merovingian, who had helped unify the Franks in the seventh century, the helmet of Bertrand de Guesclin, who led the French recovery against the English after the terrible French defeat at Poitiers, the shield of Bayard the Renaissance chivalric hero, and two hundred captured enemy colours. Behind the platform stood the new Imperial Guard.

Napoleon left his pavilion at midday, a salvo of artillery and two thousand rolling drums announced his arrival, and he took his seat on the throne, surrounded by marshals and ministers. The troops swore a Roman-style oath of loyalty to the Emperor, and then he awarded the crosses to the recipients, taking them from the glory-steeped helmet and shield in which they had been placed. A strong wind prevented the fleet from leaving port for more exercises, and the fireworks had to be postponed, but that night the Emperor entertained the legionaries outside his pavilion. He left Boulogne on 28 August to inspect the camp at Saint-Omer and then visited Charlemagne's capital Aachen on his way to Mainz, where he received the German princes.[4]

From Aachen, Talleyrand sent out another circular on 5 September, announcing that in view of Hawkesbury's doctrine that British ministers 'ought not to conspire in the country where they reside, against the laws of that country; but they are not subject to the same rules with respect to the states at which they are not accredited', the Emperor 'will not recognise the English diplomatic corps in Europe, so long as the British ministry shall not abstain from charging its ministers with any warlike agency'.[5] Cobbett, who despised Hawkesbury, accepted the logic of the French position:

> The Elector of Bavaria ordered our minister away on account of the charge preferred against him by Napoleon. Lord Hawkesbury delivers to the foreign corps diplomatic a note wherein he justifies conduct like that of which Mr. Drake was charged; whereupon Napoleon publishes an interdiction against

all our ministers in the neighbourhood of France. As we are not permitted to doubt of the 'prudence' of a doctrine promulgated by Lord Hawkesbury, we must content ourselves with the privilege of mourning its consequences.[6]

On 10 October Fouché told General Bernadotte, governor of Hanover, to arrest George Rumbold, the British representative in Hamburg, and to seize his papers. Bernadotte entrusted the operation to his aide, Nicolas-Joseph Maison, who made a personal reconnaissance of the villa at the Grindelhof, just outside the gates of Hamburg, where Rumbold lived. As aide and adviser Bernadotte gave Maison an agent sent to him by Fouché, a man called Steck (aka Charpentier), who had already undertaken the capture of a King's Messenger carrying despatches from Spencer Smith.[7]

On the night of 24/25 October French troops embarked in three boats at Harburg, a Hanoverian town on the left bank of the Elbe, and disembarked at Hamburger Berg between Altona and Hamburg. Maison and Steck went ahead with two coaches and a few soldiers, Maison having previously sent his German brother-in-law to visit Rumbold in the late afternoon to make sure that he was at home. Having posted men to prevent escape from all the doors and windows, Maison ordered Steck to announce himself as a courier from Tonningen with mail. Refusing to unlock the door, Fraser, Rumbold's servant, told Steck to deliver the parcel through the window. Checking that the troops under General Frère were close behind, Maison then broke open the door and arrested Rumbold in his bed. They tore his papers from his drawers and wrapped them up in a bed sheet. Terrified that he was about to be shot, Rumbold was instead bundled into one of the carriages, while soldiers ransacked the villa and carried off all his correspondence. According to 'a private letter from Hamburgh' cited in the not terribly trustworthy *Revolutionary Plutarch*, four people with the principal abductor General Frère spoke good

English and one was either British or American. On the previous day Rumbold had sent voluminous despatches via Husum, possibly because he had been warned, but the French seized 3000 marks in cash, just withdrawn from the bankers Thornton & Power, as well as all Rumbold's wardrobe, linen and books. He was taken across the river to Hanover, transported to Paris and confined in the Temple. After protests from the Prussian ambassador he was taken to Cherbourg and delivered to a British frigate.[8]

Fouché kept his papers, which demonstrated that Rumbold was running a spy ring in Hanover and the ports and coastal cities of north Germany, and revealed or confirmed the identities of a number of British spies. (Fouché learned, for instance, that one of Rumbold's spies had denounced Lewis Goldsmith, at that time in Warsaw, as a spy for Napoleon.) The papers proved that the *Abeille du Nord* was subsidised by the British and directed by Rumbold, and it revealed the network responsible for recruiting for the King's German Legion in Hanover. Baron d'Ompteda, based at Schwerin, had charge of the funds deposited with Thornton & Power, Count Kielmannsegge was his deputy, and they had named recruiting officers at various centres.[9]

French seizures of British diplomatic correspondence in response to real or imagined British plots had taken place either side of the arrest of Rumbold. In November the French published correspondence of June to September 1803 between Daniel and Charles Thum, who were allegedly seeking British backing through the agency of Brook Taylor, formerly Grenville's secretary and now minister at Hesse Cassel, for an uprising in the French Rhineland and the assassination of Bonaparte. Charles Thum had been arrested in March 1804 at Pfeddersheim near Worms after British diplomatic papers sent by Spencer Smith and seized by Fouché's agent Steck had supposedly exposed him.[10] Another King's Messenger called Wagstaff had his papers stolen, probably by the French, near Schwerin, the base for King's

German Legion recruiting, in November, and at about the same time the French tried to seize the banker Thornton and General Sontag, whose activities had been revealed by Rumbold's papers.

With a wave of German sympathy behind him, Napoleon made an assault on hostile journalism. Böttiger's *London und Paris* had published copies of some of Gillray's most offensive caricatures, and after a French complaint Böttiger was called to account by the Weimar domestic council in June 1804. On 9 June Duke Karl August forbade illustrations 'in which political transactions and events are ridiculed or in which named persons are mocked'. After Talleyrand ordered a copy of the journal in July, it was banned in French territory.[11] Talleyrand had Jacques Regnier's *Courier de Londres* (which enjoyed a substantial British government subsidy) banned in the Batavian Republic in August, in Hamburg in October, and in Saxony in March 1805.[12] In November 1805 the authorities in Hamburg agreed to discover and punish the editor of *Annales politiques du dix-neuvième siècle*, who turned out to be Paoli de Chagny, who had had to flee from Bavaria to Altona after Drake had been unable to pay him the promised financial support after the authorities had closed down his *Mercure de Ratisbonne*.[13]

The British government's main propaganda effort went into a second, expanded edition of *The Revolutionary Plutarch*, from which, significantly, the 'author' excluded the now embarrassing appendix reproducing *Killing No Murder*. The second edition featured a new third volume which had evidently been begun by June.[14] Sympathetic lives of Enghien, Louis XVIII and Cadoudal and a history of the war in the Vendée preceded hostile lives of half a dozen soldiers and then attacks on Consul Cambacérès, Grand Judge Régnier, Pierre Réal, Méhée, Napoleon's publicists Louis Fontanes and Marie-Joseph Blaise de Chenier, and others. Cambacérès was attacked primarily as a homosexual, for his 'unnatural debauchery', but also for granting property rights to illegitimate children and for introducing divorce for 'incompatibility of temper', which had 'caused a total dissolution in the morals of the people'.[15]

The life of Régnier stressed the prevalence of injustice in France as well as his own particular crimes – the rape of a thirteen-year-old girl prior to guillotining her lingers in the mind. The aim was to discredit the French legal system in order to prepare the ground to dismiss the report on Drake's correspondence as a 'stupid farrago of absurdity, falsehood, and forgery, the production of minds tormented by remorse for past crimes' and to cast doubt on the evidence against the plotters.

> As to Régnier's accusation and charge against the unfortunate and so barbarously murdered Duke of Enghien and General Pichegru, against Moreau, Georges, and others, they are to be received with caution and viewed with suspicion, because Buonaparte's ambition, and even safety, required at this moment a great plot. He wanted it to take away the public attention from the inefficacy of his means to invade England.

It claimed that the French police employed 132,000 spies in Paris alone (a figure that required Fouché to be paying one in six people to spy for him) while simultaneously asserting that the majority of the population of Paris was royalist.[16]

The life of Réal began with a discourse on how a pleasant face such as Réal's could disguise a foul character: 'even from viewing the picture of Napoleon Buonaparte, no man would imagine the original more atrocious than a Nero.' It sketched Réal's Jacobin background and noted his association at various times with Méhée, attributing Réal's new role as director of police to Méhée's success. This was followed in 1805 editions by a long account, 'related to the Author by persons of known probity', of the 'barbarous Police of France' in order to illustrate Réal's conduct as a police director. It claimed that around March eight thousand people had been

arrested in Paris, together with two-thirds of the population of the
Vendée. After being arrested suspects were taken by spies and by
Gendarmes d'Élite to the office of the secret police. Of this it gave
an exquisitely Gothic account:

If it was intended to inspire terror, the arrested person generally
continued shut up, chained there in what is called la Chambre
d'Enfer, or the Chamber of Hell, for 48, or even 96 hours. This
room is a large hall underground, where no light penetrates,
paved with stones, and in the wall are large iron rings, to which
the chains of the prisoner, with which his hands and feet are
bound, are fastened, and locked with a padlock. He cannot
move farther from the ring than six feet. This dark hall is large
enough to contain 150 prisoners at the same time. The only
time light is admitted into this abode of misery is when the
jailers are bringing a new victim to be chained, as they then
generally carry a lantern in their hands. Nothing but sighs and
lamentations are heard, and no consolation can be given, is
expected, or will be received, as, even here, the nearest person
to an innocent sufferer may be a *mouton*, or a spy, sent to obtain
and betray confidence. Half-a-pound of bread and two pints of
water are allowed each prisoner for each 24 hours. When carried to his first interrogatory, he does not leave the chamber of
hell by the same way he went into it, but passes through other
large subterraneous rooms, where the stench strikes one of his
senses, and blood-stained rages, instruments of torture, and
coffins, another; for these rooms are so well-lighted, that he
can see spots of blood, not only on the walls, but on the floor.
Arrived before the Secret Police Magistrate, who generally was
the barbarous Real, or the ferocious Fouché, sometimes both;
he is told that his pretended crimes have long been known to
the government, he being watched for months by the agents of
the Secret Police; of course all evasion or denial are of no other

avail than to expose himself to the rack, and certain death. If he persists in being innocent, he is carried back to the Chamber of Hell by the way that he left it, and the turnkeys shew him, en passant, the instruments of torture, explain the manner of applying them, the terrible sufferings they produce, and finish by intimating that few persons have strength enough to survive their torments.[17]

According to this account, Réal revelled in torment: Pichegru was murdered on the rack, Rolland lost the use of his leg on the rack, and Captain Wright was tortured and then had an arm and a leg removed.

In the life of Méhée the authors sought to explain the sceptical hostility of the foreign diplomatic corps, given that the correspondence that had been presented as Drake's had obviously been forged:

That Méhée was a spy first of France, and afterwards of England, is more than probable; but that his pretended correspondence with Mr. Drake, published with so much *eclat* by Bonaparte, in his official libel the Moniteur, and afterwards communicated with so much ostentation by his official libeller, Talleyrand, to the foreign diplomatic corps, are mostly forgeries, is evident from their ridiculous, absurd, and puerile content themselves ...

On the 24th of March [1804], when these pretended letters and instructions of Mr. Drake were printed, the indignation of all parties in France was great against the First Consul, for the cruel and unnecessary murder of the Duke of Enghien two days before. To divert the public attention from this crime, and to turn the public hatred from him upon England, the revolutionary assassin became a political forger. Another *coup d'etat* was besides then preparing. In four days more, or on the 28th, the slavish French Senate presented, *by orders*, an address inviting and praying their foreign tyrant, not only to change his rank and dignity, but the dynasty; to make the Corsican scoundrels, the vile and petty Buonapartes, the hereditary sovereigns of a throne which for fourteen centuries had been the hereditary property of the French Bourbons.

In comparing these epochas, it requires neither information nor genius, but common sense only, to see the internal evidence of the forgery which this publication carries with it; and those foreign ministers at Paris who looked upon it in any other light were either despicable ideots, traitors brought over by the Corsican's gold, or cowards trembling at the Corsican's bayonets.[18]

These 'despicable ideots' would probably get their just reward:

From what has happened in France during these last fifteen years, it would not be surprising if Méhée de la Touche from a known spy, were to be advanced to a place in the republican ministry; and that those foreign agents who cannot now but despise him, even in officially acknowledging his veracity, should then be obliged to dance attendance at his ante-chamber, bow at his levees, and, by his command, subscribe to future forgeries of future spies. With the exception of *some few*, all the others deserve such humiliations; because it is difficult to say which is the most disgusting to a loyal and virtuous mind, the conduct of Buonaparte, of Méhée, or of that of some members of the Foreign Diplomatic Corps at Paris.

William Vincent Barré rushed out an entire new history of the year since his last one in order to combat

the infatuation of many persons in the habit of admiring such revolutionary leaders as have acquired some sort of celebrity, through their crimes. We say *infatuation*, because persons may be infatuated with the best possible intentions.

This remark chiefly and almost exclusively applies to those foreigners who seeing the objects at a distance are but too apt to mistake fiction for reality, and thereby contact false notions and wrong opinions on men and measures.

This very detailed second part to his history, covering only 1804, and taking the story to Napoleon's coronation as Emperor, denied any connection to *The Revolutionary Plutarch* – indeed, the preface, dated 16 May 1804, was dedicated to a denial of any connection with it, in the context of a furious objection to the review of his previous work by Arthur Aikin.

Buonaparte was trying to prove that 'the English wish the ruin of the French rather than the destruction of the atrocious tyrant',[19] and this impression needed to be corrected: the English were fighting solely against the Corsican – the word 'Corsican' was constantly repeated, variously paired with despot, tyrant, upstart, imposter, artful, atrocious, insolent, odious, tiger, hyena, and also 'the lurking assassin'. In this context Barré asserted that to conspire against Buonaparte must be commendable and that the killer of Buonaparte should be rewarded. Indeed, Barré could not 'consider as guilty any of those who have been lately executed in Paris, nor even those who suffered in 1800, for having attempted to destroy Buonaparte', although he allowed that the people executed in 1800 had been rightly condemned for being guilty of killing innocent people.[20] He then produced an ingenious argument to demonstrate that the Bourbons could not possibly have had anything to do with the recent plot because it was obvious that Cadoudal and Pichegru, both being unpopular in France, were most unfit instruments to effect their restoration. Addington had insisted in April that *'the ministry had no hand, either directly nor indirectly, in the affair alluded to, and that they had never entrusted any person with such a negotiation*', and that the accusation was designed to cover the murder of the duc d'Enghien. Drake's correspondence was mostly forged, as was the correspondence of Pichegru, found on the comte d'Antraigues in 1797, and republished by the insidious Corsican. Nevertheless, he was acknowledged by foreign ambassadors.

> Thus a reputed son of an obscure lawyer in the town of Ajaccio in the island of Corsica; a revolutionary and sanguinary wretch, whose wife, mother, and sisters, have long since acquired the well-merited denomination of prostitutes, whose brothers, and other relatives, have only obtained celebrity through their horrid vices and heinous crimes; a ferocious tool of all the revolutionary jugglers, from Marat and Danton to Robespierre and Barras; a convicted assassin of Frenchmen; an atrocious robber and plunderer; a notorious imposter and hypocrite; a base and treacherous deserter from the French army in Egypt; a consummate villain, and an impudent ruffian; an acknowledged (by himself) usurper and a rebel, was qualified with the appellation of 'AUGUST' by lawful Sovereigns!!!!!
>
> ... Those Sovereigns have publicly acknowledged, that *rebellion and usurpation constitute the lawful rights to sovereignty!!!*[21]

William Cobbett continued to regret the consequences of ministerial incompetence, rejecting the line that Drake's papers were forgeries (in case anybody's perception has become blurred, it is certain that they were genuine) – 'the ministerial papers are now affecting to treat the correspondence of Mehée and Drake as a "fabrication," not recollecting, perhaps, that Lord Hawkesbury never denied its authenticity' – and reiterating the argument that in making peace with Bonaparte, Addington's ministry had already implicitly acknowledged the legitimacy of his government, effectively as fully as all governments except those of Sweden and Russia were doing now:

First to make a treaty of 'amity' with a man; solemnly to pledge yourself to discourage all attempts to disturb his government; to receive from him territories belonging to his allies; to regard these territories as your own forever; and, after all this, the moment you quarrel with him, to turn round short upon him, declare him an usurper and not entitled to the same treatment as other sovereigns or chiefs of nations; this was something which could not fail to shock the world. It does not justify the measures now taken by Buonaparté, but it gives a fatal countenance to those measures.[22]

Above all, he blamed Lord Hawkesbury for Britain's current embarrassment, for if he had been more prudent, 'the world would never have enjoyed at our expense the broad and endless laugh which has been excited by the correspondence of Mr. Drake.'[23]

It was the returned *émigré* author and publicist Louis Fontanes who recommended that Napoleon's coronation should be part of a religious ceremony. Notre Dame was chosen as the setting after the Pope had rejected Charlemagne's capital Aachen as too Protestant, and Napoleon had rejected the idea of repeating Charlemagne's journey to Rome to be crowned by the Pope as too submissive to Papal authority. Reims had unacceptable associations with traditional French royalty, but Notre Dame, cathedral of republican Paris, recently the Temple of Reason and then chief church of the Theophilanthropists, was an acceptable compromise.

Napoleon required the Pope to come to Paris to crown him, and, after tortuous negotiations, the Pope saw enough advantage for him in visiting France to outweigh the concession he was making. For Napoleon the approval of the Pope cut the ground from beneath the Bourbons and their supporters. Negotiations began in May and the Pope left Rome on 2 November, travelling slowly so that the date of the coronation had to be put back four times from 9 November to, finally, 2 December. The Pope's hopes were rewarded when on 19 November at Lyon eighty thousand people turned out to see him in pouring rain.

Buildings around the cathedral were demolished to create an open space in front and triumphal arches were created along Napoleon's route. Special costumes were designed for the event and tailors and dressmakers worked frantically to realise the designs in time. Josephine succeeded in getting herself married in a religious ceremony prior to the coronation. On 1 December Napoleon received the Senate with the results of the plebiscite on the Empire. It snowed all night and in the morning Paris was covered in a thick, white blanket. Hundreds of workers were employed clearing snow and laying sand along the route.

There were twenty thousand guests and seven hundred carriages to park; balconies along the route were rented out at exorbitant prices. Napoleon arrived in a train of twenty-five carriages escorted by six cavalry regiments.

Surrounded by the trappings of Charlemagne, in a rehearsed movement Napoleon eventually took the replica of the crown of Charlemagne from the Pope and placed it over his head, before handing it back to the Pope as he was already wearing the golden laurel.[24] He then crowned Josephine, the only queen of France to be crowned except Marie de Médicis. But France remained a republic: Napoleon was Emperor of the French and Emperor of the Republic. On 5 December Napoleon held the first distribution of the eagles in the Champ de Mars, and for the first time his soldiers swore the oath to defend their eagles.

James Gillray enjoyed this opportunity, seizing the chance to present a gloriously overblown and overdressed coronation procession, with Napoleon's train borne by obsequious European monarchs, and Josephine's by fishwives, followed by haughty republican generals with their hands bound, and Fouché leading a guard of honour of poisoners, executioners and gaolers armed with manacles and instruments of torture.

Gillray dated his print as coming out on New Year's Day 1805, and on that very same day Napoleon wrote, once again, directly to George III, proposing peace: it is most unlikely he expected his proposal to be accepted, and perhaps he only wrote to seize the opportunity to address King George, king to king, as 'Mon Frere'.[25]

20

Epilogue

After a few years had passed it occurred to the British to try to shift blame for these assassination attempts away from themselves and the Bourbons by suggesting that the Corsican tyrant had actually invented all the plots against him himself. Bizarrely enough, it fell to Lewis Goldsmith to put this idea about. After being sacked as editor of the *Argus* in February 1803 as a goodwill gesture to the British in response to the trial of Peltier, Goldsmith had a brief and not terribly successful career as a spy for Napoleon in Germany and Poland, but after returning to France he could only find drudge work as a translator. In 1809 he obtained passports and a passage to America for himself and his family, but was instead landed in England and arrested as a traitor. In prison he had a sudden change of heart and political conviction and became a publicist for the British government, writing an *Exposition of the Conduct of France towards America* (1809), and then explaining why Britain could never safely make peace with Napoleon in the magnificently scurrilous *Secret History of the Cabinet of Bonaparte* (1810), which went into six editions by March 1811.

Using the inside knowledge that he had gained working for the French government – something he admitted to quite openly in his preface – he was in a position, he claimed, to explain that the Christmas 1800 attack on Bonaparte had been a plot fabricated by Fouché in order to entrap the royalists. 'A spy was employed to engage persons of that party to meditate a conspiracy against the first Consul' and the 'infernal Machine was to be made with the approbation of the Police', but things did not go exactly as planned and the spy had to flee. The British government had nothing to do with it, of course. Having planted the idea that the bomb plot was Fouché's idea, he attributed the Grand Conspiracy to Napoleon himself, who was hoping to wipe out the Bourbons: 'Bonaparte ... formed a scheme to entice the French Princes who were in England to go to France with General Pichegru, Georges, &c. He would then have had the whole family at his mercy.'[1]

Réal and the Haute Police masterminded this plot; Réal sent Méhée to draw in British ministers; and Querelle, Lajolais and Bouvet de Lozier were all spies working for the secret police. But the plot went wrong when the ordinary police working for Prefect Dubois arrested Picot and exposed the plot prematurely. Even so, Bonaparte enjoyed some success: his mamelukes executed Enghien and strangled Pichegru in prison, and he got rid of Cadoudal.

Goldsmith's assertion that 'all the conspiracies against Bonaparte originated with himself' was given a further twist in France, where Napoleon's old friend and secretary Bourrienne, who had observed that Fouché knew more about what was going on in 1803–4 than Régnier, claimed that Fouché once actually told him: 'I created the conspiracy of Georges, of Pichegru, and of Moreau, in order to get back into the ministry'.[2]

The idea that the whole plot was invented by Bonaparte or Fouché, and that their agents provocateurs had entrapped British spies and royalist generals in a web of their own cunning devising, is at base totally implausible and can be discounted. Pierre Desmarest found the idea that the whole conspiracy was a trap organised by Bonaparte, in order to destroy Cadoudal's gang, Pichegru and

Moreau at a stroke, quite inconceivable. What government would wish or dare to run that risk? What security against murder did Bonaparte have if he deliberately chose to spend six months with bitter enemies hidden in the capital? The government had done all it could to frustrate the negotiations with Moreau, arresting Fauche-Borel and the abbé David, and though they had not prevented Lajolais from promoting negotiations between Moreau and Pichegru, the idea that he was their spy is not supported by his death on 29 September 1808 after four years in the château d'If, the prison of the man in the iron mask. The same is true of Bouvet de Lozier, who escaped from prison in 1813 and joined Louis XVIII in London, who in 1814 appointed him governor of the Ile de Réunion. He would not have been rewarded had anybody believed that he had been a traitor.[3]

However, it is equally obvious that there had been some element of successful counter-espionage and penetration of the plot. Peltier quickly reached the conclusion that Réal and Fouché had accepted an offer from Méhée to spy for them in London in an unofficial and deniable capacity but Hawkesbury's papers prove that Méhée had not been told about Cadoudal's mission.[4] Fouché doubtless obtained further insights from other spies, but although he liked people to think that he was omniscient, it is most unlikely that he knew of Cadoudal's presence in Paris prior to Querelle's revelations. His police network was nothing like as extensive or efficient as he wished it to seem in order to intimidate opponents or as his enemies liked to make out in order to depict a system of tyranny.

What Moreau was up to is also problematic. His many admirers were most reluctant to admit that he was a traitor, or that he was willing to acquiesce in the restoration of the Bourbons. In 1814 Louis XVIII paid a pension to his widow and erected a statue to him, but by then he had died fighting for the Russians against Napoleon, killed by a French cannon ball at the battle of

Dresden in 1813, having chosen Russian service ahead of leading the American forces against the British in the war of 1812. The royalists may also have believed the reports that reached London saying that Moreau had backed them further than he may really have done. Had he thrown himself at once and with zeal behind the plot it is conceivable that they might have pulled off an assassination combined with a military coup, but there is little evidence of widespread disaffection and as usual it seems that the royalists had deluded both themselves and the British government as to the strength of their support and of popular resentment against Bonaparte. Bourbon attempts to assassinate him ceased after the execution of the duc d'Enghien and without French royalist extremists providing the impulse and the instruments there were no further British attempts.

In later years the British tried to paint the execution of the duc d'Enghien as an episode that shocked Europe and led directly to the formation of the Third Coalition. The idea eventually gained widespread currency, but the French memoirs that recall the news of his death as a great shock were written after the Bourbons regained power and there is little evidence that many Frenchmen were much moved at the time. In Europe his death was barely noticed except in Russia, which had already turned against Napoleon and was preparing for war. On the other hand, most states were genuinely shocked by the revelation of the secret activities of the British, and Britain's diplomatic isolation was, for a time, alarming. The prevailing message was the French one that the British had chosen to reject Bonaparte's sincere offer of peace and had instead tried to assassinate him, a diplomatic disaster for Britain in the short term, and it was to take some years before the real Napoleon came to be seen to bear a close resemblance to the Buonaparté of British propaganda.

I have argued that Bonaparte and his friends sought in 1799–1804 to establish a viable, stable alternative to Bourbon monarchy

and it is interesting to speculate as to what might have happened
had the British government accepted Bonaparte's reiterated offers
of peace at the time that he took power in 1799, before the British
ministers had tried to assassinate him and had given him personal
reasons to hate them. Had the British accepted peace, as everybody else did, might Bonaparte's France have thrived in peace
with the world? Napoleon was no more tyrannical than any *ancien
régime* monarch, and considerably less tyrannical than most of the
regimes set up after his downfall. There is no reason to suppose
that, left to his own devices, Napoleon would have had any wish
to extend his conquests in Europe beyond France's long-sought
'natural' borders – though he might well have looked to restore
France's interests in the West and East Indies. There might eventually have been a collision between British and French interests
in their rivalry for global economic power, but for a time at least
the lion and the whale might have coexisted as rulers of their
separate spheres.

Those who, like Henry Dundas, prioritised the rivalry between
Britain and France were prepared to consider peace. The people
who considered peace out of the question were those who prioritised the restoration of the *ancien régime*. The King, the established
Church and the ruling oligarchy had most to lose if things went
wrong, and if there was a Great Terror in 1803–5 it was they who
felt it, first anxious that peace with France might encourage revolution and then, with war renewed, worried at first that the ignorant
mob might feel that they had nothing to lose from conquest by
Bonaparte. And it was they who ultimately triumphed, with the
ironic consequence that Britain itself stepped back many, many
paces and was a much less liberal and attractive country in 1815
than it had been in 1789. The riotous 'land of liberty' celebrated by
the anglomaniacs of the 1780s was transformed into the shackled,
po-faced, class-conscious society of post-Napoleonic Britain.

But simple fear of France gradually assumed more and more

importance after the emergence of Bonaparte as a dynamic general in Italy. Even as early as 1793 the exiled French politician Pierre Victor Malouet stressed the importance in British thinking on France of what he took to be irrational fears:

> I firmly believe that the sole interest of England is to preserve what she has, and remain as she is; but the development of power presented by France, in its actual state of disorganisation, excites a sort of terror as to what she might do with a good government, as if a good government would not inevitably conduce to the order, the tranquillity, the happiness of other nations. These erroneous ideas have prevailed everywhere and over all considerations.[5]

These 'erroneous' ideas were even more prevalent in 1803. In Napoleon Bonaparte the French not only had good government, but good government under a gifted general capable of harnessing national effort to a national war machine. British fear of its terrible potential and distrust of French motives was evident in the way that Talleyrand's attempt to persuade Bonaparte against war, despite all British provocation, was presented as a threat, as an element in a Machiavellian discussion of how ultimately France might best defeat Britain. Fears within government were exacerbated by knowledge of the reasons Pitt's administration and then Addington's had given the French in general and Bonaparte in particular for revenge – inciting civil war, causing financial hardship by distributing fake currency, sponsoring assassination attempts ... None of these were calculated to leave a happy impression in French minds and gave the British good reason to anticipate attempts at revenge.

Nevertheless, though fear played its part, British persistence during the Napoleonic War was ultimately driven by confidence in her ability eventually to beat her rival. It was obvious that with a crack French army over the Channel there was a chance of conquest, but most people were confident that the French would not get past the Royal Navy, or if they did, they would be trapped by it, just as Bonaparte had been trapped by Nelson in Egypt. The utter confidence of St Vincent's proud boast when commanding the Channel Fleet – 'I do not say, my Lords, that the French will not come. I say only they will not come by sea' – says everything you need to know about British immunity from a French threat thanks to the immense superiority of the Royal Navy. The odds had to change a lot before there was any real reason for fear, once everyone was satisfied that the sailors wouldn't change sides and the poor wouldn't support the French. Britain was superior to France at sea and financially, and a lot of people appreciated it. It bred an unattractive sense of national superiority and self-satisfaction that survives today even though the underlying conditions have changed totally.

In the event it was Napoleon's ever-increasing hatred for the British government that caused his downfall. The decision to beat Britain by economic means caused him to take a series of steps that made him ever more unpopular and ultimately vulnerable, culminating in the invasion of Russia when his famous luck finally ran out.

The obstinate refusal of British leaders to acknowledge Napoleon despite repeated defeats took its toll. George III became so insane in late 1810 that during 1811 the Prince of Wales finally became Prince Regent, while the old King lived in seclusion at Windsor until his death in 1820. William Pitt died of drink, exhaustion and disappointment in 1806 after seeing his latest coalition destroyed by Napoleon at the battle of Austerlitz. Henry Dundas's management of the navy between 1782 and 1800 was investigated in 1802 and he was impeached for financial mismanagement in 1806. His use of naval patronage to secure his dominant position in Scottish politics was widely resented, and although he was acquitted he retired from politics. Grenville became prime minister after the death of Pitt, but his 'broad-bottomed' administration struggled and he went into opposition in 1807. He suffered a stroke in 1823 and died in 1834. William Windham served as secretary for war in Grenville's ministry and then went into opposition; he died in 1810 as a result of an injury sustained while trying to save Frederick North's library from a fire. The Duke of Portland served in cabinet continually, and led a new ministry of Pitt's former supporters from 1807 to 1809, but his health failed and he died soon after resigning.

Lord Hawkesbury inherited his father's title of Lord Liverpool in 1808 and was prime minister from 1812 until 1827, presiding over the years of victory against Napoleon, Waterloo, and Peterloo. Addington as Lord Sidmouth was the Home Secretary who introduced the repressive measures that culminated in the Peterloo massacre. Lord Castlereagh was the Foreign Secretary who presided over the later, victorious stages of the war and the peace that installed reactionary governments throughout Europe. In 1822, possibly being blackmailed for homosexuality, possibly insane, he committed suicide. After fighting a duel against Castlereagh in 1809 over foreign policy, George Canning was more or less in the wilderness from then until Castlereagh's suicide in 1822. Much against the wishes of George IV he succeeded Castlereagh as Foreign Secretary and in 1827, much against the wishes of the Duke of Wellington, he was briefly prime minister, but his health collapsed under the strain of attempting to reconcile opposed wings of the Tory party and he died within six months of taking power.

George Hammond died aged ninety in 1853. He continued to share literary interests and political views with Canning: in 1809 at a dinner given by Hammond at his house in Spring Gardens Canning first suggested the *Quarterly Review* as a new Tory journal to John Murray, John Hookham Frere and other contributors to the *Anti-Jacobin*. In 1812 Evan Nepean was appointed governor of Bombay, where he was able to indulge his botanical enthusiasm, corresponding with Joseph Banks and sending plants and seeds to England. He was made a Fellow of the Royal Society in 1820 soon after his return, but he died in 1822. John King retired from the front line in 1806 with a post as comptroller of army accounts.

Napoleon ruled France until 1814, drawn deeper and deeper into difficulty by his attempts to unite Europe and Russia in economic warfare against Britain. In the process of bullying nations into compliance with his wish to defeat the British, he gradually grew into the role of despotic tyrant for which he had been cast by British propaganda. After Napoleon's abdication Louis XVIII ruled in 1814 but quickly became so unpopular that Napoleon was able to return to power. However, after the battle of Waterloo Napoleon was banished to the remote island of Saint Helena, where he died in 1821. Louis XVIII returned to the throne from 1815 until his death from obesity, gout and gangrene in 1824. Initially, Talleyrand was his prime minister and Fouché his minister of police, but the royalists soon unseated them and Fouché died in exile at Trieste in 1820. Talleyrand had negotiated a good deal for France at the Congress of Vienna, but stood back until under Louis-Philippe he agreed to serve as ambassador to Britain. He died in 1838. The comte d'Artois ruled France as Charles X from 1824, but his ultra-royalist measures proved unpopular and he was deposed in 1830. He died of cholera at Gorizia in 1836.

Charles-François, marquis de Rivière was imprisoned in the château de Joux in the Jura mountains until 1814. Appointed lieutenant-general of the kingdom, he organised a memorial service at the church of Saint-Paul in Paris for Pichegru, Moreau, Cadoudal and the other victims of the Great Conspiracy. Cadoudal's body had been anatomised by medical students after his execution, but his skeleton, mounted on iron wires, had been acquired by the great surgeon Baron Larrey, then inspector general of the health service, for his collection. Charles d'Hozier and Joseph Cadoudal went to Larrey and begged him to give it to them, which he did, and so Cadoudal's bones, removed from the mounting, were placed in a coffin and on 25 June 1814, ten years after his death, they were carried to the église Saint-Paul for a requiem mass, before being taken to his home village of Kerléano, where a chapel was built by public subscription to house them.[6]

Armand de Polignac and his brother Jules were imprisoned in the château de Ham in Picardy, but after they attempted to escape they were transferred to the Temple and then to Vincennes, from where they were freed in 1814, promoted and honoured. Jules was ambassador to Britain from 1822 to 1828 and foreign minister from 1829 to 1830; his ultra-royalist policies contributed to the final overthrow of the senior Bourbon line. He was imprisoned from 1830 to 1836 and then exiled to England. Both Polignacs died in 1847.

Armand Gaillard was imprisoned in the château de Bouillon in the Pyrenees until 1814, when he was ennobled by Louis XVIII and appointed governor of Brest and Oléron; he died in 1852 and was buried at Quiberville la Milon. Charles d'Hozier was imprisoned in the château de Lourdes and then the château d'If off Marseille until 1814, when the comte d'Artois made him a colonel and master of his stables. After his release from If in 1814 Louis XVIII promoted Louis Rusillon to general of brigade; eventually he retired to Switzerland and died in his home town of Yverdon.

Antoine Caron, the perfumer, was not punished for his auxiliary role in the conspiracy but was rewarded after the restoration for lending his house to royalist conspirators with the patronage of the duchesse d'Angoulême and an appointment as one of two *messagers d'état* who escorted the president of the chambers of deputies.[7]

Louis de Bourmont escaped from prison in 1804 to Portugal. When the British invaded in 1808 he offered his services to Marshal Junot and followed him to France. Nobody trusted him but in 1810 he was posted to the Army of Naples and served under Napoleon until 1814. In 1815 he was with Ney's royalist army, which deserted to Napoleon, but Bourmont deserted back to the allies on the first day of the Waterloo campaign. He gave evidence against

Ney at his trial and was made commander of a division of the royal guard. He was minister for war in 1829 but was fighting in Algeria at the time of the July revolution, after which he went into exile and plotted on behalf of the legitimate Bourbon line. He died in 1846 in the château de Bourmont.

Sidney Smith's former 'servant' Jacques de Tromelin joined Napoleon's army in 1805 and rose from captain to general of brigade; his brigade was the last to leave the field of Waterloo in 1815. He continued to serve in the army, was promoted lieutenant-general in Spain in 1823, and retired to Brittany in 1830.

If Coleridge's post as secretary to the intelligent and enlightened British commissioner in Malta, Sir Alexander Ball, was a reward for his services, the secret seems to have been kept from Coleridge himself. He arrived on 18 May 1804 and thus missed the excitement in France. His friend Robert Southey had taken up a post as secretary to the Irish chancellor in 1800 but received a government pension from 1807. Gillray had his pension renewed and worked for the government while Canning was in power; however, his eyesight was failing, he went mad after 1810, and committed suicide in 1815 just before the battle of Waterloo. Cobbett turned further away from Pitt's system of government and became a champion of the radical movement. He was imprisoned from 1810 to 1812, and fled to the United States in 1817–19 to avoid arrest for sedition. His ambition to be a member of Parliament was finally achieved at the fifth attempt in 1832, when he was elected for the newly enfranchised borough of Oldham. After the success of his *Secret History* Lewis Goldsmith became editor from January 1811 of the government-funded *Anti-Gallican Monitor*. In 1837 his only child, Georgiana, married John Singleton Copley, Lord Lyndhurst, the lord chancellor, becoming his second wife.

Friedrich Gentz drafted the King of Prussia's letter to Napoleon in 1806 and he drafted the proclamation of Austria's declaration of war in 1809; he became a close friend and confidant of Metternich

and was secretary to the Congress of Vienna. He remained mercenary to the end, noting that at the Congress of Vienna Talleyrand
gave him £22,000, while Castlereagh gave him £600 and some
fine-sounding promises. He drafted a great deal of repressive legislation to prop up decaying institutions before dying in Vienna
on 9 June 1832.

John Bowles made a fortune from the government sinecures
given him as rewards for his anti-Jacobin writing. He died in
Bath in 1819 aged sixty-eight. John Gifford died in 1818, married
with children and similarly affluent from government sinecures
and pensions. John Reeves was King's patentee for the printing of
bibles and prayer books as well as chief justice of Newfoundland
and, eventually, superintendent of aliens. He died with a fortune of
£200,000 derived from the rewards of his service to government.[8]
John Heriot was appointed governor of Chelsea Hospital. William
Vincent Barré committed suicide in Dublin in 1829.

John Wesley Wright committed suicide in the Temple after the
battle of Austerlitz (or was strangled by Mamelukes if you still
choose to believe that).

Philippe d'Auvergne committed suicide after the British and
the Bourbons failed to uphold his claim to the dukedom of
Bouillon at the Congress of Vienna, leaving him massively in
debt. His half-brother was appointed the first British governor of
Heligoland in 1807.

Julien Leclerc continued to work as a spy; he eventually received
a regular pension, which was still being paid to him when Louis
Fauche-Borel wrote his memoirs. Fauche committed suicide in
1829. In 1810 Justin Ratel was living in London with his mistress
Julienne. He had an interest in a business as a wine merchant and
was still on good terms with the Smiths. He died in 1816 after
returning to France. Nymphe de Préville moved from Münster
across Germany to Prussia and then Russia before retreating to
Queensbury in England, where both she and Louis Delaporte

were living in 1810. Later she lived in Gloucester Place and was buried in Kensal Green cemetery. Pierre-Marie Poix married and had children in England and died at Claines, Worcestershire as an English gentleman.

Sir George Rumbold died in 1807 and Sidney Smith married Rumbold's widow Caroline in 1810. Smith pursued a quixotic naval career in the Mediterranean and elsewhere, paying scant regard to Admiralty control. He turned up at Waterloo just in time to see the end of the battle and he stayed the night at Wellington's HQ. Eventually he had to move with his family to France in order to avoid creditors. He died in 1840 and was buried at Père Lachaise cemetery.

Jean-Gabriel Peltier continued to publish *l'Ambigu* and from 1806 received a secret service pension from the British government and was also rewarded by the Portuguese and Swedish. From 1807 to 1817 he was the unofficial minister-plenipotentiary in London of the Emperor of Haiti, Henri Christophe. Louis XVIII refused to reward him in 1814 so from London *L'Ambigu* criticised Bourbon policy for being too liberal. In 1822 he received a French government pension. Separated from his wife, he always lived beyond his means, his life a pattern of women, champagne and bankruptcy. He died deep in debt in the rue Montmartre in Paris in 1825.

Méhée was said to be living in Hamburg in 1807, but he contrived to draw a veil over his life from 1804 to 1814, by which time he was in France. Two anti-ultra pamphlets in 1814 drew the wrath of the royalists down on his head and he tried to deny his part in the events of 1803–4. After the fall of Napoleon in 1815 he was proscribed by the King and fled first to Switzerland and then to Brussels, where in 1817 he worked as the editor of *Le Vrai Libéral*. He was arrested there on 19 July, apparently on Castlereagh's order, but escaped again next day thanks to his mistress (he had identified her as his daughter), although the police seized her and his papers.[9] He then moved to Königsberg until he was allowed to return to France in 1819. In 1823 he was living in Paris, trying to deny authorship of the *Alliance des Jacobins*, and he died there in 1826.

Francis Drake's career was ruined by his deception by Méhée in 1804; his generous offer to be disowned by government was accepted wholeheartedly by Hawkesbury. Seeking to defend himself, Drake discovered that 'every Document whatever, relating to this affair has been withdrawn from the Foreign Office' and complained to Grenville on 25 June 1805, credibly enough, 'I was not more credulous than His Majesty's government'.[10] Hawkesbury had removed all incriminating letters from the Foreign Office files in order to preserve his own reputation, which was in at least as much danger as Drake's. His midshipman son met Napoleon on Saint Helena. Drake tried to clear his name posthumously: when he died in 1821 his will required his children to publish his papers ten years after his death. However, Hawkesbury, by then Lord Liverpool and prime minister, bought Drake's embarrassing papers from his children and paid them an annuity on condition that publication was suppressed.

Acknowledgements

The seed of this book was planted during the period when I was curating the exhibition *Bonaparte and the British*, which was shown at the British Museum in 2015. In the course of research for that project I became curious about British involvement in the assassination attempts of 1800 and 1804 and about the real motives for the vast outpouring of broadsheets, pamphlets and prints that accompanied and followed the renewal of war in 1803. This book wouldn't have been conceived without that exhibition, and for my opportunity to work on it I would like to thank Hugo Chapman, Keeper of Prints and Drawings, whose idea it was, my co-curator and friend Sheila O'Connell, and the Paul Mellon Centre for British Art who generously funded my participation.

In some parts of this book my research tries to break new ground. In other parts I owe considerable debts to the recent ground-breaking research of others – notably to the work of Simon Burrows for guiding my interpretation of the creation of Anglo-royalist propaganda, to that of Stuart Semmel, whose book *Napoleon and the British* covers some of the same ground in a rather different way, and to the work of the late Elizabeth Sparrow and of Michael Durey for opening up the world of espionage and secret service to newcomers like me.

For their kindness in answering my questions relating to

various specific issues I would like to thank Jérôme Maes, Hugues de Préville, Michel Parenty, Richard Sharp and Christopher Woodward. Helen Symington of the National Library of Scotland in Edinburgh kindly checked references in the John Murray archive in the forlorn hope of finding evidence for the authorship of the *Revolutionary Plutarch*; Tracey Earle, archivist of Messrs Coutts & Co., transcribed Lord Grenville's separate account for secret service; Alexandra Ault and Stephen Noble at the British Library made it possible for me to study the Canning papers. I would also like to thank the staff of the Bodleian Library, Oxford, Cambridge University Library, Kent archives, the Archives nationales at Pierrefitte and Philippe de Carbonnières of the Musée Carnavalet. Andrew Edmunds, Phil Craig, Pascal Dupuy, Jane Greenwood, Antony Griffiths, Annie Lyles, Mark Philp and Nigel Talbot have shared opinions and contributed thoughts. Their help has been invaluable.

For hospitality, encouragement and loyal friendship I am deeply grateful to Steve and Pauline Mobbs, Phil and Frances Craig and Juliet and Rod Rix-Standing in London, to Nicolas and Guillaume Cousin, Pascal Dupuy and their families in Paris, and to Barbara Bradshaw and her family in Oxford. The loss of her husband David while I was researching this book and of my mother a year later while I was completing it have made this a period of great sadness. I am deeply grateful for the patient support of my father during what has been a difficult time for us both.

The staff of Little, Brown have, as usual, made the process of publication a pleasure. I should like to thank my publisher Richard Beswick, Zoe Gullen who managed the project most capably, Steve Cox the copy editor, proof reader Daniel Balado, John Gilkes for maps, Linda Silverman for picture research, Marie Hrynczak for production and Mark Wells for the index. My agent Julian Alexander saw the potential of this project from the very beginning and made it happen.

Notes

3 *nivôse*, year IX

1 Miall, *Garat*, pp. 265–6.
2 BL Add MS 37851, f. 156.
3 Réal, *Indiscrétions*, p. 61.
4 The geography is difficult to describe because the street names were changed at least three times between 1798 and 1804, and the annually issued Parisian street map that I have used may not have caught up with the changes accurately. After the bomb went off the buildings to the west of the rue Saint-Nicaise were demolished and the street ceased to exist, being incorporated into the place du Carrousel. The rue de Chartres of 1798, leading east, was renamed the rue Marceau by 1800 and then the rue de Malte in 1804. If Charles Picquet's magnificent new 1804 survey is to be believed, the southern extension of the rue de la Loi, below the rue Saint-Honoré, called the rue Batave between 1798 and 1803, became the rue Marceau at that date. I have referred to it for simplicity's sake as the rue de la Loi, which is how the horse grenadier Nicolas Durand, whose account underpins this one, referred to it. Bonaparte's coach must have been in this section when the bomb went off, if it was to pause, as Durand said, at the Théâtre de la République.

1 Fair is Foul, and Foul is Fair

1 See Lignereux, 'Moment terroriste', p. 9; Salomé, 'Attentat', p. 61. The term 'terrorist' is problematically anachronistic, as it applied at the time exclusively to Jacobins and the 'Terror', but the methodology was terrorist in the modern sense.
2 See Burrows, 'British Francophone Propaganda', p. 53.

3 Sir Henry Edward Bunbury, *A Narrative of Military Transactions in the Mediterranean, 1805–1810* (privately printed, 1851), p. vii.

4 Barré, *Empire*, p. 12; *Revolutionary Plutarch*, III, pp. 141, 144; *Cobbett's Political Register*, v (1804), p. 682.

5 Much of the material was gathered together and described long ago by Ashton, Broadley and Maccunn but without much analysis of the timing and underlying causes of its creation. Stuart Semmel has covered British attitudes to Napoleon very well, but he treated the subject thematically over a long period and therefore gave little space to the significance of specific shifts during the Consulate (see, however, especially, pp. 40–6). I owe a great deal to Simon Burrows's discussion of the work of Francophone writers and their links to the British government and to Emily de Montluzin's unmasking of anti-Jacobin writers and their pensions.

6 Malmesbury, *Diaries*, II, p. 259.

7 For anglomania as it related to prints, see Clayton, *English Print*, pp. 235–82.

8 Although this book cannot be extensively illustrated, nearly all the prints that are mentioned can be seen via the British Museum's online search engine: http://www.britishmuseum.org/research/collection_online/search.aspx.

9 Mackesy, *War without Victory*, p. 38 (BL Add MS 40102, f.102).

10 Macleod, *War of Ideas*, p. 32.

11 Hampson, *Perfidy of Albion*, p. 150.

12 Hampson, *Perfidy of Albion*, p. 139.

13 Hall, *Pichegru's Treason*, p. 16.

14 Hampson, *Perfidy of Albion*, p. 139.

15 See Lutaud, *Révolutions*, pp. 225–34; Hill, *Macaulay*, pp. 212–23.

16 See especially Bertaud in *Napoléon, le monde et les Anglais*, pp. 89–95.

17 Hampson, *Perfidy of Albion*, p. 121; Bertaud in *Napoléon, le monde et les Anglais*, pp. 53–4.

2 Responding to Cataclysm

1 History of Parliament online; http://www.historyofparliamentonline.org/volume/1790-1820/member/nepean-evan-1752-1822; *Oxford DNB*.

2 BM Satires 7678–9 by Frederick George Byron for William Holland and 7824 by Isaac Cruikshank for Samuel William Fores.

3 BM Satires 7892.

4 Pigott, *Jockey Club*, part I, 5th edn 1792, preface (unpaginated).

5 *Association Papers*, preface, p. iv.

6 Dozier, *King, Constitution and Country*, pp. 57–9; Sparrow, *Secret Service*, p. 11, speculated that John Moore was a pseudonym for John King.

7 *Jackson's Oxford Journal*, 15 December 1792, reporting a meeting in the town hall of 11 December.

8 For the material culture of the English reaction to the French Revolution, see Bindman, *Shadow of the Guillotine*.

9 *Association Papers*, p. 15.

10 Manogue, 'Plight of James Ridgway'; Lutaud, *Révolutions*, pp. 231–3.

11 For Jackson see Durey, 'The Christ Church Connection'.

12 Sparrow, 'Alien Office', p. 368; Durey, *Wickham*, pp. 10–11.

13 BL Add MS 33109 f. 22.

14 BL Add MS 32731 ff. 8–9. Maddison's uncle's assistant Bode, expert at opening and resealing, taught the art to the next generation and Frederick, George, John Ernest and William Bode were Maddison's assistants.

15 Ellis, *Post Office*, pp. 65–74.

16 Wells, *Insurrection*, pp. 33–4.

17 BM Satires 8149. See Bindman, *Shadow of the Guillotine*, pp. 118–21.

18 *Parliamentary Register*, XVI (1802), p. 259.

19 TNA PRO 30/8 vol 229, ff. 291a and 292a. See Cobbett's denunciation of 'Trading Anti-Jacobins' in *Cobbett's Political Register*, XV (1809), pp. 601–11.

20 Vincent, 'Bowles', pp. 399–403 and 420.

21 Aspinall, *Politics and the Press*, p. 166. In 1805 it was said that the *Anti-Jacobin Review* and *British Critic* had a circulation of 1250 and 1500 respectively (Burrows, *French Exile Journalism*, p. 85).

22 Millard, 'Sampson Perry'; Rogers, 'Censorship and Creativity'.

23 *Gentleman's Magazine*, 1st ser., 88/1 (1818), pp. 279–80, 403. *Annual Biography and Obituary*, III (1819), pp. 311–37.

24 Hague, *Pitt*, p. 355, Pitt to Pretyman.

25 Durey, *Wickham*, pp. 42–3; *Parliamentary Register*, XXXVIII (1794), p. 246.

26 Jean Joseph Mounier and Jacques Mallet du Pan claimed that Jean Lambert Tallien was ready to cooperate. For more detail see Durey, *Wickham*, pp. 47–9.

27 Hampson, *Perfidious Albion*, p. 152; Durey, *Wickham*, pp. 47–9; Sparrow, *Secret Service*, pp. 62–4.

28 For Bayard see Sparrow, *Phantom*; on his early career, pp. 25–61.

29 Hall, *Pichegru*, p. 15.

30 Malmesbury, *Diaries*, III, p. 590.

31 Balleine, *d'Auvergne*, pp. 71–3.

32 Isaac, 'forged *assignats*', pp. 158–63; Bower, 'Economic Warfare', pp. 47–52; Perry, *Argus*, 1796, p. 246, repeated in Goldsmith, *Crimes of Cabinets*, pp. 262–3. The engraver was John Strongitharm. Balleine, *d'Auvergne*, pp. 74–5.

33 Hampson, *Perfidious Albion*, pp. 110–11.

3 *Bellum Internecinum*

1   Barrow, *Smith*, I, pp. 3–4; https://doverhistorian.com/2013/06/09/
    smiths-folly/

2   Durey, 'Escape of Sir Sidney Smith', p. 439.

3   Spencer to Windham, in Pocock, *Smith*, p. 34.

4   Durey, 'Escape of Sir Sidney Smith', p. 440. The crew of the hoy
    gunboat *Shark* mutinied in December 1795 and handed her to
    the French.

5   Aspinall, *Later Correspondence*, II, p. 470 (letter 1387). Hampson,
    Perfidious Albion, p. 150; Bowman, 'Preliminary Stages', p. 86.

6   Girtin, *Doctor*, p. 167. Wolcot, who as 'Peter Pindar' had made an
    industry out of mocking George III, stopped abruptly at this time and
    was probably paid to do so (Girtin, *Doctor*, pp. 172–6).

7   BM Satires 8710, 8693, 8709 (Alexander, *Newton*, p. 194), 8703.

8   Perry, *Argus*, p. iii. Perry was released in 1801 and became co-proprietor
    of the *Statesman* in 1809 but was broken by a legal battle with Lewis
    Goldsmith and died in debtor's prison.

9   *True Briton*, 10 November 1795.

10 *Gentleman's Magazine*, LXVI (1796), p. 78; *Caledonian Mercury*, 28 January
    1796, p. 2.

11 *An Address to the Public from the Society for the Suppression of
    Vice*, pp. 43–4.

12 Quoted in Hone, *Cause of Truth*, p. 20.

13 Durey, 'Escape of Sir Sidney Smith', pp. 441ff. Durey speculated that
    'Smith's capture had thwarted some secret plan', noting that James
    Talbot, Malmesbury's secretary, had expected a role as commissioner to
    the royalist armies in France.

14 Durey, 'Escape of Sir Sidney Smith', p. 448. It looks as if one of Frotté's
    lieutenants, Jean Picot, did his best to drink half the money. He was
    arrested for drunken riot in Bayeux in possession of £500 given to him
    by one 'Keith' (Sicotière, *Frotté*, pp. 616–17).

15 *Biographical Anecdotes* (1797), I, p. 82.

16 Trevor to Grenville 11 April 1795, quoted in Duffy, 'British Policy', p. 23.

17 See Caudrillier, *Institut Philanthropique*, p. xii.

18 See Sparrow, *Phantom*, pp. 88–9.

19 Mitchell, *Underground War*, pp. 187–91; Blanc, *Espions*, pp. 74ff.; Durey,
    Wickham, pp. 95–6.

20 Durey, *Wickham*, pp. 90–7, takes a more cautious view of the extent of
    royalist success than Mitchell, *Underground War*, pp. 140–61.

21 Hall, *Pichegru*, pp. 224–5.

22 See Ramel, *Memoirs*, pp. 172–241; Larue, *Histoire*, II, pp. 399–46; Hyde,
    Mémoires, I, pp. 204–17.

23 BL Add MS 89143/1/1/42 Canning to Frere 28 September 1798.

24　Durey, 'Escape of Sir Sidney Smith', p. 453. The circumstances are complicated because Smith's escape seems to have been an aspect of a broader project involving bribing Barras. Some of the accounts are in NMM NEP/2, a file of correspondence with Etches.

25　Durey, 'Escape of Sir Sidney Smith', pp. 449–53. Georges René Le Peley de Pléville was dismissed as minister of marine in April 1798, supposedly for disapproving of the Egyptian expedition.

26　TNA FO 27/53 Smith to Grenville, Portsmouth, 24 August 1798; Smith to Canning 26 August 1798. Rochecotte was tried and shot on 10 August 1798.

27　TNA FO 27/53 Smith to Grenville, Portsmouth, 24 August 1798; Sparrow, *Phantom*, p. 115.

28　Lloyd (ed.), *Keith Papers*, p. 67. Smith to Keith, *Antelope*, Yarmouth, 29 Jan 04, proves that Ratel sheltered Smith at Rouen.

29　The view of Mitchell, *Underground War*, pp. 217ff.

30　Grenville to Pitt 8 October 1797, *Dropmore Papers*, III, p. 378; Mitchell, *Underground War*, p. 218.

4 The Modern Alexander

1　Knight, *Organization of Victory*, p. 186.

2　Maspero-Clerc, *Peltier*, p. 140.

3　*Paris pendant l'année*, XII (1797), pp. 725–6.

4　*Paris pendant l'année*, XIII (1797), pp. 1–3n.

5　*Biographical Anecdotes* (1799 edn), I, p. iii; *Monthly Magazine*, III (1797), pp. 373–8; *Biographical Anecdotes* (1797 edn), I, pp. 165–79; *Edinburgh Magazine*, IX (1797) pp. 439–45; *New Annual Register for 1796*, pp. 184–7n; *New Jamaica Magazine*, II Sep 1798, pp. 129–35. Paoli had been living in London with a large British pension since the overthrow of George III as King of Corsica in 1796.

6　*Biographical Anecdotes* (1797 edn), I, pp. 165–79.

7　Craig, *Buonaparte*, pp. 17–19.

8　Quoted in Maccunn, *Contemporary English View*, p. 10.

9　Clayton and O'Connell, *Bonaparte and the British*, pp. 54–6.

10　Dupuy, 'Consulat', pp. 185–7; Clayton and O'Connell, *Bonaparte and the British*, pp. 58–60.

11　On Napoleon's propaganda, see especially Hanley, *Genesis of Napoleonic Propaganda, 1796–1799*.

12　Designed by a Swiss soldier who had been in Dutch pay called David Hess, advertised *Morning Post*, 26 December 1796, see Cillessen, 'Holland herboren'; during 1799 six plates from the set of twenty were copied for the *Revolutions-Almanack* published at Göttingen and the whole set was copied in Italy and published by Zatta of Venice.

13　BL Add MS 89143/1/1/38 Canning to Ellis, 19 October 1797. William

Lamb (afterwards Lord Melbourne), in a poetical congratulatory epistle, published in the *Morning Chronicle*, 17 January 1798, represents Canning as joint editor with Hammond. See Fallon, 'Piccadilly Booksellers', pp. 73–80.

14 Farington, *Diary*, III, p. 956 (28 December 1797).

15 BL Add MS 89143/1/1/38 Canning to Ellis 28 February 1798, Ellis to Canning 1 March 1798.

16 'Yet it was against his conscience, for he had been on the other side, and was brought over.' Hazlitt, *James Northcote*, p. 302. BM Satires, VIII, pp. xii–xiii. Canning's mention of the threat of the loss of his pension is a sure proof that it existed.

17 *Poetry of the Anti-Jacobin*, p. 4.

18 *Copies of Original Letters*, i, pp. ii–iii. See Simon Burrows, 'Britain and the Black Legend: the Genesis of the Anti-Napoleonic Myth' in Philp (ed.), *Resisting Napoleon*, pp. 150–2.

19 For more detail see Clayton and O'Connell, *Bonaparte and the British*.

20 Williams, *Tour in Switzerland*, II, pp. 54–7.

21 *Anti-Jacobin*, II (1798), pp. 233–4. A note explained that 'The *Courier* calls her *Miss* Williams'. The nature of Williams's relationship with John Hurford Stone, whose brother had been acquitted of treason in 1796, was the subject of lively speculation.

22 Braithwaite, *Romanticism, Publishing and Dissent*, p. 155.

23 See T. B. Howell, *A Complete Collection of State Trials*, XXVII (London, 1820), pp. 627–42. Parry was sentenced to six months in prison, fined £100 and ordered to pay £500 surety for good behaviour; he was ruined and forced to sell the paper to Daniel Stuart and Peter Street, who was in treasury pay (Bourne, *Newspapers*, p. 274; Aspinall, *Politics and the Press*, p. 208). For Grenville boasting that he had instigated prosecution see Belsham, *Reign of George* III, VII, p. 253.

24 Quoted in Bugg, *Five Long Winters*, pp. 103–4.

25 Bainbridge, *Napoleon and English Romanticism*, p. 20.

26 Goldsmith, *Secret History*, p. 58.

27 BL Add MS 29764, ff.75–6.

28 *Dropmore Papers*, v, pp. 42–4, Smith to Spencer, 6 March 1799, Spencer to Grenville, 7 May 1799; see Sparrow, *Secret Service*, pp. 186–96.

29 Pocock, *Smith*, pp. 120–1. Dwyer, *Path to Power*, pp. 443–4, believes Smith allowed Bonaparte to escape.

30 Kent Record Office, U269/O197/4 26 Oct 1799.

31 TNA FO 78/22 f.252v. 251–6, Sidney Smith to Spencer Smith, 20 October 1799.

32 Sparrow, *Secret Service*, pp. 189–90. Barré, *Consulate*, p. 142: 'It is rather astonishing that the British cruisers had kept such a bad look-out as to enable both French frigates to make their escape. But, according to Dr. Wittman, a Turkish admiral was beheaded on that account'.

33 Waresquiel, *Fouché*, pp. 357–8

34 Ségur, *Memoirs of an Aide de Camp*, p. 354.

35 Waresquiel, *Fouché*, pp. 55–6.

36 Goldsmith, *Secret History*, pp. 542–3.

37 *Revolutionary Plutarch*, III, p. 394.

38 Hyde, *Mémoires*, I, p. 251.

39 Hyde, *Mémoires*, I, p. 273.

40 Hyde, *Mémoires*, I, p. 272.

41 Dwyer, *Citizen Emperor*, pp. 28–31; Roberts, *Napoleon the Great*, p. 237.

5 The English Conspiracy

1   *Dropmore Papers*, VI, p. 53.

2   Hague, *Pitt*, p. 452. For the evidence of Bonaparte's sincerity, see Bowman, 'Preliminary Stages', pp. 112–18; although Dwyer, *Citizen Emperor*, pp. 28–31, does not share his view, I find it compelling.

3   BL Add MS 89143/1/1/123 Pitt to Canning, Hollwood 23 November 1799.

4   BL Add MS 89143/1/1/38 George Ellis to Canning n.d. [late 1799].

5   BL Add MS 89143/1/1/123 Pitt to Canning, Hollwood 3 December 1799.

6   Bowman, 'Preliminary Stages', pp. 109–18. The Alien Office took no chances with Otto, and throughout his time in London Flint had him tailed by three of their spies – see TNA FO 27–57.

7   The plans are summarised with documents in Caudrillier, *Institut Philanthropique*, pp. 19–42.

8   Ehrman, *Consuming Struggle*, p. 469; Sparrow, 'Alien Office', p. 382.

9   *Dropmore Papers*, VI, 183, Wickham to Grenville, 27 March 1800.

10 Mackesy, *War without Victory*, pp. 71–2.

11 See Lutaud, *Révolutions*, pp. 246–9. It used the translation of 1758 with certain adaptations to modern circumstances.

12 Gifford's review in *Anti-Jacobin Review*, VI, pp. 504–9.

13 See his memorial for Talleyrand in AN F/7/6247. For the Alien Office at this date see Durey, *Wickham*, pp. 106–13.

14 AN F/7/6247 'Liste alphabétique des mouchards de Paris, suivi d'une notice sur la police républicaine'.

15 *Conspiration anglaise*, pp. 84 and 154–6.

16 TNA, FO 27/56, ff. 211–12.

17 TNA, FO 27/56, f. 59.

18 Fauche-Borel, *Mémoires*, III, pp. 378–9.

19 AN F/7/6251; Alger, *British Visitors*, p. 142.

20 Napoleon, *Correspondance générale*, III, pp. 81–2, no. 4965 to General Gardanne, 11 Feb 1800.

21 Waresquiel, *Fouché*, p. 286.

22 BL Add MS 37924; Martel, *Machine infernale*, p. 67.

23 AN F/7/6251. Hauterive, *La contre-police royaliste en 1800*, p. 134.

24 BL 1195.f.20 Flint's annotated copy of *Conspiration anglaise*.

25 Waresquiel, *Fouché*, pp. 289–90.

26 Waresquiel, *Talleyrand*, p. 295.

27 These two were Bertin de Vaux and Antoine-Athanase Roux de Laborie. See Waresquiel, *Talleyrand*, pp. 295–6; AN F/7/6247, TNA FO 27/56 ff. 273–83 and 550–1.

28 *Procès contre Georges*, VI, pp. 34–5; Montgaillard, *Notice abrégée*, pp. 35–7; Maes, 'Conjuration', parts 2–3.

29 Watel, *Hyde*, pp. 33–4.

30 Sparrow, *Secret Service*, p. 137; see Larue, *Histoire*, I, pp. 399–446 and Ramel, *Memoirs*, 172–241.

31 See Durey, 'Smoking Gun', for a discussion of the word 'coup' in the context of the 1799 plot involving James Talbot that seeks to distance Grenville from assassination. It is inconvenient for Durey's argument that this 1800 'coup' produced a large explosion.

32 Watel, *Hyde*, p. 36 and notes. Hyde's friend the chevalier de Toustain was executed at Paris on 25 January 1800.

33 TNA FO 27/56 ff. 466–7; Caudrillier, 'Complot', I, p. 281.

34 Quoted in Sparrow, *Secret Service*, p. 216.

35 BL Add MS 46830, vol. 2, ff. 323–5.

36 Baring (ed.), *Windham Diary*, p. 429; Caudrillier, 'Complot', I, p. 284.

6 The Infernal Machine

1 Napoleon, *Correspondance*, VI, p. 454.

2 On 17 May 1803 the French newspaper the *Clef du Cabinet* accused Tinseau of having been 'the inventor of those mild and gentle means employed in the affair of the 3rd Nivôse (the Infernal Machine)'. In a subsequent letter to William Cobbett, Tinseau denied taking any direct or indirect part in the infernal machine or any other assassination (letter dated 25 May 1803, *Cobbett's Annual Register*, III, (1803), pp. 791–3).

3 BL Add MS 37924.

4 BL Add MS 89143/1/1/123, Canning to Pitt, 25 August 1800.

5 BL Add MS 37924, Windham diary. Hall thought this interview was with the chevalier Louis Guérin de Bruslart, Frotté's adjutant, and it may have been. From the layout of Windham's diary it is very difficult to determine which of the two was meant, although it doesn't matter hugely: both were important figures and both were in Paris for 3 *nivôse*.

6 BL Add MS 37924, Windham diary.

7 Hyde, *Mémoires*, p. 389; BL Add MS 37924, Windham diary 24 November 1800; see Hall, *Pichegru's Treason*, pp. 294–5.

8 Sparrow, *Secret Service*, p. 220.

9 AN F/7/6362.

10 TNA FO 27/56, f. 849.

11 See Lignereux, 'Moment terroriste', p. 4; Caudrillier, 'Complot', I, p. 282 – the setting is in the middle of the year, but it may really have been in order to replace Margadel after his arrest.

12 Thiry, *Machine infèrnale*, p. 154.

13 Thiry, *Machine infèrnale*, pp. 158–9. AN F/7/6271.

14 The idea that Saint-Régent was inspired by the Jacobin bomb-maker Chevalier was Fouché's: see Lignereux, 'Moment terroriste', p. 5.

15 Martel, *Machine infèrnale*, pp. 44–7.

16 Martel, *Machine infèrnale*, pp. 74–8.

17 Salomé, 'Attentat', pp. 63–4.

18 Réal, *Indiscrétions*, p. 46.

19 Roederer, *Oeuvres*, III, p. 355.

20 Martel, *Machine infèrnale*, pp. 48–53.

21 Bertaud, *Quand les enfants*, p. 34; Martel, *Machine infèrnale*, pp. 160–5.

22 Martel, *Machine infèrnale*, pp. 83–7 and 114–15.

23 Martel, *Machine infèrnale*, pp. 130–1.

24 Thiry, *Machine infèrnale*, pp. 200–01; note by Fouché 1 pluviôse IX in AN F/7/6271.

25 Martel, *Machine infèrnale*, pp. 133–4.

26 Andress, *Savage Storm*, pp. 70–4.

27 William Augustus Miles to the Marquis of Buckingham, 28 Jan 1801. Miles, *Correspondence*, II, p. 308.

28 Malmesbury, *Diaries*, IV, p. 39; this complicated issue involved principles on the Catholic question in combination with a power struggle between Pitt's friends and a court group with more direct influence on the King, as well as political calculations about the fallout from a peace negotiated from a position of disadvantage, genuine doubts about the viability of peace, and the strong desire of the outgoing government as well as the King to continue the war.

29 Malmesbury, *Diaries*, IV, p. 70.

7 The Character of Bonaparte

1 See Montluzin, *The Anti-Jacobins* and 'The *Anti-Jacobin* Revisited'.

2 *Anti-Jacobin Review*, I (1798), p. 27. Gillray was employed to etch caricatures to embellish early issues of the *Anti-Jacobin Review*, although after a year the publishers used cheaper artists and they abandoned illustration after 1799.

3 *Anti-Jacobin Review*, I (1798), pp. 34 and 172.

4 *Anti-Jacobin Review*, I (1798), p. 631.

5 *Anti-Jacobin Review*, III (1799), p. 492.

6 *Anti-Jacobin Review*, V (1800), pp. 112–14.

7 *Anti-Jacobin Review*, VI (1800), pp. 332 and 359. Despite Linda Colley's

verdict, I see little evidence of much popular sympathy for George III before 1800.

8   Maspero-Clerc, *Peltier*, pp. 90–1, TNA FO 27/53.

9   AN, F/7/6330, dossier 6959.

10 *Paris pendant l'année*, XI (1797), p. 769; when he reprinted it in 1803 (*Ambigu*, III, p. 57) Peltier claimed to have received it from the ambassador of one of the powers allied to the French Directory. While this may have been so, an agent of Wickham and aide to Condé, Jacques-Marie de Tessonet, was based at Lons-le-Saunier where the letter was supposed to have been written.

11 *Spectateur du Nord*, II (1797), pp. 105–15. In his acknowledgement in *Paris pendant l'année*, XIII (1797), p. 6n., Peltier gave a precise reference to the letter in the *Spectateur* but did not divulge his own source.

12 Burrows, *French Exile Journalism*, p. 106, Otto to Talleyrand, 30 January 1802.

13 The Portuguese translation is BL RB.23.a.35564; an Italian translation is listed in R. S. Crane and F. B. Kaye, *A Census of British Newspapers and Periodicals, 1620–1800* (Chapel Hill, N.C., 1927).

14 Ense, *Tagebücher*, pp. 9–10. He received £100 at the end of the year. *Dropmore Papers*, VI, pp. 394–5, Grenville to Carysfort, 29 November 1800.

15 Ense, *Tagebücher*, pp. 11 and 27; translation from *Edinburgh Review*, CXVII (1863), pp. 51–2.

16 Cillessen, Reichardt and Deuling, *Napoleons neue Kleider*, pp. 20–1.

17 Cillessen, Reichardt and Deuling, *Napoleons neue Kleider*, pp. 14–16.

18 Semmel, *Napoleon and the British*, p. 24, citing Burdon, *Various Thoughts*, pp. 154–6.

19 *Morning Post*, 7 December 1799; *Monthly Magazine*, IX (1800), p. 291.

20 Cobbett, *Political Proteus*, pp. 88–9.

21 *Morning Post*, 2 January 1800.

22 *Morning Post*, 6 February 1800.

23 *Anti-Jacobin Review*, VI (1800), p. 461.

24 Bowman, 'Preliminary Stages', p. 108n.

25 *Morning Post*, 3 February 1800; *Sun*, 16 October 1799. See Goldsmith, *Crimes of Cabinets*, pp. 200–9 and 280–305.

26 Lignereux, 'Moment terroriste', pp. 3–5, tabulates the attempts on Bonaparte's life. BL Add MS 27,337 f.81 to Canning (27 October 1800). Canning's handling of Gillray matches Burrows's assessment of the way the government handled French journalists: Burrows, *French Exile Journalism*, pp. 129–30.

27 *Prospectus of a New Daily Paper to be entitled The Porcupine By William Cobbett*, September 1800.

28 *Anti-Jacobin Review*, VII (1800), p. vi.

29 Burrows, *French Exile Journalism*, p. 109.

30   *Courier*, 17 January 1801.

31   TNA FO 95/2/5 ff. 526–7.

32   Burrows, *French Exile Journalism*, p. 109; TNA FO 27/66, Hawkesbury to the bishop of Arras, 16 April.

33   *Anti-Jacobin Review*, VIII (1801), p. 20.

34   *Anti-Jacobin Review*, IX (1801), p. 87; *Critical Review*, XXXI (1801), p. 216.

35   *Anti-Jacobin Review*, VIII (1801), pp. 475–82. Starhemberg was named in XIII (1802), p. 446.

36   *Le Grand Homme*, p. 11n. 'On sait que la fille de Madame Bonaparte n'est pas celle de son mari; on sait aussi que le héros n'ignoroit pas, en épousant Madame de Beauharnois, que son ami Barras lui faisoit un double présent.'

37   *Dropmore Papers*, VII, pp. 73–4.

38   Fell, *Batavian Republic* (1801), pp. 346–9; *Monthly Review*, XXXVII (1802), p. 308.

39   Goldsmith, *Crimes of Cabinets*, pp. 160, 219.

40   Goldsmith, *Crimes of Cabinets*, pp. 231–2.

41   BL Add MS 33110, ff. 179–82.

8 The Peace and the Press

1   History of Parliament online. The comments are those of Lord Boringdon and Richard Wellesley, Lord Mornington.

2   WYRO, Lucas diary, XX, ff. 61 and 63.

3   Roffe, *My diary of sixty-three days*, pp. 15–16.

4   Otto to Talleyrand, 6 Oct 1801, in Morieux, 'An Inundation', p. 217.

5   Thomas Crabb Robinson to his brother Henry, Bury St Edmunds, 20 October 1801, in Sadler, *Diary, Reminiscences and Correspondence*, p. 57.

6   *Anti-Jacobin Review*, XI (1802), p. 465; its publisher Robinson was one of those listed as taking the *Argus*, awarded, like Ridgway, a triple exclamation mark on the home secretary's list. BL Add MS 33110, f. 179. *Anti-Jacobin Review*, XII (1802), p. 482, XIII (1802), p. 507.

7   *Cobbett's Political Register*, VIII (1805), pp. 978–9.

8   Cobbett to Windham, 10 October 1801, BL Add MS 37869, f.14.

9   Cobbett, *Letters to the Right Honourable Lord Hawkesbury*, pp. 17–18, 26–8.

10   BL Add MS 37853, f.17.

11   BL Add MS 37853 f. 17 Cobbett to Windham 24 November 1801 and f. 110 undated, but late 1803.

12   BL Add MS 89143/1/163 Grenville to Canning, 12 January 1802.

13   Russell, *Memorials and Correspondence*, III, p. 349, Fox to Grey, 22 October 1801.

14   WYRO, Lucas diary, XX, f. 114.

15 Burrows, *French Exile Journalism*, p. 110; Peltier, *Paris pendant l'année*, XXXIV (1801), pp. 337–8 and 444.

16 Burrows, *French Exile Journalism*, p. 112; Napoleon, *Correspondance générale*, III, p. 899, no. 6749, 2 February 1802.

17 Burrows, *French Exile Journalism*, pp. 112–13.

18 On the mistreatment of Wickham's former secretary see Hall, *Pichegru*, pp. 327–8 and TNA FO 27/56 ff. 279–81 Flint to Frere, 29 May 1800 and FO 27/58 Le Clerc to Hammond, 25 and 29 Aug 1801.

19 Andréossy was appointed in May but was not in London until November. Napoleon, *Correspondance générale*, III, p. 988, no. 6924.

20 Burrows, *French Exile Journalism*, p. 111; TNA FO 95/638 Arras to Dutheil, 26 June 1802; Dutheil to Arras, 30 June; Arras to Dutheil, 6 July 1802.

21 Burrows, *French Exile Journalism*, p. 34. The owners were Samuel Swinton and Alexandre de Calonne.

22 BL Add MS 37869, ff. 1, 17, 119; Caudrillier, 'Complot', 1, pp. 285–6.

23 Burrows, *French Exile Journalism*, p. 25. The Treasury solicitor's file copy of number one was bought on 16 August and the last date referred to in the text is 13 July.

24 Maspero-Clerc, *Peltier*, p. 174.

25 Translated in *Cobbett's Annual Register*, II (1802), pp. 179–81.

26 Ziegler, *Addington*, p. 165; Burrows, *French Exile Journalism*, p. 119.

27 Napoleon, *Correspondance générale*, III, p. 1065, no. 7090; that it was *Bell's Weekly Messenger* is proved by Tinseau's letter to Cobbett dated 25 May 1803 referring to it as 'the only English paper that has the honour to be permitted to circulate in France'. *Cobbett's Annual Register*, III (1803), p. 791.

28 TNA FO 27/63, 28 August 1802.

29 Baring (ed.), *Windham Diary*, pp. 439–40.

30 BL Add MS 33109, ff. 398 and 406–7.

31 WYRO, Lucas Diary, XXI, f. 23.

32 *Ambigu*, I (1802), p. 172.

33 *Ambigu*, I (1802), pp. 218–19.

34 WYRO, Lucas diary, XXI, f. 50.

35 Dwyer, *Citizen Emperor*, p. 110.

36 Coleridge, *Essays*, II, pp. 490n and 501–2.

37 Cobbett, *Political Proteus*, p. 183; Bourne, *English Newspapers*, p. 275, from *Gentleman's Magazine*, June 1838, p. 578.

38 See Maspero-Clerc, *Peltier*, pp. 163–6. I find it suspicious that the ultra-loyal Royal Academician Joseph Farington was one of the jurors.

39 Peltier, *Trial*, p. 83.

40 Burrows, *French Exile Journalism*, p. 86; BL Add MS 51463.

41 Burrows, *French Exile Journalism*, p. 108; Bourrienne, *Mémoires*, IV, pp. 305–7.

42   Cobbett, *Political Proteus*, p. 162.
43   Bugg, *Five Long Winters*, pp. 105–6.

9 Rousing the Nation

1   Sparrow, *Secret Service*, p. 263; Castlereagh, *Letters and Despatches*, IV,
     pp. 58–62.
2   *Historisches Lexikon der Schweiz*, http://www.hls-dhs-dss.ch/textes/f/
     F17853.php, http://www.hls-dhs-dss.ch/textes/d/D24147.php; Mitchell,
     Underground War, p. 206.
3   Hone, *Cause of Truth*, p. 106.
4   Fox's letter is in Moore, *Sheridan*, p. 312.
5   Sparrow, *Phantom*, p. 150; Bayard to Pelham in TNA HO 95/638.
6   *Political Proteus*, p. 206.
7   Wilson, *British Expedition to Egypt*, pp. 74–7.
8   Rose, *Life of Napoleon*, I, pp. 203–4; Shorter (ed.), *Napoleon and his Fellow
     Travellers*, pp. 252–4.
9   Bourrienne, *Mémoires*, II, pp. 222–7, set out the extenuating
     circumstances for the massacre of what he said was 4000 Albanians and
     the long deliberations in council that preceded it; and on pp. 257–64
     he strongly defended the decision to administer fatal doses of opium to
     what he said were about sixty plague victims, without knowing whether
     or not the opium was finally administered. See Roberts, *Napoleon the
     Great*, pp. 189–92 and 128–9. Dwyer takes a harsher view and, after
     allowing for the normality of hideous behaviour in the sacking of a city,
     finds the cold-blooded executions shocking (*Path to Power*, pp. 416–22).
10   Randolph, *Wilson*, I, p. 220. He certainly discussed the issue with Joseph
     Fourier at the Lazaretto, Toulon, in 1801: 'From Fourier I heard much
     of Buonaparte: especially his reasons for the massacre of Jaffa and for
     poisoning his own sick at Acre. He talks well on all subjects and is one
     of the best-informed men I ever met with.'
11   Randolph, *Wilson*, I, pp. 238–9.
12   *Cobbett's Annual Register*, II (1802), pp. 385–8; *Anti-Jacobin Review*, XIII
     (1802), pp. 337–9.
13   BL Add MS 37869 f.129. See *Histoire de l'expédition de l'armée britannique
     en Égypte*; the French-language version of the frontispiece is dated 7
     April 1803; *Gentleman's Magazine*, 27 (1829), p. 646.
14   *Anti-Jacobin Review*, XIV (1803), p. 222.
15   Wilson's reply was printed *inter alia* in 'The Tender Mercies of Bonaparte
     in Egypt! Britons, Beware!', *Edinburgh Review*, II (1804), pp. 330–3.
     The reviewer did not believe that Pitt was the author of the *Machine
     infernale* either.
16   *Anti-Jacobin Review*, XIV (1803), p. 495.
17   The information may have come from Louis Dupérou. The captured

papers of 1800 in AN F/7/6247 included a 'Liste alphabétique des Mouchards de Paris suivi par quelques Notices sur la Police républicaine'.

18 *Anti-Jacobin Review*, XIV (1803), pp. 28–35.

19 On 10 August 1803 Carysfort wrote to Grenville to ask him, 'as the notions which circulate upon the continent at the present conjuncture may materially affect this country, both now and at future periods, I could wish to have a hint from you what points I should particularly recommend to Gentz, and what turn I should endeavour to give to his work before I write to him.' *Dropmore Papers*, VII, pp. 186–7.

20 See Clayton and O'Connell, *Bonaparte and the British*, p. 13.

21 *Cobbett's Weekly Political Register*, XXXIII (1818), p. 626.

22 Hone, *Three Trials*, pp. 57 and 59.

23 Greatheed, *Englishman in Paris*, pp. 105–6. See Roberts, *Napoleon the Great*, pp. 321–2.

24 Browning, *Whitworth*, pp. 133–4.

25 Malmesbury, *Diaries*, IV, p. 258; Roberts, *Napoleon the Great*, p. 324.

26 Rachel Charlotte Biggs to Nicholas Vansittart, 4 December 1812, in BL Add MS 31234, ff. 23–4; Semmel, *Napoleon and the British*, p. 42. Mrs Biggs was the same person who came up with the idea for the Royal Jubilee in 1809, though, as we see, she was not the innocent member of the public that Linda Colley took her to be (*Britons*, pp. 217–9). See Major and Murden, *Georgian Heroine*.

27 Cobbett's Annual Register, IV (1803), p. 130–42.

28 Cobbett, *Political Proteus*, p. 80.

29 *British Critic*, XXII (1803), p. 214.

30 Wheeler and Broadley, *Invasion*, II, p. 275; p. 281 has a shorter version.

31 *European Magazine*, XLIV (1803), pp. 130–1; see Semmel, *Napoleon and the British*, p. 43.

32 *Loyalist*, I, pp. 3–4.

33 Dibdin, *Professional Life*, 1803, I, pp. 7–8. Wheeler and Broadley, *Invasion*, II, p. 249. Cox Jensen, *Napoleon and British Song*, esp. pp. 57–8.

34 Cox Jensen, *Napoleon and British Song*, p. 61.

35 Wheeler and Broadley, *Invasion*, II, p. 260.

36 More's song is sometimes dated to 1798, but it includes references that can only belong to 1803. See Franklin and Philp, *Napoleon*, pp. 32–3. On song generally, see Cox Jensen.

37 *Morning Post* (26 November 1803).

38 Dundas to lord lieutenants, 6 April 1798, cited in Cookson, *British Armed Nation*, p. 212.

39 Cookson, *British Armed Nation*, pp. 212–13.

40 *Cobbett's Annual Register*, IV (1803), pp. 706–17.

41 *Cobbett's Political Register*, VIII (1805), pp. 979–80.

42 *Fraser's Magazine*, XXIX (1844), p. 571.

10 Grand Conspiracy

1   Caudrillier, 'Complot', II, p. 263.

2   Fauche-Borel, *Mémoires*, II, p. 391, and III, p. 3.

3   AN F/7/6451 dossier 37; Roberts, *Napoleon the Great*, pp. 333–4; Blanc, *Espions*, pp. 226–34.

4   Roberts, *Napoleon the Great*, p. 333.

5   TNA FO 27/80 5 July 1810, Smith memorial and Sidmouth to Wellesley. Sparrow, *Secret Service*, p. 275.

6   Windham, *Diary*, p. 440; Caudrillier, 'Complot', II, p. 259.

7   For the atrocity see Lignereux, 'Moment terroriste', p. 7. On their arrest, Savary, *Memoirs* I part II, pp. 17–18. According to Leclerc's 1 February bulletin from Paris they had been arrested on the information of Pierre-Martin de Laubéypie, in London to investigate fake French banknotes on behalf of the Bank of France, but also charged with infiltrating *chouan* circles. He had warned the Foreign Office about Laubéypie, and they should not have ignored the warning. However, they were arrested before Laubéypie arrived in London, AN F/7/6361 and TNA FO 27/70 f. 256 Paris 1 Feb 1804. On Laubéypie's mission see FO 95/4/3 f. 155.

8   Roberts, *Napoleon the Great*, p. 334, assumes that 'abduct' meant assassinate.

9   Caudrillier, 'Complot', II, pp. 259ff. Montgaillard, *Notice abrégée*, pp. 8–9.

10 *Procès de Georges*, p. 307.

11 He also told Hobart that a French agent in Jersey, thought to be a spy, 'has been ordered away'. Sparrow, *Secret Service*, p. 272.

12 TNA WO 1/924, ff. 101–4; Balleine, *Auvergne*, p. 84.

13 TNA WO 1/924, f. 327.

14 Browning, *Whitworth*, p. 131; Sparrow, *Secret Service*, p. 263.

15 Sparrow, *Secret Service*, p. 267.

16 BM 1981,U.203 and 1985,0119.391. The epigrammatic French evidently posed problems for the translator.

17 *Ambigu*, II (1803), p. 66.

18 *Ambigu*, II (1803), p. 118.

19 TNA FO 27/69 letter of 23 July 1803.

20 Burrows, *French Exile Journalism*, p. 133.

21 *Ambigu*, III (1803), pp. 57–8.

22 *Ambigu*, III (1803), pp. 221–4 and IV (1804), pp. 9–17.

23 Tinseau also produced *The Empire of Germany divided into Departments* and a *Statistical View of the French Republic* (1803).

24 http://www.culture.gouv.fr/documentation/memoire/HTML/IVR31/IA62000656/INDEX.HTM

25 http://preville.chez-alice.fr/divers/personnages.htm#nymphe

26 *Biographie Universelle* (Paris, Michaut: 1844), Supplement, vol. 76, pp. 94–6.

11 Reactivating the Spies

1 Roberts, *Napoleon the Great*, p. 325.
2 TNA FO 27/69.
3 Sparrow, *Secret Service*, p. 279.
4 TNA FO 27/69.
5 AN F/7/6361.
6 TNA FO 27/69.
7 TNA FO 27/70, f. 42; Adm 2/1361.
8 Barrow, *Smith*, II, p. 127.
9 Malmesbury, *Diaries*, IV, p. 294; 'informed him [Pitt] of all I knew relative to the plot in France' in April 1804, but given that the British side of it was being directed from Pitt's own home, it is implausible that he was not already well versed in its details.
10 https://doverhistorian.com/2013/06/09/smiths-folly/
11 ADM 2/1361 July–December 1803.
12 Markham, *Correspondence*, p. 31.
13 Bonner-Smith (ed.), *Letters of St. Vincent*, II, p. 394.
14 Nicolay, *Boulogne Camp.*, pp. 3–5, 20–2, 111–12.
15 AN F/7/6361.
16 AN F/7/6362, Bonaparte to Régnier, 25 August 1803; Napoleon, *Correspondance*, VIII, pp. 623–4.
17 F/7/6362 'Rapport au grand juge ministre de Justice par le citoyen Fardel sur sa mission à Boulogne sur Mer', Boulogne, 8 September 1803.
18 AN F/7/6361; F/7/6365; Maes, 'Conjuration', part 7.
19 TNA FO 27/69, 27/70 f. 52ff.

12 Atrocities of the Corsican Demon

1 *Anti-Jacobin Review*, XV (1803), pp. 332–3.
2 Advertised in the *Morning Chronicle*, 21 November 1803, as published at 10s. 6d. by Thomas Hurst.
3 BL Add MS 37869, f. 129.
4 *Gentleman's Magazine*, XCIX (1829), pp. 645–6.
5 *Revolutionary Plutarch*, II, 1804, p. 172n, referring to pregnancy and poisoning of washerwoman's daughter and pleasure in hospitals and anatomy. 'These particulars of Buonaparte are taken from a work called *Les Annales du Terrorisme*, printed by Desenne, at Paris, in 1795, or *an* iv, page 59, 60 and 62. In February, 1798, the Author, then a prisoner, was in company with Philipeaux at Paris, who confirmed the above mentioned particulars in the presence of d'Ab .... t, at present a Corsican Colonel of Artillery.' If true, candidates might include Sidney Smith, John Wesley Wright and Antoine Viscovitch as well, perhaps, as Pichegru's aide Louis Rusillon and his friend Jean-Baptiste

Couchery. It seems plausible that the work might have been informed by Pichegru's circle in Brompton and Couchery wrote for Regnier and Peltier. It is sometimes ascribed to Lewis Goldsmith, but he was not the author as he was working for the other side at the time, and sometimes to 'Stewarton', to whom similar later works are attributed but who is otherwise unknown.

6 For example, III, pp. 341–69.

7 I have tried to give page references to both the first and second editions of *The Revolutionary Plutarch*.

8 *Anti-Jacobin Review*, XVII (1804), p. 289. 'But as the author has appealed to the public for the truth of his facts, and as thousands of persons now living are able to confute them, if they be not what his authorities state them to be, there is strong presumptive evidence of their authenticity, and, if they remain uncontradicted, we may safely receive them as facts [!].'

9 Oxford, Bodleian Library, Curzon.b.9 (59). BL 806.k.1 (III).

10 BL 806.k.1 (8 is *Such is Buonaparte!*; 74 contains the advertisement for the *History of Buonaparte*).

11 *Revolutionary Plutarch*, II, pp. 160–6/182–8; *Anti-Gallican*, pp. 310–12, taken from the *British Press*.

12 *Anti-Gallican*, pp. 381–9; *Loyalist*, I, pp. 166–8 (number X, 1 October 1803), reprinting the broadsheet *Ring the Alarum Bell* no. III, BL 806.k.1 (75).

13 *Revolutionary Plutarch*, II, p. 138. 2nd edn p. 159.

14 Barré, *Consulate*, p. 2; *Important History*, p. 3.

15 *Revolutionary Plutarch*, II, pp. 170–2, 2nd edn 194–5.

16 *Cobbett's Annual Register*, IV (1803), p. 64; *Loyalist*, I, p. 50; genuine words from Dwyer, *Path to Power*, p. 143.

17 *Anti-Gallican*, p. 382; *Important History*, p. 4; *Loyalist*, I, p. 208; BL 806.k.1 (7); BM 1866,0407.982–5.

18 *Revolutionary Plutarch*, II, pp. 176–82/199–204; *Anti-Gallican*, p. 382; *Important History*, p. 4.

19 *Revolutionary Plutarch*, II, pp. 314 and 322/342 and 350.

20 Barré, *Consulate*, pp. 206–7.

21 *Revolutionary Plutarch*, II, pp. 194–9 and 202/217–22 and 215; *Ambigu*, III (1803), pp. 57–8.

22 *Revolutionary Plutarch*, II, p. 204/227.

23 *Loyalist*, I, p. 49.

24 Barré, *Consulate*, p. 142; *Revolutionary Plutarch*, II, p. 329/358.

25 Barré, *Consulate*, p. 299.

26 The author claimed to have had the story from Guidal (a potential culprit), who told him in May 1801 and was subsequently rusticated by Fouché. Guidal was disgraced on 27 March 1804 and was eventually executed in 1812 for his participation in that year's attempted coup.

Reading between the lines, Guidal was probably one of those republicans who were courted by Anglo-royalists to test out their willingness to play a part in the proposed coup of 1804.

27 *Revolutionary Plutarch*, II, p. 283/309.
28 *Important History*, p. 12.
29 *Anti-Jacobin Review*, XVI (1803), pp. 199–200.
30 *Revolutionary Plutarch*, II, pp. 344–51 and 368/374–82 and 400.
31 *Revolutionary Plutarch*, II, p. 383/415.
32 *Revolutionary Plutarch*, I, pp. 377–84/372–8; *Loyalist*, pp. 37–40.
33 *Anti-Jacobin Review*, XV (1803), pp. 509–30. The fall from the brothel window is p. 512, the 'hatred' p. 521.
34 *Anti-Jacobin Review*, XIV (1803), p. 498; *Revolutionary Plutarch*, 2nd edn, I, p. 130.
35 *Revolutionary Plutarch*, 2nd edn, I, p. 145.
36 *Revolutionary Plutarch*, II, p. 34/I, p. 248.
37 *Buonaparteana*, p. iv.
38 Barré, *Consulate*, p. 22.
39 BL 806.k.1 (11); Wheeler and Broadley, *Invasion*, II, p. 284.
40 BL 806.k.1 (45); *Ambigu*, V (1804), p. 437.
41 Cillessen, Reichardt and Deuling, *Napoleons neue Kleider*, pp. 21–2, 257 and 185–6; Banerji and Donald, *Gillray Observed*, pp. 11–14.
42 *European Magazine*, XLV (1804), p. 56; also published as an endorsement in later editions of *Revolutionary Plutarch*.
43 *Annual Review and History of Literature*, II (1803), p. 510; denied in Barré, *Empire*, p. vii. Arthur Aikin was the son of John.

13 Landing the Assassins

1   TNA FO 27/80, memorandum of the spy 'L. Smith'.
2   *Procès de Georges*, I, p. 140; correspondence accounts for July.
3   Pocock's statement in *Thirst for Glory*, p. 158, that Wright landed Cadoudal from the brig *Vincejo* is incorrect, as the brig was still unavailable for want of officers on 10 January 1804 (Markham, *Correspondence*, p. 133).
4   Markham, *Correspondence*, pp. 31, 127.
5   TNA Adm 51/4415; Adm 36/15501.
6   Lloyd, *Keith Papers*, p. 33.
7   Markham, *Correspondence*, pp. 121, 158.
8   Lloyd (ed.), *Keith Papers*, p. 31.
9   Napoleon, *Correspondance générale*, IV, p. 235, no. 7871.
10 Maes, 'Conjuration', part 4.
11 Ségur, *Memoirs of an Aide de Camp*, pp. 96–7.
12 Fauriel, *Derniers jours*, p. 184n.
13 TNA FO 27/71 'Note'.

14 Rusillon's evidence under interrogation, *Procès de Georges*, I, p. 53.
    Lajolais evidence, Hall, *Pichegru*, pp. 310–12.

15 *Ambigu*, IV, p. 357. TNA FO 27/71. In his analysis Peltier may well have
    been trying to shift blame onto Moreau, but there can be little doubt of
    Moreau's deep involvement in the plot.

16 TNA FO 27/69.

17 Lloyd (ed.), *Keith Papers*, p. 55.

18 According to Maes, 'Conjuration', part 5.

19 Lloyd (ed.), *Keith Papers*, p. 57.

20 Markham, *Correspondence*, pp. 121–2 and 125.

21 Lloyd (ed.), *Keith Papers*, p. 59.

22 Lloyd (ed.), *Keith Papers*, p. 65.

23 Markham, *Correspondence*, p. 132.

24 TNA Adm 1/4353; Hall, *Pichegru*, p. 312.

25 Markham, *Correspondence*, pp. 133–4.

26 Markham, *Correspondence*, pp. 137–8.

27 According to Fauriel, Moreau delayed the meeting for three days on the
    pretext of having a hunting party and set it for the evening of 27 January,
    but Fauriel's aim was to clear Moreau of involvement in the plot; it is
    difficult to see how it could have got so far without greater involvement
    from Moreau than Fauriel allows. Fauriel, *Derniers jours*, p. 184.

28 AN F/7/6361 and TNA FO 27/70 II.

29 *Courier de Londres*, 6–17 January 1804, beginning pp. 13–16 with text as
    in Lutaud, *Révolutions*, A5 (p. 305). On 13 January (p. 32) the *Courier*
    announced that the pamphlet would be published separately on Monday
    16 by Prosper & Co. for 1s. 3d. This was the *Traduction du Pamphlet qui
    a fait mourir l'Usurpateur Cromwell, titulé Tuer n'est pas Assassiner, dédié à
    Napoléon Buonaparté*, printed by Cox, Fils et Baylis but according to the
    title page also sold by Prosper.

30 See Lutaud, *Révolutions*, pp. 269–81. Lutaud (p. 285) was on the
    right track but incorrect in believing that the *Lettre d'un Anglais* was
    distributed either by Méhée de la Touche or by Georges. Although it
    is possible that copies were printed and distributed by other channels
    as well as by Drake it is certain that Drake handled printing and
    distribution of one edition because there are receipts in his accounts (BL
    Add MS 38569 f. 113).

31 *European Magazine*, XLV (1804), p. 56; *Anti-Jacobin Review*, XVII
    (1804), p. 302.

32 Yorke, *Anti-Corsican*, p. 129. See Semmel, *Napoleon and the British*, p. 128.

33 Rémusat, *Mémoires*, I, pp. 309–10; Lutaud, *Révolutions*, pp. 339 and 369.
    The articles and the *Lettre à Bonaparte* were reprinted in the *Moniteur*.
    Henry Redhead Yorke's letters as Galgacus to the *Star* from 2 August
    1803 were collected in *The Anti-Corsican, or War of Liberty*, 1804.

34 Malmesbury, *Diaries*, IV, p. 287.

14 Méhée de la Touche

1   *Biographical Anecdotes*, II, p. 418; *Revolutionary Plutarch*, III, p. 296.

2   TNA FO 95/4/3 ff. 186–9.

3   TNA FO 27/69 Doyle to Pelham 5 February 1803 and to Hammond 6 February 1803.

4   TNA FO 27/69 Doyle to Pelham 13 March 1803; Cobban, 'Méhée', p. 102.

5   TNA FO 27/69 Doyle to Hawkesbury 23 March 1803 refers to a letter from Hawkesbury of 18 March.

6   Blanc, *Espions*, p. 241, and see Moleville's account in Lutaud, *Révolutions*, pp. 309–11.

7   *Cobbett's Political Register*, VI (1804), pp. 782–3.

8   Méhée, *Alliance*, pp. 69–70; *Ambigu*, V (1804), p. 429.

9   *Ambigu*, V (1804), p. 427; Barré, *Empire*, pp. 98, 235, 293–4.

10 TNA FO 27/69 undated, filed in March.

11 TNA FO 95/4/3 ff. 145–6.

12 The piece printed in *Revolutionary Plutarch*, III, pp. 341–69, appears to be genuine.

13 TNA FO 27/80 Moleville memorandum, 3 March 1810.

14 TNA FO 95/4/3 ff. 193–210; Méhée, *Alliance*, pp. 34–6; Cobban, 'Méhée', p. 104; Fayet, *Recherches historiques*, I, p. 130.

15 Malmesbury, *Diaries*, IV, pp. 262–3.

16 The payments are recorded in TNA HO 387/6/9, the first, interestingly, on 11 May, before war was declared.

17 *Biographical Anecdotes*, II, pp. 412–19.

18 *Ambigu*, I (1802), p. 152.

19 Barré, *Consulate*, pp. 278–9.

20 Barré, *Empire*, pp. 298–309.

21 See Lutaud, *Révolutions*, pp. 225–34; Hill, *Macaulay*, pp. 212–23.

22 Barré, *Empire*, pp. 299–304. Lutaud (*Révolutions*, pp. 303–5) was not aware of Barré's transcription and claimed that the only known version of this text was in Détré, *Apologistes*, pp. 284–6. Détré gave no source for his version of the preface and Lutaud assumed that he owned a copy of a pamphlet but it is possible that he took the text from Barré. It differs from Barré's only very slightly in that 'sixth edition' is written by Détré as 'this edition'. Nevertheless, their conclusion that this was the text of a version written by Méhée and circulated in France in 1803–4 and almost certainly that of the *Lettre d'un Anglais à Bonaparte* seems correct. Lutaud (*Révolutions*, p. 280) suggests that the different preface that appeared in the *Courier de Londres* may have been written by Jean-Baptiste Couchery.

23 TNA FO 95/4/3 f. 185.

24 TNA FO 95/4/3 ff. 190–2.

25 TNA FO 83/4, to Drake, 2 Oct 1803. Cobban, 'Méhée', p. 104.

26 Fayet, *Recherches historiques*, I, pp. 138–41.

27 Fayet, *Recherches historiques*, I, pp. 141–3.

28 Napoleon, *Correspondance*, IX, pp. 92–3.

29 Méhée, *Alliance*, p. 138.

30 BL Add MS 38569 f. 113.

31 Lutaud, *Révolutions*, p. 285, notes that Méhée's pamphlet referred to
    the hero of a popular French story, *Le Conte de la Ramée, grenadier de
    Champagne* (1784), and that his name is an anagram of *armée*, and that
    the text was probably supposed to be a version of the address to the
    soldiers of Cromwell that was an integral part of *Killing No Murder*.

32 BL Add MS 38569 f. 5.

33 TNA FO 27/80 Moleville memorandum, 3 March 1810.

34 Blanc, *Espions*, p. 240.

35 Roederer, *Oeuvres*, III, p. 363.

36 Fayet, *Recherches historiques*, I, p. 138, gives the letter to Shée in which
    Méhée made this claim. Waresquiel argues that although there is no
    surviving documentary evidence in the police files or secret accounts to
    prove that Fouché sent Méhée to London, the two men knew each other
    well enough for there to be little doubt about it.

15 Paris in Panic

1 Desmarest, *Témoignages historiques*, pp. 89–90.

2 Savary, *Memoirs*, I part II, pp. 15–18.

3 Napoleon, *Correspondance*, IX, p. 272.

4 Waresquiel, *Fouché*, pp. 394–5.

5 Blanc, *Espions*, pp. 225–35.

6 Réal, *Indiscrétions*, pp. 53–61; Desmarest, *Témoignages historiques*, pp.
   91–2; Savary, *Memoirs*, I part II, pp. 26–7; TNA FO 27/70 for the
   measures taken; Fauriel, *Derniers jours*, p. 206.

7 Ségur, *Memoirs of an Aide de Camp*, p. 99.

8 Méhée, *Alliance*, pp. 185–7 (this letter reached Drake on 11 February); BL
   Add MS 38358 f. 98v confirms Méhée was not told about Cadoudal.

9 Napoleon, *Correspondance*, IX, p. 288.

10 *Ambigu*, IV (1804), pp. 136–7.

11 TNA FO 27/70 f. 256.

12 The detailed account of the meetings is derived from a report to the
    Foreign Office that was probably written by the spy Désiré Joliclerc in
    TNA FO 27/70 f. 406ff.

13 As Sir John Hall noted astutely: *Pichegru*, pp. 317–19. Macdonald was not
    put on trial but Napoleon did not employ him again until 1809.

14 TNA FO 27/70 ff. 372–3; *Ambigu*, V (1804), p. 53.

15 Réal, *Indiscrétions*, pp. 54–63 with more detail.

16 TNA FO 27/70 f. 372.

17 Savary, *Memoirs*, I part II, pp. 17–25.

18 The *Leyden Gazette*, quoted in *Ambigu*, IV (1804), p. 356, gave a different version of this arrest in which Mme Denand, when arrested, attempted to hide a glove, which proved to contain a note with another rendezvous and an English coin. The police replaced her with another *cabaretière* and next day captured Picot after he had matched the token, but lost the people following him.

19 Fauriel, *Derniers jours*, pp. 231–3. Dubois hated Fouché and his former private secretary Fauriel, and the feeling was mutual.

20 *Ambigu*, IV, pp. 355–7, reprinting a supplement to the *Leyden Gazette* of 21 February. Desmarest, *Témoignages historiques*, p. 95, gives a slightly different version.

21 Maes, 'Conjuration', part 5.

22 Savary, *Memoirs*, I part II, pp. 17–25; Fayet, *Recherches historiques*, I, p. 159n.

23 Markham, *Correspondence*, pp. 140–1.

24 AN F/7/6361 report on what agents had learned through deception from Philippe's wife.

25 Markham, *Correspondence*, p. 158.

26 TNA Adm 2/1362 Marsden to Patton, 6 March 1804.

27 TNA FO 27/70 Rapport de M. Brebillon sur la parte de la Correspondance, et les moyens de la réparer, London, 23 April 1804.

28 See Savary's report of 17 February in Fayet, *Recherches historiques*, I, pp. 158–9 and AN F/7/6361, Réal's report to Régnier of 17 May 1804.

29 TNA FO 27/70 Rapport de M. Brebillon.

30 AN F/7/6361 explanation of accounts, interrogation of Flouets; AN F/7/6362.

31 AN F/7/6362 report of Dumont to Réal, 14 April 1804.

32 Desmarest, *Témoignages historiques*, pp. 95–6.

33 Olivier Blanc argued (*Espions*, p. 234) that Bouvet was a traitor from the start, but I find that theory unlikely, particularly as he was rewarded in 1814, which would not have happened had his fellow conspirators thought he had been a traitor. It is also most unlikely that Bonaparte would have imprisoned him for ten years had he been a plant.

34 Grasilier, 'Par qui fut livré', p. 10; Hall, *Pichegru*, pp. 316–18; TNA FO 27/70 ff. 406–9 'Particulars relative to General Pichegru, received 11 June 1804'; f. 410 Jean-Baptiste Couchery to Hammond, 12 June 1804.

35 Morand, 'Un journal napoléonien de propagande', pp. 801–2.

36 BL Add MS 38569 Drake to Hawkesbury, 21 Feb 1804.

37 Grasilier, 'Par qui fut livré', pp. 9–14; Hall, *Pichegru*, pp. 342–3. TNA FO 27/70.

38 *Ambigu*, IV (1804), pp. 274–6.

39 Desmarest, *Témoignages historiques*, p. 138.

40   *Gazette d'Hambourg* reprinted in *Ambigu*, IV (1804), pp. 426–7; Ségur, *Memoirs of an Aide de Camp*, p. 104; Hall, *Pichegru*, p. 340.

41   Savary, *Memoirs*, I part II, pp. 26–7; *Ambigu*, IV (1804), pp. 364–5.

42   *Ambigu*, V (1804), pp. 211–12, from the *Moniteur*; Fayet, *Recherches historiques*, I, pp. 228–30; Lenotre, *Cadoudal*, pp. 199–203.

16   Worse than a Crime

1   Réal, *Indiscrétions*, pp. 110–12; Savary, *Memoirs*, I part II, pp. 33–4. Artois had got as far as Portsmouth in 1800 (TNA FO 27/56).

2   Fayet, *Recherches historiques*, I, p. 196. Louis XVIII had always refused his consent to their marriage but Fayet believed it to have taken place.

3   Fayet, *Recherches historiques*, I, pp. 204–5.

4   Bertaud, *Enghien*, p. 320.

5   Bertaud, *Enghien*, p. 335.

6   Much of this seems to have been learned on his second visit to de Mussey on 27 February 1804. Fayet, *Recherches historiques*, I, p. 167.

7   Fayet, *Recherches historiques*, I, pp. 205–6.

8   AN F/7/6417. Lentz is sceptical about the authenticity of this report (*Savary*, p. 77).

9   Bertaud, *Enghien*, pp. 343–4.

10   Waresquiel thinks Fouché manipulated Bonaparte (*Fouché*, pp. 396–7). Réal's account (*Indiscrétions*, pp. 107–19) is not as candid as it might be – he must surely have known more about Méhée's activities and the supposed threat from the east than he admits, and it seems likely that with Méhée's help Fouché and Réal and probably also Talleyrand pushed Bonaparte towards precipitate action against Enghien.

11   Fayet, *Recherches historiques*, I, pp. 212–13 and 223–8; Bertaud, *Enghien*, p. 345.

12   Savary, *Memoirs*, I part II, pp. 36–7.

13   Fayet, *Recherches historiques*, II, pp. 44–7.

14   Bertaud, *Enghien*, p. 357.

15   Roberts, *Napoleon the Great*, p. 337.

16   Rémusat, *Mémoires*, I, pp. 312–24.

17   Réal, *Indiscrétions*, p. 116.

18   Savary, *Memoirs*, I part II, pp. 40–4.

19   Fayet, *Recherches historiques*, I, pp. 251–66.

20   Waresquiel, *Fouché*, p. 397.

21   Réal, *Indiscrétions*, p. 119.

22   TNA FO 27/71 as an item in Ratel's expenses.

17 The Eagle Does Not Catch Flies

1   TNA FO 27/70, my translation.
2   BL Add MS 38569, ff. 53–5.
3   BL Add MS 38569, ff. 55–63.
4   *Cobbett's Political Register*, v (1804), pp. 347–8.
5   *Cobbett's Political Register*, v (1804), pp. 412–16.
6   Fayet, *Recherches historiques*, ii, p. 140.
7   *Cobbett's Political Register*, v (1804), pp. 436–7.
8   TNA FO 27/70.
9   TNA PC 1/3596.
10 TNA FO 27/71 report of Stevenot.
11 *Ambigu*, v (1804), pp. 213–14.
12 *Ambigu*, v (1804), pp. 212–13 and 224–5; Napoleon, *Correspondance*, ix, p. 389.
13 *Ambigu*, v (1804), pp. 218–20; Napoleon, *Correspondance*, ix, pp. 398–9.
14 BL Add MS 38569, f. 83; Sparrow, *Secret Service*, p. 302.
15 Rosey's report is printed in Fayet, *Recherches historiques*, ii, pp. 264–77.
16 Sparrow, *Secret Service*, p. 303.
17 TNA FO 353/82; Sparrow, *Secret Service*, pp. 301–2.
18 BL Add MS 38571 ff. 63–75.
19 BL Add MS 38569 No.17 28 March 1804 89.
20 TNA FO 9/28.
21 BL Add MS 38569 No.21 144 3 April 1804.
22 BL Add MS 38569 f. 150; FO 353/74.
23 *Cobbett's Political Register*, v (1804), pp. 606–8, and vi (1804), pp. 765–71.
24 Sparrow, *Secret Service*, p. 305.
25 Méhée, *Alliance*, p. 264.
26 *Cobbett's Political Register*, v (1804), pp. 629–30.

18 Trials and Executions

1   TNA FO 27/70 report of Poix; AN F/7/6362, report of Dumont to Réal, 14 April 1804.
2   *Ambigu*, v (1804), pp. 143–7 'Meurtre du Général Pichegru'.
3   Hall, *Pichegru*, pp. 348–51. Desmarest, *Témoignages historiques*, p. 145.
4   Barré, *Empire*, pp. 260–1.
5   TNA FO 27/70 and 71. There was a discussion of the Velocifers in the *Oberdeutscher Justitz und Polizey Anzeiger*, December 1804, pp. 303–7.
6   TNA FO 27/71 'Comte des dépenses faites par Mr. le Moine'.
7   Barré, *Empire*, p. 311.
8   Fayet, *Recherches historiques*, ii, p. 145.

9   *Cobbett's Political Register*, v (1804), p. 697.

10 *Anti-Jacobin Review*, XVII (1804), pp. i–x.

11 *Ambigu*, IV (1804), p. 414; TNA FO 27/71 'Note'.

12 Markham, *Correspondence*, p. 174; Bonner-Smith, *Letters of St. Vincent*,
    II, p. 401.

13 See TNA WO 1/750 Talleyrand to Harrowby, 28 August 1804, in
    which the French authorities explained that Wright had been caught
    red-handed landing Jean-Marie and two others. They presumably didn't
    catch them. That one was Guillemot is speculation, but the timing fits.
    Guillemot was denounced by a courier in November, was captured on
    15 December by a patrol of eleven hussars, and shot on 5 January 1805
    near Vannes.

14 *Naval Chronicle*, XII (1804), pp. 15–16 (Julien's report) or XXXIV (1815), pp.
    441–4 (life of Wright).

15 *Times*, 24 March 1804 and 11 June 1804, in Fayet, *Recherches historiques*,
    II, pp. 151–2. The alleged source of the letter published by the ministerial
    newspapers was the usual *Nouvelles à la Main*.

16 TNA FO 27/80, 29 June 1810.

17 Fayet, *Recherches historiques*, II, p. 181.

18 *Ambigu*, v (1804), pp. 62–3; Dwyer, *Citizen Emperor*, p. 139.

19 TNA FO 27/70 Rapport de Mr Durieux. AN F/7/6362 Jugement
    rendu par la Commission Militaire Spéciale séante au Palais de
    Justice à Rouen.

19 The Emperor Napoleon

1   These paragraphs are dependent on Dwyer, *Citizen Emperor*, pp. 124–7
    and 135–44.

2   Gentz quoted by Dwyer, *Citizen Emperor*, p. 131; *Ambigu*, v (1804), p.
    437; *Cobbett's Political Register*, v (1804), p. 754.

3   Nicolay, *Boulogne Camp*, pp. 122–5.

4   Nicolay, *Boulogne Camp*, pp. 297–308; Dwyer, *Citizen Emperor*,
    pp. 148–52.

5   *Cobbett's Political Register*, VI (1804), pp. 888–9.

6   *Cobbett's Political Register*, VI (1804), pp. 934–5.

7   See Waresquiel, *Fouché*, pp. 393–4.

8   See Grasilier, 'Enlèvement de Rumbold'; Malmesbury, *Diaries*,
    IV, p. 331.

9   AN F/7/6451. (F/7/6448-52 are the surviving Rumbold papers, lacking
    anything Fouché might have seen fit to remove.)

10 *Moniteur*, 17 September and 18 November 1804.

11 Cillessen, Reichardt and Deuling, *Napoleons neue Kleider*, p. 22; Banerji
    and Donald, *Gillray Observed*, p. 14.

12 See Burrows, 'British Francophone Propaganda', p. 44.

13 TNA FO 38/5. On 25 September 1804 Paoli wrote from Altona asking for a 200-*louis* pension and pointing out that he was now in a place where he could write pamphlets and even a journal but did not have the means. A letter written in London on 24 March 1805 discusses a project to set up a paper in Stralsund in Sweden, but for authorisation Chagny needed the sort of official backing that the British government was unwilling to give because they didn't want it known on the Continent that they were paying a journalist to write in their favour (FO 27/71).

14 Cadoudal is still alive in the text, but a footnote gives an account of his execution.

15 *Revolutionary Plutarch*, III, pp. 244 and 246.

16 *Revolutionary Plutarch*, III, pp. 260–1 and 283–5.

17 *Revolutionary Plutarch*, III, pp. 316–17.

18 *Revolutionary Plutarch*, III, pp. 370–3.

19 Barré, *Empire*, p. 99.

20 Barré, *Empire*, p. 225.

21 Barré, *Empire*, pp. 419–50.

22 *Cobbett's Political Register*, VI (1804), pp. 823–4.

23 *Cobbett's Political Register*, VI (1804), p. 223.

24 Roberts, *Napoleon the Great*, p. 355.

25 TNA FO 27/71.

20 Epilogue

1   Goldsmith, *Secret History*, pp. 140 and 152.

2   Goldsmith, *Secret History*, pp. 160–78; Bourrienne, *Mémoires*, V, pp. 272–5, and VI, p. 294. See also Fauriel, *Derniers jours*, p. 215.

3   Desmarest, *Témoignages historiques*, pp. 102–3.

4   *Ambigu*, V (1804), p. 424; BL Add MS 38358, f. 98v.

5   Pierre Victor Malouet in London to Jacques Mallet du Pan, 16 August 1793, in A. Sayous (ed.), *Memoirs and Correspondence of Mallet du Pan*, 2 vols (London, 1852) I, pp. 383–5.

6   Lenotre, *Cadoudal*, pp. 252–4; Fayet, *Recherches historiques*, II, p. 181n.

7   Réal, *Indiscrétions*, pp. 95–100.

8   According to John Lewis Mallet, who knew Reeves well, as Reeves had generously provided a home for his father Jacques Mallet du Pan when he fled to England. Mallet, *Mallet du Pan and the French Revolution*, p. 291.

9   Vane (ed.), *Castlereagh Correspondence*, XI, pp. 357, 358, 364.

10 BL Add Ms 69068. Sparrow, *Secret Service*, p. 300.

Select Bibliography

London, British Library (BL)

Add MSS 16919, 16921, 16922, 16925, 16927, 16929 Papers of the
Association for Preserving Liberty and Property

Add MS 27337 Gillray papers

Add MS 29764 Sheridan papers

Add MS 31234 ff. 23–5 Rachel Charlotte Biggs to Vansittart

Add MS 32731 ff. 7–11 on the Secret Office of the Post Office

Add MS 33109 Portland papers

Add MS 33110, ff. 179–82 Report from Freeling to Pelham on British
subscribers to the *Argus*

Add MS 37851 Windham correspondence including secret
service accounts

Add MS 37853 Windham correspondence with William Cobbett

Add MS 37869 Windham correspondence

Add MS 37923 Windham diary 1798–9

Add MS 37924 Windham diary 1800

Add MS 38357–8 Hawkesbury papers 1801–5

Add MS 38569 Drake correspondence with Hawkesbury

Add MS 38571 Spencer Smith correspondence with Hawkesbury

Add MS 46822 Drake correspondence with Grenville and Whitworth

Add MS 46830 part 2 Drake correspondence with Tinseau d'Amondans

Add MS 51462–4 Secret service payments

Add MS 69076 Grenville's secret service accounts

Add MS 89143 Canning papers

648.c.26/19 collection of broadsheets of c.1793

806.k.1 collection of broadsheets c.1803
1851.c.3 collection of broadsheets c.1803

London, Coutts Bank Archive

Lord Grenville's account GH

London, The National Archives (TNA)

Adm 1/2695 Captains' letters, Wright
Adm 2/1361 Admiralty out letters July–December 1803
Adm 2/1362 Admiralty out letters 1804
Adm 36/15501 Muster book of *Basilisk*
Adm 36/17022 Muster book of *Bonetta*
Adm 41/42 Muster books of *Favorite*, *Flirt*, *Fly* armed cutters
Adm 41/44 Muster book of *Griffin* armed cutter
Adm 51/1499 Captain's log, *Hound*
Adm 51/4023 Captain's logs, *Speculator* hired armed lugger and *Stag* hired
    armed cutter
Adm 51/4415 Captain's log, *Basilisk*
EXT 9/34 Letters from James Walsh on activities of Coleridge,
    Wordsworth and Thelwall at Alfoxton
FO 9/28 Bavaria 1804, Drake correspondence
FO 27/53 France 1798
FO 27/56 France 1799
FO27/57 Surveillance of Otto
FO 27/69 France 1801
FO 27/70 France 1802–4
FO 27/71 France 1804–5
FO 27/80 France 1810, memorials of Moleville and 'L. Smith'
FO 27/359 France 1826, memorial of Flint
FO 38/7 Advices and Intelligences from various Persons employed by the
    British Government on the Frontiers of Holland 1803
FO 78/20 Sublime Porte 1799
FO 82/3 Württemberg 1804
FO 95/2/5 Secret intelligence from Paris 1800–1
FO 95/4/3 Méhée documentation
FO 95/638 Bulletins from Paris 1802
FO 353/80 Intelligence from France and Germany

FO 353/81 Gentz to Jackson 1803–6
FO 353/82 Correspondence between Jackson and Spencer Smith
HO 42/64/64 Duke of Portland's secret service accounts
HO 69/8/41 Bouillon papers 1795
HO 69/28 Bouillon papers 1800
HO 387/2/4 John King secret service vouchers
HO 387/3 Secret service payments
HO 387/4/5 Charles William Flint account given 23 Aug 1800 on his
    leaving England
HO 387/5-10 Secret service accounts
PC 1/120A/204 Letter announcing discovery of Cadoudal plot
PC 1/3596 Order to cruiser commanders to try to save fleeing conspirators
PRO 30/8/229/2 Secret service payments
PROB 11/1476/97 Will of John Wesley Wright 1798
PROB 11/1579/331 Will of Justin Ratel
PROB 11/1583/55 Will of Arabella Williams
PROB 11/2025/337 Will of Pierre-Marie Poix dit Durieux
TS 11/578/1893 Brief against James Belcher, bookseller of Birmingham
TS 11/175/702 Brief against William Holland, printseller
WO 1/397 Intelligence – various agents on the Continent 1799–1803
WO 1/750 Case of Captain Wright
WO 1/923 Bouillon correspondence 1800–1801
WO 1/924 Bouillon correspondence 1802–5

London, National Maritime Museum (NMM)

MSS/84/014/1 c.40 Secret service docs 1790–1804
MSS/84/014/2 c.40 Secret service docs 1790–1804
NEP/1 Sixty-seven letters from William May
NEP/2 Fifty-four letters from R. C. Etches, W. Wilby and Sir W.
    Sidney Smith
NEP/3 Secret account book of the Admiralty, kept by Charles Wright,
    1795–1804; accounts and letters from Nepean, 1783–1803
NEP/6 Letters from Sir John Jervis (later Earl St Vincent) to
    Nepean, 1801–03

Kent Record Office, Maidstone (KRO)

U269/O197/4 26 Sidney Smith correspondence in Egypt

U1590/S5/O4/3 Sidney Smith correspondence with Pitt 1794–1804
U1590/S5/O5/5 Letters from General Edward Smith

Oxford, Bodleian Library

Curzon Collection of prints, broadsheets etc. relating to Napoleon, formerly belonging to A. M. Broadley

Paris, Archives Nationales (AN)

F/7/6247 chiefly *conspiration anglaise*
F/7/6250 chiefly Hyde de Neuville
F/7/6251 dossier Williams, dossier Ratel
F/7/6271 chiefly *machine infernale*
F/7/6329 Andréossy at Dover
F/7/6336 Goldsmith in Germany
F/7/6361 Boulogne/Abbeville correspondence
F/7/6362 Boulogne/Abbeville correspondence
F/7/6364 dossiers Poix, Leclerc
F/7/6365 dossier Préville and other interrogations
F/7/6371 on Ratel with correspondence intercepted at Calais
F/7/6448-51 Rumbold papers

West Yorkshire Record Office (WYRO)

Lucas diary: Diary of Amabel, Lady Lucas, available online at: https://library.hud.ac.uk/calmview/Record.aspx?src=CalmView. Catalog&id=Yorke

Ambigu
Annual Biography and Obituary
Annual Review and History of Literature
Antidote, ou l'année philosophique et littéraire
Anti-Jacobin
Anti-Jacobin Review
Cobbett's Political Register
Critical Review
Edinburgh Magazine

European Magazine
Gentleman's Magazine
Monthly Magazine
New Annual Register
Paris pendant l'année
The Parliamentary Register

Caledonian Mercury
True Briton

An Address to the Public from the Society for the Suppression of Vice, instituted, in London, 1802: containing an account of the proceedings of the society, from its original institution, 1803

Adolphus, John, *Biographical Memoirs of the French Revolution*, 2 vols, London: Cadell and Davies, 1799

——, *Footsteps of Blood; or the March of the Republicans*, London: Hatchard, 1803

Adresse à Bonaparte, London, 1803

Alexander, David, *Richard Newton and English Caricature in the 1790s*, Manchester: MUP, 1998

Alger, John Goldsworth, *Napoleon's British Visitors and Captives, 1801–1815*, London: Archibald Constable, 1904

Andress, David, *The Savage Storm: Britain on the Brink in the Age of Napoleon*, London: Little, Brown, 2012

The Anti-Gallican, or Standard of British Loyalty, Religion and Liberty, London: Verner & Hood and Asperne, 1804

Ashton, John, *British Caricature and Satire on Napoleon I*, 2 vols, London: Chatto & Windus, 1884

Aspinall, Arthur, *Politics and the Press c.1780–1850*, Home & Van Thal, 1949

—— (ed.), *The Later Correspondence of George III*, 5 vols (1962–70)

Association Papers, London: Sewell etc., 1793

The Atrocities of the Corsican Demon, or a glance at Buonaparté, London: Lane, Newman & Co., 1803

Bainbridge, Simon, *Napoleon and English Romanticism*, Cambridge: CUP, 1995

Balleine, G. R., *The Tragedy of Philippe d'Auvergne*, London and Chichester, Phillimore & Co., 1973

Banerji, Christiane and Diana Donald, *Gillray Observed: the Earliest Account of his Caricatures in* London und Paris, Cambridge: CUP, 1999

Baring, Mrs Henry (ed.), *The Diary of the Right Hon. William Windham 1784–1810*, London: Longmans, 1866

Barker, Hannah, *Newspapers, Politics, and Public Opinion in Late Eighteenth-Century England*, Oxford: Clarendon, 1998

Barré, William Vincent, *History of the French Consulate, under Napoleon Buonaparte*, London: Thomas Hurst, 1804

——, *The Rise, Progress, Decline and Fall, of Buonaparte's Empire in France*, London: J. Badcock, 1805

Barrell, John, *The Spirit of Despotism: Invasions of Privacy in the 1790s*, Oxford: OUP, 2006

Barrow, John, *The Life and Correspondence of Admiral Sir William Sidney Smith*, 2 vols, London: Richard Bentley, 1848

Belsham, William, *Memoirs of the Reign of George III from his accession, to the peace of Amiens*, 8 vols, 6th edn, London: R. Phillips, 1808

Bertaud, Jean-Paul, *Le duc d'Enghien*, Paris: Fayard, 2001

——, *Quand les enfants parlaient de gloire: l'armée au coeur de la France de Napoléon*, Paris: Aubier, coll. historique, 2006

——, Alan Forrest, Annie Jourdan, *Napoléon, le monde et les Anglais: guerre des mots et des images*, Paris: Editions Autrement, 2004

Bew, John, *Castlereagh: a Life*, Oxford: OUP, 2012

Bickley, Francis L. (ed.), *The Diaries of Sylvester Douglas, Lord Glenbervie*, 2 vols, London: Constable, 1928

Bigard, Louis, *Le Comte Réal, ancien jacobin. De la Commune Révolutionnaire de Paris à la Police Générale de l'Empire*, Versailles, 1937

Bills, Mark, *Samuel William Fores, Satirist: Caricatures from the Reform Club*, exhibition catalogue, Gainsborough's House, Sudbury, 2014

Bindman, David, *The Shadow of the Guillotine: Britain and the French Revolution*, exhibition catalogue, London: British Museum, 1989

Biographical Anecdotes of the Founders of the French Republic, London: R. Phillips, 2 vols, 1797 (2nd edn, 1799)

Blanc, Olivier, *Les espions de la Révolution et de l'Empire*, Paris: Perrin, 1995

BM Satires: *Catalogue of Political and Personal Satires preserved in the Department of Prints and Drawings of the British Museum*, VI–VIII, ed. M. D. George, 1942–9

Bonner-Smith, Davis (ed.), *Letters of Admiral of the Fleet, the Earl of St. Vincent, whilst the First Lord of the Admiralty, 1801–1804*, 2 vols, London: Navy Records Society, 1922 and 1927

Bourne, H. R. Fox, *English Newspapers: Chapters in the History of Journalism*, 2 vols, London: Chatto & Windus, 1887

Bourrienne, Louis Antoine Fauvelet de, *Mémoires de M. Bourrienne ministre d'état de Napoléon*, 10 vols, Paris: Ladvocat, 1829–30

Bower, Peter, 'Economic Warfare as a Deliberate Weapon', in V. H. Hewitt (ed.), *The Banker's Art: Studies in Paper Money* London: British Museum Press, 1995, pp. 46–63

Bowman, H. M., 'Preliminary Stages of the Peace of Amiens', University of Toronto Studies, History, Second Series, 1, pp. 77–155

Braithwaite, Helen, *Romanticism, Publishing and Dissent: Joseph Johnson and the Cause of Liberty*, London: Palgrave Macmillan, 2003

Broadley, Arthur Meyrick, *Napoleon in Caricature*, 2 vols, London: John Lane, 1911

Browning, Oscar, *England and Napoleon in 1803, being the despatches of Lord Whitworth and others*, London: Longmans, 1887

Bugg, John, *Five Long Winters: the Trials of British Romanticism*, Stanford University Press, 2014

Buonaparteana, or sketches to serve for an Inquiry into the Virtues of the Buonaparte Family, Bath, 1804

Burdon, William, *Various Thoughts on Politicks, Morality, and Literature*, Newcastle: for the author, 1800

——, *The Life and Character of Buonaparte from his birth to the 15th of August, 1804*, Newcastle: Anderson, 1804

Burrows, Simon, *French Exile Journalism and European Politics, 1792–1814*, Woodbridge: Boydell & Brewer, 2000

——, 'Culture and Misperception: The Law and the Press in the Outbreak of War in 1803', *International History Review*, XVII (1996), pp. 793–818

——, 'The Struggle for European Opinion in the Napoleonic Wars: British Francophone Propaganda, 1803–1814', *French History*, 11:1 (1997), pp. 29–53

Cambacérès, Jean-Jacques Régis de, *Mémoires inédits*, Paris: Perrin, 1999

Cannadine, David (ed.), *Trafalgar in History: a Battle and its Afterlife*, London: Palgrave Macmillan, 2006

Caudrillier, G., 'Le Complot de l'An XII', *Revue Historique*, Sep–Dec 1900, pp. 278ff; Jan–Apr 1901, pp. 257ff; Jan–Apr 1902, pp. 57ff

——, *L'Association Royaliste de l'Institut Philanthropique à Bordeaux et la conspiration anglaise en France pendant la 2e coalition*, thèse, Paris, 1908

Chatel de Brancion, Laurence, *Le Sacre de Napoléon: le rêve de changer le monde*, Paris: Perrin, 2004

Cillessen, Wolfgang, Rolf Reichardt and Christian Deuling (eds), *Napoleons neue Kleider: Pariser und Londoner Karikaturen im klassischen Weimer*, Berlin: G + H Verlag, 2006

Cillessen, Wolfgang, '"Holland herboren – Europa in noo" Die Hollandia regenerata des David Hess und ihre europäische Rezeption', in Alberto Milano (ed.), *Commercio delle stampe e diffusione delle immagini nei secoli XVIII e XIX*, Rovereto: ViaDellaTerra, 2008

Clayton, Tim, *The English Print 1688–1802*, New Haven and London: Yale University Press, 1997

—— and Sheila O'Connell, *Bonaparte and the British: prints and propaganda in the age of Napoleon*, exhibition catalogue, London: British Museum, 2015

Cobban, Alfred, 'The Great Mystification of Méhée de la Touche', *Historical Research*, 41, 1968, pp. 100–6

——, 'British secret service in France, 1784–1792', *Aspects of the French Revolution* (1968), pp. 192–224

Cobbett, William, *Letters to the Right Honourable Lord Hawkesbury and the Right Honourable Henry Addington on the Peace with Buonaparté*, London: Cox & Baylis, 1802

——, *Letter to Sheridan*, 1803

——, *The Political Proteus*, London: Cox, Son & Baylis, 1804

Coleridge, Samuel Taylor, *Essays on his Own Times*, 2 vols, London: William Pickering, 1850

Colley, Linda, *Britons: Forging the Nation, 1707–1837*, New Haven and London: Yale University Press, 1992

Conspiration anglaise, Paris: Imprimerie de la République, 1801

Cookson, J. E., *The Friends of Peace: Anti-War Liberalism in England 1793–1815*, Cambridge, 1982

——, *The British Armed Nation, 1793–1815*, Oxford: Clarendon Press, 1997

Copies of Original Letters from the Army of General Bonaparte in Egypt, intercepted by the Fleet under Admiral Lord Nelson, 3 vols, London: J. Wright, 1798–1800

Cox Jensen, Oskar, *Napoleon and British Song, 1797–1822*, London: Palgrave Macmillan, 2015

Craig, William, *Anecdotes of General Buonaparte*, London, 1798

Davies, Huw, 'Diplomats as spymasters', *Journal of Military History*, 76, 2012, pp. 37–68

Desbrière, Edouard, *Projets et tentatives de débarquement aux Îles Britanniques, 1793–1805*, 4 vols, Paris, 1900–2

Desmarest, Pierre Marie, *Témoignages historiques ou, quinze ans de haute police sous Napoléon*, Paris: Alphonse Levavasseur, 1833

Détré, Charles, *Les Apologistes du Crime suivis de Tuer n'est pas Assassiner par le colonel Silas Titus*, Paris: Éditions de l'Humanité Nouvelle, 1901

Dibdin, Charles, *The Professional Life of Mr Dibdin*, 4 vols, London: the author, 1803

Dickinson, H. T. (ed.), *Britain and the French Revolution, 1789–1815*, London: Macmillan, 1989

Dictionnaire des Jacobins vivans, Hamburg, 1799

Donald, Diana, *The Age of Caricature: Satirical Prints in the Reign of George III*, London and New Haven: Yale University Press, 1996

Dozier, Robert R., *For King, Constitution and Country: the English Loyalists and the French Revolution*, University Press of Kentucky, 1983

Dropmore Papers, *The Papers of J. B. Fortescue preserved at Dropmore*, ed. W. Fitzpatrick and F. Bickley, 10 vols, London: HMSO, 1892–1927

Dubroca, Louis, *Life of Bonaparte, First Consul of France*, London: G. and J. Robinson, 1802

——, *Mémoires pour servir à l'histoire des attentats du gouvernement anglais contre toutes les puissances de l'Europe*, Paris: Dubroca, 1803

Duffy, Michael, 'British Policy in the War against Revolutionary France', in Colin Joes (ed.), *Britain and Revolutionary France: Conflict, Subversion and Propaganda*, Exeter: University of Exeter, 1983

Dupuy, Pascal, 'Le 18 Brumaire en Grande-Bretagne: le témoignage de la presse et de la caricature', *Annales Historiques de la Révolution Française*, 1999, pp. 773–88

——, 'La caricature anglaise face à la France en révolution (1789–1802)', *Dix-Huitième Siècle*, 32 (2000), pp. 307–20

——, 'La Révolution française dans la caricature et la presse anglaise sous le Consulat', in Wolfgang Cillessen and Rolf Reichardt (eds), *Revolution and Counter-Revolution in European Prints from 1789 to 1889*, Hildesheim: Olms, 2010

Durey, Michael, *William Wickham, Master Spy: The Secret War Against the French Revolution*, London: Pickering & Chatto, 2009

——, 'The British Secret Service and the Escape of Sir Sidney Smith from Paris in 1798', *History*, 84, 1999, pp. 437–57

——, 'Lord Grenville and the Smoking Gun: the Plot to assassinate the French Directory in 1798–1799', *Historical Journal*, 45, 2002, pp. 547–68

——, 'William Wickham, the Christ Church Connection and the Rise and Fall of the Security Service in Britain, 1793–1801', *English Historical Review*, CXXI, 2006, pp. 714–45

Dwyer, Philip, *Napoleon: The Path to Power*, London: Bloomsbury, 2007

——, *Citizen Emperor: Napoleon in Power 1799–1815*, London: Bloomsbury, 2013

Ebbinghaus, Therese, *Napoleon, England und die Presse (1800–1803)*, Munich and Berlin: Oldenbourg, 1914

Edmonds, Charles (ed.), *Poetry of the Anti-Jacobin: comprising the celebrated political and satirical poems, of The Rt. Hon. G. Canning, John Hookham Frere, W. Pitt, the Marquis Wellesley, G. Ellis, W. Gifford, the Earl of Carlisle, and others*, London: Sampson Low, 1890

Ehrman, John, *The Younger Pitt. III. The Consuming Struggle*, Palo Alto, CA: Stanford University Press, 1996

Elliott, Marianne, *Partners in Revolution: the United Irishmen and France*, London: Yale University Press, 1982

Ellis, Kenneth, *The Post Office in the Eighteenth Century*, Oxford: OUP, 1958

Ense, K. A. Varnhagen von, *Tagebücher von Friedrich von Gentz*, Leipzig: Brockhaus, 1861

Fallon, David, 'Piccadilly Booksellers and Conservative Sociability' in Kevin Gilmartin (ed.), *Sociable Places: Locating Culture in Romantic-Period Britain*, Cambridge: CUP, 2017, pp. 70–93

Farington, Joseph, *The Diary of Joseph Farington*, vols I–VI ed. K. Garlick and A. Macintyre; VII–XVI ed. K. Cave, London: Yale University Press, 1978–84.

Fauche-Borel, Louis, *Mémoires de Fauche-Borel*, 4 vols, Paris: Moutardier, 1829

Fauriel, Claude Charles, *Les derniers jours du Consulat*, ed. Lodovic Lalanne, Paris: Calmann Lévy, 1886

Fayet, Auguste Nougarède de, *Recherches historiques sur le procès et la condamnation du duc d'Enghien*, 2 vols, Paris: Comptoir des Imprimeurs-Unis, 1844

Fell, Ralph, *A Tour of the Batavian Republic*, London: R. Phillips, 1801

Ford, John, *Ackermann, 1783–1983: the business of art*, London, 1983

Franklin, Alexandra, and Mark Philp, *Napoleon and the Invasion of Britain*, Bodleian Library, Oxford, 2003

Frere, W. E. and Sir B. (eds), *The Works of the Right Hon. John Hookham Frere*, London, 1874

Gatrell, Vic, *City of Laughter: Sex and Satire in Eighteenth-Century London*, London: Atlantic Books, 2006

Gentz, Frederick, *De l'Etat de l'Europe avant et après la Révolution Française*, London: Cox, Fils et Baylis, 1802

——, *A Vindication of Europe and Great Britain from Misrepresentation and Aspertion. Translated and Abridged from Mr Gentz's Answer to Mr Hauterive*, London: Stockdale, 1803

——, *On the State of Europe, before and after the French Revolution*, translated by John Charles Herries, London: Hatchard, 1804

George, Mary Dorothy, *English Political Caricature*, 2 vols, Oxford University Press, 1959

Geyl, Pieter, *Napoleon: For and Against*, London: Jonathan Cape, 1949

Gilmartin, Kevin (ed.), *Sociable Places: Locating culture in Romantic Period Britain*, Cambridge: CUP, 2017

Girtin, Tom, *Doctor with Two Aunts*, London: Hutchinson, 1959

Glorious Defeat of the French Gunboats! . . . to which is added a true and circumstantial Account of the Escape of that Gallant Hero Sir Sidney Smith [London, 1799]

Glover, Michael, *A Very Slippery Fellow: the Life of Sir Robert Wilson 1777–1849*, Oxford: OUP, 1977

Goldsmith, Lewis, *The Crimes of Cabinets or, a Review of their Plans and Aggressions for the Annihilation of the Liberties of France*, London: J. S. Jordan, 1801

——, *The Secret History of the Cabinet of Bonaparte*, London: Richardson and Hatchard, 1810

Grainger, John D., *The Amiens Truce: Britain and Bonaparte, 1801–1803*, Woodbridge: Boydell Press, 2004

Grasilier, Léonce, 'Enlèvement de Rumbold', *Nouvelle Revue Rétrospective*, 1901, pp. 369–84

——, *Par qui fut livré le Général Pichegru*, Paris: Lucien Dorbon, 1906

Greatheed, Bertie, *An Englishman in Paris, 1803. The Journal of Bertie Greatheed*, ed. J. C. T. Bury and J. C. Barry, London: Geoffrey Bles, 1953

Grenby, M. O., *The Anti-Jacobin Novel: British Conservatism and the French Revolution*, Cambridge: CUP, 2001

Hague, William, *William Pitt the Younger*, London: HarperCollins, 2004

Hall, Sir John, *General Pichegru's Treason*, London: Smith, Elder & Co., 1915

Hampson, Norman, *The Perfidy of Albion: French Perceptions of England during the French Revolution*, London: Macmillan, 1998

Hanley, Wayne, *The Genesis of Napoleonic Propaganda, 1796–1799*, New York: Columbia University Press, 2002

Harris, Bob, *Politics and the Rise of the Press: Britain and France 1620–1800*, London: Routledge, 1996

Hauterive, Alexandre-Maurice Blanc d', *De l'Etat de la France à la fin de l'An* VIII, Paris: Henrics, 1800

Hauterive, Ernest d', *La contre-police royaliste en 1800*, Paris: Perrin, 1931

Hazard, Paul, 'Le Spectateur du Nord', *Revue d'histoire littéraire de la France*, XIII (1906), pp. 26–50.

Hazlitt, William, *Conversations of James Northcote, Esq. R.A.*, London: Henry Colburn and Richard Bentley, 1830

Hill, Bridget, *The Republican Virago: the Life and Times of Catharine Macaulay, Historian*, Oxford: Clarendon Press, 1992

Holmes, Richard, *Coleridge: Early Visions*, London: HarperCollins, 1998

Hone, J. Ann, *For the Cause of Truth: Radicalism in London 1796–1821*, Oxford: Clarendon Press, 1982

Hone, William, *The Three Trials of William Hone for Publishing Three Parodies*, London: William Tegg & Co., 1876

[Huddesford, George], *Buonaparte: an Heroic Ballad*, London: Hatchard, 1803

Huerta, Carlos de la, *The Great Conspiracy: Britain's Secret War against Revolutionary France*, Stroud: Amberley Publishing, 2016

Humphreys, John L., *Piccadilly Bookmen: Memorials of the House of Hatchard*, London: Hatchard, 1893

Hutt, Maurice, *Chouannerie and counter-revolution*, 2 vols, Cambridge, 1983

Hyde, Guillaume, *Mémoires et souvenirs du baron Hyde de Neuville*, Paris: Plon, 1888

The Important History of the Atrocious Life and Actions of Napoleon Buonaparte, Ginger, 1803

Isaac, Peter, 'Sir John Swinburne and the forged *assignats* from Haughton Mill', *Archaeologia Aeliana* 5th Series, vol. 18, 1990, pp. 158–63

Jackson, Lady (ed.), *The Diaries and Letters of Sir George Jackson*, 2 vols, London: Richard Bentley, 1872

Jones, Colin (ed.), *Britain and Revolutionary France: Conflict Subversion and Propaganda*, Exeter: University of Exeter, 1983

Kennedy, Deborah, *Helen Maria Williams and the Age of Revolution*, Bucknell University Press, 2002

Knight, Roger, *Britain Against Napoleon: the organization of victory, 1793–1815*, London: Allen Lane, 2013

Lachouque, Henry, *Sous la République et Napoleon. Un gentilhomme d'aventure. Le général de Tromelin*, Bloud & Gay, 1960

Lanzac de Laborie, L. de, *Mémorial de J. de Norvins*, II: 1793–1802, Paris: Plon, 1896

Lean, E. Tangye, *The Napoleonists: A Study in Political Disaffection 1760–1960*, Oxford: OUP, 1970

Lenotre, Georges, *Georges Cadoudal*, Paris: Bernard Grasset, 1929

Lentz, Thierry, *Savary: le séide de Napoléon (1774–1833)*, Paris: Editions Serpenoise, 1993

——, *Le Grand Consulat 1799–1804*, Paris: Fayard, 1999

Lettre d'un Anglais à Bonaparte, 1803

The Life of Napoleone Buonaparte, containing an account of his parentage, Education, Military Expeditions, Assassinations, and Avowed Intention of Invasions; the greater part from the original information of a gentleman resident at Paris, Manchester, 1803

Lignereux, Aurélien, 'Le moment terroriste de la chouannerie: des atteintes à l'ordre public aux attentats contre le Premier Consul', La Révolution française [online], 1/2012, put online 18 March 2012, consulted 16 March 2016. URL: http://lrf.revues.org/390

Lipscombe, Nick, 'Napoleon's Obsession: the Invasion of England', *British Journal for Military History*, 1:3 (2015), pp. 115–33

Lloyd, Christopher (ed.), *The Keith Papers: Volume III*, Navy Records Society, 96 1955

The Loyalist: containing original and select papers; intended to rouse and animate the British Nation during the present Important Crisis, London: Hatchard, Bickerstaff, Asperne and Symonds, 1803

Lutaud, Olivier, *Des Révolutions d'Angleterre à la Révolution Française: le Tyrannicide et Killing no Murder*, La Haye: Martinus Nijhoff, 1973

Maccunn, F. J., *The Contemporary English View of Napoleon*, London: G. Bell, 1914

Macdonald, Simon, 'English Language Newspapers in Revolutionary France', *Journal for Eighteenth-Century Studies*, 36, 2013, pp. 17–33

Mackereth, George, *An Historical Account of the Transactions of Napoleone Buonaparte First Consul of the French Republic*, London, 1801

Mackesy, Piers, *War without Victory: the Downfall of Pitt 1799–1802*, Oxford: OUP, 1984

Macleod, Emma Vincent, *A War of Ideas. British Attitudes to the Wars Against Revolutionary France, 1792–1802*, Aldershot: Ashgate, 1998

Maes, Jérôme, 'La Conjuration menée par Georges Cadoudal', parts 1–7, *Le Tréport Magazine*, http://www.ville-le-treport.fr/loisirs_sport_culture-87.html

Mallet, Bernard, *Mallet du Pan and the French Revolution*, London: Longmans, 1902

Malmesbury, Third Earl (ed.), *Diaries and Correspondence of James Harris, First Earl of Malmesbury*, 4 vols, London: Richard Bentley, 1844

Mann, Golo, *Secretary of Europe; the Life of Friedrich Gentz, Enemy of Napoleon*, New Haven: Yale University Press, 1946

Manogue, Ralph A. 'The Plight of James Ridgway, London Bookseller and Publisher, and the Newgate Radicals 1792–1797', *Wordsworth Circle*, 27.3, Summer 1996, pp. 158–65

Markham, Sir Clements (ed.), *The Correspondence of Admiral John Markham, 1801–1807*, Navy Records Society, 28 (1904)

Martel, Arnaud Louis Raoul, *Étude sur l'affaire de la machine infernale du 3 nivôse an IX*, Paris: Lachaud, 1870

Maspero-Clerc, Hélène, *Un journaliste contre-révolutionaire: Jean-Gabriel Peltier (1760–1825)*, Paris: Société des études robespierristes, 1973

Mee, Jon, *Print, Publicity, and Popular Radicalism in the 1790s: The Laurel of Liberty*, Cambridge: CUP, 2016

Méhée de la Touche, Jean Claude Hippolyte, *Réponse au C^{en}. Garat, par le C^{en}. Méhée* [Paris, n.d.]

——, Alliance des Jacobins de France avec le ministère anglais, Paris: Imprimerie de la République, 1804

——, *Die Verathärischen Plane Englands und der Jakobiner wider des Kaysers, und die Freyheit des Franz. Volks*, Strasbourg, 1804

Miall, Bernard, *Pierre Garat, Singer and Exquisite: his life and world (1762–1823)*, New York: Charles Scribner's Sons, 1913

Michaud, Jean François, *Les Adieux à Bonaparte*, London and Paris, 1799

——, *Les Derniers Adieux à Bonaparte Victorieux*, London and Paris, 1800

Miles, Charles Popham (ed.), *The Correspondence of William Augustus Miles on the French Revolution*, 2 vols, London: Longmans, Green and Co., 1890

Millard, Lorraine, 'Sampson Perry: a forgotten radical and his House of Commons Libel', unpublished thesis, University of Queensland, 2015

Mitchell, Harvey, *The Underground War against Revolutionary France*, Oxford: Clarendon Press, 1965

Montgaillard, Maurice comte de, *Notice abrégée sur la vie, le caractère et les crimes des principaux assassins aux gages de l'Angleterre, qui sont aujourd'hui traduits devant le Tribunal de la Seine*, Paris, 1804

——, *Mémoires secrets de J. G. M. de Montgaillard, pendant les années de son émigration, contenant de nouvelles informations sur la caractère des Princes français et sur les intrigues des Agens de l'Angleterre*, Paris, 1803

Montlosier, François-Dominique-Reynaud de, *Mémoires sur la révolution française, le consulat, l'empire, la restoration, et les principaux événements qui l'ont suivie* (2 vols., 1829)

Montluzin, Emily L. de, *The Anti-Jacobins, 1798–1800: the early contributors to the 'Anti-Jacobin Review'*, London: Macmillan, 1988

——, 'The *Anti-Jacobin* Revisited: Newly Identified Contributions to the Anti-Jacobin Review during the Editorial Regime of John Gifford, 1798–1806', *Library*, IV (2003), pp. 278–302

Moore, Thomas, *Memoirs of the Life of the Right Honourable Richard Brinsley Sheridan*, 2 vols, London: Longmans, 1826

Moores, John Richard, *Representations of France in English Satiric Prints 1740–1832*, London: Palgrave Macmillan, 2015

Morand, Paul, 'Un journal napoléonien de propagande', *Revue des Deux Mondes*, August 1938, pp. 781–804

Moreau et Pichegru, au 18 fructidor An V, . . ., Paris: Bertrand-Pottier, 1804

Morieux, Renaud, '"An Inundation from our Shores": Travelling across the Channel around the Peace of Amiens', in Philp (ed.), *Resisting Napoleon*, pp. 217–40

Napoleon, *Correspondance de Napoléon 1er publiée par ordre de l'Empereur Napoléon III*, 32 vols, Paris: Plon, 1858–70

——, *Correspondance générale*, Paris: Fayard, 2004–

Newenham, Thomas, *The Warning Drum, a Call to the People of England to Resist Invaders*, London: Debrett, Hatchard, Ginger and Asperne, 1803

Nicholson, Eirwen, 'Consumers and Spectators: The Public of the Political Print in Eighteenth-Century England', *History*, 81 (January 1996), pp. 5–21

Nicolay, Fernand, *Napoleon at the Boulogne Camp*, New York: John Lane, 1907

Patten, Robert L., *George Cruikshank's Life, Times and Art*, London, 1992

Peltier, Jean-Gabriel, *The Trial of John Peltier, Esq, for a libel against Napoleon Buonaparte, First Consul of the French Republic*, London: Cox, Son & Baylis, 1803

Perry, Sampson, *The Argus, or General Observer*, London: H. D. Symonds, 1796

Philp, Mark (ed.), *The French Revolution and British Popular Politics*, Cambridge: CUP, 1991

——, 'Vulgar Conservatism, 1992–3', *English Historical Review*, 110:435 (1995), pp. 42–69

—— (ed.), *Resisting Napoleon: The British Response to the threat of invasion 1797–1815*, Aldershot: Ashgate, 2006

Pichegru et Moreau, Paris, 1804

Pigott, Charles, *The Jockey Club*, 3 parts, London: H. D. Symonds, 1792

Pitt, William, *The Speeches of the Right Honourable William Pitt in the House of Commons*, III, London: Longmans, 1817

Pivoteau, Sébastien, 'L'appartenance à un complot: une accusation à géométrie variable. L'exemple des usages politiques de la conspiration de Pichegru sous le Directoire', *Journée d'étude sur 'Les appartenances de l'Antiquité à nos jours'*, Apr 2008, Limoges, France, pp. 65–75, 2009

Pocock, Tom, *A Thirst for Glory: the Life of Admiral Sir Sidney Smith*, London: Aurum Press, 1996

——, *The Terror before Trafalgar: Nelson, Napoleon and the Secret War*, London: John Murray, 2002

Poetry of the Anti-Jacobin, 2nd edn, London: Wright, 1800

Polden, Patrick, 'John Reeves as Superintendent of Aliens 1803–1814', *Legal History*, 3 (1982) 31–51

Procès instruit par le Tribunal Criminel du Département de la Seine contre les nommés Saint-Réjant, Carbon, et autres, prévenus de conspiration contre la personne du Premier Consul, 2 vols, Paris 1801

Procès instruit par le Cour de Justice Criminelle et Spéciale du Département de la Seine, séante à Paris, le Tribunal Criminel du Département de la Seine contre Georges, Pichegru et Autres, 6 vols, Paris: Patris, 1804

Ramel, Jean-Pierre, *Memoirs of Adj. Gen. Ramel*, transl. C. L. Pelichet, Norwich, n.d.

Randolph, Herbert, *Life of General Sir Robert Wilson*, 2 vols, London: John Murray, 1862

Rapp, Jean, *Mémoires des contemporains*, Paris: Bossange, 1823

Réal, Pierre, *Indiscrétions. 1798–1830. Souvenirs anecdotiques et politiques tirés du porte-feuille d'un fonctionnaire de l'Empire*, I, Paris: Dufey, 1835

Régnier, Claude Ambroise, *Rapport du grand-juge, ministre de la justice, au gouvernement. Paris, le 27 pluviôse an XII*, Paris: Imprimerie de la République, 1804

——, *Rapport du grand-juge au premier consul*, Paris: Imprimerie de la République, 1804

——, *Second Rapport du Grand Juge, relatif aux trames du nommé Drake, ministre d'Angleterre à Munich et du nommé Spencer-Smith, ministre d'Angleterre à Stutgard, contre la France et le Premier Consul*, Paris: Imprimerie de la République, 1804

Reiff, Paul. F., *Friedrich Gentz, an Opponent of the French Revolution and Napoleon*, Urbana-Champaign, Ill.: The University, 1912

Rémusat, Paul de (ed.), *Mémoires de Madame de Rémusat*, I, Paris: Calmann Lévy, 1880

The Revolutionary Plutarch, 3 vols, London: John Murray, 1804

Rivière, Charles-François, *Mémoires Posthumes ... de Charles-François, duc de Rivière*, Paris: Ladvocat, 1829

Roberts, Andrew, *Napoleon the Great*, London: Allen Lane, 2014

Roe, Nicholas, *Wordsworth and Coleridge: the Radical Years*, Oxford: Clarendon Press, 1988

Roederer, A. M., *Oeuvres du comte P. L. Roederer*, III, Paris: Firmin Didot, 1854

Roffe, Robert Cabbell, *My diary of sixty-three days: with memorandums of occasional trips into Kent*, ed. Edwin Roffe, privately printed, 1858

Rogers, Rachel, 'Censorship and Creativity: The Case of Sampson Perry, Radical Editor in 1790s Paris and London', *Revue LISA/ LISA e-journal* [online], vol. XI – n° I | 2013, put online 30 May 2013, consulted 13 February 2017. URL: http://lisa.revues.org/5205; DOI: 10.4000/lisa.5205

Rose, John Holland, *The Life of Napoleon I*, 2 vols, London: George Bell, 1907

Russell, Lord John (ed.), *Memorials and Correspondence of Charles James Fox*, 4 vols, London: Richard Bentley, 1853–7

Sadler, Thomas (ed.), *Diary, Reminiscences, and Correspondence of Henry Crabb Robinson*, 2 vols, London: Macmillan, 1872

Salomé, Karine, 'L'attentat de la rue Nicaise en 1800: l'irruption d'une violence inédite?', *Revue d'histoire du XIXe siècle*, 40 (2010), pp. 59–75

Sarratt, [Jacob], *Life of Buonaparte, in which the Atrocious Deeds which he has perpetrated in order to attain his elevated Station are faithfully recorded*, London: Tegg and Castleman [1803]

Savant, Jean, *Les Espions de Napoleon*, Paris: Hachette, 1957

Savary, Anne Jean Marie René, *Memoirs of the Duke of Rovigo (M. Savary)*, 1, London: Henry Colburn, 1828

Ségur, Philippe de, *Memoirs of an Aide de Camp of Napoleon 1800–1812*, 1896, republished Stroud: Nonsuch, 2005

Semmel, Stuart, *Napoleon and the British*, New Haven and London: Yale University Press, 2004

Sherwig, J. M., *Guineas and Gunpowder: British foreign aid in the wars with France 1793–1815*, Cambridge, Mass., 1969

Shorter, Clement (ed.), *Napoleon and his Fellow Travellers*, London: Cassell, 1908,

Sicotière, Louis de la, *Louis de Frotté et les insurrections normandes, 1793–1832*, 1, Paris: Plon, 1889

Sparrow, Elizabeth, 'The Alien Office, 1792–1806', *The Historical Journal*, 33, 1990, pp. 361–84

——, 'The Swiss and Swabian Agencies, 1795–1801', *The Historical Journal*, 35, 1992, pp. 861–84

——, 'Secret Service under Pitt's Administrations, 1792–1806', *History*, 83, 1998, pp. 280–94

——, *Secret Service: British Agents in France, 1792–1815*, Woodbridge: Boydell, 1999

——, *Phantom of the Guillotine: The Real Scarlet Pimpernel, Louis Bayard – Louis Duval 1769–1844*, Penzance: Carn Press, 2013

Speck, W. A., *Robert Southey: Entire Man of Letters*, New Haven and London: Yale University Press, 2006

[Starhemberg, Ludwig Josef Maximilian von], *Le Grand Homme*, London, 1800

Thiry, Jean, *La machine infernale*, Berger-Levrault, 1952

Thomson, Oliver, *Mass Persuasion in History: an Analysis of the Development of Propaganda Techniques*, Edinburgh, 1977

——, *Easily Led: a History of Propaganda*, Stroud: Sutton, 1999

Tinseau, Charles-Léon, *A Letter to Buonaparté*, London: Cox, Son & Baylis, 1803

——, *The Empire of Germany divided into Departments*, trans. W. Cobbett, London: E. Harding, 1803

Tolstoy, Nicolai, *The Half-Mad Lord: Thomas Pitt 2nd Baron Camelford (1775–1804)*, London: Jonathan Cape, 1978

Traduction du Pamphlet qui a fait mourir l'Usurpateur Cromwell, titulé Tuer n'est pas Assassiner, dédié à Napoléon Buonaparté, London: Cox, Fils et Baylis, 1804

Trotter, John Bernard, *Memoirs of the latter years of the Right Honourable Charles James Fox*, London, 1811

Vane, Charles (ed.), *Memoirs and Correspondence of Viscount Castlereagh*, 12 vols, London: Henry Colburn, 1849–53

Vincent, Emma, '"The real grounds of the present war": John Bowles and the French revolutionary wars, 1792–1802', *History*, new ser., 78 (1993), pp. 393–420

Wardroper, John, *Kings, Lords and Wicked Libellers: Satire and Protest 1760–1837*, London: John Murray, 1973

Waresquiel, Emmanuel de, *Talleyrand: le prince immobile*, Paris: Fayard, 2003

——, *Talleyrand: dernières nouvelles du diable*, Paris, 2011

——, *Fouché: les silences de la pieuvre*, Paris: Tallendier, 2014

Watel, Françoise, *Jean-Guillaume Hyde de Neuville (1776–1857) Conspirateur et diplomate*, Paris: Ministry of Foreign Affairs, 1997

Weber, Paul, *On the Road to Rebellion: the United Irishmen and Hamburg 1796–1803*, Dublin: Four Courts Press, 1997

Wells, Roger, *Insurrection: the British Experience 1795–1803*, Gloucester: Alan Sutton, 1986

Wheeler, H. F. B., and Arthur Meyrick Broadley, *Napoleon and the Invasion of England: the Story of the Great Terror*, 2 vols, London: John Lane, 1908

Wickham, William, *The Correspondence of the Right Honourable William Wickham*, 2 vols, London: Richard Bentley, 1870

Williams, Helen Maria, *A Tour in Switzerland; or, a view of the present State of the Governments and Manners of those Cantons: with comparative Sketches of the present State of Paris*, London: G. G. and J. Robinson, 1798

Wilson, Robert Thomas, *History of the British Expedition to Egypt*, London: T. Egerton, 1802

Wimet, Pierre-André, 'Le manoir de Godincthun et son énigme', *Revue de Boulogne*, 328, mai/juin 1970, pp. 423–9

[Yorke, Henry Redhead], *The Anti-Corsican, or War of Liberty*, London: Richardson, 1804

Ziegler, Philip, *Addington: a Life of Henry Addington, first Viscount Sidmouth*, London, 1965

Index

Aachen, 330, 340

Abbeville, 195–200, 265–7, 312–13

Addington, Henry: and anti-Napoleon propaganda, 11; becomes Prime Minister (14 March 1801), 107, 108; and Peace of Amiens, 125, 130–1, 132, 142, 144, 145, 339–40; and Sheridan, 125–6, 132, 144, 147; and *émigré* journalism issue, 133–4, 135; and Cadoudal, 135; warns Heriot over *True Briton*, 138; and return to war, 147, 156; Gillray's mocking of, 153, 154, 156; friendship with King, 163; levée en masse legislation, 165; and reactivation of correspondence (1803), 187, 189; and Méhée's plan, 241; ministry under strain (March-April 1804), 295, 298; denies French allegations (April 1804), 309–10, 338–9; resignation of (May 1804), 317; trial of Cobbett for seditious libel, 320; as repressive Home Secretary (as Lord Sidmouth), 350

Aikin, Arthur, *Annual Review and History of Literature*, 220–1

Aikin, John, 59–60, 115, 338

Aitken, Ann, 47

Aitken, James, 47

Alarum Bell (periodical), 160, 161

Alien Office, 31, 36–7, 85, 112, 121, 171, 185–6, 239–40, 242, 258

Aliens Act (January 1793), 31, 133–4, 241–2

American War of Independence, 15, 16, 19, 24, 26, 33, 39

Amiens, 85, 197

Amiens, Peace of (1801–3), 12–13, 125–36, 138–41, 142–5, 156, 213; as recognition of Napoleon's legitimacy, 108, 339–40; shift in liberal British opinion during, 125–6, 132, 142–3, 145, 147–8, 165–9; *Moniteur* article by Napoleon, 136–7, 141–2; resumption of war (May 1803), 144–5, 155–8, 162–4; and Swiss crisis, 146–7; anti-Napoleon propaganda during, 148–55, 157–69

Andréossy, Antoine-François, 134, 151, 174

Angoulême, Louis Antoine, duc d', 277

Angoulême, Marie Thérèse, duchesse d', 352

Annales du Terrorisme, 203, 208

Annales politiques du dix-neuvième siècle (Chagny journal), 333

Answer from M. Méhée to M. Garat (pamphlet), 202

Anti-Gallican (periodical), 160–1, 204, 205, 206, 208

Anti-Gallican Monitor, 353

Antigallican Songster (song collection), 33

Anti-Jacobin, or Weekly Examiner, 62–3, 64, 65, 68, 109, 110, 350

Anti-Jacobin Review, 35, 84, 109–11, 117, 120, 121–2, 151–3, 203, 206, 214; opposes peace with France, 129, 131, 135; life of Fouché in, 152, 216; life of Talleyrand in, 215–16; review of *The Revolutionary Plutarch*, 220, 235; view of 'Grand Conspiracy', 317–18

Antraigues, Emmanuel-Henri-Louis de Launay, comte d', 37, 52, 56, 339

Argus (English-language journal in Paris), 123–4, 141, 268–9

Argus (radical journal), 35, 47, 69

Arras, Louis-Antoine-Marc-Hilaire de Conzié, bishop of, 136, 138, 251

Artois, Charles Philippe, comte d', 50, 82, 83, 86, 92, 93–4, 99, 134, 172, 278; Paris network of, 77, 83; and 'Grand Conspiracy', 171, 228, 233, 277, 279, 283–4; rules France as Charles X, 351, 352

Asperne, James, 159–60, 161, 234–5

Asseline, Jean-René, bishop of Boulogne, 85, 181

Association for Preserving Liberty and Property, 28–30, 32, 33, 48, 157

The Atrocities of the Corsican Demon (book), 205

Augereau, General Pierre, 53, 217

Austerlitz, battle of (December 1805), 349, 354

Austria, 19, 82, 83, 93, 106, 170, 281, 327

Auvergne, Philippe d' (prince de Bouillon), 39, 43, 48–9, 175, 244, 249, 299; and Channel Islands correspondence, 39–40, 83, 175–6; and 'Infernal Machine' plot, 95, 97; suicide of after Congress of Vienna, 354

Bachelier, Marie-Françoise, 195–6

Baden, 278–84, 285, 286

Badini, Carlo Francesco, 143–4, 268–9

Ball, Sir Alexander, 353

Barbier-Walbonne, Lavinie, 2

Barras, Paul, 52, 61, 75, 121–2, 207, 208, 209, 210

Barré, William Vincent, 151, 202, 239, 242–4, 315, 316, 318; *The History of the French Consulate, under Napoleon Bonaparte*, 201–2, 206–7, 210, 212, 217–18, 220; second part to his history (1804), 337–9; suicide of (1829), 354

Barrois, Pierre, Colonel, 289

Barthélemy, François, 46, 52, 53, 91

Batavian Republic, 333

Bavaria, Elector of, 307, 330

Bayard, Louis, 37, 55, 56, 99, 148, 170, 180

Bayard, shield of, 330

Beauharnais, Eugène de, 191, 214

Beauharnais, Josephine (Napoleon's wife), 2–3, 6–7, 16, 61, 89, 191, 214, 239, 288; scurrilous biographies of, 209–10; crowned at Notre Dame (2 December 1804), 341

Belleisle (Brittany), 92–3

Bell's Weekly Messenger, 138, 143–4, 268

Beloe, William, 34

Benoit Laisné (escape guide), 266–7, 298, 312

Bernadotte, Jean-Baptiste, General, 331

Berry, Charles Ferdinand, duc de, 277

Berthier, Louis-Alexandre, General, 2, 191, 225

Bessières, Jean-Baptiste, General, 2

Bewick, Thomas, 40

Bickerstaff, Robert, 161

Biggs, Rachel Charlotte, 157

Biographical Anecdotes (1797), 60, 115–16, 202, 236, 241

Biville, hamlet of (near Le Tréport), 86, 97, 174, 175, 198, 224–5, 228–9, 233, 260, 262, 263–4

Blaise de Chenier, Marie-Joseph, 333–4

Boilly, Louis, 153

Bonaparte, Caroline (sister of Napoleon), 2, 6, 215

Bonaparte, Jérôme (brother of Napoleon), 215

Bonaparte, Joseph (brother of Napoleon), 288

Bonaparte, Lucien (brother of Napoleon), 214

Bonaparte, Pauline (sister of Napoleon), 179, 215

Bonaparte à un Anglais (pamphlet), 251

Bonneuil, Michelle de, 172–3, 256

booksellers and publishers: prosecution of in Britain, 26, 30, 47, 69, 154; denunciations of in Britain, 29, 30; loyalist, 160–2

Botherel, Félicité, comte de, 279

Böttiger, Karl August, 114–15, 219, 333

Bougainville, Marie Joséphine Flore, Madame de, 40

Bouillon, Godefroy de la Tour d'Auvergne, duc de, 39

Boulogne, 85–6, 98, 172, 180–3, 187–9, 199–200; Nelson's raid on (August 1801), 127; and Napoleon, 191–2, 193, 328–30

Bourbon, Louis Henri, duc de (son of prince de Condé), 277

Bourbon dynasty: absolutism of, 20, 25, 50–1; restoration issue, 20, 34, 36, 37, 50–1, 77, 81, 95, 113, 327, 347; Napoleon's anger at princes in London, 135; 'Bourbon prince' during 'Grand Conspiracy', 228, 235, 259, 263, 277–80, 283–4; ill-feeling against in France (1804), 284; Enghien's execution as signal to, 291, 346; Barré on, 338–9; final overthrow of senior line (1830), 351, 352, 353; *see also* Artois, comte d'; Condé, prince de; Enghien, Louis Antoine, duc d'; Provence, comte de ('comte de Lille', future Louis XVIII)

Bourmont, Louis de Ghaisne, comte de, 87, 97, 104, 105, 352–3

Bourrienne, Louis Antoine Fauvelet de, 144, 214, 344

Bouven, abbé, *Eloge funèbre de S. A. S. Mr le duc d'Enghien*, 291

Bouvet de Lozier, Athanase-Hyacinthe, 174–5, 227, 256, 261, 267, 300, 322–3, 344, 345

Bowles, John, 33–4, 48, 109, 120, 121, 203–4, 354

Boze, Joseph, 128

Bradyll, Thomas, 163

Brest, 49, 82, 85, 90, 175, 180, 185

Britain: political and social system, 10, 12, 19–20, 27, 29; love of exaggeration and caricature, 13; Anglo-French struggle for global primacy, 15; France as 'natural enemy' of, 15; as 'modern Carthage', 22–3; French refugees to, 27–8, 31; paranoia and panic (autumn 1792), 28; economic war on France (from 1793), 40; 'Gagging Acts' (1795), 46–8; Austrian subsidy (1800), 82, 83; domestic unrest (1799–1800), 106; Paris embassy, 140–1, 176–7; rejects French Empire, 327; as illiberal in post-Napoleonic period, 347; confidence in ultimate victory, 348–9; sense of national superiority, 349; *see also* espionage, British; Paris correspondence

British Critic (periodical), 34, 159

British Neptune (weekly newspaper), 161, 204

British Press (weekly newspaper), 161, 214

Bruix, Vice-Admiral Eustace de, 191, 329

Brunswick, Charles William Ferdinand, Duke of, 19

Bruslart, Louis Guérin, chevalier de, 105

Bulletin de Paris, 113

Buonaparte Massacring Fifteen Hundred Persons at Toulon (print), 209

Buonaparte Massacring Three Thousand Eight Hundred Men at Jaffa (print), 209

Buonaparteana (1804), 217

Buonaparte's Confession of the Massacre at Jaffa (poster), 209

Buonaparte's True Character, 218

Burban, Louis, 273, 274

Burdon, William, 115, 148

Burke, Edmund, 19, 30, 33, 36, 38, 61; *Reflections on the Revolution in France*, 17, 25, 27

Burns, Robert, 162

Cadoudal, Georges: in London (July 1800), 3, 94, 96; and Saint-Régent, 4; and failed rising (late autumn 1799), 87; flees to London (April 1800), 87–8; and British expeditionary force (May 1800), 92–3; and 'Infernal Machine' plot, 94, 96, 97, 98, 99, 100, 103, 104; in Britain after 'Infernal Machine', 135, 137, 138–9, 172; Picot and Lebourgeois arrests, 174; and Channel Islands correspondence, 176; and route through Le Tréport, 195, 198; landing in France (August 1803), 222, 223–6; in France (from August 1803), 226–8, 233, 255, 258, 260, 261, 269; royalist reinforcements (autumn 1803), 228–9; Querelle's revelations, 257, 258, 260; in hiding (Paris, February–March 1804), 272–3; arrest of (9 March 1804), 273–5, 283; interrogation of, 275, 283, 314; trial of (May–June 1804), 319, 320, 321–2; execution of (25 June 1804), 323; life of in *The Revolutionary Plutarch*, 333; fate of skeleton of, 351–2

Cadoudal, Joseph, 351–2

Calliole, Jean-François, 274–5

Cambacérès, Jean-Jacques Régis de, 210, 284–5, 328, 333

Cambridge Intelligencer, 69–70, 111, 144–5

Camelford, Thomas Pitt, 2nd Baron, 171, 177

Camus, Rosalie le, 98, 193

Canning, George, 17, 30–1, 53, 62, 112, 127, 131, 160; and Pichegru, 54, 96; and the *Anti-Jacobin*, 62–3, 64, 68; and propaganda, 62–3, 66–7, 68, 119, 153–4; opposes peace with France, 79–81; and 'Infernal Machine' plot, 96; later political career of, 350, 353

Carbon, François-Jean, 4, 98, 100, 101, 103, 104–5, 106

caricatures and prints, 13, 21–2, 25, 29, 30, 33, 209, 310, 320; pro-government in Britain, 33; and 'Gagging Acts', 46–7;

caricatures and prints – *continued*
of Napoleon, 62, 118–19, 131–2, 153–4, 155, 156, 163–4, 166–7, 177–9, 218–19, 291, 341–2; and Böttiger, 114–15, 125; *The Child and Champion of Jacobinism, New Christened* , 128; positive images of George III, 162–3; invasion prints, 163–4; *A Consular Attempt at a Crown*, 177, 218; French caricatures of Drake, 310–11; *Mr Drake's Reply to his Calumniators!!* (Holland), 311; *see also* Gillray, James

Caron, Antoine, 98, 273, 274, 300, 352
Carthage, 22–3
Castlereagh, Robert Stewart, Viscount, 146–7, 172, 173, 350, 354
Catholicism: dechristianisation during Revolution, 35–6, 48, 75, 76, 340; Napoleon imposes peace on Pope (1797), 58; British nonconformist hatred of, 61; Civil Constitution of the Clergy, 76; Napoleon's restoration of, 77, 87, 126; Napoleon's coronation at Notre Dame (2 December 1804), 340–2
Caulaincourt, Armand de, 285, 286
César (Bonaparte's coachman), 2, 5, 6, 101
Chagny, Paoli de (journalist in Ratisbon), 246, 249, 305, 333
Channel Islands, 39–40, 82, 83, 88, 138, 175, 176, 237–8, 249, 299–300
Charlemagne, 328, 330, 340, 341
Charles I, King, 21
Charlotte, Queen, 15, 16
Chateaubriand, Armand de, 40
chouans (royalist insurgents of western France), 3, 43, 82, 85, 116–17; 'Infernal Machine' assassination plot, 3–7, 9, 95–106; British aid to, 4, 9, 38, 39–40, 42, 87, 116–17; failure of coup (September 1797), 53, 54; failed rising of (late autumn 1799), 86, 87, 92; and 'Grand Conspiracy', 225–6, 228, 255–7, 300–1
Churchill, Winston, 14
ciphers and codes, 32, 90–1, 246–7, 266, 292, 305, 308
Civil List, 33
civil war, English, 21
Cobbett, William, 11, 141, 142, 143, 148, 154, 318, 320, 322; *Porcupine* (journal), 119–20, 129; and propaganda, 119–20, 157–9, 161, 205–6, 208; opposes peace with France, 129–30, 131, 135;

Weekly Political Register (journal), 131, 151, 159, 205–6, 207–8, 295–6; *Important Considerations*, 157–9, 161, 177; and resumption of war (May 1803), 157–9, 161; *Letter to Sheridan* (October 1803), 165–8; on Méhée, 239; and British involvement in 'Grand Conspiracy', 295–6, 297, 309–10, 316–17, 339; contempt for Hawkesbury, 316–17, 330–1, 340; trial for seditious libel, 320; on proclamation of Empire, 328; move to radicalism, 353
Cold Bath Fields prison, 31
Coleridge, Samuel Taylor, 17, 50, 65, 115, 116–17, 118, 353; and press freedom, 29, 141–2; shift of position (1802), 132, 141–3
Colman, George, 162
Combremont, Mme, 192, 193
Condé, Louis Joseph, prince de, 42–3, 171, 211, 277, 278–9, 280, 281, 304
Condé army, 82, 277; on the Rhine, 42–3, 45, 280–1, 282, 283, 304; Spencer Smith's role, 234, 281, 292; Wickham's role, 281
Cornwallis, William, Admiral, 228
Costard de Saint-Léger, Mme, 227
Coster de Saint-Victor, Jean-Baptiste, 98, 103, 105, 106, 173, 227, 261, 323
Cosway, Maria, 62
Couchery, Jean-Baptiste, 259, 268
Couchery, Victor, 259, 268, 271, 272
the *Courier*, 68, 69, 129, 131, 135, 316
Courier de Londres, 113, 134, 176, 179, 234, 243, 268–9, 333
Cox, Son & Baylis (printers), 136, 161, 204, 205
Les Crimes des Républicains en Italie, 211
Critical Review, 34, 117, 121
Cromwell, Oliver, 21, 22, 77, 84
Cruikshank, Isaac, 62

Dagobert I, Merovingian king, 329–30
Danican, Auguste, General, *Les Brigands démasqués*, 204, 209
David, abbé Pierre, 171–2, 345
David, Jacques Louis, 65
Davout, Louis Nicolas General, 191
Decrès, Denis, 191
Delaporte, abbé Louis, 181, 193, 194, 266–7, 312, 313, 316, 354
Delpierre, Louis, 193–4
Denand, Jean-Baptiste, 227, 260–1
Denis, Catherine, 266

Index

Denmark, 316

Denon, Vivant, 328

Desgenettes, René, 150

Desmarest, Pierre, 102, 106, 174, 256, 257–8, 271, 275, 344–5

de Sol de Grisolles, Louis, 175, 226, 255–6, 257–8

Despard, Edward, 143

Destavigny (police officer), 274, 275

Deville, Victor, 301

Dibdin, Charles, 162

Dibdin, Thomas, 162

The Dictionnaire des Jacobins Vivans (by 'Quelqu'un'), 204

Didelot, François Charles Luce, 234, 281, 283

Dieppois, Jean, 196, 313, 325

Dossonville, Jean-Baptiste, 91, 270

Doyle, John, General, 237–8, 239

Drake, Francis (Ambassador in Munich), 190, 244–8, 249–52, 257, 269–71, 280, 293–5, 302–3, 305–7, 330–1; as consul at Genoa, 37; publishes *Lettre d'un anglais à Bonaparte*, 234, 250; correspondence of published by French, 294–5, 302, 307–8, 309–10, 318, 334, 336, 338–9, 340; and Talleyrand's circular letter, 302, 308, 316; French caricatures of, 310–11; post-1804 life of, 356

Dubois, Louis Nicolas, 104–5, 252, 261, 272–3, 275, 300, 344

Dubroca, Louis, *Life of Bonaparte*, 129

Dubuisson, Jean-Baptiste-Antoine (vicomte de la Boulaye), 182, 267

Dubuisson, Pierre, 300

Duchâtelet, Mlle, 181, 193, 313

Ducorps, Louis, 226

Dumont, André, 265–6, 267, 312–13

Dumouriez, Charles François, General, 282, 283, 285, 287

Dundas, Henry, 18, 19, 24, 36, 80, 107, 125, 164–5, 347, 349

Dupérou, Louis, 84–5, 88, 89, 91–2, 98–9

Duponchel, Jacques-Joseph, 195, 196, 200, 264–5, 325

Dupuis, Julie, 298, 313

Dusouliers, Lucie, 312

Dutancourt, Pierre, 288, 289

Dutheil, Jean-François, 83, 85, 92, 121

Duval, Françoise, 313

Edinburgh Review, 60

Egypt, 57, 66–7, 71, 72–3, 116, 156, 211, 349

Ellenborough, Edward Law, 1st Baron, Lord Chief Justice, 143, 320

Ellis, George, 53, 63, 64, 80

émigrés in Britain: writers, 58–9, 111–13, 133–4, 135–6, 138, 139–40, 143–4, 177–9 *see also* Peltier, Jean-Gabriel; and Portland Whigs, 36; and Windham, 38, 39; Anglo-royalist strategy (1795), 42–3, 45; factionalism of, 50, 51; French-language press in London, 59, 111–13, 134, 177–9; and Napoleon's meeting with royalists (1799), 77; Napoleon lifts ban on (1800), 97, 113, 126, 134

Enghien, Louis-Antoine-Henri, duc d', 277–8, 279–85, 333; capture of (15 March 1804), 285–8, 303; trial and execution of (20/21 March 1804), 288–91, 304, 309, 316, 318, 346

English Revolution, seventeenth-century, 21–2, 77, 84

l'Escault (Mlle Duchâtelet's house), 181, 193, 194

espionage, British: aid to *chouans*, 4, 9, 38, 39–40, 42, 87, 116–17; Churchill's WW2 methods, 14; growth of systems in Britain, 14; George III as source of funds for, 20; and Nepean at Home Office, 24–5; mail interception in Britain, 31–2; Secret Office of Post Office, 31–2; British secret service payments, 33, 34, 35, 82; Flint at the Alien Office, 37–8, 85; Wickham's role, 37–8, 42; 'the Channel Islands correspondence', 39–40, 83, 175–6, 249; Marcouf islands correspondence, 44–5, 55, 56, 83; plan to manipulate 1797 elections, 51–2; Anglo-royalist network unravels (May 1800), 88; Talon replaces Dupérou in Paris, 98–9, 105; *see also* Paris correspondence

espionage, French republican: use of double agents, 89 *see also* Méhée de la Touche, Jean-Claude; Napoleon's propaganda, 62; Fouché's spy network, 75, 88–9, 97–8, 99, 172, 256; Talleyrand's spy network, 76, 89, 172–3

Etches, Richard Cadman, 54

Ettenheim, 278, 281–3, 285, 292

Eu (town near Le Tréport), 90, 175, 195, 198, 225, 226, 227–8, 260, 264

European Magazine, 160, 219, 234–5

Even, Joseph-Laurent, 228

Evening Mail, 29–30

Fairburn, John, 161
Fardel, Pierre, 90, 193–4
Farington, Joseph, 63
Fauche-Borel, Louis, 171–2, 345, 354
Fell, Ralph, 122
Fiévée, Joseph, *Lettres sur l'Angleterre*, 140
Fishguard, French landings at (1797), 50
Flint, Charles William, 37–8, 85, 88, 91–2, 171, 185–6, 189
the Flouets (Nymphe's relations in Abbeville), 197, 312–13
Flower, Benjamin, 69–70, 111, 144–5
Fontanes, Louis de, 77, 333, 340
Fores, Samuel William, 47, 155, 163, 164, 291
Forfait, Pierre, 191
Fouché, Joseph, 12–13, 88–9, 90–2, 135, 323, 326, 328, 331–2, 344, 345; sacked by Napoleon (September 1802), 12, 152, 256; hatred of Talleyrand, 74, 77, 89; physical appearance of, 74; background of, 74–5; spy network of, 75, 88–9, 97–8, 99, 172, 256; and Bourmont, 87, 97, 104, 105; arrest of Dupérou, 88, 89, 91–2; intelligence before 'Infernal Machine', 96, 97–8, 99; foils Jacobin bomb plot (November 1800), 99–100; investigation of 'Infernal Machine' plot, 102–6, 120; life of in *The Revolutionary Plutarch*, 203, 212, 216; and Enghien, 284, 285, 290–1; death in exile (1820), 351
Fox, Charles James, 17, 25, 46, 79, 125–6, 132, 142–3, 147, 295; George III's hatred of, 16, 297–8; public image as Jacobin traitor, 48; on suppression of press, 69, 70; visit to Bonaparte (September 1802), 140
France: revolutionary calendar, 1, 35, 126; Anglo-French struggle for global primacy, 15; republican Rome comparisons, 22–3; currency forged by British, 40; failed 13 vendémiaire coup (5 October 1795), 45, 61, 209; Directory, 46, 52, 53; 1797 elections, 51–3; 18 *fructidor* (4 September 1797), 53; Bonaparte's Army of Italy, 61, 66, 180, 241, 281, 289, 347–8; Brumaire coup (9 November 1799), 74, 79, 109, 110, 115; proclamation of Empire, 321, 326–8; new symbols for Empire, 328, 341; plebiscite on Empire, 328, 341; Napoleon in Boulogne

(July-August 1804), 328–30; refuses recognition of English diplomats, 330–1; seizures of British diplomatic correspondence, 331, 332–3; arrest of Rumbold in Hamburg, 331–3; Napoleon's coronation at Notre Dame (2 December 1804), 340–2; *see also* royalists, French
Francis II, Emperor of Austria, 327
Freeling, Francis, 28, 32, 48
French Revolution (1789): reactions to in Britain, 16–17, 18–19, 25–6; comparisons with English Revolution, 21–2, 77, 84; French refugees to Britain, 27–8, 31; dechristianisation, 35–6, 48, 75, 76, 340; the Terror (1793–4), 35–6; Fouché's role in, 75; September massacres, 112, 240, 242
French Revolutionary Wars (1792–1802): Quiberon expedition (1795), 4, 42, 43; Pitt's initial reluctance to join, 18–19; French invasion of Low Countries, 19; Prussia and Austria attack France (July 1792), 19; George III's view of, 19–20, 46, 53; Bourbon restoration issue, 20, 34, 36, 37, 50–1, 77, 81, 95, 113, 347; in Austrian Netherlands (1794–5), 40–1; Anglo-royalist strategy (1795), 42–3, 45; campaigns against in Britain, 45–6, 69; Bonaparte's victories in Italy (1796), 49, 58, 61, 347–8; royalist risings in west defeated (1796), 49; French attempt on Ireland, 49–50; peace negotiations (1797), 53, 57; Battle of the Nile (August 1798), 66, 116, 122, 211, 349; Napoleon's peace offer (December 1799), 78, 79–81, 116, 117, 118, 213, 347; Anglo-royalist strategy (1800), 79, 82–3, 88; peace at Lunéville (9 February 1801), 106
Frere, John Hookham, 63, 64, 88, 91, 350
Frotté, Louis de, 43, 44, 49, 56, 87, 213
A Full True and Particular Account (broadside), 204

Gaillard, Armand, 301–2, 322–3, 352
Gaillard, Raoul, 174–5, 198, 225, 226, 233, 261, 274, 301–2
Gallien, Jean Antoine, 196, 264–5
Garat, Pierre, 1, 2
Gentz, Friedrich, 113–14, 152–3, 327, 353–4
George, Prince of Wales, 16, 26, 45–6, 349
George III, King: and American War,

15, 16, 19, 26; character and outlook of, 15–16, 19–20, 26, 27; hatred of Fox, 16, 297–8; view of Jacobinism, 18, 19, 27; supports war against France, 19–20, 53, 81, 108, 347; liking for Nepean, 24; caricature and ridicule of, 25–6; bouts of insanity, 26, 35, 108, 349; 'wicked and seditious Writings' banned, 27; hostile portrayals of outlawed, 29, 46; abused by mob (1795), 46; support for French 'purs' ('ultras'), 51; Napoleon's offers of peace, 78, 79–81, 116, 117, 118, 213, 342, 347; potshots taken at (1800), 106; opposes Peace of Amiens, 125; and resumption of war (1803), 154, 155, 157; positive caricatures of, 162–3; falls ill (February 1804), 295, 306

Gifford, John, 35, 84, 109, 120, 121, 151, 203–4, 354; opposes peace with France, 129, 130, 131; view of 'Grand Conspiracy', 317–18

Gifford, William, 63

Gillray, James, 17, 64–5, 66–7, 114–15, 118–19, 153–4, 156, 333, 341–2, 353; *Le Triomphe de la Liberté en l'élargissement de la Bastille*, 17; *The Hopes of the Party*, 25; *The Presentation – or – The Wise Mens Offering*, 47; plates for *Hollandia Regenerata*, 62; *Apotheosis of Hoche*, 64, 65; *The Friend of Humanity and the Knife-Grinder*, 64; *French Habits*, 65; *The Apples and the Horse-Turds* , 118; *Democracy; – or – a Sketch of the Life of Buonaparte*, 118–19; *Political Dreamings* , 131–2; *Introduction of Citizen Volpone and his Suite* , 132; *Lilliputian Substitutes* , 132; *Preliminaries of Peace* , 132; *Evacuation of Malta*, 153; *Armed-Heroes*, 156, 219; *Maniac-Ravings*, 156, 219; *John Bull and the Alarmist*, 159, 219; *Death of the Corsican Fox*, 163; *The King of Brobdingnag and Gulliver*, 163, 219; *Buonapartè. 48 Hours after Landing!*, 164; *Hand-Writing upon the Wall*, 218; *The Arms of France*, 218–19; *The Corsican Carcase-Butcher's Reckoning Day*, 218–19; *The Corsican-Pest; – or – Beelzebub going to Supper*, 219

Ginger, John, 160, 204, 206, 207, 208, 209, 219

Globe, 214

Godincthun (Ratel's house near Boulogne), 85–6, 181, 192–3, 197

Goldsmith, Lewis, 71, 76–7, 123–4, 252–3, 332, 343–4, 353

Goldsmith, Oliver, 16

'Grand Conspiracy': Pichegru-Moreau rapprochement idea, 170–2, 222, 228, 233, 255, 258–9, 267–8, 314–15, 345; preparations for, 170–2, 173–7, 180–3, 195, 198, 222–4; and Le Tréport, 174, 175, 195, 198, 224–5; use of Royal Navy cutters, 176, 190–1, 197–8, 223–4, 225, 229–33, 261–5; chains of safe houses to Paris, 182–3, 226, 227, 260, 301; landings at Le Tréport (December 1803), 198–200; landings in France (August 1803), 223–6; Napoleon strengthens guard on coast, 225; Cloche d'Or (Paris headquarters), 226–7, 260–1; journey to Paris, 226–7; conspirators' arrival in Paris, 227–8, 233–4; and the 'Bourbon prince', 228, 235, 259, 263, 277–80, 283–4; further landing of royalists (autumn 1803), 228–9; network unravels, 255–62, 264–8, 270–5, 298–302, 312–13; and Méhée, 257, 269–70, 280; Querelle talks after arrest, 257, 258, 260; inside the Tuileries, 259–60; attempted landing of reinforcements (February 1804), 260, 261–2, 263–4, 277; Savary uncovers Le Tréport/Biville network, 260, 261–2, 264–6, 312–13; French penetration of plot, 260–1, 268, 271–2, 345; allegations of British government involvement, 268–9, 295–7, 307–10, 316–18, 334, 336–7, 338–9, 346; interrogations, 275, 283, 313, 314; report of Grand Judge Régnier, 279, 307, 308, 309, 318; British theories on exposure of, 293–4; attempts to rescue prisoners/fugitives, 299–300, 318–19; escape to Britain of Cadoudal's officers, 318; trials (May-June 1804), 319, 320, 321–2; pamphlet war during trials, 320–1; trial verdicts, 322–3; executions, 323, 325; Barré on, 338–9; as 'plot fabricated by Napoleon', 344; Moreau's motives during, 345, 346

Le Grand Homme (Count Starhemberg pamphlet), 121–2, 153

Grenville, Lord, 19, 24, 30, 69–70, 93, 97, 114, 295, 297–8, 320, 322; personality of, 18, 141; supports Bourbon restoration, 36, 37, 57, 81; and Wickham, 36, 37–8, 42; and Sir Sidney

Grenville, Lord – *continued*
    Smith, 43, 71, 72, 73; opposes peace
        with France, 53, 57, 79, 80, 81–2, 108,
        122, 125, 131, 141; as prime minister,
        349–50; later life of, 350
Grunstein, Colonel, 280, 282, 286, 287
Guesclin, Bertrand de, 330
Guillemot, Pierre, 135, 318
Guiton, Aimé, 289

Haiti, Henri Christophe, Emperor of,
    355
Hamburg, 331–2, 333
Hammond, George, 63, 186, 187, 188–9,
    191, 197, 238–9, 350
Hanot, Mme (of Herly), 313–14
Hanover, 15, 20, 32, 156, 317, 331, 332
Hardwicke, Lord, 320
Hatchard, James, 160, 161, 208–9, 219
Hauterive, Alexandre-Maurice Blanc d',
    123, 152
Hawkesbury, Robert Jenkinson, Lord,
    121, 126–7, 135, 138–9, 305–6, 307;
    and 'Grand Conspiracy', 191, 270–1,
    293–4, 310, 316–17; and Méhée, 238–9,
    240, 244–5; circular letter (early May
    1804), 316–17, 330–1, 339; Cobbett's
    contempt for, 316–17, 330–1, 340; as
    prime minister (1812–27, as Lord
    Liverpool), 350, 356; suppresses
    Drake's posthumous papers, 356
Haydn, Josef, *Creation*, 1–2, 7
Heligoland, 316
Henry-Larivière, Pierre, 242
Heriot, John, 28, 35, 63–4, 131, 138, 354
Hermilly, Jean-Marie, 222, 225, 229, 299,
    318
Herries, Guillaume, 75
Herries, John Charles, 152
The History of Buonaparte (large sheet),
    205
Hizay, Marie, 273, 322
Hobart, Robert, Lord, 175, 176
Hoche, General, 49–50, 64
Hohenlinden, Battle of (2 December
    1800), 106, 170
Holland, William, 30, 155, 163, 164, 311
Hone, William, 154
Hood, Samuel, Admiral Lord, 43
Horn, Alexander, 250, 251
Horné, Etienne, 225, 226
Hortense (Josephine's daughter), 2, 7,
    140, 214
Houat, island of, 92

Hozier, Ambroise d', 258
Hozier, Charles d', 103, 105, 174–5, 226,
    227, 301, 302, 322–3, 351, 352
Hulin, Pierre-Augustin, 289
Hume, David, *History of England*, 21
Humphrey, Hannah, 130, 219
Huskisson, William, 31, 36
Hussein, Saddam, 14
Hyde de Neuville, Guillaume, 52,
    77, 82, 83–5, 86, 87–8, 92, 94, 193;
    correspondence of captured (May
    1800), 88, 89, 90–2; and 'Infernal
    Machine' plot, 97, 99, 105; at safe
    house in Paris (November 1800), 98,
    273

Iles Saint-Marcouf, 44–5, 55, 56
The Important History (pamphlet), 13,
    204, 206, 207, 208, 213
'Infernal Machine' (rue Nicaise
    assassination attempt, 24 December
    1800), 3–7, 100–1, 213; bomb's late
    detonation, 6, 101; casualties and
    damage, 6, 7, 101, 102; aftermath of,
    6–7, 101–2; device as first of its kind,
    9; initially blamed on Jacobins, 9;
    British funding and promotion of,
    9–10, 97, 120–1, 142; origins of plot,
    94, 95; planning and preparations
    for, 95–100, 118–19; choice of bomb
    as method, 96, 99–100; Fouché's
    intelligence beforehand, 96, 97–8, 99;
    police investigation into, 102–6, 120;
    arbitrary punishment of Jacobins after,
    104, 120; Carbon and Saint-Régent
    executed, 106; British press reaction,
    120; Goldsmith's version of, 253, 344;
    as 'plot fabricated by Napoleon', 253;
    Barré on, 338
invisible (sympathetic) ink, 245, 247, 248,
    294
Iraq War (from 2003), 14
Ivernois, François d', 114

Jackson, Cyril, 30, 36
Jacobins, French: initially blamed for
    'Infernal Machine', 9, 102, 103–4,
    120; Committee of Correspondence
    and of Propaganda, 11; club in rue
    Saint-Jacques, 26–7, 242; associated
    with vice by anti-Jacobins, 47–8; the
    Mountain in National Assembly, 75;
    Fouché foils bomb plot (November
    1800), 99–100

Jaffa, 149–51

Johnson, Joseph, 69

Joliclerc, Désiré, 268, 271–2

Jordan, Jeremiah, 69

Journal des Hommes Libres, 237

journalism in Britain: French *émigré* writers, 58–9, 111–13, 133–4, 135–6, 138, 139–40, 143–4, 177–9 *see also* Peltier, Jean-Gabriel; government involvement in, 13, 28, 34–5, 62–5, 119, 141, 204, 333; issue of free speech, 13, 14, 16, 64, 141–2, 143–4, 168; suppression of opposition voices, 13, 28–30; seditious libel, 14, 35, 48, 69–70, 320; pamphleteers in government pay, 33–4, 35; prosecutions of radicals, 35; reaction to 'Infernal Machine' plot, 120; Cobbett attacks for hypocrisy, 165–8

journalism in France: Napoleon's suppression of, 12–13, 84, 212–13, 249, 333; Hyde launches newspapers in Paris, 84; Michaud's anti-Napoleon pamphlets, 84, 88; English language, 123–4, 141, 268–9

journals and newspapers: suppression of in Britain, 13, 28–30, 46, 69–70; English liberal/radical, 23, 34, 59–60, 68, 69–70, 111, 115, 116–17, 121, 129, 132, 144–5; French-language press in London, 59, 111–13, 134, 177–9, 333; role of during Amiens, 126, 129–31, 132, 136–8, 142–5, 148, 151–3, 156–62, 165–9; Napoleon bans English newspapers, 138, 139; *see also* press, English loyalist

Joyaux, Aimé-Augustin-Alexis (Villeneuve), 98, 99, 100, 103, 105, 225–6, 261, 273, 274; condemned to death in his absence, 106; capture of (25 March 1804), 300; execution of (25 June 1804), 323

Julien, Joseph-Louis-Victor, General, 319

Keith, George Elphinstone, Admiral Lord, 189–90, 191, 223, 224, 229–30, 231–3, 263, 264, 299, 318

Keith, John, 54, 71, 72, 173

Kemble, John Philip, 162

Kielmannsegge, Friedrich von, Count, 332

Killing No Murder pamphlet (1657), 22, 30, 84, 95, 203, 221, 234–5, 243–4, 268–9, 333

King, John, 30–1, 36, 245, 351

King's German Legion in Hanover, 156, 332

Kléber, Jean-Baptiste, General, 73, 212

Klinglin, Jean-Jacques-Joseph de, Austrian general, 248, 281

La Chaussée, Charles, comte de, 96, 104

La Poterie (near Saint-Pierre-en-Val), 226, 233

Lagrimaudière, Yves, 261

Lahorie, General Victor, 268

Lajolais, Catherine, 222, 281, 286

Lajolais, General Frédéric, 222, 228, 233, 259, 267, 281, 322–3, 344, 345; arrest of (15 February 1804), 268, 271

Lamothe, maréchal de logis, 281–2, 283

Lannes, Jean, General, 2, 5

Larrey, Dominique-Jean, Baron, 351

Larue, Isaac-Étienne de, 90, 91

Laubéypie, Martin, 186, 268

Lauriston, Jacques, General, 191

Le Tréport, 86, 89–90, 97, 174, 175, 195–200, 261–2, 263–4

Leblond, Louis, 313–14

Lebourgeois, Charles, 173–4, 255–6, 283

Leclerc, Julien, 52, 99, 188, 234, 259–60, 313, 325; and rebuilding of Paris network, 92; Pichegru-Moreau rapprochement idea, 170, 171; and network in France (from early 1802), 172, 180–3, 194, 195, 196, 197–9, 264–5; escapes arrest (15 February 1804), 265; code keys of discovered, 266, 292; escapes to London, 298, 299, 312; letter to Ratel (16 March 1804), 298–9; hopes to re-establish Paris correspondence, 315–16; at Westerstede (July 1804), 316; later life of, 354

Lecourbe, Claude-Jacques, General, 321

Lefevre, Louis, 98, 183, 193

Lefort, Robert, 187, 193

Leinhart, Captain, 304

Lelièvre de Saint-Rémy, 231

Léridant, Louis, 273, 274, 275, 322

Lettre de La Ramée à ses camarades de l'armée, 244, 245, 250–1

Lettre d'un Anglais à Bonaparte (version of *Killing No Murder*), 234, 243, 245, 250, 268–9

Leval, Jean-François, General, 280

Lille, comte de (Louis XVIII) *see* Provence, comte de ('comte de Lille', future Louis XVIII)

Limoëlan, Joseph Picot de, 4, 5, 6, 98, 99, 101, 103, 105, 106
Liston, Robert, 172
Locminé, Battle of (1796), 4
London Corresponding Society, 36–7, 45
London und Paris (Saxon journal), 219, 333
Long, Charles, 35
Louis XVI, King, 21; execution of, 22, 50, 61
Louisiana, 185
The Loyalist (periodical), 160, 161, 208–9, 215
Lucas, Amabel, Lady, 127–8, 133, 139, 140–1
Lunéville, Treaty of, 285
Lyndhurst, John Singleton Copley, Lord, 353

Macaulay, Catharine, 22
Macdonald, General Jacques, 171, 258, 259
Mackereth, George, 122
Mackintosh, James, 143
Maddison, John, 31–2
Maison, Nicolas-Joseph, 331
Mallet, François, 55–6, 83, 85
Mallet du Pan, Jacques, 113
Malmesbury, James Harris, Earl of, 15, 38, 53, 57, 107, 156, 235, 241
Malouet, Pierre Victor, 348
Malta, 66, 116, 147, 153, 155, 156, 211, 353
Mansel, Mr, 320
Marboeuf, Charles Louis de, 60
Marengo, Battle of (14 June 1800), 93
Maret, Hugues-Bernard, 294–5
Margadel, Charles-Nicolas, chevalier de, 82, 83, 97–8
Marie-Antoinette, 16
Markham, Captain John, 223, 229, 230–1
Marmont, Auguste de, General, 191, 323
Marsden, William, 299
Masclet, Amé, 172, 193
Masséna, André, General, 188
Massignon, Jean-Baptiste, 226
Méhée, Jean, 242
Méhée de la Touche, Jean-Claude, 236, 237–44, 256, 285, 286, 293, 334, 345; 'escape from Oléron', 237, 243, 252; 'Jacobin committee' of, 240–1, 244–5, 249–51, 257, 293, 294, 305, 307; sent to Drake in Bavaria (September 1803), 244–8; arrival at Paris (3 November 1803), 248–9; correspondence with

Drake from Paris, 249–52, 257, 269–70, 294–5, 302, 339, 340; fictional Jacobin general, 250, 280, 293, 294, 302; works with and for Napoleon, 252, 253, 280, 305; Lewis Goldsmith on, 252–3, 344; *L'Antidote* (journal), 253; imprisonments, 253; and 'Grand Conspiracy', 257, 269–70, 280, 344; *Alliance des Jacobins* (pamphlet), 308–9, 311, 355; life of in *The Revolutionary Plutarch*, 333, 336–7; post-1804 life of, 355–6
Mengaud, Joseph, 53, 88–9, 91, 177, 192
Menou, Jacques-François de, 212
Mercure Britannique, 243
Mercure de Ratisbonne, 249, 305, 333
Mérille, Jean, 261
Merry, Anthony, 127, 138
Michaud, Jean François, 84, 88
Milton, John, *Areopagitica*, 22
Mirabeau, Honoré-Gabriel Riqueti, comte de, *Sur la liberté de la presse* (1788), 22
Moleville, Antoine-François Bertrand de, 239, 240, 241, 242, 245, 246–7, 251, 252, 307
Moncey, Bon-Adrien Jeannot de, General, 193, 259, 268
Monck, George, 21, 77, 84, 291
Moniteur, 120, 156, 258, 260, 261, 263–4, 289, 292–3, 295, 302; article by Napoleon (8 August 1802), 136–7, 141–2
Monnier, Pierre, 226
Montagu, Rear-Admiral Robert, 190–1, 197, 223, 229
Montgaillard, Maurice comte de, 328
Monthly Magazine, 23, 34, 59–60, 115
Montlosier, François-Dominique-Reynaud de, 113, 134
More, Hannah, 'A King or a Consul?', 163
Moreau, General Jean Victor, 156, 188, 203, 213, 217, 218, 248, 284; victory at Hohenlinden (2 December 1800), 106, 170; and Pichegru, 170–1, 222, 228, 233, 255, 258–9, 267–8, 314–15, 345; and 'Grand Conspiracy', 227, 228; motives of in 'Grand Conspiracy', 259, 345, 346; arrest of (15 February 1804), 268, 271, 304; loyalty of Rhine frontier troops to, 281; low 'ultra' opinion of, 282; Cobbett on, 295–6; trial of

(May–June 1804), 320, 321–2; letter to
Napoleon (1 March 1804), 321; light
sentence given to, 322–3; death of at
battle of Dresden (1813), 345–6

Morning Chronicle, 66, 131, 132, 235, 269,
297

Morning Post, 115, 116–17, 129, 131, 132,
141–2, 166

Morpeth, George Howard, Lord, 309

Murat, Joachim, 257, 313

Murray, John, 350

Mussey, de (agent of comte de Lille), 248

Napoleon: height of, 4, 61, 153, 218;
British propaganda against, 9–11, 12,
66–7, 109–11, 148–53, 156–65, 168–9,
201–9, 210–13, 217–18, 219–21; enduring
perceptions of, 10, 12, 118–19, 153;
suppression of press, 12–13, 84, 212–13,
249, 333; passion for 'Ossian', 16, 59,
136; form of name of, 23, 58; and 13
vendémiaire (5 October 1795), 45, 61,
209; victories in Italy (1796), 49, 58, 61,
347–8; in Egypt, 57, 66–7, 71, 116, 211,
349; initial French *émigré* attitudes to,
58–9; British liberal admiration for,
59–60, 62, 67–8, 70, 79, 109, 110, 115–18,
122–3, 124; early biographies of, 59–61;
caricatures of, 62, 67, 118–19, 131–2,
153–4, 155, 156, 163–4, 166–7, 177–9,
218–19, 341–2; printed portraits of, 62;
commands Army of England, 65–6;
Gillray's caricatures of, 66–7, 118–19,
131–2, 153–4, 156, 164, 218–19, 341–2;
and Bourbon restoration issue, 71,
72–3, 74, 77, 95, 113; departure/escape
from Egypt, 71, 72–4, 189, 319; aim for
viable, stable alternative to Bourbons,
74, 124, 137, 148, 346–7; Brumaire coup
(9 November 1799), 74, 79, 109, 110, 115;
restores religion, 77, 87, 126; meeting
with royalists (December 1799), 77–8;
peace offers by, 78, 79–82, 116, 117, 118,
213, 342, 347; measures to conciliate
royalists (1799), 86–7; lifts ban on
émigrés (October 1800), 97, 113, 126,
134, 165; blames Jacobins for 'Infernal
Machine', 102, 103–4; English loyalist
press vilification of, 109–11, 119–20,
121–2, 124, 316, 317–18; atrocity stories,
112–13, 143, 148–51, 179, 180, 204–13;
shift in Liberal British opinion on
(1801–3), 125–6, 132, 142–3, 145, 147–8,
165–9; popularity in Britain during

peace, 128–30; complaints against
émigré journalism, 133–4, 135–6, 138,
143–4; and Cadoudal's presence in
Britain, 135, 137, 172; *Moniteur* article
(8 August 1802), 136–7, 141–2; Jaffa
hospital poisoning story, 143, 149–50,
179, 212; accosts Whitworth (March
1803), 154–5, 156; resumption of war
(May 1803), 155–6; invasion force
(1803), 185, 250, 251, 323; Boulogne
as headquarters (June 1803), 191–2,
193; scurrilous biographies of (1803),
201–9, 210–13, 217–18, 219–21; and
Méhée, 249, 252, 253, 280; security
crisis (January 1804), 255–8, 260; and
Enghien, 280–91; and destruction
of Anglo-royalist networks, 301–2;
becomes Emperor (May 1804), 326–8;
visit to Boulogne (July–August 1804),
328–30; coronation at Notre Dame
(2 December 1804), 340–2; increased
despotism in later years, 346, 351; and
economic warfare, 349, 351; Saint
Helena exile (1815–21), 351

Nares, Robert, 34

Nelson, Horatio, 39, 71, 72; victory at the
Nile (August 1798), 66, 116, 122, 211,
349; raid on Boulogne (August 1801),
127

Nepean, Evan, 24–5, 28, 30, 36–7, 54, 189,
190–1, 223, 232, 350–1

Netherlands, 40–1

New Annual Register, 60

Newton, Richard, 62

Ney, Michel, General 191, 353

nonconformism, 61, 109–10, 111

Offenburg, 248, 270, 280, 281, 282, 286

Ompteda, Christian Friedrich Wilhelm,
Baron d', 332

Ordener, Michel, 285, 286–7

Ordre, Claude-Guillaume-Victor du
Wicquet, baron d', 86, 87, 98, 182–3,
194, 197

'Ossian', 16, 136

Osvalt, Catherine, 261

Otto, Louis-Guillaume, 82, 120, 121,
133–4, 135, 138; as peace negotiator, 127,
128; and Méhée, 246, 247, 248

Ottoman Empire, 43, 56–7, 71–2

Paine, Thomas, 25–6, 27, 29, 30

Paoli, Pasquale, 59, 60–1

Pâques, Inspector, 300

Paris correspondence: 'Paris Committee' of royalist agents, 37–8, 52–3, 55–6; Channel Islands, 39–40, 83, 175, 176, 249; Marcouf islands correspondence, 44–5, 55, 56, 83; Rouen end of, 55–6, 83; Smith re-establishes network in Paris, 55–6; Amiens and Boulogne route, 85–6, 98, 172, 180–3, 187–9, 192–200; route through Le Tréport, 86, 89–90, 97, 174, 175, 195–200; Leclerc and Bayard (December 1800), 99; Leclerc takes over, 172, 180–3; reactivation of networks (1803), 185–91, 192–200; police activity around Boulogne (August 1803), 192–4; Boulogne–Abbeville network broken, 260–8; captured correspondence of Boulogne agents, 266, 281, 292–3; Leclerc's code keys discovered, 266, 292

Parry, John, 69

Patton, Philip, Admiral, 232, 264

Pelham, Thomas, Lord, 107, 139, 239–40, 241

Peltier, Jean-Gabriel, 218, 239, 293, 314, 318, 327–8, 355; *Paris pendant l'Année* (1795–1802), 58–9, 84, 112, 120, 131, 133, 134, 178, 211; background of, 112; *Le Dernier Tableau de Paris*, 112; *Les Actes des Apôtres*, 112, 134; the *Ambigu*, 135–6, 139–40, 177–9, 314, 355; trial of (February 1803), 140, 143–4, 168, 178, 297, 343; later life of, 355

Péricault, abbé, 283

Perry, James, 131, 132

Perry, Sampson, 35, 47

Peterloo massacre (August 1819), 350

Petit (police officer), 273–4, 275

Phélippeaux, Antoine de, 52, 54–5, 71, 202, 207

Philippe, Jean-Louis, 195–6, 313, 325

Phillips, Richard, 60, 69, 241

Pichegru, Jean-Charles, 82, 147, 203, 213, 217–18, 248, 282, 283, 339; victory in Netherlands, 40–1; defection to Anglo-royalist cause, 42–3, 45, 51–2, 314; elected president of the Five Hundred, 52–3; deportation and escape from Sinnamary, 53, 54, 90, 91; in London (July 1800), 94, 96; and Moreau, 170–1, 222, 228, 233, 255, 258–9, 267–8, 314–15, 345; and the 'Grand Conspiracy', 195, 222, 228; in London (1803–4), 228, 233; in Paris (January/February 1804), 233,

255, 258–9, 260, 267–8, 271; arrest of (28 February 1804), 272, 296, 303; imprisonment in Temple, 272, 275; loyalty of Rhine frontier troops to, 281; Cobbett on, 295–6; suicide of (April 1804), 314–15

Picot, Jean, 173–4, 255–6

Picot, Louis, 225–6, 227, 233, 261, 283, 344

Pigott, Charles, *The Jockey Club*, 26, 30

Pillichody, Colonel Louis, 146, 147

Piogé the Pitiless, 255–6

Pitt, William: aid to 'Infernal Machine' plotters, 9; and anti-Napoleon propaganda, 11; and British ruling system, 12; government's suppression of opposition voices, 13, 28–30, 36–7, 46–8, 69–70; and Churchill's WW2 methods, 14; as leading British politician, 17–18, 81; lifestyle of, 17–18, 70, 349; initial opposition to war, 18–19; and Bourbon restoration issue, 20, 36, 80, 81, 83; Portland Whigs join, 20, 36; use of patronage, 20–1, 69; anti-Jacobinism of, 26–7; and naval rearmament, 28; unpopularity of ministry, 45–6, 106; negotiations with Directory (1795), 46; peace negotiations (1797), 53, 57; and the *Anti-Jacobin*, 62, 63; liberal hatred of, 70, 169; and Napoleon's peace offer (December 1799), 79–81; 'child and champion' phrase, 83, 129; and 'Infernal Machine' plot, 96, 97; supports peace (1801), 106–7; resignation of (16 February 1801), 107, 124, 125; Coleridge on, 132; encouragement of volunteering, 164–5; as Warden of the Cinque Ports, 190; George III rejects ministry including Fox, 297–8; return to office (May 1804), 317; death of (1806), 350

Place, Francis, 48

poetry, English 'Jacobin', 65

Poix, Antoine, 181, 192, 313

Poix, Celestine, 181, 193

Poix, Claudin, 172, 181, 194, 313

Poix, Joachim, 172, 181

Poix, Pierre-Marie (La Rose), 181–2, 187, 192, 194, 196, 197, 199–200, 264; escapes arrest (15 February 1804), 265; solo campaign of damage limitation, 266–7, 312, 313–14; arrest of (9 June 1804), 323–4; escapes to London, 324–5; later life of, 355 policing: and Napoleon, 12–13, 152, 256, 257–8; and Nepean, 24–5; expanded police force in Britain, 27–8, 31; Westminster Police Bill, 27–8, 31; continental system of, 28; and Fouché, 75, 88–9, 91, 99, 102, 152, 216, 256, 345; Anglo-royalist penetration in Paris, 85, 99, 105; 'Infernal Machine' investigation, 102–6, 120; in Boulogne area, 191, 192–5, 260–8, 312–14; and 'Grand Conspiracy', 223, 255–8, 260–1, 267–8, 269–70, 271–5, 299–302, 314–15; *Revolutionary Plutarch* on French police, 334–6

Polignac, Armand de, 229, 259, 272, 321, 322–3, 352

Polignac, Jules, 233, 259, 272, 322, 352

Porter, Robert Ker, 208–9

Portland, William Cavendish-Bentinck, Duke of, 20, 36, 93, 139, 350

Post Office, 28, 31–2

press, English loyalist, 119–20, 124, 142, 204–9, 215, 219, 234–5, 316–18, 321; British government funded, 13, 28, 34–5, 62–5, 111, 119, 138, 141, 160–1, 333, 353; denunciations of print and bookshops, 29–30; Canning's *Anti-Jacobin*, 62–5, 68, 109, 160; role of during Amiens, 126, 129–31, 132, 136–8, 142–3, 145, 148, 151–3, 156–62, 165–9; *see also Anti-Jacobin Review*

Préville, Godefroy, chevalier de Roussel de, 182, 194

Préville, Nymphe de ('la Belle'), 182, 197, 266–7, 312, 316, 325, 354–5

Price, Charles, 44

prints *see* caricatures and prints

propaganda: British against Napoleon, 9–10, 12, 66–7, 109–11, 148–53, 156–65, 168–9, 201–9, 210–13, 217–18, 219–21; French royalist, 10, 84, 88, 112–13, 135–6, 139–40, 177–80; derivation of word, 11–12; Napoleon's, 12, 62, 89, 91; public opinion as new concern in 1790s, 12; British campaign as highly successful, 12–13; degrees of exaggeration, 13; British before Napoleonic Wars, 13–14; use of word 'Corsican', 23, 338, 339; pro-government in Britain, 33; association of Jacobinism with vice, 47–8; and Canning, 62–5, 66–7, 68, 119, 153–4; Gillray's caricatures of Bonaparte, 66–7, 118–19, 131–2, 153–4,

156, 164, 218–19, 341–2; *Intercepted Letters*, 66–7, 117–18, 212; English loyalist press, 109–11, 119–20, 121–2, 124, 129–30, 151–3, 156–62, 204, 316, 317–18; repetition technique, 111, 314; French-language press in London, 111–13, 134, 177–9, 333; Napoleon's alleged atrocities, 112–13, 143, 148–51, 179, 180, 204–13; and Peltier, 112–13, 120, 139–40, 177–9; and German opinion, 114–15; assassination references in, 118–19, 120, 136, 140, 177–9, 218–19, 220–1, 234–5, 268–9; and William Cobbett, 119–20, 157–9, 161, 205–6, 207–8; government placards/posters/handbills, 159–60, 166; as national unifying force, 168–9; scurrilous biographies of Napoleon, 201–9, 210–13, 217–18, 219–21; and Enghien's death, 291, 316, 318; British countering 'Grand Conspiracy' allegations, 333–5; plots as invented by Napoleon or Fouché, 343–5

Provence, comte de ('comte de Lille', future Louis XVIII), 37, 50, 51, 179, 180, 248, 277, 278, 279, 286, 345; Napoleon's letter to (September 1800), 95; life of in *The Revolutionary Plutarch*, 333; rules as King Louis XVIII (1814 and 1815–24), 351, 355

Prussia, 19

Quarterly Review, 350

Quennehen, Prosper, 197, 267, 312, 313

Querelle, Pierre, 226, 255–7, 258, 260, 270, 319, 344, 345

Quiberon expedition (1795), 4, 42, 43

Rance, Colonel, 289

Rapp, Jean, 2–3, 7

Ratel, abbé Justin ('The Monk'), 83, 90, 97–8, 105, 180, 181, 194, 298–9, 354; and Smith's escape from Temple gaol, 55, 56; background of, 56; and Paris end of correspondence, 56, 85; correspondence via Amiens and Boulogne, 85–6; evades arrest (May 1800), 88; leaves France for London (early 1802), 172; runs network from London, 186, 187, 188–9, 192, 195, 197, 198; on Spencer Smith at Stuttgart, 234, 281, 292; hopes to re-establish Paris correspondence (April 1804), 315, 316; releases Poix from Hull prison, 325

Ratisbon, 246, 249, 305

Réal, Pierre, 242, 253, 257, 267, 281, 288, 290; and 'Infernal Machine' investigation, 102, 104; and 'Grand Conspiracy', 260, 269, 272, 314–15, 344, 345; life of in *The Revolutionary Plutarch*, 333, 334–6

Rebuffet, Etienne, 275

Red Book of Bourrienne, 214

Redesdale, John Mitford, Baron, 320

Reeves, John, 27, 28–9, 32, 33, 46, 48, 157, 354

Regnaud de Saint-Jean-d'Angély, Michel, 172, 326

Régnier, Grand Judge Claude Ambroise, 193, 248–9, 253, 255, 257, 271, 284–5, 301–2; report on 'Grand Conspiracy', 279, 307, 308, 309, 318; life of in *The Revolutionary Plutarch*, 333, 334

Regnier, Jacques, 134, 135, 333

Reich, baronne de, 281, 283, 285, 286

Rémusat, Claire de, 288

Réponse au Cen. Garat, par le Cen. Méhée (pamphlet), 253

The Revolutionary Plutarch, 13, 202–4, 205, 206, 207, 209–11, 212–17, 219–21, 236, 243; reviews of, 220, 234–5; on arrest of Rumbold, 331–2; second, expanded edition, 333–7

Rey, Jean-Baptiste, 2

Reims, 340

Ridgway, James, 30

Rivière, Charles-François de, 92, 96–7, 99, 233, 271, 272, 319, 322–3, 351

Roberts, Percy, 129, 155

Robespierre, Maximilien, 36, 67, 75, 205, 209

Rochecotte, Fortuné Guyon, comte de, 52, 55, 56

Rochelle, Etienne-François, 228, 268, 272, 322–3

Roger, Michel, 98, 100, 103, 105, 222, 228, 261, 323

Rohan-Rochefort, Charlotte de, 278, 286, 287, 288, 290

Rolland, Henri, 233, 268, 271, 322

Rome, republican, 22–3

Rose, George, 28, 35

Rosey, Captain (aide to fictional general), 280, 286, 293, 294, 302–3, 304, 305

Roussel de Bedoine, Madeleine de, 182

Rowlandson, Thomas, *The Contrast*, 33

Royal Navy, 9, 18, 82, 97, 154, 348–9; evacuation of Toulon, 43–4; mutinies in the Channel fleet (1797), 50; cutters used during 'Grand Conspiracy', 176, 190–1, 197–8, 223–4, 225, 229–33, 261–5; and rescue of 'Grand Conspiracy' fugitives, 299, 318–19

royalists, French: and anti-Napoleon propaganda, 10, 84, 88, 112–13, 135–6, 139–40, 177–80; and absolutism, 20, 25, 50–1; and English history, 21–2, 77, 84; chains of safe houses, 40, 54–5, 98, 174, 175–6, 182–3, 199, 226, 227, 260, 301; and 'war of assignats', 40; Normandy network, 43, 44, 56; Quiberon expedition (1795), 43; failed coup in Paris (5 October 1795), 45, 61; risings in western France (1796), 49; factions, 50, 51, 52; constitutional monarchists, 50–1, 52, 113; death of Louis XVII (June 1795), 51; 'purs' ('ultras'), 51, 52, 57; deportations to Sinnamary (September 1797), 53; failure of coup (September 1797), 53, 54, 55; meeting with Napoleon (December 1799), 77–8; Margadel's *coup essentiel* plan (1800), 82, 83–4, 92, 93; Dupérou's 'counter-police', 84–5; Boulogne spy network, 85–6, 98, 172, 180–3, 187–9, 192–200; Anglo-royalist network unravels (May 1800), 88; landing near Le Tréport ambushed (May 1800), 89–90, 195; reactivation of networks (1803), 185–91, 192–200; network unravels (early 1804), 255–62, 264–8, 270–5, 298–302, 312–13; *see also* chouans (royalist insurgents of western France); *émigrés* in Britain; Paris correspondence

Rumbold, George, 156, 173, 331–3, 355

Rusillon, François-Louis, 52, 147, 233, 259, 272, 319, 322–3, 352

Russia, 327, 339, 345–6; troops in Channel Islands (1799–1800), 82, 88; Napoleon's invasion of (1812), 349

Saint-Domingue (Haiti), 213

La Sainte Famille (supposed pamphlet), 203, 212, 215

Saint-Hilaire, Edouard de la Haye, 98, 103, 105, 318; condemned to death in his absence, 106

Saint-Régent, Pierre Robinault de, 4, 5, 6, 98, 99, 100, 101, 103, 105; and possible second attempt plan, 104;

arrest, trial and execution of, 106
Saint-Rémy, Lelièvre de, 187, 192, 196, 197, 231
Saumarez, Admiral Sir James, 176
Saumarez, Thomas, 237–8
Savary, General, 255, 256, 260, 261–2, 264–7, 277, 289, 290, 312–13
Saxony, 333
Schilling, Baron, 287
Schmidt, Lieutenant, 282, 283, 286, 287
Scott, Walter, 162
Sébastiani, Horace, 156
Ségur, Louis-Philippe, comte de, 1
Ségur, Philippe de, 227
Shakespeare, William, 16, 162
Shée, Henri, 248, 252, 253, 280, 281–2, 286, 303
Shepheard, William, 223
Sheridan, Richard Brinsley, 16, 116, 125–6, 132, 144, 147–8, 155, 162, 165
Shirley, William, 162
Smith, Colonel Charles Douglas, 190, 196–7, 200
Smith, General Edward, 190, 230
Smith, George, 320
Smith, Sir Sidney: background of, 43; at Toulon, 43–4; Earl Spencer on, 44; and Iles Saint-Marcouf, 44–5, 55, 56; captured by the French (April 1796), 48–9; rescue from Temple gaol (1798), 54–5, 207; re-establishes intelligence network in Paris, 55–6; at Constantinople, 56–7, 71–3; and Napoleon's departure from Egypt, 71, 72–4, 189, 319; defends Acre against Bonaparte, 71–2, 111, 122; Fauche meets, 171; commands *Antelope* (1803), 176, 186; and reactivation of networks (1803), 185, 189, 190, 197, 198; and Paris network, 185–8; covets Downs station, 189, 190, 230; exiled to the Belgian coast (1803), 189–90; later life of, 355; marries Rumbold's widow Caroline (1810), 355
Smith, Spencer, 73, 190, 283, 292–3, 308; at Constantinople, 43, 56–7, 71; as ambassador to Stuttgart, 234, 281, 302–5; seizure of diplomatic papers sent by, 331, 332
Sneyd, John, 64
Society for the Suppression of Vice, 47, 48
songs, 33, 160, 161, 162, 163
Sontag, General, 332–3

Soult, Jean-de-Dieu, General, 191
Southey, Robert, 17, 64, 65, 70, 353
Spanish succession, War of, 15
Spectateur du Nord, 113
Spencer, George, Earl, 44, 72, 73
Spère, Julienne (Ratel's mistress), 86, 90, 98, 172, 192–3, 194, 354
Spin, Pierre-Antoine, 175, 227, 273, 300, 301
St Vincent, John Jervis, Earl, 71, 189, 191, 223, 229, 264, 318, 349
Starhemberg, Ludwig, Count von, 121–2, 153
Sterne, Laurence, 16
Strasbourg, 247, 248, 280, 281, 285, 286
Stuart, Daniel, 142
Such is Buonaparte! (poster), 205
Summary View (pamphlet), 204
Sun (newspaper founded 1792), 28, 34–5, 63–4, 80, 118, 129, 131
Sweden, 327, 339
Swift, Jonathan, *Gulliver's Travels*, 163
Switzerland, 36, 37, 46, 52, 53, 67–8, 213; Helvetic Republic established (1798), 68, 113, 146; crisis in (1802), 146–7
Symonds, Henry Delahay, 26, 30, 47, 161
Syria, 148–51

Talbot, James, 176–7
Talleyrand, Charles Maurice, 135, 144, 152, 203, 212–13, 333, 348; hatred of Fouché, 74, 77, 89; physical appearance of, 74, 75–6, 215–16; spy network of, 76, 89, 172–3; background of, 76–7; Lewis Goldsmith on, 76–7; and Dupérou, 85, 89; and *émigré* journalism, 133, 134, 135; life of in *Anti-Jacobin Review*, 215–16; and Enghien, 284–5, 290–1; circular letter exposing Drake, 302, 308, 316; refuses recognition of English diplomats, 330–1; career after Napoleon, 351; at Congress of Vienna, 351, 354
Tallien, Thérèse, 210, 212
Talon, Antoine Omer, 98–9, 105
Taylor, Brook, 304, 332
Tessonet, Jacques-Marie de, 250
Testolini, Gaetano, 62
theatre, 162
Théâtre de la République et des Arts, Paris, 1–2
Thelwall, John, 50
Theophilanthropists, 340
Third Coalition, 346, 349

Thornton (banker), 332–3
Thoyras, Rapin de, *History of England* (1724–7), 21
Thum, Daniel and Charles, 332
Thumery, General de, 282, 287
Thuriot, Judge Jacques-Alexis, 275, 314
Tierney, George, 83
the Times, 129, 130–1, 136, 316, 321
Tinseau, Charles-Léoleclern, 94, 96, 179–80, 190
Tiraceau, Mme, 192–3
Toulon, 43–4, 61; massacre at, 96–7, 180, 207–9
Toussaint Louverture, François-Dominique, 213
Treasonable and Seditious Practices Act (1795), 46
Troche, Gaston, 222, 225, 260, 262, 319
Troche, Michel, 90, 175
Tromelin, Jacques Boudin de, 45, 49, 54–5, 134
Tromelin, Henriette de, 303
Troubridge, Thomas, 189, 224
True Briton, 34–5, 63–4, 111, 131, 138
Tuttelet, Pierre, 187, 194
Twenty Thousand Pounds Reward, 218

Vansittart, Nicholas, 138
Velocifers (light carriages), 315–16
Verlingues, Captain, 193, 194
Veyrat, Chief Inspector Pierre, 192–3
Vidor, Françoise, 313, 314
Vidor, Jacques, 313, 314
Vienna, Congress of (1814–15), 351, 354
Viscovitch, Antoine, 54, 71, 176–7

Wakefield, Gilbert, 69, 70, 110–11
Walmer Castle, Kent, 190, 231

Walsh, James, 50
Waterloo, Battle of (June 1815), 351, 353, 355
West, Temple, 163
Whigs, 16, 17, 20, 36
Whitbread, Samuel, 117
Whitworth, Charles, 140–1, 144, 154–5, 156, 177
Wickham, William, 42, 49, 51, 52, 55, 82–3, 93, 185–6; and Switzerland, 36, 37, 46, 53, 68, 113, 147; investigates LRC, 36–7
Williams, Arabella, 86, 90
Williams, Helen Maria, 67–8, 90, 113, 122
Willot, Amédée, 53, 82, 91, 242, 251
Wilson, Sir Robert, *History of the British Expedition to Egypt*, 148–51, 202, 211
Windham, William, 4, 38–9, 88, 119, 123, 173, 295, 320, 322; and 'Infernal Machine' plot, 4, 94, 96, 97; support for French 'purs' ('ultras'), 51; opposes peace with France, 79, 107, 108, 125, 131; death of (1810), 350
Wittman, William, *Travels in Turkey, Asia Minor and Syria*, 151
Wolcot, John, 46
Wordsworth, William, 17, 50, 162
Wright, John Wesley, 44–5, 49, 56, 71, 176; and 'Grand Conspiracy', 190–1, 196, 198, 200, 223–4, 229–30, 231, 233, 263–4, 299, 318–19; French capture of (May 1804), 319–20; suicide of after Austerlitz, 354
Württemberg, 234, 283, 305, 308

York, Frederick, Duke of, 40
Yorke, Charles, 128, 175
Yorke, Henry Redhead, 130, 138, 235